RESEARCH IN MARITIME HISTORY
NO. 14

GLOBAL MARKETS: THE INTERNATIONALIZATION OF THE SEA TRANSPORT INDUSTRIES SINCE 1850

Edited By

David J. Starkey and Gelina Harlaftis

International Maritime Economic History Association

St. John's, Newfoundland
1998

ISSN -1188-3928
ISBN -0-9681288-4-X

Research in Maritime History is available free of charge to members of the International Maritime Economic History Association. The price to others is US$15 per copy.

Back issues of *Research in Maritime History* are available:

No. 1 (1991)	David M. Williams and Andrew P. White (comps.), *A Select Bibliography of British and Irish University Theses about Maritime History, 1792-1990*
No. 2 (1992)	Lewis R. Fischer (ed.), *From Wheel House to Counting House: Essays in Maritime Business History in Honour of Professor Peter Neville Davies*
No. 3 (1992)	Lewis R. Fischer and Walter Minchinton (eds.), *People of the Northern Seas*
No. 4 (1993)	Simon Ville (ed.), *Shipbuilding in the United Kingdom in the Nineteenth Century: A Regional Approach*
No. 5 (1993)	Peter N. Davies (ed.), *The Diary of John Holt*
No. 6 (1994)	Simon P. Ville and David M. Williams (eds.), *Management, Finance and Industrial Reslations in Maritime Industries: Essays in International Maritime and Business History*
No. 7 (1994)	Lewis R. Fischer (ed.), *The Market for Seamen in the Age of Sail*
No. 8 (1995)	Gordon Read and Michael Stammers (comps.), *Guide to the Records of Merseyside Maritime Museum*
No. 9 (1995)	Frank Broeze (ed.), *Maritime History at the Crossroads: A Critical Review of Recent Historiography*
No. 10 (1996)	Nancy Redmayne Ross (ed.), *The Diary of a Maritimer, 1816-1901: The Life and Times of Joseph Salter*
No. 11 (1997)	Faye Margaret Kert, *Prize and Prejudice: Privateering and Naval Prize in Atlantic Canada in the War of 1812*
No. 12 (1997)	Malcolm Tull, *A Community Enterprise: The History of the Port of Fremantle, 1897 to 1997*
No. 13 (1997)	Paul C. van Royen, Jaap R. Bruijn and Jan Lucassen, *"Those Emblems of Hell"? European Sailors and the Maritime Labour Market, 1570-1870*

Research in Maritime History would like to thank Memorial University of Newfoundland for its generous financial assistance in support of this volume.

CONTENTS

CONTRIBUTIONS

ABOUT THE EDITORS

DAVID J. STARKEY is Wilson Family Lecturer in Maritime History at the University of Hull. A specialist on various aspects of British maritime history, he is the author of *British Privateering Enterprise in the Eighteenth Century* (Exeter, 1990); and co-editor of *Pirates and Privateers: New Perspectives on the War on Trade in the Eighteenth and Nineteenth Centuries* (Exeter, 1997).

GELINA HARLAFTIS is Assistant Professor of Maritime History at the University of Piraeus. An expert on Greek maritime history, her books include *Greek Shipowners and Greece, 1945-1975: From Separate Development to Mutual Interdependence* (London, 1993); and *A History of Greek-owned Shipping: The Making of an International Tramp Fleet, 1830 to the Present Day* (London, 1996).

CONTRIBUTORS

BJØRN L. BASBERG is Senior Lecturer in economic history at Trondheim Business School. His research interests include nineteenth- and twentieth-century maritime history, especially whaling, with an emphasis on technology and innovation.

JOCHEN BLÄSING is a Professor in the Faculty of Economics at Tilburg University. A specialist in German-Dutch economic relations and modern business history, he is the author of *Mensen en spanningen: sociaal-economische geschiedenis van de N.V. Provinciale Noordbrabantsche Electriciteits-Maatschappij 1914-1985* (Leiden, 1992).

FRANK BROEZE is Professor of History at the University of Western Australia and Vice-President of the IMEHA. He has published widely on themes in economic and maritime history, and his most recently books are *Gateways of Asia. Port Cities of Asia in the 13th-20th Centuries* (London, 1997); and *Island Nation. A History of Australians and the Sea* (St. Leonards, NSW, 1998).

WILLIAM H. FLAYHART is Professor and Chair of the Department of History and Political Science at Delaware State University, where he has taught since 1970. During 1994-1995 he was Visiting Professor of Maritime History at the University of Leiden.

SHIN GOTO teaches Business History in the Department of International Business and Management at Kanagawa University. He has worked on innovation in Japanese shipping and shipbuilding since 1920. His recent research centres on the relationship between the contractual nexus and corporate behaviour.

ROBERT GREENHILL is a member of the Department of Business Studies at London Guildhall University. His research has focussed on the involvement of British business in Latin America during the nineteenth and twentieth centuries. Dr. Greenhill has a special interest in Britain's maritime history and history of the commodity trades.

POUL HOLM is Research Professor of Nordic Maritime History at the Centre for Maritime and Regional History in Esbjerg, Denmark. He is presently directing a research project on coastal heritage management. His latest book is *Proteiner fra havet. Esbjergs fiskemelsindustri 1948-1998* (Esbjerg, 1998).

ADRIAN JARVIS is Curator of Port History at Merseyside Maritime Museum and Co-director of the Centre for Port and Maritime History, a joint venture by the Museum and the University of Liverpool. He has published two monographs on the history of the Port of Liverpool and numerous papers on that and allied topics, as well as a book on Samuel Smiles which examines the historiography of technology.

LEWIS JOHNMAN is the Quintin Hogg Research Fellow in History at the University of Westminster. He is currently working on a study of the British shipbuilding industry since 1945.

VASSILIS KARDASIS teaches economic history in the Department of Economics at the University of Crete. He has published extensively on nineteenth-century Greek maritime history.

YRJÖ KAUKIAINEN is Professor of European History at the University of Helsinki. He has published on maritime history, demographic history and economic and social history, mainly in the eighteenth and nineteenth centuries. His recent books include *Sailing into Twilight. Finnish Shipping in an Age of Transport Revolution, 1860-1914* (Helsinki, 1991) and *A History of Finnish Shipping* (London, 1993).

KATAYAMA KUNIO is Professor of Economics and International Transport at Osaka Gakuin University. A specialist in pre-1939 Japanese shipping, his most recent book in Japanese is *Expansion of Modern Japanese Shipping into Asia* (Tokyo, 1996).

TON LANGENHUYZEN teaches in the Faculty of Economics at Tilburg University, where he specializes in the history of European Integration and business history. His most recent publication is "Joodse achtergronden van de Osse industrie," in J. Cahen and A. van de Sande (eds.), *Joods leven in Brabant* (Den Bosch, 1996).

LARS U. SCHOLL is an historian at the Deutsches Schiffahrtsmuseum and an external lecturer in maritime history at the University of Hamburg. A specialist in nineteenth- and twentieth-century German maritime history with a particular interest in shipping and shipbuilding, he is the author of several books on German marine artists. He is also the Chair of the Editorial Board of the *International Journal of Maritime History* and President of the German Commission for Maritime History.

EDWARD W. SLOAN is the Charles H. Northam Professor History at Trinity College, Connecticut, and for three decades has lectured and led graduate seminars of the Munson Institute at Mystic Seaport Museum. With several other Munson Institute faculty, he is co-author of the forthcoming *America and the Sea*, published by Mystic Seaport Press.

MARIKO TATSUKI is currently a Professor at Keisen University specializing in economics and the history of the Japanese economy.

JOHN THEOTOKAS is Adjunct Lecturer in the Department of Business Administration at the University of the Aegean. He has a particular interest in the management of shipping companies.

WILLIAM D. WRAY is Associate Professor of History at the University of British Columbia. He is the author of *Mitsubishi and the NYK, 1870-1914: Business Strategy in the Japanese Shipping Industry* (Cambridge, MA, 1984); and editor of *Managing Industrial Enterprise: Cases from Japan's Prewar Experience* (Cambridge, MA, 1989). He is presently completing a manuscript entitled "Riding a Tsunami: Japan's NYK Line and World War I."

Introduction

David J. Starkey and Gelina Harlaftis

> ...exuberant energy, wealth, power and arrogance... propelled Europeans into all corners of the globe and by the mid-nineteenth century created a single world-wide economic and maritime system.[1]

The internationalization of the world economy has been one of the defining characteristics of the nineteenth and twentieth centuries. A direct result of European expansionism and industrialization, this process has been facilitated by, and has stimulated, profound improvements in transportation and communications. While revolutions in land, air and sea transport have played a significant part in extending the scope of economic activity, remarkable advances in the means of information dissemination have greatly expedited the flow of intelligence and data upon which the business decisions of producers and consumers are based. Due to such developments, the world has become smaller in a metaphorical sense; but, at the same time, the spatial expansion of the world's commodity, labour and capital markets has been such that they have become literally global in extent.

Global Markets is concerned with the part that the sea transport industries have played in this process. Such a subject area provides an excellent vantage point from which to examine the emergence and development of the international economy, for the sea transport industries, by their very nature, are both intrinsic to, and influenced by, the economic and political interactions between nations. Accordingly, studies of shipping and shipping-related activities provide insights into the nature of phenomena which are labelled, often very imprecisely, "internationalization" and "globalization." The former is directly derived from the concept of the nation state, though it implies rather more than the simple

[1]Frank Broeze, *Island Nation. A History of Australians and the Sea* (St. Leonards, NSW, 1998), 38.

exchanges between bordering states that the term "international" might be taken to mean. Instead, internationalization implies a process of becoming, an ongoing evolution entailing the emergence of multilateral, spatially dispersed and regular links between nations. This gradual process is well illustrated by the pace and pattern of the geographical spread of shipping routes from the mid-nineteenth century (see Wray's chapter). "Globalization" is more contentious. While not all observers accept the validity of the concept, some arguing that if anything it forms simply a phase in the internationalization process (Johnman), those who view it as a distinct phenomenon offer different interpretations as to its meaning, scope and location in an historical context (Greenhill, Scholl, Jarvis, Goto). Most commentators, however, would concur that globalization is a process by which nation states and nationally-based business institutions are superposed (and sometimes undermined) by transnational economic, information and political networks (Holm).

But how did internationalization and globalization come about? Which forces have conditioned their evolution? What have been, and will be, the consequences of these phenomena? The authors in this volume address four main issues relating to these broad questions: information, networks and cooperation in transoceanic shipping (Kaukiainen, Sloan, Greenhill, Wray); the expansion of markets (Blasing and Langenhuyzen, Flayhart, Katayama, Tatsuki); technological change (Scholl, Jarvis, Holm, Basberg); and the adaptability of entrepreneurs, institutions and nation states to changing business environments (Kardasis, Theotakis, Johnman, Goto, Broeze).

The first of these issues relates to the efforts of firms to reduce the commercial risks inherent in shipping operations by improving information flows and collaborating with actual and potential competitors. While such strategies are generally associated with the rapidly growing prominence of steamships, railways and the telegraph in the second half of the nineteenth century, they were actually deployed much earlier. For instance, international freight markets, based on the transmission and receipt of an adequate supply of accurate information, were emerging well before 1850. As the case of Peter Malm of Jakobstad indicates, Scandinavian sailing vessel owners had developed strong links with business "friends" in various Mediterranean ports, contacts who in turn had commercial and family links further afield. Via such networks, data on freight rates, commodity markets and other items of local knowledge vital to the prosperity of shipping companies, were relayed back to shipowners to inform the decision-making process. Reliable, trustworthy local agents were at the heart of this system. In the proliferation of correspondence between Malm and his shipmasters and agents, and in the formalisation of charterparties, bills of lading and other forms of the necessary paperwork, many of which were translated into the appropriate European language, there are clear signs that the nucleus of a relatively sophisticated international freight market had developed by the 1830s (Kaukiainen).

Collusion with rivals was a further risk-averting devise favoured by shipowners. Widely considered to have been a child of the 1870s, the international cartel was in fact born at least two decades earlier when the Cunard and Collins Lines entered into an agreement to set freight rates and share revenues on their seemingly competitive transatlantic routes. With the powerful banking enterprise of the Brown Brother acting as midwife, this innovative agreement — conceived, ironically, as that icon of trade discrimination, the British Navigation system, was being dismantled — remained secret until well into the twentieth century (Sloan). Only marginally more visible were the shipping conferences, the first of which is customarily deemed to have been established on the London-Calcutta route in 1875. Essentially oligopolistic arrangements, conferences represented a response by established operators to the profit-reducing threat posed by the entry of newcomers into their trades. Precisely how effective conferences were in stemming the tide of market forces is difficult to calculate. However, the psychological benefits — chiefly in terms of that intangible asset, business confidence — accruing from being a member of the club rather than an excluded outsider, were highly significant (Greenhill).

Conferences also played an important role in the internationalization of shipping. On many lines, the established operators, and initiators of cartels, were British shipping companies, while the new entrants to the market were generally based in other countries. This gave a nationalistic edge to the situation, as the newcomers were obliged to devise means to counter the advantages held by the dominant, Anglocentric oligopoly. In the case of Japan, this entailed the emergence of alliances between shipping enterpises which in stages passed from passive participation to co-regimism in markets initially dominated by British firms. At the same time, national alliances operating on an increasingly worldwide scale were obliged to co-operate with other, sometimes rival, national groups to handle day-to-day matters such as freight solicitation, overseas agency, brokerage, international transactions and short-term financing. Such transnational linkages formed strands in a global web which has been evolving since the 1890s. As the development of Japanese shipping enterprise shows, national alliances and global webs have overlapped and existed co-terminously over the last century (Wray).

Market expansion is the second principal issue discussed in this volume. The sea transport industries are essentially conditioned by the level and character of international sea-borne trade, itself a function of regional specialization and the international division of labour. Sustained population growth, mass migration and the spread of industrialization meant that the level of world trade expanded more than ten times faster than world production during the 1870-1914 period, greatly increasing the demand for shipping services.[2] Exploiting these propitious conditions, shipowners and traders built up their operations and inaugurated new routes. In the Netherlands, the sea transport industries were transformed as the rapid industrialization of the Ruhr region of Germany precipitated the massive growth of transit traffic in bulk raw materials on the Rhine. This led to the reorientation of the Dutch shipping industry away from the protected colonial staple trades towards the Eurocentric transit trade, a shift that galvanized the port industry, especially in Rotterdam, as well as obliging the shipbuilding industry to "modernize" its techniques and products (Blasing and Langenhuyzen). Industrial development in the United States likewise impacted upon the transport sector and encouraged firms such as the Pennsylvania Railroad Company to invest in sea, as well as land, transport in an attempt to expand its business by establishing transatlantic shipping services at the port of Philadelphia. This attempt to provide a unitary service from Europe to the mid-western states of America involved the establishment of an American steamship line, efforts to operate a shipping company based overseas, and the acquisition of

---

[2]A.G. Kenwood and A.L. Lougheed, *The Growth of the International Economy 1820-1960* (London, 1971), 90-91.

foreign liner services. The investment of railroad capital in other industries and other countries ultimately led in the 1890s to the revival of America's stake in the highly competitive environment of the North Atlantic passenger liner trade (Flayhart).

In the Far East, the Japanese sought to expand their shipping interests from the early years of the Meiji Restoration in 1868. Such plans did not come to fruition until the 1890s when the House of Representatives, shipping firms and influential academics began to urge the government to support and subsidize the establishment of new Japanese ocean-going services. Before 1895, commercial, rather than military, motives underpinned this lobbying (Katayama). In the years down to the First World War, Japanese shipping companies, notably NYK and OSK, greatly developed their liner interests, a trend that was given a substantial boost during the First World War when the virtual withdrawal of British shipping and British goods exposed many markets to penetration by operators from Asian states. The Japanese, whose manufacturing base was burgeoning, exploited this opportunity more than any other power, and continued to build up their shipping and trade interests during the interwar years, a period in which the sea transport industries of many other countries, especially Britain, struggled. Accordingly, having already established themselves on the routes of the northern hemisphere, Japanese liner companies developed a range of southern hemisphere services to Australia, Africa and South America (Tatsuki).

A third issue, technological change, is then considered. Over the centuries, this has been a critical factor in facilitating, or perhaps determining (Jarvis), the development of the sea transport industries. For instance, seminal advances in shipping technology, such as the evolution of the three-masted, ocean-going ship in the fifteenth century, the steel-hulled steamer in the late nineteenth century and the tankers and containerships of the modern era, have been fundamental to the improvements in the range and efficiency of sea-borne trade and, with it, economic activity in general. Similarly, on land, the application of civil engineering skills has led to great productivity gains, as capital works like the construction of the Suez and Panama Canals reduced travel time between distant regions of the world, and infrastructural developments, like the building of larger, deeper docks served by more effective cargo-handling equipment, has greatly enhanced the efficiency of ports.

There have been other significant, if less epoch-making, technical advances. The establishment of telegraph systems, for example, between Europe and the rest of the world not only facilitated the increase of world trade from 1840 onwards, but also changed fundamentally the organisation and management of shipping companies. Before telegraphy the only way of passing information from one part of the world to the other was by letter. While this form of transmission permitted the growth of nascent freight markets (Kaukiainen), in the age of sail it still took months for Europeans to receive messages from the Far East, and weeks from the Americas. The introduction of the telegraph in the 1840s, and the gradual diffusion of submarine cables all over the world, effected a revolution in the exchange of commercial and other information. A British entrepreneur could now direct his business from his office in London without having to travel abroad. Before the First World War, Britain owned two-thirds of the world's submarine cable network, thereby strengthening its position as the pre-eminent trading nation. Aboard ship, the wireless proved to be a highly beneficial invention, as it improved the safety of vessel operation by linking ship to shore and providing the master with access to intelligence of climatic and navigational hazards (Scholl). Advances in cargo handling and storage were also extremely valuable, especially in respect of the transport of perishable cargoes. Indeed, the transoceanic movement of many foodstuffs only developed once refrigeration became viable in ships and warehouses. Pioneering voyages between the northern and southern hemispheres, especially on routes linking Europe with Latin America, Australia and New Zealand, started in the 1860s, and within three decades effective forms of mechanical refrigeration had resulted from a successful combination of theory and practice. Moreover, much less time was spent in port by steamships due to the development of bulk cargo handling techniques in the main European and American ports (Jarvis).

The fishing and whaling industries entail the transport of productive factors and products over the seas and have therefore shared in the benefits afforded by technological advances in shipping. However, these industries are primarily concerned with exploiting marine resources, an objective which has been greatly influenced by technological change. In the fisheries, for example, the adoption of the trawl net, the application of steam propulsion, and, on land, the utilization of railways are some of the technical advances that have enhanced the catching effort since the mid-nineteenth century (Holm). Likewise, the advent of "modern" whaling, with the deployment of Svend Foyn's steam catcher boat and harpoon gun, dramatically improved the efficiency of whaling operations (Basberg). At the same time, such technological progress gave an added impetus to the internationalization process, as fishermen and whalermen in other countries imitated or imported the new techniques. As a result, there has been an increase in competition in the fishing and whaling industries, a marked growth in output, and a massive, possibly devastating, contraction in the resource base which sustains these activities.

Internationalization and globalization have altered the business environment in which entrepreneurs, companies and nation states work. How individuals and institutions have adapted to the problems and opportunities thrown up by such broadening horizons is the fourth issue to be addressed in this volume. A range of responses have been apparent in the sea transport industries. Given that Greeks have emerged as major players in the twentieth-century tramp shipping market, assembling large companies operating on a worldwide scale, it might might be anticipated that the organisation and management of these enterprises would have changed considerably during the course of their development. However, this has not been the case, despite the efforts of entrepreneurs such as Demetrios Moraitis to adopt new business practices and enter new markets. This celebrated shipowner, a native of the island of Andros, attempted to raise capital by establishing multi-participant tramp shipping ventures in which the smallest of small savers could invest. He also endeavoured to form the first Greek transatlantic line with the intention of profiting from the carriage of emigrants from the eastern Mediterranean to New York, thereby encroaching upon a business dominated by Italian and German companies. Though these initiatives took place between 1893 and 1908 — a period when the prevailing international trend very much favoured the development of joint stock enterprises, mergers and large holding corporations — they both failed to break the mould of the family-dominated institutional structure of Greek shipping (Kardasis). Indeed, in marked contrast to the "Chandlerian paradigm," the Greek tramp shipping industry has continued throughout the twentieth century to rely to an extraordinary extent on the family as a business unit and has therefore yet to undergo the transition from "personal" to "managerial" capitalism. It would seem that tramp shipping, the most vibrant sector of Greece's sea transport industries, still retains the characteristics that were shaped in the first phase of the internationalization process in the mid-nineteenth century (Theotokas).

During the late nineteenth and much of the twentieth century, as the experience of the Greek shipping industry testifies, non-British liner firms, to compete effectively in the international arena, needed to reach agreements with British shipping lines, while non-British tramp owners had to be linked to the world's most important maritime centre, the British market. Shipbuilding was a further spoke in this Anglocentric wheel, for it was in Britain that much of the world's steamship tonnage was built and exchanged on the second hand market. Even though British shipbuilding had experienced relative decline since the early 1890s, when over eighty percent of the world's tonnage had been completed in British yards, this remained the single most productive national industry in the late 1940s. Yet, as world shipbuilding output mushroomed during the so-called "Long Boom" of 1945-1973, the relative contraction of British production not only continued but gathered pace. Various reasons have been advanced for this competitive and comparative failure, including the institutional rigidity of shipbuilding firms, labour relations and state policy. In this volume, Johnman argues that the underlying explanation for this extraordinary failure was the inability of British shipyard owners to adapt to changes in the business environment, more particularly their reluctance to adopt a positive approach to the sustained growth of an increasingly international market.

Less conservative attitudes to the internationalization of the sea transport industries can be discerned elsewhere. In Japan, for instance, the state has acted to try to arrest the "hollowing out" of the shipping industry, a widespread phenomenon in which the procurement and deployment of foreign productive factors leads inexorably to decreases in domestic investment and employment. The Japanese government's response has entailed the negotiation of revised manning arrangements so that Japanese shipowners are now permitted to recruit low-wage foreign seamen as well as relatively expensive Japanese seafarers. Moreover,vessel registration procedures have been liberalized to permit a broader definition of "Japanese" shipping, and tacit support has been afforded to the "flagging out" of a large proportion of the merchant fleet — practices commonly used by the economically advanced maritime nations since the 1960s (Goto). In this, modern governments are merely following a well-trod path, for nation states have long since sought to support their shipping interests, be it in the form of the erection or abolition of protective systems like the Navigation Laws, the provision of direct and indirect subsidies, or flag discrimination.

State financial aid has also played a role, albeit relatively minor, in the "container revolution" that has transformed liner shipping since the 1960s. In this sector, the creation of a sophisticated, "intermodal" transport chain, the links of which extend from producer to consumer, has involved the development of integrated shipping, port, railway and highway services, and entailed huge investments in ever larger vessels, rolling stock, road linkages and port infrastructure. The immense financial requirements of this business, and the massive volume of freight moved in containers, has had a profound impact on the world's sea transport industries. In the shipping industry, mergers, take-overs and new forms of collaboration have occurred, leading to the formation of international networks dubbed the "Global Alliance" and the "Grand Alliance." Such amalgamations have expanded their activities to all the oceans of the world and revived the notion of the "round-the-world" service. Technological developments in cargo-handling and vessel construction have enabled ports and shipbuilders to keep pace with — at times, to force the pace of — the expansion in the scale of shipping operations. At the same time, the adaptability of the human agents in this process of change has been demonstrated, as seafarers have accepted new working practices, entrepreneurs have sunk capital into experimental technology, and shipping companies have joined forces with erstwhile rivals (Broeze).

In essence, therefore, containerization not only embraces the four central themes of this volume — business networks and alliances, market expansion, technological change, and adaptability to change — but also highlights the extent to which internationalization and globalization have influenced the development of the sea transport industries. Yet, as a number of contributors to this volume imply, these processes have still to run their full course.

International Freight Markets in the 1830s and 1840s: The Experience of a Major Finnish Shipowner

Yrjö Kaukiainen

There is a common belief that truly international, or global, freight markets only became possible after the introduction of steam shipping and telegraph communication. It is obvious, however, that some very important developments in maritime trade took place during the era of sail, well before these crucial technological innovations occurred.

In the late 1950s and 1960s, Douglass C. North published a series of articles on the long-run development of freight rates and shipping productivity.[1] In these, he claimed that the costs of seaborne transport declined almost continuously from the mid-seventeenth century until the First World War, thus effectively diminishing the proportion of freight in the prices of overseas products ("freight ratio"). According to North, the fall in the real cost of shipping was steepest in the first half of the nineteenth century, that is, long before the transition from sail to steam.[2] So far, no one else has attempted any comparable long-term analysis.

North explained this secular trend in terms of a long-run improvement in shipping productivity. He did not ascribe this solely to technological change, but also to market factors such as "the expansion in the volume of international trade" and institutional changes like "the ending of navigation laws and other artificial impediments to multilateral shipping."[3] This is not surprising for a scholar who is best known as an neo-classical institutionalist and has claimed that "improvements in human

[1]See, in particular, Douglass C. North, "Ocean Freight Rates and Economic Development 1750-1913," *Journal of Economic History*, XVIII (1958), 537-555; and North, "Sources of Productivity Change in Ocean Shipping, 1600-1850," *Journal of Political Economy*, LXXVI (1968), 953-970.

[2]North, "Sources of Productivity," 954, esp. note 4.

[3]North, "Ocean Freight Rates," 541.

organization" were probably as important for economic growth as technological development.[4]

However, while North studied the development of hull forms, ship sizes and manning ratios in some detail he did not devote as much attention to the evolution of freight markets. It is true that he identified "the reduction of time idle in port or in ballast"[5] as an important contributor to the growth of shipping productivity, but he proceeded no further. Yet this seems to be one of the most interesting aspects of this complex problem: it is quite tempting to suppose that periods of unemployment, whether in port or sailing with ballast, reflect the failure of the market to transmit potential freighters' needs to actual carriers. If this is true the reduction of "idle time" depended — more or less — on the development of the networks and institutions of the market.

The importance of such factors can only be estimated if we know how the freight markets worked — what were the institutions and best everyday practices — and how did they change? This chapter addresses such questions. As it considers only a short period of time — the 1830s and 1840s — it does not provide a long term comparative analysis. Yet this is an important period, for in these decades the Navigation Laws were still in force and it is possible to form some idea as to what kinds of "impediments to multilateral shipping" such laws, as well as practices and traditions arising out of them, actually presented. The period is also, according to Douglass C. North, a period of rapid productivity growth; therefore, if productivity and markets were linked, the latter should show some signs of change or development.

The Case and the Source Material

Research into everyday business practices inevitably calls for a micro-level approach. It also requires source material which offers a detailed, day-to-day picture of what individual shipmasters did while staying in port. Quantitative data on the number of days in port can certainly give useful background information but, since they normally do not divulge the reasons for long stays, they reveal very little about the efficiency of

---

[4]For example, see North, "Institutions and Productivity in History" (http://econwpa.wustl.edu/eprints/eh/papers/9411/9411006.abs.).

[5]North, "Ocean Freight Rates," 541.

freight markets. Equally, a high proportion of time sailing in ballast did not necessarily reflect market inefficiencies or inadequate information flows, because it was often due to an imbalance in the supply of cargo on certain trade routes. While the source material which sheds most light on such problems is the correspondence which masters conducted with shipowners and other business partners, charter-parties and other agreements can also provide valuable information.

Such records exist for a few Finnish trading-houses; as far as the 1830s and 1840s are concerned, probably the most useful are those of Peter Malm, Jr. (1800-1868), from the small Ostrobothnian town of Jakobstad (Pietarsaari). While the correspondence and other material is well preserved,[6] Malm was one of the foremost Finnish shipowners of his time whose vessels sailed far afield in international ocean trades. It may be doubted whether data concerning such a peripheral actor can be regarded as representative, but in reality the domicile of a shipowner was not quite as important as one might think. National commercial laws and customs were relatively uniform all over Western Europe and were applied to all business "friends" and customers irrespective of nationality. Thus, Peter Malm not only transmitted money by bills of exchange similar to those of British businessmen, his ships and masters worked within the same freight market infrastructure, whether in Marseille, Rio de Janeiro or London. Provided the shipowner was engaged in truly international freight trades and had access to normal services and sources of

---

[6]The most important parts of the archives of the Malm trading house containing correspondence, ships' accounts and charter parties are preserved in the Finnish National Archives in Helsinki. But part of the original archive has remained in Jakobstad, either in the town museum (which occupies Malm's old house) or the local town archives. Unfortunately, the materials in the National Archives have never been properly organized. The bulk of the letters received have been provisionally organized according to year and sender, but some correspondence still remains totally unsorted in bags and cardboard boxes. Thus, there are gaps in the material for at least the mid-1830s and early 1840s, which means that for such years some random parts of the alphabet are missing. These gaps are very difficult to fill, as the totally unorganized archives still amount to 50-60 metres of shelving. Nonetheless, all the material in its original state, even including parts which now are unaccessible, was used by a well-qualified maritime historian (and a former professor of Scandinavian history in Åbo Akademi), Oscar Nikula, who starting in the 1930s wrote the history of the house: Oscar Nikula, *Malmska handelshuset i Jakobstad* (Helsingfors, 1948). Although the institutions and practices of freight markets were not the author's real interests, the book offers some data with which gaps in correspondence can be bridged. Moreover, it contains a wealth of fairly detailed background information.

information, his experiences can be taken as a typical reflection of the market environment.

Peter Malm fits this model. He was the oldest son in a family which had been engaged for two generations in foreign trade and shipping. As well as studying at local high school and Åbo University, he had spent two years in England for practical studies and visited Germany and Denmark.[7] After establishing himself as a foreign-trading merchant, Peter Malm entered blue-water shipping in 1826 when he launched his first full-rigged ship. Return on investment was obviously satisfactory as the tonnage increased at a rapid rate, and in 1842 Malm commanded eleven blue-water ships of a total tonnage of almost 2900 Swedish *lasts*, a fleet larger than any other merchant in Finland. Shipwrecks and sales diminished his shipping stock by about a half over the next seven or eight years, but a renewed expansion was imminent when the Crimean War broke out.[8]

Although Peter Malm did not stay abroad for long periods after starting his own business, he was kept up to date by correspondence, newspaper, such as the *Hamburger Börsenhalle*,[9] and personal contacts. Three of his brothers became master mariners, the second oldest, Arvid (1808-1845), being engaged in foreign shipbrokers' offices such as Sörensen, Son and Co. in Liverpool, 1829-1833; Sack, Weber and Co. in Liverpool, 1836-1837; and F. Bonnin in Marseille, 1838-1842.[10] Malm could also rely on a wide network of business "friends," his most important connections being in Stockholm (Dan. Sutthoff and Co.), Riga (Westberg and Co.), St. Petersburg (Gustaf Sterky and Son), Elsinore

---

[7]In Liverpool, he apprenticed in a trading house (Sörensen, Son and Co.) with Scandinavian connections and was later a minor shareholder in the firm. He seems to have been fluent in English and German and also knew some French (and because Swedish was his mother tongue, he understood Danish and Norwegian). *Ibid.*, 62-63.

[8]In 1830, Malm owned three ships and brigs of a total of 490 lasts; in 1838, the corresponding figures were eight and 1791; in 1846, eleven and 2518; and in 1853, eight and 1850. In addition, he normally owned a few coastal vessels. *Ibid.*, 512-517 (ship list).

[9]Malm Archives (Helsinki), Letters Received (hereafter MA, LR), Capt. Idman to P. Malm, London, 22 October 1845; Idman to P. Malm, Marseilles, 11 April 1848.

[10]Nikula, *Malmska handelshuset*, 56-59; MA, LR, Arvid Malm to P. Malm, 28 September and 28 October 1838.

(Louise sal. Holms Enka, later associated with Julius Schierbeck), Hamburg (Jacobi and Suse), Marseille (J. and B. Magnan de Kothen, Wessel and Co.) and Genoa (Steurenberg and Casanova). The hub of this network was the London house of Rew, Prescott and Co., which specialized in selling Scandinavian timber products, some from the firm's own sawmills in Sweden. Not only did this house sell Malm's exports and arrange for the financing of different transactions but it also acted as an intermediary between Malm and his shipmasters, reporting the whereabouts of the latter and giving them advice and intelligence when necessary. As well as these first-rate friends, Malm had contacts with many other shipbrokers, while he also had access to the networks which his principal business partners had built.[11] Thus, Malm's shipmasters, even when far from home, had numerous sources of basic information.

International Shipping in the 1830s and 1840s

Peter Malm started operating in the international freight markets before the abolition of the old mercantilist system. The British Navigation Acts and their counterparts in France, Spain, Sweden and other countries had created a framework in which bilateral rather than multilateral trade and shipping was the rule. While nations generally prescribed that their own cargoes should be carried by their own vessels, there were also customs and dues which discriminated against all foreign carriers. Even the Dutch Republic, the main advocate of the freedom of seas and trade, decreed that its colonial trade was reserved for chartered companies, such as the VOC.[12]

But there were countries and regions such as Russia, the German free towns and a number of Italian states, which did not erect Navigation Laws. Thus, outsiders could enter the carrying trades between certain foreign countries, especially in the Baltic and the Mediterranean. For

---

[11]Nikula, *Malmska handelshuset*, 103-105, 111-115, 135-140; MA, LR (in particular those from Rew, Prescott and Co.).

[12]For example, see Hans Chr. Johansen, "Danish Shipping Services as a Link between the Mediterranean and the Baltic 1750-1850," in L.R. Fischer and H.W. Nordvik (eds.), *Shipping and Trade, 1750-1950: Essays in International Maritime Economic History* (Pontefract, 1990), 15-16; Sarah Palmer, *Politics, Shipping and the Repeal of Navigation Laws* (Manchester, 1990), 40-42; and C.R. Boxer, *The Dutch Seaborne Empire 1600-1800* (St. Ives, 1990), 101-103.

example, Dutch, Danish and Swedish ships dominated the trades between the Western Mediterranean and the Baltic in the late eighteenth century, and also carried freight between different Mediterranean ports. Similarly, Dutch and English ships carried most of Russia's foreign trade.[13]

In the early nineteenth century, more trades were opened to international competition. After the old Dutch East India Company collapsed, vessels of all nations were allowed to carry goods from Batavia and other Dutch East India ports.[14] Almost simultaneously, South American shipping became free. After the King of Portugal had fled to Brazil, Britain persuaded him in 1808 to open the ports of the colony to the ships of "all friendly nations," a liberal policy that continued after Brazil was declared independent in 1825. The disintegration of the Spanish American Empire had similar ramifications, with the new republics of La Plata, Columbia and Chile attracting European shipping.[15]

Even the British colonial system provided some opportunities for "interlopers." In the West Indies, foreign ships and transit trade were allowed in some free ports and there were exceptions concerning certain commodities. The end of the East India Company's monopoly in 1833 did not directly affect foreign shipping but it anticipated a more liberal colonial and trade policy. More important in the short run was the series of reciprocity treaties signed between Britain and various states from 1815

---

[13]Johansen, "Danish Shipping Services ," 16-20; and Yrjö Kaukiainen, *A History of Finnish Shipping* (London, 1993), 41-43.

[14]For example, see Femme S. Gaastra and Jaap R. Bruijn, "The Dutch East India Company's Shipping, 1602-1795, in a Comparative Perspective," in J.R. Bruijn and F.S. Gaastra (eds.), *Ships, Sailors and Spices, East India Companies and Their Shipping in the 16th, 17th and 18th Centuries* (Amsterdam, 1993), 206. Actually, the VOC had chartered foreign vessels even before this; *Concordia* from Jakobstad sailed with a cargo from Batavia to Amsterdam in 1784-1785 (see Nikula, *Malmska handelshuset*, 27-28). From 1795, Dutch East India trade was mainly carried on by Danish vessels in order to avoid English blockades; see Ole Feldbaek, "Dutch Batavia Trade via Copenhagen, 1795-1807," *Scandinavian Economic History Review*, XXI (1973), 43.

[15]C.R. Boxer, *The Portuguese Seaborne Empire 1415-1825* (Aylesbury, 1973), 204-205. In 1808, a couple of ships from St. Petersburg sailed to Brazil and the first Swedish ship did so in 1809. The "opening" of Spain's former colonies created a speculative boom in Britain, in particular; see Nikula, *Malmska handelshuset*, 90-94. But it must be noted that already in the eighteenth century a few Finnish ships had carried cargo between Cadiz and Spain's American possessions; see Kaukiainen, *Finnish Shipping*, 42.

onwards which allowed the vessels of the partner country to trade in British ports, and *vice-versa.* Although these agreements did not mean that the restrictions relating to coastal and colonial trades had been abolished, they effectively promoted free trade, if not free shipping.[16] Even foreign carriers sailing to British ports gained because their ships were no longer burdened by high customs or dues, and so their competitiveness improved.

Thus, the old mercantilist system was weakening before the abolition of the British Navigation Laws in 1850. While there had been trades with true international competition before the Napoleonic Wars, they were much more important in the 1830s and 1840s. In addition to the South American trades, the routes between Northwest Europe and the Dutch East Indies became increasingly internationalized. After the Peace of Adrianople in 1829, this was also true of the Eastern Mediterranean and the Black Sea. Against this, most of the great shipping arteries within the British Empire, and between Britain and North America, still remained closed to outsiders.

Peter Malm's Ships on Foreign Freight Markets

Peter Malm deployed his vessels in much the same way as other Finnish (and Swedish) shipowners. In late summer or autumn, those at home embarked with tar and timber, normally for a Mediterranean port. The cargo was sold at the destination and freight opportunities were investigated. If a profitable freight was found, the ship or brig sailed foreign, often for years; otherwise, a cargo of salt was bought in Hyéres, Cagliari, Cadiz or Lisbon and carried to the Baltic at first open water. Such a cargo normally terminated a long cross-freighting tour, the salt in most cases being sold in Riga, St. Petersburg, Wiborg or Stockholm, though sometimes it was brought home.

Peter Malm had — in addition to his brothers — some very able shipmasters. In particular, P.G. Idman (1796-1856, in Malm's service from 1839) and P.G. Böckelman (1808-1888; in Malm's service from at least 1836) stand out. The former, although born in Jakobstad, received his master's certificate in Stockholm in 1818 and commanded ships of a

---

[16]Palmer, *Politics,*, 50-52; the circular of the Finnish Customs Office, 16 October 1843, concerning the Reciprocity agreement between Russia and Britain, 30 December 1842/11 January 1843, *Finlands Författnings Samling* (1843), 250.

major Stockholm shipowner for almost ten years.[17] Böckelman, evidently possessed keen commercial skills, for he took care of the firm's office in 1837 when the patron was away from Jakobstad. He also owned a third of the ship which was in his command and became its sole owner in 1847.[18] Both captains seem to have had a good first-hand knowledge of freight markets and shipbrokers in various European ports, as is demonstrated in long and detailed letters to their employer.

How they, and other masters, managed the business transactions depended on whether their ship was selling an export cargo or trying to find a freight. It also varied from one area and port to another.

Selling the Export Cargo

When Malm's ships sailed to the Mediterranean with tar and timber, the commodities were carried at the owner's risk; purchase agreements were not normally made in advance. Thus the master's first task after entering Marseille, Genoa, Leghorn or Cadiz, and clearing customs, was to offer the goods for sale. Old business friends, such as Magnan de Kothen, Wessel and Co. or Steurenberg and Casanova, seem to have been given some priority, at least they were contacted first, but they enjoyed no real option rights. Instead, masters usually contacted several houses for offers. As most of the Scandinavian timber and tar arrived within a short period around the end of the year, the markets could fluctuate rapidly. Therefore, it was common for masters to correspond with houses in other ports, and then consider sailing there if prices seemed higher.[19]

---

[17]Idman had visited Valparaiso in 1821, the second Swedish master ever to arrive at that port; Nikula, *Malmska handelshuset*, 174-177.

[18]Nikula, *Malmska handelshuset*, 128; MA, LR, P.G. Böckelman to P. Malm, 14 June and 29 July 1844, and 16 April 1847. Obviously, he was fluent in both English and German, and, in the 1840s when sailing in trades to and from Hamburg, he almost made the city his second home. His wife accompanied him on voyages and their youngest daughter was schooled in Hamburg.

[19]MA, LR, Capt. Forbus to P. Malm, Genoa, 15 December 1832; Capt. Humble to P. Malm, Marseille, 17 January 1832, and Leghorn, 6 November 1833; Capt. Idman to P. Malm, Marseilles, 3 April 1840, Marseilles, 1 January 1845, and Marseilles, 11 April 1848; Capt. Juttre to P. Malm, Genoa, 5 February 1848; and Capt. Nyman to P. Malm, Marseilles, 22 March 1847, and Marseilles, 17 November 1848.

In the 1830s, Malm exported little to Britain, but this trade increased around the turn of the decade and again after 1842, when the customs of non-empire timber products were lowered. In addition to London, cargoes were often sent to Liverpool, because freight could normally be found easily there. Unlike in the Mediterranean ports, a commission merchant or consignee was contacted in advance to sell the tar and timber; if the cargo went to London it was regularly sold by Rew, Prescott and Co., sometimes the goods being left in their care.[20]

In Mediterranean ports, bargaining might take a long time, particularly when demand was slack. Unfortunately, the captains' letters only seldom reveal precisely how long it took to sell the cargo. In 1832, there were two instances (Marseille and Genoa) in which the goods were sold only six and eight weeks after the ship had entered port; in contrast, in 1840 (Marseille) a cargo was sold in less than ten days.[21] Since unloading was begun only after the goods were sold, this process implied a direct increase in port time. If letters were sent to other ports, the main constraint was the speed of mail, for no reference is made to the optical telegraph. In the 1830s, an answer to a letter sent from Genoa to Marseille could take at least a week and in the case of Cadiz the time was double. This very constraint accounted for the fact that commission merchants were rarely used in Mediterranean ports. Although Malm regularly received information on local prices, this was, at best, one month old when it reached Jakobstad. It was risky to make firm decisions on such data because, before a ship finally reached the intended port, the age of that data had increased by anything between one and three months, and the market situation might have changed considerably.[22]

---

[20]For example, MA, LR, Capt. Alcenius to P. Malm, Bristol, 1 February 1841; Capt. Fr. Malm to P. Malm, London, 31 October 1842; and Rew, Prescott and Co., 13 October 1837; and Nikula, *Malmska handelshuset.*, 138-139 and 205-208.

[21]MA, LR, Humble to P. Malm, Marseilles, 17 January and 3 March 1832; Magnan de Kothen to P. Malm, 13 February 1832; Forbus to P. Malm, Genoa, 15 December 1832 and 9 February 1833; and Idman to P. Malm, Marseilles, 3 and 10 April 1840.

[22]Delivery times are calculated according to postal stamps on letters. Malm also recorded when he answered a letter, sometimes also when he received it. In the late 1830s, a letter from Marseilles reached Strasburg in three days and Grisslehamn (where mail crossed the Aaland Sea to the Finnish side) in about twenty days. In winter, however, times

Communications with Britain were faster. In summer, a letter from London could reach Jakobstad in two weeks. As cargoes could reach Britain in three or four weeks, it was less risky to commission a merchant in advance. In 1840, Malm sold two shiploads of deals to Bristol and Gloucester on f.o.b. terms, the buyers paying a freight of four pounds per standard. In 1848, a consignment of sawn wood was sold to Marseille on similar terms but such sales remained exceptional until the 1860s.[23]

Compared with the timber and tar trade, buying an import cargo of salt was normally a fairly simple and quick business. Malm's business friends in Marseille, Genoa or Leghorn either sold salt themselves or acted as agents between the master and salt traders in Hyéres or Cagliari. Salt was also bought from Torlades and Co. (Lisbon and St. Ybes), who might be regarded as permanent business partners of Malm (as well as many other Finnish and Scandinavian firms).[24]

Looking for Freight in the Mediterranean

As the shipmasters started to sell their cargo they also began to look for further employment. Carrying freight between foreign ports, at least during the winter months when the Baltic was blocked with ice, was of great importance to the overall profitability of shipping and, therefore, prospects for such earnings might affect the transactions with the buyers of tar and timber. It was not uncommon for the latter to make their bids more attractive by promising to arrange a freight agreement.[25]

Some of Malm's permanent business contacts sent him data on freight rates and, since they knew the local markets and had a number of business links, both in their cities and farther afield, they were reasonably efficient agents. Yet, this was a very simple type of freight market, a

could be much longer. See Fernand Braudel, *The Structures of Everyday Life* (London, 1988), 424-428.

[23]Nikula, *Malmska handelshuset*, 201 and 209-210. These transactions were made through a travelling agent, Adolphus Lindgren, who visited Finland in 1839; MA, LR, Idman to P. Malm, Marseille, 11 April 1848.

[24]MA, LR, Humble to P. Malm, Hyéres, 9 April 1832, and Lisbon, 24 April 1833; and Forbus to P. Malm, Genoa, 9 February 1833, and Trapani, 11 March 1833.

[25]See MA, LR, Humble to P. Malm, Marseilles, 17 January 1832.

"spot" market in which the ship had to be on the spot to make a contract. When Malm's ships arrived in Marseille, Genoa or another Mediterranean port, the masters had little idea as to whether there was demand for cargo space until they saw the number of ships in port and visited the houses of Magnan de Kothen, Casanova and other merchants. The same applies to other Scandinavian ships and therefore these spot markets could fluctuate quite suddenly. For example, in January 1832, the port of Marseille was full of freight-seekers and, according to Magnan de Kothen, the prospects seemed quite dull.[26]

Indeed, this was typical throughout the early 1830s. Although the peace of Adrianople (1829) pacified the eastern Mediterranean, and France delivered a fatal blow to Barbary piracy by conquering Algiers, declining business cycles and the onslaught of cholera combined to keep freight markets in a fairly pessimistic state.[27] Thus it was no wonder that Malm's captains were not very successful in finding freight from the western Mediterranean, and until 1834, at least, they mainly carried salt to the Baltic. After 1835, however, freight markets improved and Malm's ships were able to find employment both within the Mediterranean and in the trades to Western Europe or South America, as well as in the grain trade from the Black Sea. Although freight levels sank in the early 1840s there was no real slump until 1848, the "mad year" in Europe.

In one respect the picture remained unaltered until the end of the 1840s: ships carrying Finnish products to Mediterranean ports continued to enter local freight markets without prearranged contracts. The masters, however, learned to widen their search beyond local merchant communities. Whether that had happened in the early 1830s cannot be established from the correspondence, but it had certainly become almost standard practice by the end of the decade. For example, in 1838, Captain Böckelman, while loading timber in Segna (Dalmatia), wrote to both Marseille and Trieste in order to obtain a new freight in advance.[28]

---

[26]MA, LR, Humble to P. Malm, Marseilles, 17 January 1832. See also Humble to P. Malm, Seville, 5 December 1832; John D. Schau (Sevilla) to P. Malm, 27 November 1832; Capt. Rudolphi to P. Malm, Marseilles, 4 March 1837; F. Wessel (Marseilles) to P. Malm, 11 February 1837; and Nikula, *Malmska handelshuset*, 112-120.

[27]Nikula, *Malmska handelshuset*, 108-110. The same story can be found in North's freight indices; see "Sources of Productivity," appendix, col. 9.

[28]MA, LR, Böckelman to P. Malm, Segna, 4 August 1838.

Likewise, P.G. Idman, after arriving in Marseille in 1840, not only contacted local brokers but wrote to shipbrokers in both Trieste and Amsterdam. Perhaps it was because of his (and Böckelman's) advice that even other masters started to contact shipbrokers farther afield — in any case Idman gave hints to his colleagues and even wrote to Amsterdam on behalf of one of them. At least once Idman wrote to Amsterdam already from Elsinore, although the answer only arrived after he had been in Marseille for some time.[29]

Contacting Dutch brokers, however, did not mean that information on Mediterranean freight opportunities was to be found in Amsterdam. Rather, the masters were planning ahead and looking for contracts to carry goods from the Dutch East Indies to Europe (indirectly, this also shows that there was practically no contact between the Mediterranean and East Asian freight markets). If an East Asian return freight was found the local Mediterranean market could be used to supply an outward cargo. At least Marseille and southern Spanish ports had contacts with South America, and Malm's ships actually found a number of freights in this direction.

That Malm's masters corresponded with Trieste (mainly with shipbroker Lazarovich), and frequently loaded and discharged cargoes there, suggests that it had a special position in the Mediterranean freight market. Being the main outlet for the Habsburg Empire it obviously had more or less regular contacts both within and without the Mediterranean. On at least one occasion a Malm-owned ship found a cargo there which had nothing to do with local trade: Thus, in 1838, Captain Böckelman (who then was in Marseille) negotiated a freight of raisins from Cesme (Turkey) to Hamburg.[30]

It seems that little changed during the 1830s and 1840s. As late as 1848, Mediterranean freight markets were predominantly local and masters wanting to know the prospects in other major ports had to rely on writing letters.[31] Only one important change can be recorded: Marseille

---

[29]MA, LR, Idman to P. Malm, Marseilles, 10 April and 30 May 1840, Trieste, 8 March 1844, Marseilles, 18 May and 18 June 1844, and Marseilles, 1 January 1845.

[30]MA, LR, Böckelman to P. Malm, Marseilles, 27 November 1838.

[31]See MA, LR, Capt. Nyman to P. Malm, Marseilles, 17 November 1848; and Capt. Juttre to P. Malm, Genoa, 5 February 1848.

grew gradually in importance, at least as far as the Black Sea grain trade was concerned and this affected its freight market. As grain traders, Greeks in particular, formed wide networks local brokers were able to arrange freight not only for Marseille but for Britain. Yet the market does not seem to have been very efficient; for Malm's ships frequently sailed to the Black Sea "on speculation," without a signed freight agreement.[32]

Freight Markets in the Baltic

Malm's ships quite often returned to the Baltic from the Mediterranean with cargoes of salt for home, or sometimes freight for Riga or Cronstadt. Sometimes, they were chartered to carry salt to Bergen and from there the standard freight was herring to Cronstadt. Such ships were not always ordered home but tried instead to find a new cargo which would take them back to wider waters.

In such a situation, the best prospects were to carry timber products from Riga, St. Petersburg or Wiborg to British ports.[33] In all these places, the freight markets were just as localized as they were in most Mediterranean ports. Both Riga and St. Petersburg had important British merchant colonies and good contacts with the British Isles, but no signs of communication (or market integration) between them were found. In one respect the business was really traditional: in Riga, Malm's masters always addressed his permanent business friend, Westberg and Co., who then did their best by contacting their own friends (including local British traders) in order to find an acceptable freight. It seems probable that the situation was the same in St. Petersburg (Sterky and Son). In Wiborg, on the other hand, Malm had several business connections (Rosenius and Seseman, Tichanoff, etc.) and sometimes these even combined their goods to furnish a full cargo.

Such adherence to permanent business contacts may reflect the fact that Malm was able to exert much tighter control over Baltic

---

[32]See MA, LR, Nyman to P. Malm, Marseilles, 22 March 1847; Idman to P. Malm, Marseilles, 18 May 1844 and 1 January 1845, and Odessa, 2 May 1845. Also, see Gelina Harlaftis, *A History of Greek-Owned Shipping. The Making of an International Tramp Fleet, 1830 to the Present Day* (London, 1996), 40-41 and 53.

[33]It must be remembered that the British Navigation Laws forbade Finnish ships to carry goods like Swedish timber to Britain.

transactions than those farther afield. He regularly sold the salt cargo in advance and may then even have corresponded on freight prospects. On the other hand, the relatively primitive nature of the market may have contributed — if anything, communications were worse than in Central Europe, particularly during the winter. A striking example is the case of the ship *Hercules*. After unloading salt in Tallinn in December she was frozen in the port. The master, wanting to secure a freight agreement for next spring in good time, instead of sending a letter to Westberg, travelled himself by sleigh to Riga to discuss the prospects *tête a tête*.[34]

The Baltic freight market was efficient in one respect, for Malm's ships found acceptable freight there during the early 1830s.[35] The fact that Malm normally had time and opportunity to arrange freight in advance may, of course, have contributed. This was also a very simple and straightforward business: freight agreements were concluded only after a trade transaction had been finalized. However, since the wood trade fluctuated a lot — and varied seasonally — hardly any selling was done on long-term. This factor obviously kept the freight market primitive; and it was practically impossible to conclude a freight agreement in advance.

West European Freight Market

Considering Peter Malm's own working experiences in Liverpool and the key role which Rew, Prescott and Co. had in his financial transactions, one might have expected that the British freight market was very important to him. However, the restrictions posed by Navigation Acts and customs discrimination against non-empire timber products made it a problematic market. Even during the late 1830s, the overall number of freight charter parties negotiated with British merchants or agents seems not to have exceeded those concluded in Marseille, Cette, or other South European ports.

---

[34]Nikula, *Malmska handelshuset*, 132; and MA, LR, Westberg and Co. to P. Malm, 24 February/8 March, 17/29 March, and 21 April/3 May 1838.

[35]Only one case was found when a Malm-owned ship did not find acceptable freight in spite of arriving fairly early in Riga; the master regarded the offered rates as too low and preferred to bring grain to Jakobstad instead. MA, LR, Forbus to P. Malm, Riga, 30 May 1833.

In three cases the freight agreements concerned typical British exports, coal, iron and rock salt (which could be carried by ships of any nationality) and two of them were concluded in the port where the cargo had been taken in; thus they were simple spot markets similar to those governing typical Mediterranean freights. In three cases, however, there was a more complicated transaction: two entailed sailing to Archangel or Onega to take a timber cargo to Liverpool, while the third contract, which started with the carriage of emigrants from Liverpool to New York, included a return cargo. Not surprisingly, all three were arranged by Sack and Weber, with whom Arvid Malm was employed at the time.

In the 1840s, Malm's involvement in the West European freight market increased substantially. However, this was not related to European trades but South American and East Asian shipping, which soon employed all his best ships. Yet the role of British shipbrokers and other agents grew hardly at all: in the cases covered by correspondence, the number of charter parties negotiated by British agents remained about the same as in the preceding decade. On the other hand, a growing number of freight agreements were made with Dutch and Hamburg agents. This relationship probably reflected the fact that Britain still excluded foreign carriers from much of her colonial trade. This led to a bitter experience for Captain Böckelman in 1844. He concluded a charter party in Hamburg for coal from Newport to Ceylon, but this was soon cancelled as being contrary to British law.[36] This, however, was the only such case in the Malm archive.

Those interested in long-distance trades found better opportunities in two other directions: first, in the trades between the Netherlands and its East Indian possessions, and, second, between Hamburg and South America. The centre of the former trade was, of course, Amsterdam. It was still an important entrepot for East Indian colonial goods such as tea, coffee, sugar and spices, and there were several houses which regularly shipped such produce. As far as Malm's ships were concerned, the key figure in that market was the shipbroker Henrik Gullen. Clearly, Captain Idman had known him for some time, and in one letter he explained why he so often sought the services of this gentleman:

---

[36]MA, LR, Rew, Prescott and Co. to P. Malm, 9 and 23 July, and 20 August 1844; and Böckelman to P. Malm, Hamburg, 2 and 29 July 1844. It is possible that someone had misinterpreted the trade agreement between Britain and Russia, 30 December 1842/11 January 1843.

> anyone who in Amsterdam is looking for such freight [from Batavia to West Europe] should contact Mr. Gullen, who in this respect is collaborating with another shipbroker, a son-in-law to van Straten who always can offer these freights.[37]

Gullen could also be approached by correspondence from the Mediterranean and other ports, but in such cases the masters dealt directly with him. However, it seems that some Hamburg houses also acted as agents for Amsterdam traders; at least in 1842, Idman signed a charterparty there on a cargo for van Straten (from Batavia to Amsterdam), and his letter suggests that no less than two local houses, Knohr and Burchardt and Jacobi and Suse (Malm's old business friend), had been involved as middlemen.[38]

The charter parties concluded by Malm's captains in Hamburg reflect similar market conditions — even though they concerned mainly import shipments on the account of local commercial houses. Hamburg's trade with Brazil (coffee) and Chile (nitrates, copper ore) had expanded so rapidly that there was demand for more (or maybe cheaper) tonnage than the old "Free and Hanse Town" commanded. There were occasional direct imports from British India, as two of Malm's ships indicate.

If Idman was a central figure in dealings with Amsterdam, the same key role in relation to Hamburg was performed by Captain Böckelman. From 1840, he conducted regular business with Hamburg houses and helped other Malm masters to find freight in his favourite market. Initially his principal agent was Jacobi and Suse, but after a freight dispute in 1843, regular contacts were established with a shipbroker, August Bolten.[39] In a few cases, British merchants or agents arranged a South American charter party for Malm's captains: thus, in 1841, while in Hull with the *Syphide,* a cargo of salt from Setubal to Montevideo was

---

[37]MA, LR, Idman to P. Malm, Trieste, 8 March 1844.

[38]MA, LR, Idman to P. Malm, Hamburg, 6 October 1842.

[39]MA, LR, Böckelman to P. Malm, Hamburg, 4 July 1843; August Bolten is mentioned for the first time in a letter from Rew, Prescott and Co. to P. Malm, 23 July 1844. Interestingly, Böckelman even tried to offer his ship to carry emigrants from Hamburg to New Zealand — obviously such emigration was already substantial: Böckelman to P. Malm, Batavia, 8 January 1845.

negotiated (probably by Rew, Prescott and Co) for Böckelman, plus a return trip from the Philippines to Europe. Likewise, the *Hercules* (Capt. Idman) obtained a cargo of gunpowder and general goods to Rio in 1845. At least one master (Roos, ship *Otto*) managed to conclude a good freight from Havana (which was a free port) to Rotterdam with an outward freight of coal from Newport. More regularly, however, Malm's, as well as other Finnish ships, were finding Black Sea freight on the British market.[40] Since the most important exporting ports belonged to Russia, Finnish ships were able to carry their products to Britain without violating the Navigation Laws. Predictably, Rew, Prescott and Co. helped to establish contacts between masters and shipbrokers.[41]

The Malm correspondence suggests that the freight markets of Britain (especially London and Liverpool), Amsterdam and Hamburg were more developed than those of the Mediterranean, even including Trieste and Marseille. There are signs that some degree of integration existed between them. Thus, it was possible to conclude, in Hamburg, a return freight to Britain or Amsterdam or an outward coal freight from Wales.[42] It is also interesting to note that a British agent was able to arrange a charter party concerning a shipment of salt from Portugal to South America. However, it must be pointed out that there was no evidence of an Amsterdam broker negotiating anything "foreign," nor of a British agent "selling" anything concerning Amsterdam or Hamburg. It is also instructive that Captain Idman, while staying in London in 1845, still wrote to Hamburg, and that Captain Sylvander, while in Liverpool

---

[40]For the Havana freight, see MA, LR, Rew, Prescott and Co. to P. Malm, 18 July 1845; and Nikula, *Malmska handelshuset*, 123-124 and 196-197. At least one freight was carried on the account of Ralli Brothers (London), which also had offices in Marseilles, Constantinople, Odessa, Kerch and Taganrog; see Capt. Nyman to P. Malm, Sligo, 21 June 1847. It seems that before the repeal of the Corn Laws, the bulk of imports consisted of linseed and tallow. This is also reflected in the fact that the standard Black Sea charter parties had long since reckoned freight rates in relation to tallow.

[41]MA, LR, Rew, Prescott and Co. to P. Malm, 4 and 25 October 1844, 26 August 1845 and 6 June 1846.

[42]See also the other offer he received via August Bolten: MA, LR, Böckelman to P. Malm, Hamburg, 11 July 1845.

during 1843, not only contacted "most local shipbrokers but even corresponded...with the major ports of trade around the North Sea."[43]

This example may be interpreted as showing that even British local freight markets were not really integrated. It is clear that there were networks of merchant and shipbrokers specializing in different areas (like the Baltic or the Black Sea) or on customers of different nationalities.[44] It is also true that the Baltic Exchange was already in existence but the system was not yet as efficient as was to be the case in subsequent decades. An overall impression is that the tempo of business was slow throughout the 1830s and 1840s, so that Rew, Prescott and Co., after being asked for a freight by Captain Julius Malm in 1837, promised to "bait their hooks" (that is, start asking for offers), and that shipbrokers, not only in London but also in Odessa, informed Malm of freight opportunities, and sent actual offers, to faraway Jakobstad by mail.[45]

Looking for Freight in South America and East Asia

Malm's ships normally sailed for other continents with charter parties which more or less determined precisely what they were expected to do. Thus, they seldom went freight-seeking to South American or East Asian ports, as the evidence provided by Idman's (barque *Hercules*) three-year-long circumnavigation (1844-1847); and three other cases, testifies. European ships sailing in search of freights in Brazil normally expected to find a shipload of coffee or sugar to be returned. But if the master had no firm contract with an importer he was, once again, faced with a spot market in which prospects could fluctuate widely. For example, in 1842, Idman quickly located a return cargo in Rio after selling a shipload of

---

[43]MA, LR, Rew, Prescott and Co. to P. Malm, 10 October 1845; and Capt. Sylvander to P. Malm, Liverpool, 5 November 1843.

[44]For example, the London firm Sack, Bremer and Co. told P. Malm (MA, LR, 30 January 1845) that it was a "Schiffs Mäkler...für die herren Rheder in Lübeck, Wismar, Rostock, Barth, Stralsund..." Another company, Windle and Co., introduced itself as a specialist in the Norwegian trade that wanted to expand to serve Finnish shipping as well (to P. Malm, 14 April 1837).

[45]MA, LR, Rew, Prescott and Co., 21 March 1837; W. T. Mentzer (Odessa) to P. Malm, 14/26 March, 4/15 August and 7/19 November 1841; and H.J. Menger (Odessa) to P. Malm, 15/27 January 1843.

timber,[46] but three years later he was less fortunate. Due to rain, supplies of coffee were limited and those that there available were bought by American ships which were buying cargoes exactly as Finnish ships did in Mediterranean salt ports. Accordingly, freights sank so low that Idman decided to accept a small cargo from Rio and Paranagua to Valparaiso and then sail "on speculation" to Batavia.[47]

In Valparaiso, Idman found that supply and demand for cargo space were better balanced than in Rio. This was also the experience of Captain Sylvander (barque *Veloce*) who arrived there two months later. The latter had a charter party to carry a cargo for a Hamburg firm but since this had gone bankrupt in the meantime (the information had arrived to Valparaiso via Panama), he also had to resort to the local freight market. Both managed to find a freight: Sylvander a mixed cargo of cocoa and copper, Idman some mixed cargo and despatches which the French government sent to Otaheiti (Tahiti).[48]

When Idman was in Batavia and Surabaya almost four years earlier, he had found that ships with a charter party from Europe were paid less than those which had sailed "on speculation" to operate in the spot market.[49] This time, however, on arriving at Batavia on Epiphany, 1847, he was told that good freights had been offered a month ago but

---

[46]The buyer of timber was a German-origin house which also was exporting coffee to Hamburg. Whether its offer for a homeward freight affected the selling decision cannot be ascertained as Idman's letters from Brazil (which Nikula had at his disposal) could not be found.

[47]MA, LR, Idman to P. Malm, Rio de Janeiro, 6 January, 17 February and 5 March 1846. Idman's addressee (the receiver of gunpowder, etc.) was Mr. O. Ralli, who also traded with coffee to Mediterranean ports, and for some time Idman hoped for a freight to Constantinople. Idman's chances may have been impaired by the fact that *Hercules* was regarded as large for a coffee-carrier (Idman to P. Malm, Paranagua, 2 April 1846).

[48]MA, LR, Sylvander to P. Malm, Valparaiso, 26 July and 16 September, Guayaquil, 14 and 30 October, Valparaiso, 24 December and Huasco, 29 December 1846; Idman to P. Malm, Valparaiso, 14 and 26 July, and Callao, 5 September 1846. In the former case, several foreign houses in Guayaquil and Valparaiso sent their goods with him for Hamburg, with which they obviously had regular trade. Idman, again, must have known a few local merchants from his earlier visits and this may have helped him to obtain a government cargo.

[49]MA, LR, Idman to P. Malm, Surabaya, 10 April 1843.

now there was nothing to be had. The reason for such a sudden slump was extraordinary: the steamer carrying mail from Amsterdam had been wrecked. Another steamer then came from Singapore on 16 January and with it arrived two different mail consignments. Obviously they contained firm orders, as now the business picked up. Idman found a cargo and sailed for Rotterdam.[50]

It is quite clear that the ocean freight markets in Brazil, Chile and the Dutch East Indies were not local like those in the Mediterranean. Such a substantial proportion of freight agreements were made beforehand in Europe that they were rather "appendages" or "satellites" to the corresponding markets in Western Europe. On the other hand, it is equally obvious that the advance freight contracts did not equate supply and demand, and therefore there was also a "spot" market so that sailing "on speculation" was a realistic alternative in the 1840s. Such an option may have been rendered more attractive by the existence of some demand for coastal transport, both on the Plate River and in Southeast Asia.[51]

Freight Markets in the 1830s and 1840s

Although Peter Malm's ships sailed far and wide, their voyages were too few and restricted to be taken as a representative sample of the overall conditions of world shipping. The data is also biased because it barely touches those ocean trades which were still closed to "interlopers," such as British colonial trade, and shipping between Britain and the United States. Nevertheless, the material offers a rather good insight into the conditions under which ships of non-colonial, small nations operated, for there are many references to Swedish, Danish, Norwegian and German vessels in the same ports as those from Jakobstad.[52]

---

[50]MA, LR, Idman to P. Malm, Batavia, 29 January 1847.

[51]According to Idman, a number of British and French and even a few German and Scandinavian ships traded on the River Plate. MA, LR, Idman to P. Malm, Paranagua, 2 April 1846.

[52]See MA, LR, Idman to P. Malm, Surabaya, 10 April 1843; Amsterdam, 19 November 1843; Trieste, 8 March 1844; Marseille, 18 June 1844; Marseille, 1 January 1845; Rio de Janeiro, 6 January 1846; Törnvik to P. Malm, Montevideo, 24 February 1842; and Batavia, 10 June 1844; Böckelman to P. Malm, Hamburg, 21 June 1844.

In one respect, Malm's correspondence is more widely relevant: it offers numerous examples of the general constraints which affected the development of freight markets practically everywhere. The most important of these was the quality of communication and the stock of information which could be found in different localities. Limitations and imperfections in these respects also meant that there was a substantial opportunity cost which can be interpreted as the price of information.

It is not difficult to understand that freight markets were heavily dependent on communication. In essence, they were all based on the exchange of information between those who needed cargo space and those who could supply it. But freight markets relied on information in another sense, because of their close connections with commodity markets. Decisions concerning maritime transport were always preceded by decisions on overseas mercantile trade; thus, the better the flow of information between these two markets, the more they were co-ordinated.[53] The experiences of Captain Idman in 1847 in Batavia indicate the problem of delayed information. In more extreme cases, a paucity of information could result in the total integration of trade and transport, as the examples of Malm's Mediterranean exports show. The East Asian old colonial trade represented an almost equally primitive system: orders to buy typically arrived at the port of loading with the ship which was to carry the goods. In terms of the time required in buying or selling the cargo, this was a fairly clumsy way of doing business but, due to slow or inadequate communications, it was the only practical way.

The 1830s and 1840s were a time of transformation. While the overland carriage of mail on many routes still relied on poor roads and horses, the advent of steam was already improving communication at certain critical points. Not only was the railway of practical importance for postal connections in Britain, Belgium, Northern Germany and the Habsburg Empire, but steamships were making coastal traffic and the crossing of the Channel speedier and more regular than ever before. Already by the mid-1840s mail was arriving in Batavia by steamer via the Mediterranean and the Red Sea, a faster route than by the Cape. Mail could even reach Chile via Panama faster than a ship could sail there round the Horn. Thus, communications had started to improve markedly

---

[53]The first freight markets formed part of commodity exchanges (bourses) and these were not only local but even regionally specialized. Thus, for example, the Baltic Exchange initially specialized in the wholesale trade of Russian and Baltic products.

before the days of the telegraph, not only in Europe but between Europe and other continents.

The crucial point was not the improved speed of communication, but the fact that it made possible a more flexible and faster carrying system by freeing it, to some degree, from a physical partnership with mercantile transactions. In the present context, such a development is best exemplified by the East Asian trade: it was only after information travelled to Batavia faster than a sailing ship rounding the Cape that a real freight market was born. Thus, it would seem that a central element in the emergence of modern international maritime transport was the gradual differentiation of commodity and freight markets. This was, of course, a slow change which is difficult to chart accurately, but one relevant indicator seems to be the development of freight agency or shipbroking as an independent profession. While information on freight opportunities was still regularly furnished by ordinary merchants and trading houses, Peter Malm's correspondence reveals that specialized shipbrokers (Ge. *Makler*, Swedish *mäklare*) were to be found in large and important trading and communication centres such as Trieste, Marseille, London, Liverpool, Amsterdam and Hamburg. Another factor contributing to such specialization was the growth of bulk cargo (grain, coal) transport.

Another aspect of the development of freight markets was the fact that it became increasingly common to conclude freight agreements in advance, at least a few months before the actual loading. As this generally concerned cargoes imported into the major West European centres (and charters negotiated in close co-operation with the importing merchants) it was not a complex operation, and the "advance" only involved the time required to sail a ship to a loading port. Yet, in principle this was much more than a simple "spot" market: while the contract need not be made in the loading place, neither did it have to be arranged in the port of destination. The shipmaster (or owner) therefore could plan ahead and try to find a combination of "outward" and "homeward" cargoes.

This development not only depended on improvements in communication, but also quite on institutions, practice, and instruments of transaction. First, it may be supposed that since trading with different "futures" (commodities to be delivered in future) was a well-established tradition,[54] such trade (eg. grain imports) helped advance freight contracting. Second, the basic instruments of freight trade, charter parties,[55] developed so as to make it easier and less risky to sign the agreement as a "future." Malm's correspondence includes several cases in which the agreement only included rather general clauses which later could be defined according to actual needs and circumstances. For example, the ports of loading and/or discharge could be stipulated in general terms (or by listing a few alternatives and a port where final orders were to be found), while it was even possible to change the commodity to be carried as the payment could be adjusted by using what was later to be known as freight scales.[56] Some leeway was afforded by specifying a generous number of lay days (demurrage) so that an unexpectedly early arrival did not cause too unpleasant a surprise.

Malm's correspondence shows that such "general-clause" charter parties were in everyday usage in the 1840s. Practically all the cargoes his ships carried from East Asia, South America or the Black Sea were finalized only after arrival at loading ports. For example, in June 1846, Captain Törnvik wrote from Odessa that he did not know whether he was to carry wheat or rye until the actual loading started, inferring that this was common practice: "you never get any beforehand information from these Gentlemen." He also related that on his arrival there was very little

---

[54]See Herman van der Wee, "Monetary, Credit and Banking Systems," in E.E. Rich and C.H. Wilson (eds.), *The Cambridge Economic History of Europe: vol V, The Economic Organization of Early Modern Europe* (Cambridge, 1977), 331-332.

[55]In the early nineteenth century, charter parties seem to have assumed fairly standard forms. Malm's correspondence includes cases in which a *pro forma* charter party (most obviously a printed form) was sent by the agent in question in order to show the standard clauses of the trade. See MA, LR. Böckelman to P. Malm, Hamburg, 30 June 1845; Törnvik, Rotterdam, May (between 29 April and 29 May) 1843.

[56]Normally, the basic freight was agreed in terms of certain standard commodities. If it was changed to another, the freight rate was determined according to the volume or weight requirements of the replacement in relation to the original commodity. The change of the port of discharge could also be compensated for by additions or reductions to the basic rate. See Seth Svensson (ed.), *Gebers handelslexikon* (Stockholm, 1927), 391. Disputes which arose after Böckelman's Chilean cargo and Idman's return from Batavia, both in 1843, indicate that at least the principle of freight scales was known at the time even if there was some friction in their application. MA, LR, Böckelman to P. Malm, Hamburg, 4 July 1843; and Idman to P. Malm, Amsterdam, 10 and 19 November 1843.

demand for shipping and "no one wanted to have anything to do with the ship."[57] On two different occasions he observed that all the lay-days were used specifically because business was slack.[58] Perhaps the most novel agreement was that which Captain Törnvik concluded in Liverpool in 1841. While it concerned a geographically defined trip to East Asia it was essentially a time charter.[59] Yet it should be noted that many of these practices may have had a long tradition. Thus, freight scales have much in common with the way in which the English East India Company computed freight cost for different commodities and even the idea of time-chartering is basically no different from the long-term chartering of ships which the company had practised since 1659.[60]

It is clear that in spite of some improvements international freight markets were far from perfect. Thus, ships could pile up in Rio as there was no system to warn prospective freight-seekers. Ships also used to sail to the Black Sea and East Asia without a concluded charter party, "on speculation." As the correspondence of Captain Idman shows, this happened when no acceptable freight was found in advance, and also because it was expected that better agreements could be made on the spot market. It is, indeed, logical to expect that by concluding a charter party in advance one was paying an opportunity cost for not being caught unemployed in some odd corner of the world.[61] Such risk-taking which was common much later in more peripheral trades, indicates clearly that freight-market information was far from perfect in the 1830s and 1840s, and that transactions involved a cost, at least an opportunity cost, well above zero.

---

[57]MA, LR, Törnvik to P. Malm, Odessa, 26 June 1846.

[58]MA, LR, Törnvik to P. Malm, Montevideo, 14 April 1842; and Antwerp, 16 November 1846.

[59]MA, LR, Törnvik to P. Malm, Manila, 5 August and 22 September 1842; and Nikula, *Malmska handelshuset*, 187-188.

[60]K.N. Chaudhuri, "The English East India Company's Shipping (c. 1660-1760)," in Bruijn and Gaastra (eds.), *Ships, Sailors, Spices*, 51-52 and 61.

[61]See MA, LR, Idman to P. Malm, Soerabaya, 10 April 1843, Amsterdam and Neudiep, 12 December 1843; and Marseille, 18 May 1844.

Conclusion

Evidence from Peter Malm's correspondence indicates that markets were not only changing but improving. In line with the logic of Douglass C. North's analysis, the question arises as to how much this improved the productivity of shipping by decreasing the number of days spent in port? Answering such a question using a limited number of cases — less than a hundred — is risky: while there is nothing to suggest that Malm's ships were behaving abnormally there is no guarantee that they were typical or representative. Moreover, freight market failures were not always directly reflected in port times: as ships performed various, chronologically overlapping tasks during one and the same stay, a delay in one did not always add to total time. Finally, it may even be supposed that the slow tempo of freight business was reflected in the tempo of port activities: if freight agreements could have been concluded more quickly this would have put pressure on stevedoring and other port work (as was clearly seen in the late nineteenth century after the growth of regular liner services). Therefore, conclusions can only be drawn with due caution.

Some general points do emerge. First, the experiences of Peter Malm's ships paint a picture of gradually improving efficiency. Typically, they stayed between forty and fifty days in ports where they were either loading or unloading or doing both.[62] Compared with corresponding averages for sailing vessels in the 1860s and 1870s — between thirty and thirty-five days[63] — these stays were markedly longer. On the other hand, it is clear that they represent an improvement on eighteenth-century levels, particularly those evident in East Asian trades. While the typical eighteenth-century East Indiaman stayed between 100 and 200 days in India or China,[64] Malm's ships, on average (eight cases), cleared such

[62]This figure only refers to vessels for which fairly accurate itineraries could be compiled and for stays with fairly precise times of entrance and clearance. As the total was only seventy-eight cases, it seems better to speak of typical rather than average durations.

[63]See Yrjö Kaukiainen, "Seamen Ashore," *The Northern Mariner/Le Marin du Nord*, VI, No. 3 (July 1996), 40-41, with references also to Eric W. Sager and Gerald E. Panting.

[64]See E. Göbel, "Danish Companies' Shipping to Asia, 1610-1807," in Bruijn and Gaastra (eds.), *Ships, Sailors, Spices*, 105.

ports forty-two days after arrival and only once stayed in Batavia for more than two months.

That the old-fashioned integration of freight and commodity markets involved loss of time is apparent in Malm's Mediterranean exports. This is clearly seen in port-times: on average, visits of this type took over seventy days. However, these included some cases in which a new ship was coppered, but even if this was disregarded, the average was still more than sixty days. Of the other port visits exceeding sixty days, only six were due to problems in finding further employment.[65] Four of these were in Rio and Valparaiso, one in New York and one in Hamburg. This spatial distribution seems to confirm the assertion that West European freight markets were more efficient than South American. Ten to twenty days, over and above the average of forty to fifty days in port is a substantial delay, comparable with time lost due to repairs. Therefore, to claim that freight market development was an important element in the overall growth of shipping productivity seems fully justified. Of course, this was a complex long-term process and the evolution of ships and navigational skills were also an essential element in it.[66] Equally important was the development of port technology and management; in fact, it is possible that port times decreased even more rapidly than passage times.[67]

The most important single factor contributing to the improvement of freight markets was the speed of communication. This may have been linked with the simultaneous growth in international trade which increased the demand for more rapid flows of information. But there must also have been a backward linkage: increasingly efficient freight markets and falling

---

[65]In other such cases, the ship was taken into a dry or floating dock for re-coppering or repairs four times. On two of these occasions, both unloading and loading took place.

[66]It is indicative that all Malm's ships sailed from East Asia to Europe in a much shorter time than did late-eighteenth-century East Indiamen. Rather than sailing for some 200 days (including, of course, stops at the Cape and Atlantic Islands), Malm's vessels managed the passage in an average of 148 days (eight cases, the longest passage being 174 and the shortest 122 days); see Göbel, "Danish Companies' Shipping." In the 1860s and 1870s, corresponding times were normally shorter, with 120-140 days typical for a bulk-carrier. As ships no longer stopped at the Cape or the Atlantic Islands, the improvement of speed through the water was not equally great.

[67]While Malm's ships spent about forty-six percent of total time in ports, the proportion for Finnish ships in the 1860s and 1870s was about forty percent.

transport costs stimulated the growth of trade. It is interesting that, while North claimed that the improvement of shipping efficiency was fastest in the first half of the nineteenth century, the fastest growth in the volume of world exports seem to have taken place slightly later, between the 1840s and 1870s.[68]

Perhaps even more important is the fact that before the abolition of the British Navigation Laws there was at least a nucleus of an international freight market. Although still spatially restricted and not equally effective everywhere it was truly competitive in the sense that participation was unrestricted by any institutional constraints. Moreover, the most advanced segment, the West European, already possessed many features and practices — separate freight and commodity markets, advance chartering, specialized shipbrokers — which were important in the later development of international, or global, markets.

---

[68]See Angus Maddison, *Phases of Capitalist Development* (Oxford, 1982), 254, table F6.

The First (and Very Secret) International Steamship Cartel, 1850-1856

Edward W. Sloan

The nineteenth-century internationalization of maritime industries is especially well demonstrated through the efforts of two leading steamship lines — one British, the other American — together with an Anglo-American banking firm of international eminence, to rationalize the competitive environment of mid-nineteenth century steam liner service on the major transatlantic shipping route for passengers and cargo. This effort to achieve stability, predictability, and profitability involved the creation of the first major international cartel in oceangoing steamship operations.[1] A particularly distinctive and essential element of this cartel was the role of a transatlantic financial institution in both initiating and maintaining an arrangement that provided for the setting of minimum freight rates and sharing of revenues while serving to forestall direct competition from rival shipping firms on both sides of the Atlantic Ocean.

While this inter-firm shipping agreement was stipulated and enforced through a formal contractual arrangement, it was kept secret so successfully that both the agreement and its specific provisions were not known publicly until well over a century had elapsed.[2] Consequently, historians of shipping conferences customarily date the initiation of such agreements among major steamship competitors at 1875, with the Calcutta Conference of steam liner companies trading between the United Kingdom

[1]It may be argued that previous efforts among small coastal and regional carriers constitute examples of international steamship cartels, but the magnitude and impact of this international transoceanic agreement among such dominant and celebrated liner operators as Cunard and Collins appears to place their arrangement in a special category without precedent.

[2]E.W. Sloan, "Collins versus Cunard: The Realities of a North Atlantic Steamship Rivalry, 1850-1858," *International Journal of Maritime History*, IV (1992), 87-89 and 99-100.

and India.[3] A slightly earlier attempt to create such a self-regulating association occurred in 1868 when several New York-based steamship lines formed the Transatlantic Shipping Conference; however, nothing of substance came from the efforts of these firms until 1902.[4]

The first, and very secret, international steamship cartel had its origins in the late 1840s. At that time the British and North American Royal Steam Packet Company, known popularly as the Cunard Line in recognition of its promoter and largest single shareholder, Samuel Cunard, had operated successfully against both domestic and foreign competitors since beginning its transatlantic service in 1840. Now there was a new and dangerous challenge: the American-based New York and Liverpool United States Mail Steamship Company, which was being formed by a highly successful operator of transatlantic sailing packets, Edward Knight Collins.[5]

This "Collins Line," as it was customarily identified, was a major financial undertaking for its time. To compete directly with the well-established Cunard Line required a fleet of ocean-going steamships of sufficient number and quality to attract a major portion of the transatlantic passenger and cargo business conducted between New York and Liverpool.[6] To promote his enterprise successfully and to raise the unprecedented amount of capital required to build and operate his projected fleet of steamships, Edward Collins turned to the internationally respected and powerful banking enterprise of the Brown Brothers.

William Brown was the senior partner of Brown, Shipley and Co., Ltd. in Liverpool; his younger brother, James, was the senior partner of

---

[3]E.W. Zimmermann, *Zimmermann on Ocean Shipping* (New York, 1921), 462-463; B.M. Deakin, in collaboration with T. Seward, *Shipping Conferences: A Study of Their Origins, Development and Economic Practices* (Cambridge, 1973), 23-24; D. Marx, Jr., *International Shipping Cartels: A Study of Industrial Self-Regulation by Shipping Conferences* (Princeton, NJ, 1953), 46; and L.C. Kendall, *The Business of Shipping* (Centreville, MD, 1983), 282-284.

[4]Marx, *International Shipping Cartels*, 46.

[5]F.E. Hyde, *Cunard and the North Atlantic, 1840-1973: A History of Shipping and Financial Management* (London, 1975), 37-45.

[6]D.B. Tyler, *Steam Conquers the Atlantic* (New York, 1939), chapters 9-15; C. Ridgely-Nevitt, *American Steamships on the Atlantic* (Newark, DE, 1981), chapter 9; and R. Whitney, "The Unlucky Collins Line," *American Heritage*, VIII (1957), 48-53.

Brown Brothers and Co. in New York City. These two brothers held the largest ownership shares in their respective firms, and by pooling their capital they operated essentially as a single transatlantic banking enterprise.[7] Brown Shipley and Co. had served as commercial agents in Liverpool for Edward Collins's remarkably successful line of transatlantic sailing packets, popularly known as the "Dramatic Line," and Brown, Shipley would continue their agency relationship with Collins as he moved into steam. James Brown, in New York City, was the largest single investor in the new Collins Line of steamships, and throughout the shipping firm's existence he served as the company president. William Brown, as one of the great merchant bankers of Britain, became a member of Parliament and an renowned philanthropist. He also, significantly, was an initial and major investor in the Cunard Line.[8]

In the complex, sensitive, and mutually suspicious business relationship between the transatlantic competitors, William Brown was of critical importance.[9] In fact, notwithstanding their public prominence, Samuel Cunard and Edward Collins were relatively minor participants compared to William Brown, his brother James, and the managing director of the Cunard Line, Charles MacIver.[10]

MacIver provided the initiative for the secret agreement between the two shipping firms. For several years, especially following the United States Congress's authorization in 1847 of funds for steamship line subsidies, MacIver and Samuel Cunard had recognized the serious threat that the newly organized Collins Line presented: a large, well financed, and subsidized steamship service that would compete directly with the comparably well-subsidized Cunard Line on the Liverpool-New York

---

[7]E.J. Perkins, *Financing Anglo-American Trade: The House of Brown, 1800-1880* (Cambridge, MA, 1975), chapters 2-4.

[8]Sloan, "Collins versus Cunard," 85-89; and Hyde, *Cunard and the North Atlantic*, 13.

[9]For example, Brown, Shipley and Co. Ltd. Archives, London, (BS&Co.), William Brown Letterbooks (hereafter cited as WB Letterbooks), William Brown to James Brown, 30 December 1853.

[10]Sloan, "Collins versus Cunard," 83-86 and 99-100.

route.[11] Samuel Cunard wrote MacIver on 1 May 1847 that for the first time since beginning operations they were faced with "formidable opposition," that the Collins steamers would be different from other and earlier competitors through not just matching the Cunard Line's "improvements" but adding their own, all to the end of offering a superior service. Moreover, Cunard prophetically warned: "we shall also have National prejudices to contend with."[12]

Such national prejudice was rampant throughout the 1840s and 1850s on both sides of the Atlantic. For many Americans, the Collins Line both symbolized and objectified the New World's challenge to British superiority in technology and industrial production, a superiority that often found expression in openly contemptuous British observations about "Brother Jonathan" and American pretensions.

Edward Knight Collins, like so many of his fellow Americans, for years had bristled at such patronizing remarks and argued for the necessity of an American response. In a petition of 15 January 1852 for increased government support, Collins said it was his patriotic duty to respond to a perceived British threat to American independence, as exemplified by the Cunard Line's effort to maintain the maritime supremacy of England. "Relying on the national objects in view, and the national character of the enterprise," Collins asserted, "we have not been content to regard it as a commercial speculation, but have considered ourselves embarked in a contest of maritime skill and superiority."[13]

Senator William H. Seward of New York put the matter even more firmly several months later, at the time the United States Congress was considering Collins's petition for a large subsidy increase. This was, in Seward's words:

---

[11]J.E. Saugstad, *Shipping and Shipbuilding Subsidies* (Washington, DC, 1932), 51-53, 233-235.

[12]University of Liverpool, Business Archives (ULBA), Cunard Archives (CA), Samuel Cunard to Charles MacIver, 1 May 1847.

[13]United States, Congress, 32nd Congress, 1st Session, Senate Misc. Doc. No. 17 (1852), "Memorial of E.K. Collins and His Associates...," 1; see also New York Historical Society (NYHS), Brown Brothers and Co. Mss. (BB&Co.), Collins Line File, draft of a letter from Joseph Shipley to an unidentified congressman, 1 February 1852.

> a contest for the ultimate empire of the ocean...the struggle for the freedom of commerce and command of the seas...The field of battle is chosen, not by us, but by the enemy...We must meet our adversary on that field, not elsewhere, and we must meet him, or surrender the whole nation's cause without a blow.[14]

In light of these and countless other rhetorical flourishes of similar heat and conviction, it should be clear why any understanding, let alone formal agreement, between the Collins Line and the Cunard Line had to be held in strictest confidence among the participants.[15] Both firms were receiving substantial public support, and not just for carrying the oceanic mails but also for providing steam vessels that could be taken by their respective governments for wartime use. Had knowledge of their arrangement become public, one may imagine the outraged response of American congressmen and senators, if only through a sense of patriotism betrayed. One may also assume a comparable level of outrage in the British Parliament, notwithstanding William Brown's presence as member for South Lancashire.

Yet business was business, and the prospect of a commercial battle for the Atlantic was the last thing that the Cunard interests desired. Once the Collins Line went into operation, with the maiden voyage of the *Atlantic* late in the spring of 1850, Charles MacIver recognized the need to act swiftly. Even before formally warning his partners that the Cunard Line would lose much of its transatlantic business to Collins, MacIver moved to stabilize the competitive situation.[16] To do this it was necessary to bring the Collins Line into a suitable arrangement that would avoid ruinous rate-cutting and other predatory practices that might easily drive both firms into unprofitable operations, or even financial ruin. Yet Edward Collins, with characteristic bravado, had already asserted his

---

[14]*U.S. Congressional Globe*, 32 Congress, 1 Session (27 April 1852), 1199-1202.

[15]For example, BS&Co., WB Letterbooks, William Brown to Samuel Cunard, 20 May 1853.

[16]Hyde, *Cunard and the North Atlantic*, 38; F.E. Hyde, "Cunard and North Atlantic Steamship Agreements, 1850-1914," in B.M. Ratcliffe (ed.), *Great Britain and Her World, 1750-1914: Essays in Honour of W.O. Henderson* (Manchester, 1975), 266-267.

intention to drive the Cunarders off the Atlantic. How could such a threat be diverted?

The solution for MacIver was to gain the support of James Brown, as the Collins Line's President, leading stockholder, and major creditor. But James Brown for years had been an enthusiast of Edward Collins's "steam scheme" and with persistent and uncritical optimism had envisioned enormous profits stemming from the irresistible splendour and speed offered to eager shippers and passengers alike by the Collins Line. Moreover, among the New York partners, James was not alone in his conviction that the Collins project was sure to succeed. Early in 1846 his brother, Stewart, was writing to the Liverpool branch about Collins's proposed transatlantic liner service: "I think he *will* make *this* go. His plan is to get large patronage from our government."[17] In May of the following year James wrote to William that Collins's efforts over the previous seven years were about to be realized, and that the steamship line would be profitable even without considering the $385,000 annual government subsidy for carrying the mail. Collins, James insisted, would surmount the British competition in steam just as he had done with his celebrated transatlantic sailing packet line; "and the more I look into it the more assured I am to take a good interest in it." Moreover, he reminded William, the Liverpool branch of Brown Brothers would benefit considerably from commissions received on passage money because the Collins steamships would be so fast that they would attract a great number of passengers travelling first class. Collins, James stated, "estimates the comm. at Liverpool from $25-35,000 per annum."[18]

Once the Collins proposal had been approved by the United States government, James became more than ever convinced that enormous profits lay within reach of anyone who chose to invest in the steamship line. At the beginning of January 1848 James wrote to his brother, George, urging him to subscribe for stock in the enterprise. Collins, he insisted, had been very careful in calculating the expenses of the project and now was saying that current projections showed expenses to be even less than initially estimated. Even with an increase in the amount of these expenses, James stated, "still we think it promises ample remuneration

---

[17]NYHS, BB&Co., Chronological File, Stewart Brown (New York) to Joseph Shipley (Liverpool), 31 March 1846.

[18]BS&Co., WB Letterbooks, James Brown to William Brown, 14 May 1847.

certainly not less than 25% per annum and may be 50%." Accordingly, James assured his brother, "If you take $200,000 you will never regret it. It will pay you better than any investment you have two or three times over."[19]

Still in its formative period, oceangoing steam was inefficient, unreliable, and expensive.[20] Rapid changes in the technology of steam propulsion and shipbuilding made matters even more unpredictable. The move from paddlewheel to screw propulsion, and from wood to iron hulls, was already under way, yet both the Cunard and Collins steamers currently on the Atlantic run were wooden-hulled paddlewheelers. Major investment in larger, faster, and more technologically advanced steamships was unavoidable and imminent. The rapid obsolescence that both technological innovations and extraordinary wear and tear imposed on the wooden-hulled paddlewheelers required continual infusion of additional funds, not just for substantial repairs but also for improvements and new construction.

William Brown clearly recognized the need for such continuing and heavy commitment of capital funds;[21] this was no time for Cunard or Collins to enter a rate war that would cut heavily into their capital resources and might discourage further investment.[22] William had always been "fixed and determined" to avoid any investment, either by the firm or for his own account, in Collins's steam project. His continual warnings, however, had failed to dissuade his younger brother or temper James's optimism for the steamship line. Now that the line actually had begun its transatlantic service, James Brown had to be brought, however unwillingly, to recognize the harsh realities of competition and of making a profit in oceangoing steam liner service. A level-headed, informed, and influential voice was essential to dispel the euphoria that such a novel and glamorous enterprise as the Collins Line encouraged among the New

---

[19]NYHS, BB&Co., Collins Line File, James Brown to George Brown, 1 January 1848.

[20]E.W. Sloan, "The Evolution of Seagoing Steam: Stages in a Maritime Revolution," *Log of Mystic Seaport*, XLIII (Winter 1992), 87-98.

[21]BS&Co., WB Letterbooks, William Brown to James Brown, 11 September and 25 October 1851.

[22]For example, *ibid.*, William Brown to James Brown, 21-22 January 1852.

York partners and their fellow investors. Who could temper the uncritical and excessive enthusiasm of James Brown better than his older brother and financial mentor, William?

In 1800, aged sixteen, William Brown had emigrated with his parents from Ireland to America. The patriarch of the family, Alexander Brown, had already established his modest reputation as a linen trade merchant and auctioneer in Belfast. Arriving in America, he settled in Baltimore with his family and started the firm of Alexander Brown and Sons as exporters to Europe of flax and cotton and importers of linen. William, the eldest son and reputedly "cleverest of the family," remained in America for nearly ten years before leaving for Liverpool to open another branch of the family business. Soon William became recognized as "a leader of Liverpool commerce" through expanding the scope of his business, both through buying general merchandise on the firm's own account and through serving as commercial agent for American shippers and shipping firms. As Chairman of the Board of Directors of the Bank of Liverpool and one of its major investors by the early 1830s, William established his reputation as a leading banker as well as merchant.[23]

Business flourished, and after the death of his father in 1834 William moved beyond operating his own Liverpool-based firm while serving as Liverpool representative for Alex. Brown and Co. to becoming senior partner in the Brown Brothers transatlantic enterprises. By the mid-1830s he had augmented the firm's capital and by 1839 was celebrated as the "head and soul of the establishment of Brown, Shipley and Company." In 1836 he was reported as doing £10,000,000 in business, but in the following year a severe banking crisis imperilled both the firm and William's own fortune. At this point he persuaded the Bank of England to loan him up to £2,000,000, said to be "larger than had ever yet been made to any private individual in the world." With these funds and the endorsement of his financial probity and acumen that such funds represented, William survived the crisis and was able to repay the entire

---

[23]For much of the information on William Brown, including certain material quoted from his letterbooks, I am indebted to John R. Killick, Leeds University Business School, who has prepared an authoritative and detailed entry on William Brown for a forthcoming volume in the *Dictionary of National Biography*.

amount borrowed, with interest, within six months.[24] In the decades that followed, William became a major political force in Britain, enjoying an unopposed election to Parliament as member for South Lancashire in 1846, after an earlier defeat at the polls. A strong supporter of free trade, William worked to repeal the Corn Laws and to expand commercial relations with the United States in line with his own business interests. In 1844 Richard Cobden had remarked that William Brown "has in his hands one-sixth part of the trade between this country and the United States."[25] William Brown, in fact, more than once successfully served as mediator between Britain and the United States so that in 1858 his transatlantic political, commercial, and financial role had expanded to the point where the American consul to Liverpool, Nathaniel Hawthorne, said that William "grasped, as it were, England with his right hand and America with his left."[26]

Noted for his honesty and energy, although "provokingly inaudible" in his occasional remarks, William held the respect of his Parliamentary colleagues for his shrewd, informed, and temperate conduct of the government's affairs rather than for any force of personality or flair for the dramatic. Indeed, he was often underestimated because of his small stature, weak voice, severe myopia, and somewhat diffident manner: "poor little Mr. Brown," Nathaniel Hawthorne observed privately in 1857, "an exceedingly unpretending old gentleman in black, small, withered, white haired, pale, quiet and respectable."[27]

James, on the other hand, was venturesome to the point of aggravation, at least as William viewed his younger brother's business behaviour. Deceptively similar to William in outward appearance and with a "marked peculiarity of manner" resulting from the severe myopia, or "Brownsight," that he shared with his elder brother, James Brown may

---

[24]Killick, "William Brown," 2-10; Perkins, *Financing Anglo-American Trade*, 19-21 and 38-40; and H.R. Fox Bourne, *English Merchants: Memoirs in Illustration of the Progress of British Commerce* (2 vols., London, 1866), II, 300-310.

[25]Quoted in Bourne, *English Merchants*, II, 313.

[26]*Ibid.*, II, 308 and 318.

[27]*Ibid.*, II, 314-315; Nathaniel Hawthorne, *The English Notebooks* (New York, 1962), 458 and 460 (entry for 19 April 1857); and Killick, "William Brown," 12-14 and 18-19.

have impressed those outside of the family as possessing a staunch financial conservatism equal to William's, but his "quick, nervous step" and "ardent temperament" suggest otherwise. James, as his family minister recalled, possessed a lightning-quick intellect and great intuitive judgement that led him to instant and strong opinions about others, so that he either despised them or was vigorously supportive; thus the total acceptance of Edward Knight Collins and the "steam scheme" was entirely characteristic of James Brown. Unlike his older and more cautious brother, James "was too confiding to be exempt at times from the errors of others. His confidence, whenever he gave it was unlimited. From his friends he withheld no trust, but was as open and as simple as a little child."[28] James's unqualified faith in the Collins project mirrored the conviction he often expressed in a favourite business maxim: "there is such a thing as being over-careful and over-suspicious of the integrity of parties with whom we are dealing; it makes the house unpopular. Better to be taken in and lose a little occasionally, than to be so rigid as to make parties afraid to approach you."[29]

When it came to the matter of steamships the price for such optimism and credulity could be formidable. James's heavy and growing financial commitments to the Collins Line resulted in "locking up" a large portion of the Brown Brothers's total working capital, so that the firm's correspondence flowing from Liverpool to New York frequently called sharp attention to the problem of "lockups" as the Collins Line expenses mounted.[30] With his own firm so financially entangled just at the time the Collins Line was beginning operations, William realized, a costly rate-war between Collins and Cunard was unacceptable. Accordingly, as early as March 1849 William had already begun to explore the possibility of an accommodation between the rival steamship firms. "How unpleasant it would be," William wrote Cunard's agents, the MacIvers, "for your vessels and those coming to us to be carrying on a war of mutual injuries." William then explained that he had asked his brother James "to see Mr

---

[28]J.C. Brown, *A Hundred Years of Merchant Banking: A History of Brown Brothers and Company; Brown, Shipley & Company; and the Allied Firms, etc*. (New York, 1909), 230-234. John Crosby Brown was the fifth son of James Brown.

[29]F.R. Kent, *The Story of Alexander Brown & Sons* (Baltimore, 1925), 208.

[30]Perkins, *Financing Anglo-American Trade*, 35 and 49-59.

Cunard...and if possible to make such arrangements as would prevent injury to either concern."[31] Fortunately for William Brown, Charles MacIver saw matters in the same light.

On 29 May 1850, only a month after the *Atlantic*'s initial voyage to Liverpool and before any of her three sister ships had entered service, MacIver satisfactorily completed his negotiations with William Brown and his Liverpool-based banking associates. Acting as agents for their respective firms, Charles MacIver (for the Cunard Line) and William Brown, Joseph Shipley, and their partner Francis A. Hamilton (for the Collins Line) signed the Articles of Agreement that created the first international oceanic steamship cartel.

The main elements of this agreement provided for fixing minimum rates for passengers and cargo, while permitting either firm to charge higher rates for passengers; and a pooling and subsequent allocation of gross revenues. Each firm would report such revenues for stipulated periods, and at the end of each year there would be an accounting in which gross revenues would be aggregated and then compared to a prescribed formula by which the Cunard Line would receive two-thirds and the Collins Line one-third of the total. Any discrepancy between the actual and prescribed percentage of the total would be resolved by a transfer of funds.[32]

This agreement took effect on 25 May 1850 and remained in force in one form or another until it was finally suspended on 11 November 1856, following the disappearance early that year of the Collins Line's *Pacific*. The loss of the *Pacific*, coupled with the earlier sinking of her sister ship *Arctic* in September 1854, placed too great a burden on the firm, so that by the time a replacement vessel, the huge *Adriatic*, went into service late in 1857 the Collins Line was on the verge of bankruptcy and any resumption of the secret agreement with Cunard was hopeless.[33]

---

[31]BS&Co., WB Letterbooks, William Brown to D. and C. MacIver, 8 March 1849, as quoted in Killick, "William Brown," 11.

[32]ULBA, CA, Revised draft of "Articles of Agreement...[29 May 1850]."

[33]*Ibid.*, "Memorandum of Agreement...[between Messrs. Brown Shipley and Co. and Charles MacIver]," 11 November 1856; Sloan, "Collins versus Cunard," 96; Hyde, *Cunard and the North Atlantic*, 40-44; and Hyde, "Cunard and the North Atlantic Steamship Agreements, 1850-1914," 266-268.

For most of the time that the agreement was in force the two firms maintained this special business association without difficulty, yet on occasion there were accusations of sharp practice that threatened to destabilize the relationship. Early in July 1853, Charles MacIver — clearly agitated — wrote privately to a Brown, Shipley partner, Francis Hamilton, complaining that the Collins Line was publicly advertising in London that it would take families across the Atlantic at reduced rates and that such rate-cutting had "placed me in a very awkward position with our folks." At first, MacIver stated, he had believed this advertisement for lower rates to be confined to a special fare for children that the two firms together had arranged by agreement, so that he had "set it down as indiscreet zeal on the part of your London agent in giving the widest publicity to what was after all a private part of the arrangement between us which was not to appear in print, nor does it appear in your advertisement here." However, MacIver continued, after further examination of the issue by "our people" he feared that the Collins Line was in serious breach of the agreement, and that sufficient evidence of this was the great disparity in the number of passengers recently travelling to America on Collins Line steamships compared to those on the Cunarders. MacIver insisted:

> The inference will be too strong for me to bear up against — my logic will go but little way to prove that parties advertising to carry passengers at a reduced rate did not do it, & to that & that alone will be attributed the difference. I regret this exceedingly, & regret it all the more because it looks so like truth that I would be called a fool to say I disbelieve it, and if I attempt to defend on any fanciful ground such as American prejudices or preferences for their own steamers the reply is certain: "How is it exhibited on your Boston steamers Mr. MacIver you carry lower there, & you get the passengers they carry lower on the New York line, & they get them, & we give you fair warning Mr. MacIver that we will not allow the assumed or real prejudices of the Americans to enable other people to fatten at our experience, therefore you will require to bring down your rates to such a point as will give us our legitimate share of the traffic, or failing in that make the portion which goes past us not very much worth the having."

MacIver continued by asking Francis Hamilton to consider this problem and to try to come up with a plan to place passenger rates on the same basis as those for cargo. MacIver then cautioned:

> it's the only fair or proper footing to insure any lasting working arrangement, for its quite evident to me that under no circumstances can I contemplate at present would our company likely to be worse off without an agreement at all than with the present; no bargain can be expected to exist which is not to conduce to mutual benefit.

He concluded by reminding Hamilton of a similar arrangement entered into earlier with the Grand Trunk Railway, "but even if [that] were to be proposed at this moment, I would have suggested to your acceding to it for mutual security & protection, and on that ground alone."[34]

William Brown soon took up this issue with his brother James. Writing in mid-September, William explained the position of Brown, Shipley and Co. and its exasperation with the meddling of Edward Collins:

> We are very much annoyed by Collins promising free passages & making engagements on your side in complete violation of our honora[able] engagement with Mr. McIver; unless it is put a stop to pray inform him that we will not be the instruments through which to break faith & that he must find less scrupulous agents. In fact we must be left to make all arrangements here or we cannot act at all.

Remarking on the "difficulties that Collins creates," William encouraged his brother to take a firm hand over the American line's operations:

> The House [Brown, Shipley and Co.] will write you as Chairman of the Co. that it may come before the Board,

---

[34]ULBA, CA, Papers used by Francis Hyde, Prof. F.E. Hyde papers, Cunard Archives Associated Deposits, Charles MacIver to Francis A. Hamilton, 2 July 1853.

> but you may wish to strengthen their hands by reading a part of this to Collins — I put my opinion & views strongly, for it is your interest that he should be aware of our feelings & be governed by the views of men of better judgement."[35]

The partners at Brown, Shipley and Co. managed to curb Collins's aggressive practices and smooth MacIver's ruffled feathers over the passenger rate issue, but then they had to contend with an accusation by James Brown that MacIver was undercutting the Collins Line on freight rates by having the Cunard Line use its smaller screw steamers to carry cargo to Jersey City, rather than New York, yet scheduling their sailing from Liverpool on the same day the Collins liners made their regular departure for New York. "It would seem that it is a direct interference & especially so as they keep down the rate by these to the old price of £3 in place of raising their rate to £5, keeping the £1 difference in the rates." There might be some excuse for this practice, James pointed out, "if there was Goods enough to fill both...but as we were not full it seems going in the face of our agreement, & so different from their former views to put on the Screws only when other Screws were interfering either with our Ships or theirs." James then added a stern postscript:

> Since writing the foregoing I have seen Mr. Collins & he agrees with me that if Mr. McIver pursues this course, we see no remedy but dropping our rate for freight as it will not do to come away with but half cargo. We desire to act in good faith & we expect the same from Mr. McIver.[36]

William quickly replied to James, warning him and Collins to back away from any confrontation with MacIver:

---

[35]BS&Co., WB Letterbooks, William Brown to James Brown, 18 September 1853.

[36]ULBA, CA, Papers used by Francis Hyde, Prof. F.E. Hyde papers, Cunard Archives Associated Deposits, James Brown to Brown Shipley and Co., 13 December 1853.

> I cannot too strongly impress on you the importance of not going to war with McIvers Company — they are people of immense strength & command of Boats that would beat you out of the field. Although things may arise which appear on your side unfair, yet you may rest assured if you were here you would consider that the benefits are greatly in your favor — It would be a trial of purse who could do each other most harm.[37]

The good offices of William Brown and his partners once again smoothed over the disagreement, so that the secret arrangement between the two steamship lines to maintain minimum rates while discouraging new competitors remained in force.

From William Brown's perspective any problem between the two shipping firms arose from the actions of Edward Collins. As William had advised James in July 1853, "it is very annoying that Collins is so unmanageable — you have the votes & you must exercise your power to control him."[38] In addition to keeping Collins under control and encouraging more judicious financial management from James, William believed that it was his own responsibility, as senior partner of Brown, Shipley and Co., to maintain a consistently high level of transatlantic accord. Writing to Samuel Cunard in May 1853, William encouraged greater coordination between the two shipping lines and a more frequent and systematic scheduling of sailings. In a statement that acknowledged the private, as distinct from the public, nature of the competition, William assured Cunard that "I am sure such an arrangement would harmonize the jealousies that now exist, not with us but with the public."[39]

William Brown's preoccupation with controlling competition and minimizing transatlantic discord was matched by his ever-growing concern for James's commitment of so much money to the Collins Line. Following the tragic loss of the *Arctic* in September 1854, William became more dubious than ever about the financial viability of the Collins

---

[37]BS&Co., WB Letterbooks, William Brown to James Brown, 30 December 1883.

[38]*Ibid.*, William Brown to James Brown, 26 July 1853.

[39]*Ibid.*, William Brown to Samuel Cunard, 20 May 1853.

Line, and at one point believed he had an ideal solution for all these problems. At this moment Britain and France were embroiled in the Crimean War and there was a pressing demand for steamships to serve as transports if not as naval auxiliaries. What if the three remaining Collins Line steamships — *Atlantic*, *Baltic*, and *Pacific* — could be sold as a package to foreign investors and for a price that would essentially recover James's investment and, in turn, free the Brown Brothers from their lockup difficulties?

Early in January 1855, after previous consultation with James, William Brown wrote a "strictly confidential" letter to the Earl of Clarendon (currently Foreign Secretary in the ministry of Lord Aberdeen) about the possible sale of "some first class large American steamers capable of carrying an armament & probably about 1000 men, & in every way suitable for transports." If the British government were not interested, William added, would the Foreign Office find out from the French Minister if his government might be interested in such a purchase? Of course, this matter had to be kept quiet "as in case it became known it would be injurious to the owners in the U. States."[40] Two days later, following an encouraging response from Lord Clarendon, William wrote James that he was waiting to hear from the British government before approaching the French about the steamers. Warning James that "no time should be lost in giving us final instructions & the lowest limits," William made it clear that he needed more authority in these negotiations. As it was:

> I carry on the correspondence in my name to keep the negotiation private — You must perceive that if this Govt. are willing to give a fair price for these steamers we cannot expect they will make an offer & wait your answer — that would bind them & leave you at liberty to accept or not.[41]

On the same day William wrote Lord Clarendon another private letter to reveal that the three steamers were those of the Collins Line. "No vessels were ever built more faithfully," William maintained, "& they

---

[40] *Ibid.*, William Brown to The Earl of Clarendon, 10 January 1855.

[41] *Ibid.*, William Brown to James Brown, 12 January 1855.

have all just got new Brass Tubes in their Boilers." If the Admiralty approved of their purchase, he added, there as yet was no set asking price but "we know they consider them worth fully £150,000 each." After all, William reminded Lord Clarendon, "there are no vessels that come into this Port better known or which have been more admired, looked at, & examined." Moreover,

> no money has been spared to keep them up in the highest state of efficiency — As to speed there is nothing that floats faster. Cunard & they have run many a race against time & I think if anything Collins has the advantage going westward in the face of westerly winds — their accommodations for passengers are very large.

As a final observation, William (attentive as ever to his own business interests) admitted that "we shall regret their sale as we shall lose the agency."[42]

For a time the sale of the Collins steamships (and the consequent end of the Collins Line) appeared likely. William persisted in his efforts to encourage Lord Clarendon and tried to arrange for an official, if private, survey of the *Atlantic*. Still lacking were any definite instructions from the New York owners, but William hoped to have them by early February.[43] However, prospects for any sale of the Collins liners to a foreign government grew dimmer by the day. On 25 January William wrote James that he had received a note from Lord Clarendon saying that the British government had given up the idea of such a purchase. There was still the possibility of sale to the French, but this now appeared unlikely. "Had I been furnished with a Power of Attorney & your limits," William stated,

> I possibly might have been able to have closed with the British Govt. at once, but their now declining looks like there being more prospect of peace — The same feeling

---

[42]*Ibid.*, William Brown to The Earl of Clarendon, Foreign Office, London, 12 January 1855.

[43]*Ibid.*, William Brown to Lord Clarendon, 22 January 1855.

> may actuate the French Govt., but it is impossible to say what turn affairs may take.

Yet if the Collins Line stayed in business and went ahead to build a necessary replacement vessel for the lost *Arctic,* what did this mean for the Brown Brothers's financial picture, especially that portion attributable to James? "In event of building a new ship," William inquired, "out of what funds is she to be paid for — they cannot expect you to advance the money."[44]

By early February William had almost lost hope of selling the steamers to any foreign government. "We have not yet heard from France," he wrote James.

> I therefore fear they are not disposed to purchase the steamers — we shall no doubt have final instructions, & your definite views by the 12 ins. — Something may turn up with the new Ministry or from France that may open a negotiation for a sale; if so I will be within reach to act.[45]

After being invited by the Queen on 4 February to form a new government, in the hopes of bringing the Crimean War to an end, an elderly Lord Palmerston assembled his new ministry by the next evening with Clarendon continuing as Foreign Secretary. Two weeks later William wrote to say there now was no chance of selling steamers to the French government, since "the Emperor would nationalize no more Foreign Ships."[46] For William Brown this was a depressing conclusion to his persistent efforts to lift from his brother, as well as their transatlantic banking enterprise, a financial burden that only was to become heavier.

While the formal agreement between the two shipping lines remained in force the Collins Line was unquestionably an effective competitor. Although the first year's reconciliation produced a small payment to the Collins Line of £1427, this was a result of irregularities in

---

[44]*Ibid.*, William Brown to James Brown, 25 January 1855.

[45]*Ibid.*, William Brown to James Brown, 2 February 1855.

[46]*Ibid.*, William Brown to James Brown, 16 February 1855.

the Cunarder's Havre trade as it related to the entire transatlantic business of the two firms. For the Liverpool-North American run the American Line had produced thirty-five percent of aggregate gross revenues. The following year, 1851, resulted in a balance of £10,836 to be paid by the Collins Line to Cunard for the Liverpool-North America voyages. Over this period the American steamships produced nearly thirty-eight percent of total revenues during the main shipping season, when the Cunarders ran two vessels for every one Collins liner, and over forty-six percent of the revenues when both lines ran alternately each week.

For 1852 the American percentage of a rapidly-growing transatlantic business was greater than the year before; of a total £396,185 in gross revenues, the Collins Line generated £162,708, or forty-one percent, so that before adjustments for the Havre trade the Collins Line owed £30,646 to its competitor. A revision and renewal of the agreement then put accounts on a different fiscal-year basis, so that the next comparable data, for the period covering 1 April 1853 through 31 March 1854 shows a similar departure from the initial stipulated division. Of a total of £539,243 total gross revenues, the Collins Line produced £215,734, or exactly forty percent. The "excess earnings" of the Collins Line for this period amounted to £34,153, so that in accordance with a revised payment schedule the Cunard Line received a flat £5,000. For the same fiscal period for 1854-1855 the payment to the Cunard Line was again £5,000, on the basis of the Collins Line's £21,165 "excess" revenues. This figure, however, was considerably affected both by a number of Cunarders being drawn from the Atlantic route to serve the British forces during the Crimean War and by the loss in September 1854 of the Collins liner *Arctic*. Even so, when the Cunarders were running two vessels for every one Collins liner the American portion of gross revenues was over thirty-nine percent of the total.[47]

With the Collins Line consistently producing more than its stipulated share of the pooled revenues there may be some question about William Brown's judgement in his initial negotiations with Charles

---

[47]ULBA, CA, "Summary of the Statements of the Earnings..." For the 1854-1855 period, see also NYHS, BB&Co., Collins File, Brown, Shipley and Co. to James Brown, 31 July 1855, which states: "there is due as per agreement £5000 to the British Company & you please authorize us to pay the same at your earliest convenience. You will observe that the carrying capacity of the steamers is estimated in accordance with the terms of the agreement."

MacIver. Had William, with his customary skepticism about Collins and the steamship line, been too generous with the Cunard interests? Was a different division of revenues, in favour of the Collins Line, ever possible, and would such a division have made a significant change in the Collins Line's fortunes? To answer these questions it is necessary to examine the conditions of steamship competition on the Atlantic during the 1840s and early 1850s.

Beginning its transatlantic operations in 1840, the Cunard Line had successfully withstood challenges from both British and American competitors, such as the British and American Steam Navigation Company, the Great Western Steamship Company, and the Ocean Steam Navigation Company.[48] That these other firms barely survived or even went out of business while the Cunard Line maintained and enlarged its oceangoing presence suggests the hazardous nature of early steamship enterprise and the strength of the Cunard operation. By April 1850, when the first of the Collins steamships began the New York-Liverpool run, the Cunard Line had nine steamers sailing from Liverpool to Halifax and Boston or directly to New York. Moreover, by this time the Cunard Line had under construction or in the planning stages other and considerably larger steamships — notably *Asia* [1850], *Africa* [1850], and *Arabia* [1852] — that were intended to match the Collins liners for size, speed, and comfort.[49] In addition to the subsidized transatlantic steamers Cunard operated steamship lines to the Mediterranean and to the West Indies. The vessels in these lines were smaller and not ideally suited to the North Atlantic, but they permitted Cunard a flexibility in scheduling and financing operations that Collins could never match with only his four huge and expensive steamships.

By selling off his interests in sailing packets, both transatlantic and coastal, Collins had concentrated his risk as well as his investment capital. The Cunard Line, with far greater resources, could afford to engage in rate wars and other forms of cut-throat competition, even if it involved running the transatlantic steamers at a loss. Collins, without a fifth steamship as originally planned, with no other vessels in reserve, and with a chronic shortage of working capital, could not long afford such competition. A cartel form of agreement that undervalued the potential

---

[48]Tyler, *Steam Conquers the Atlantic*, chapters 3-9.

[49]Hyde, *Cunard and the North Atlantic*, 27-31 and 326-327.

earning capabilities of the Collins Line — assuming all four steamships remained in regular service without interruption and with a steadily growing supply of passenger and cargo revenues — was still preferable to no such agreement at all.

In any case, the financial situation of the Collins Line was so shaky at the outset and so rapidly worsened that a larger share of pooled revenues would have made only a marginal difference in the "bottom line" result, which was a consistent operating loss throughout the life of the Collins Line. The projected cost of his steamships had fallen appallingly short of actual expenditures, so that additional capital had to be poured into the enterprise just to get the ships into service. To his chagrin, James Brown soon had to commit, through the loan of funds, an amount equalling ten times his initial equity investment, and the heavy burden of interest payments and debt amortization placed on the Collins Line only added to the shipping firm's excess of operating expenditures over revenues.[50]

Thus while the figures indicate that the Collins Line was briefly a formidable and troublesome competitor, especially as it benefitted from increasing annual subsidy payments, they also demonstrate the American firm's failure to gain dominance on the Atlantic. For the Cunard Line the secret agreement worked as intended; a potentially hazardous, cut-throat competition was avoided. By a calculated policy of risk aversion when possible or balancing risk elements when necessary, the Cunarders throughout the 1850s enjoyed a reasonably stable, predictable, and profitable business on the major transatlantic route from Liverpool to New York. The Collins Line, on the other hand, struggled to break even at best, and despite a large increase in its subsidy payments after 1852 the firm never paid a cent in dividends to its shareholders and finally declared bankruptcy early in 1858.

Despite the failure of the Collins Line operation, the agreement with Cunard had succeeded in forestalling the emergence of rival firms on either side of the Atlantic. To be sure, Commodore Cornelius Vanderbilt launched his own enterprise in 1855 as an alternative to the Collins Line, first offering to operate an unsubsidized transatlantic steamship liner service and later proposing a liner service to Southampton, England, for

---

[50]For a comment on James Brown's growing disillusionment, see NYHS, BB&Co., Collins File, John A. Brown (Philadelphia) to Joseph Shipley (Wilmington, DE), 16 November 1857.

half the amount of the Collins Line subsidy. Moreover, by 1851 there existed a different form of steamship travel, with the unsubsidized immigrant service that William Inman provided between Liverpool and Philadelphia.[51] Yet neither Vanderbilt's nor Inman's shipping operations can be held accountable for the Collins Line's failure or the difficulties that preceded it. The failure of the Collins Line, as William Brown above all others recognized, was of its own making.

William Brown never had been at all sanguine about the Collins Line or its promoter, so from the early 1840s through the late 1850s he steadily discouraged his brother James from persisting in his support of the Collins Line.[52] William, far more than his brother and others in the New York office, recognized the staggering cost demanded for achieving unprecedented speed and luxury on the Atlantic run, and he recoiled at the prospect of such a necessary outlay of funds. Each time a new demand for funds arose, William and his Liverpool partners pleaded with James and his partners in New York to resist further financial commitments to the Collins Line.[53] Clearly expressing the level of the Liverpool partners' frustration and apprehension is a letter of 4 May 1855 to the New York office concerning the financing of the proposed new Collins steamship *Adriatic*:

> We should have been very glad if you could, by a sale of the boats or in some other way, have washed your hands of the whole concern; for apart from all other considerations it is mortifying to be implicated even

[51]Tyler, *Steam Conquers the Atlantic*, 194, 220 and 223-242 (for Vanderbilt); 197-198, 212, 256-257 and 378-379 (for Inman).

[52]BS&Co., WB Letterbooks, William Brown to James Brown, 2 June 1847, 23 January 1848, and 29 January 1851; William Brown to US Mail Steam Ship Co. [Collins Line], 16 August 1851.

[53]*Ibid.*, William Brown to US Mail Steam Ship Co., 16 August 1851; William Brown to James Brown, 28 October 1851; William Brown to John Brown, 14 November 1851. NYHS, BB&Co., Chronological File, Mark Collet to Francis Hamilton, 2 May 1856; and Brown, Shipley and Co. to Brown Brothers and Co., 29 January 1858.

unwillingly & indirectly in the expenditure which you justly stigmatize as disgraceful.[54]

At an early stage of the transatlantic rivalry Charles MacIver had perceptively observed, "The Collins people are pretty much in the situation of finding that breaking our windows with sovereigns, though very fine fun, is too costly to keep on."[55] Without question, William Brown shared these sentiments; moreover, like MacIver, he realized the futility of attaining stable, predictable, and profitable results through unrestricted competition in this formative era of oceangoing steam liner enterprise. Accordingly, he sought to limit such competition through an arrangement that necessarily had to be shielded from public knowledge, while at the same time he and his Liverpool partners urged his brother to scale back if not abandon his unwise commitments to the Collins Line.[56] That the Collins "steam scheme" would end in such disaster confirmed the soundness of William Brown's business judgement. That both the Collins Line and the Cunard Line could compete so vigorously while holding off new entrants and maintaining passenger and cargo rates at a level that for Cunard, at least, was profitable also confirmed William Brown's shrewd business sense in shaping such a restrictive transatlantic shipping arrangement. The collapse of this American challenge to British maritime dominance did not result from the secret agreement that created the first international steamship cartel, but in spite of it.

Yet any valuable lesson learned from this experience was not to be shared among the larger maritime community of that era. The persistent secrecy surrounding the relatively brief operations of this cartel assured that it would not serve as a precedent for future shipping combinations and conferences. What remains significant is the still

---

[54]NYHS, BB& Co., Collins File, Brown, Shipley and Co. to Brown Brothers and Co., 4 May 1855. See also NYHS, BB&Co., Chronological File, Brown, Shipley and Co. to Brown Brothers and Co., 26 January 1855.

[55]ULBA, CA, T.E. Hughes, "History of Cunard Line" (unpublished mss., ca. 1904), chapter 5.

[56]For example, NYHS, BB& Co., Chronological File [typewritten extract in Collins Line File]; William Brown to James Brown, 26 July 1853; Brown Shipley and Co. to Brown Brothers and Co., 26 January 1855; and NYHS, BB& Co., Collins Line File, Brown Shipley and Co. to Brown Brothers and Co., 4 May 1855.

relevant example that the Cunard and Collins Lines provide for understanding problems in the development and maintenance of shipping conferences, especially those of international, even global, reach. Also looming large in this experience is the critical role of non-shipping elements, particularly international banking interests in their own self-interested search for protection from a ruinously competitive struggle. That national prestige, political posturing, and major commitments of public funds were also involved certainly complicated the issue and unquestionably shaped the intense, continual, and remarkably successful effort to keep this international shipping cartel shrouded in secrecy for so long.

Competition or Co-operation in the Global Shipping Industry: The Origins and Impact of the Conference System for British Shipowners before 1914

Robert G. Greenhill

"Globalisation," Martin Wolf wrote recently in the *Financial Times*, "is a word that now leaps readily to every tongue. Like the idea or loathe it, few deny its existence or understate its significance."[1] Yet the idea of freer trade in goods and services combined with largely unfettered capital movements is not really very new. Economic historians may indeed be as familiar with the concept in a much earlier context as in a late twentieth-century one. From about the middle of the nineteenth century regional economic networks began to coalesce to create not just international groupings in which several countries participated, but globalization whereby the world economy functioned more or less as a whole. Production expanded under conditions of comparative cost advantage so that exports represented nearly ten percent of the world's output. Moreover, during the second half of the nineteenth century most countries had in practice adopted an internationally acceptable system of fixed exchange rates through the gold standard. In addition, net overseas lending and borrowing before 1914 was a much higher fraction of national income than it is today and the first multinational companies had begun to generate transactions within the international economy. And, unlike today, emigration remained at a buoyant level as labour moved more or less freely between countries. Economic activity was clearly multilateral in the decades before the First World War rather than bilateral. What brought all this about?

Today, information technology lies behind the growing integration of the global economy but 150 years ago the permissive technology which underpinned the trend towards globalization was that which lowered the cost of transport and communication. Globalization occurred before 1914 because transport became a fraction of the end user price of products. It was now worthwhile to import into Europe wheat and meat from as far

[1] *Financial Times*, 1 October 1997 and 8 January 1998.

away as Argentina or Australia because lower transport charges had removed the protection which distance had earlier given to European farmers. Improved steamships and the compound engine, as well as railroads, spread rapidly throughout the globe. In addition, the telegraph and the cable transformed information flows and made them accessible to all. If technological change made globalization feasible, then liberalization made it happen. Free trade, a succession of commercial treaties and few restrictions on capital movements all created a largely deregulated business environment in the late nineteenth century, despite the partial return to tariffs from the 1870s. For shipowners the abandonment of the Navigation Laws opened up the world's shipping trades to competition.[2] Technological change and liberalization thus complemented each other in the development of a global economy in which the factors of production freely crossed frontiers.

The results of globalization were double-edged; while new markets became available, increased competition also appeared. This was particularly true for British shipowners who, from the 1870s, began to experience not only lower prices for their services (and, hence, lower profits) but fiercer competition on their routes. British shipping had dominated the ocean-going trade routes from the 1850s when the globalization of world markets bought about the internationalization of the sea transport industries. The early industrialization of Britain's shipyards, which ensured the rapid application of iron, and then steel, and steam power, enabled her shipowners to meet new demands. The country's rising population required more foodstuffs and the increased manufacturing capacity created a ready export trade. A two-way trade of food and raw materials inwards, and coal and industrial goods outwards, formed the basis of the demand for British tonnage. Imperial possessions, which provided a major source of imports and an export market, demanded an efficient communications network and Britain's substantial entrepot trade, founded on her maritime lead and her geographical position between Europe and the Americas, helped to confirm an already strong position in shipping. Even by 1890, when newly industrialized nations were developing their own fleets, Britain's fleet still represented nearly forty percent of world tonnage. Britain's shipping industry was

---

[2]See, for example, Sarah Palmer, *Politics, Shipping and the Repeal of the Navigation Laws* (Manchester, 1990).

broadly based on both tramp ships and liners. There were also sailing vessels, although by the end of the century they were of much less importance. Corporate size ranged from small single-ship enterprises to companies owning huge fleets.[3] And British shipping embraced every major trading route across the oceans.

How did shipowners respond to the changed market conditions of the last quarter of the nineteenth century? One of the outcomes was to formulate a strategy against the competitive and profit-reducing threats, which culminated in the creation of shipping conferences, essentially cartels or oligopolistic arrangements whereby sellers, independent but associated shipping companies, combined to set prices and services to their customers, usually merchants and shippers. The seaborne passenger trade, especially the emigrant sector, also experienced cartel-like arrangements. Conferences, so called because shipowners and their representatives met in conferences to decide tactics, were designed to protect the interests of members through price-fixing and market-sharing techniques and to exclude competitors from a trade. Usually a conference covered one leg of a voyage between a range of ports and a shipping line serving many routes was likely to be a member of several conferences. Collusion between businessmen such as shipowners can, of course, take many forms: from the oral gentleman's agreement and the casual exchange of market information to something much more formal and explicit. Shipping conferences were therefore only one form of alliance between companies.

The literature on shipping conferences is rather sparse compared to the extensive publications on other aspects of ship operation — technological change, company history, entrepreneurship and so on. While there is brief reference to shipping conferences in works on the history of cartels, books devoted exclusively to conference arrangements are small in number.[4] Francis Hyde and colleagues at the University of Liverpool from the 1960s filled part of the gap in the literature with a series of scholarly company histories which analysed shipping conferences

---

[3]Ronald Hope, *A New History of British Shipping* (London, 1990), 306 ff.

[4]The best known are D. Marx, *International Shipping Cartels: A Study of Industrial Self-Regulation by Shipping Conferences* (Princeton, NJ, 1953); and B.M. Deakin, *Shipping Conferences: A Study of Their Origins, Development and Economic Practices* (Cambridge, 1973).

from the point of view of their chosen firm.[5] Most recently Gordon Boyce has turned to the issue of conferences in his book on the rise of large-scale enterprise in British shipping after 1870.[6] This *lacuna* in the history of British shipping may be explained on a number of grounds: the sensitive nature of the issues involved, the largely secretive nature of the work and the failure to preserve substantial conference archives. Formal agreements left some written records but informal ones rarely did so.

The failure to recognise the significance of shipping conferences may, of course, be part of a wider indifference towards the importance of cartels and oligopoly in the years before 1914, a period normally associated with the existence of large numbers of small firms and underpinned by assumptions that perfect competition, as well as free trade and *laissez-faire*, would distribute resources to ensure maximum allocative efficiency. Nevertheless, this ignorance, if true in earlier years, needs to be revised. As early as 1776 Adam Smith argued in *The Wealth of Nations* that "people of the same trade seldom meet together, even for merriment or diversion, but the conversation ends in conspiracy against the Publick or in some contrivance to raise prices."[7] Now recent scholarship has begun to recognise the growth of cartels from the late nineteenth century. C.H. Lee noted the failure of business historians to describe the realities of nineteenth-century markets, while there have been case studies of cartels in a variety of industries.[8] "British business," Oliver Westall recently wrote, "has usually faced markets characterised by varying degrees of oligopolistic competition." He went on to argue that Victorian entrepreneurs late in the nineteenth century had three strategic options:

---

[5]For example, Francis E. Hyde, *Blue Funnel* (Liverpool, 1957); and Hyde, *Shipping Enterprise and Management, 1830-1939* (Liverpool, 1967).

[6]Gordon H. Boyce, *Information, Mediation and Institutional Development: the Rise of Large-Scale Enterprise in British Shipping, 1870-1919* (Manchester, 1995).

[7]Adam Smith, *Wealth of Nations* (2 vols., London, 1776), I, 145.

[8]C.H. Lee, "Corporate Behaviour in Theory and History: I — The Evolution of Theory," *Business History*, XXXII (1990), 17-31. Industrial case studies of cartels include S. Jones, "Price Associations and Competition in the British Pin Industry," *Economic History Review*, Second series, XXVI (1973), 237-253; and L. Pressnell, "Cartels and Competition in British Banking: A Background Study," *Banca Nazionale de Lavoro Quarterly Review*, XXIII (1970), 373-406.

competition, collusion or integration, and very often chose the second to avoid painful rivalry.[9] "In the late nineteenth century," argued Frank Dobbin in 1994, "cartellisation became widespread in British industry."[10] More recently still, Helen Mercer in her hidden history of British anti-trust policies noted that in the mid-1880s British cartels were largely limited to shipping conferences, and that seventeen cartels could be detected in the transportation industries by 1914, of which the majority were in shipping.[11]

This chapter takes another look at the history of shipping conferences. It examines their operation within the context of changing world trading patterns before the First World War. The first part traces their origin and identifies the reasons for their emergence during the last quarter of the nineteenth century. The second section assesses the influence of shipping conferences before 1914. How did conferences operate? What were the criticisms levelled against them? How successful were they in maintaining anti-competitive practices? The final part of the paper briefly draws some of the threads together.

Origins of Shipping Conferences

This section will examine the reasons for the establishment of shipping conferences from the last quarter of the nineteenth century from two directions: those factors which drove individual shipping companies to explore and secure some degree of collective action with rivals and the market variables which produced a climate conducive for collective action. Monopolistic agreements or cartels between sellers in the same industry or trade have been found in many societies and cultures dating back to earliest times. Unfettered competition may offer benefits to consumers as a whole but "it is a nuisance from the point of view of most businessmen," argued Machlup. "There may be a few hardy individual-

---

[9]Oliver M. Westall, "The Competitive Environment of British Business, 1850-1914," in M. Kirby and M. Rose (eds.), *Business Enterprise in Modern Britain from the Eighteenth to the Twentieth Century* (London, 1994), 207-235.

[10]Frank Dobbin, *Forging Industrial Policy: The United States, Britain and France in the Railway Age* (Cambridge, 1994), 203.

[11]Helen Mercer, *Constructing a Competitive Order: The Hidden History of British Anti-trust Policies* (Cambridge, 1995), 11-12.

ists," he continued, "among those who enjoy vigorous competition as long as they are stronger than their opponents...and make enough money for comfort. But those that are losing ground and those that are losing money...regard unrestrained competition as an uncivilised way of doing business."[12] Collusion is seen as a way of easing the pressures of competition by united action as well as realising higher aggregate profits. Co-operation obviates the dangerous consequences of independent action and reduces the complexities of interdependence. Firms no longer need to speculate about the likely reactions of their rivals.

Despite apparent examples of cartels from the ancient classical world and from medieval Europe, most writers suggest that cartels are of a much more modern origin, sometimes associating them with the German crisis of 1873 when prices broke. Stocking and Watkin regarded the institutional forms of cartels as relatively new to the late nineteenth century. Although cartel practices were old, the movement was young, "the product," they argued, "of a mature...industrial society."[13] By the end of the nineteenth century in Britain, Clapham observed, "a number of trade associations, more or less formal, covered a good part of the industrial field," especially in iron and steel, textiles and the electrical and chemical industries.[14] "From the end of the nineteenth century in industrial capitalist economies," argued Mercer, "large firms, cartels, 'trusts' and all manner of collusive organisations were supplanting the 'invisible hand' of the market."[15]

What factors drove British shipowners into the conference system at the end of the century? While it is true to say that cartels are not

---

[12]F. Machlup, *The Economics of Sellers' Competition: Model Analysis of Sellers' Conduct* (Baltimore, 1952), 434. I owe this reference and some others which follow to Dr. J.Lipczynski to whom I am also indebted for allowing me to see a draft of two of the chapters of his PhD thesis which dealt with some of the theoretical approaches to the study of cartels, see J. Lipczynski, "Selected Aspects of Cartel Stability" (Unpublished PhD thesis, London School of Economics, 1994). Dr. Lipczynski is, of course, not responsible for any of the opinions expressed in this chapter.

[13]G. Stocking and M. Watkins, *Cartels or Competition?* (New York, 1948), 5.

[14]J.H. Clapham, *An Economic History of Modern Britain* (3 vols., Cambridge, 1938), III, 213.

[15]Mercer, *Constructing a Competitive Order*, 1.

exclusively the children of distress, depressed business conditions when prices and profit margins were falling played an important part in the development of shipping conferences before 1914. Firms are naturally concerned with measures of performance, such as profitability, and years of poor performance can eventually lead to the exploration of strategies to establish an "accommodation" with rivals. Poor returns could result from weak demand side impulses such as a general economic depression, or from supply side influences due to an increasingly competitive industry trimming prices and profit margins. From their peak in the early 1870s freight rates fell fairly constantly, the result of overcapacity as the supply of available tonnage outstripped the demand for cargo space, a development caused largely, but not only, by the constant application of technological change to the shipping industry, which increased its efficiency. It is no coincidence that what is generally regarded as the first of the modern conferences started in the Calcutta trades in the early 1870s. The threat to profits motivated shipowners to counter short-run variations in prices and demand in favour of long-run stability, which would enable them to earn a reasonable return on capital employed. Conferences which immunized their members against a reduction in prices by a series of agreements may be seen as a defensive mechanism in times of economic hardship.

Depression does not, of course, tell the whole story. If collusion through the conference system and profitability are negatively related then it might be expected that in more buoyant times when freight rates rose the incentive to combine would be weaker or conferences would fold. Once conferences had become a recognised strategy for shipowners, firms did not wait for conditions to become critical in a depression but would quickly move to prevent excess competition and offset falling rates. Hence, conferences became a more or less permanent feature of the business environment for shipowners and shippers alike, operating in good and bad times. After 1900, when it appeared that conferences had applied a brake to the fall in rates, there was naturally every incentive to maintain the collusive arrangements. There was something like a ratchet effect whereby shipowners were unlikely to return to the wholesale cut-throat conditions which had previously existed.

Similarly, some authorities have suggested that firms in a declining industry are more likely to collude than those in expanding industries in an attempt to restore rates of growth and return to some historical level. Declining industries may experience a breakdown in orderly marketing or tacit collusion as firms desperately undercut rivals to maintain their positions. This sudden lack of discipline may force firms to adopt more overt and specific forms of collusion. But the problem with this argument is that shipping can hardly be regarded as a declining industry in the late nineteenth century.

If depression is only one of the reasons for shipping conferences, and then, possibly, only at their inception, what other factors might be involved? One possibility might be that the risk emanating from variable levels of demand often forced firms into collective solutions. An important source of uncertainty is a shipowner's exposure to lumpiness and infrequency of orders, the presence of which may generate a feeling of insecurity that forces firms to consider more overt collusion. Large and infrequent orders may be said to characterize many of the world's carrying trades which were dependent on shipping primary commodities subject to annual harvest peaks and slumps. Brazilian coffee picked around June and July provided a boost to orders for tonnage which dried up some months later when the crop had been shipped. It temporarily attracted outside tonnage which creamed off the trade at low rates to the detriment of the regular lines. Undercutting of the regular carriers is more likely to occur where orders are large and infrequent rather than small and regular and some footloose firms, typically tramp shipowners, may be operating under very short time horizons. They were therefore willing to accept the immediate "gain" of a large order rather than worry about the "cost" of future retaliation that may or may not be realised.

Uncertainty can be very much lessened by the provision of useful market information, the desire for which may itself be a powerful drive towards some form of agreement that could guarantee a steady flow. All firms require information on which to make their decisions and the importance and extent of this information will depend on the degree of the industry's interdependence. The effects of information exchange are to make firms less vulnerable, more sensitive to each other's actions and more aware of market positions. Conference membership was unlikely to reveal the strategic thinking and/or the timing of long-term investment plans of rival shipowners, highly desirable as this information was, since no one wants to suffer the consequences of under or over investment in new tonnage. But it probably brought positive short-run benefits to shipowners in the form of the exchange of commercial information.[16]

Firms like shipping companies which heavily invest in capital intensive assets are in fact most vulnerable when making investment decisions. Of course, the huge capital investments which the large liner firms made, for example, on the North and South Atlantic runs, are themselves barriers to entry which reduce the likelihood of genuinely contestable markets. But the presence in shipping of a high ratio of fixed to variable costs is an additional source of instability since any fall in demand or price will substantially damage a capital intensive company which has every incentive to maintain a long-run rate stability, possibly through collusion.[17]

Further, firms with similar costs will find it easier to collude than those where cost differences are pronounced. It might be argued that the differences in cost functions within German and British liner companies would be marginal. Fixed costs were likely to be similar in so far as they ordered tonnage from the same, usually British, yards and the running costs of crew, victualling and so on would not be markedly different before 1914. Nor at this point had competitive advantages been established by nations whose flags exempted them from maritime regulations, a problem more for the interwar years and beyond. As a result, shipowning members of a conference can accept an agreed rate which should be profitable for all. In the mining/extractive industries, on the other hand, another area where cartels have flourished, very different cost structures exist because of the wide variety of deposits, at different depths and thicknesses, and consequently there is a wide variety in marginal costs. These problems do not rule out cartels in mining — indeed they have often flourished, as examples like Chilean nitrates before 1914 and OPEC in our own time, can demonstrate. But such collusion in mining may be much more difficult to sustain since a single price may not reflect the differences in cost.

It is also possible that market variables created a business climate in the late nineteenth century favourable to the creation of shipping conferences. One of the most commonly analysed variables is the level of

---

[16]Boyce, *Information, Mediation,* 159-164.

[17]H.J. Molenaar and E. van de Voorde (eds.), *Competition Policy in Liner Shipping* (Antwerp, 1994), 112.

industrial concentration. One hypothesis is that collusion is facilitated by the high concentration of a few firms in an industry, since the lines of communication and co-ordination between existing and potential conference members are simpler. As early as 1906, when concern about shipping conferences was at a height in the United Kingdom, one of the first writers on cartels noted that "the formation of a Trust or Cartel requires that in the first place the parties shall be few in number to come to terms readily."[18] The expected relationship would be a positive one between concentration and collusion and negative between the number of firms and collusion. Firms find it easier to establish collusive solutions to their commercial problems in industries characterized by high levels of concentration.

In the case of shipping, concentration ratios undoubtedly rose from the last quarter of the nineteenth century, especially in the years just before the First World War, when a number of mergers, take-overs and amalgamations produced seven huge groups, notably P&O, Royal Mail and Furness Withy, which between them controlled about fifty percent of British shipping by 1914.[19] Evidence suggests that a four or five firm concentration ratio of about fifty percent is typical of cartels and the routes subject to conferences were narrowly defined in order to keep the number of participants small. It is well known that there were separate agreements from different European ports on outward conferences to, say, the Far East or Latin America. Furness Withy and Royal Mail, which dominated the shipment of refrigerated meat between Argentina and the United Kingdom, exploited their control of specialised tonnage to establish an oligopoly in their contractual relations with the meat packing companies. In 1916, for example, the two companies co-operated on a joint account for the Brazilian trade and affirmed "that neither party nor their associated companies will sign any meat contract...without previous consultation and agreement together."[20] Perhaps, the highest concentration

---

[18]D.H. MacGregor, "Shipping Conferences," *Economic Journal*, XIX (1909), 504-512.

[19]E.T. Chamberlain, *Liner Predominance in Transoceanic Shipping* (Washington, 1928), 20 ff.

[20]See freight agreements and pooling in the refrigerated meat trades of Argentina and Brazil in the Furness-Withy archives at the National Maritime Museum, Greenwich, FWS/E/3/1.

was to be found in the Elder Dempster-Woermann Line conference from West African ports to Europe.[21] Rates tended to be more competitive on runs between cities like London and Buenos Aires where many lines competed but much less so at intermediate ports where fewer lines called.

On the other hand, very high concentration ratios may only require tacit co-operation between producers who can organise themselves automatically, while a slightly lower level of concentration after the entry of new firms requires a more formal, overt arrangement. Hence, if an industry experiences changes in structural conditions, such as the entry of new firms, tacit forms of collusion may not work. This point may therefore also help to explain the timing of the creation of shipping conferences in the last quarter of the nineteenth century. Before 1870, the number of steamship companies on any route was small and tacit co-operation was possible, as in the case of the relationship between the Royal Mail Steam Packet Company and Compagnie Générale Transatlantique in the 1860s to the Caribbean.[22] Explicit collusion between two liner firms like these with an almost homogenous product was possible but hardly necessary. There was already an understanding, a commercial culture, not to rock the boat. After 1870, with the growth of new lines and an increasingly diffuse membership, more formal and explicit conference arrangements had to be introduced. A relatively high level of concentration on a shipping route will by definition also ensure that the fringe of non-participants in a conference will be small.

The size distribution of firms is yet another variable which can affect their ability to collude. Where firms in an industry are of roughly equal size, it is argued that the chances of collusion are enhanced. The large size of the British liner groups and the countervailing power of the large German concentrations like Hamburg-Amerika and Norddeutsche-lloyd, which dominated the conference system, offer some support to this argument. However, the divergence of views between large and smaller shipowners in a conference may be exaggerated. It is clear that most conferences included smaller members, yet this asymmetry in market shares still led to stability when the smaller members were willing to

---

[21]Charlotte Leubuscher, *The West African Shipping Trade, 1909-1959* (Leiden, 1963).

[22]M. Barbance, *Histoire de la compagnie générale transatlantique: un siècle d'exploration maritime* (Paris, 1955), 87.

follow the lead of the larger, knowing that the deeper pockets of the large shipowner could be used to punish the small if they stepped out of line. Indeed, small shipping companies had much to gain from joining a conference of larger members in terms of stability and protection from their possible predatory or discriminatory pricing policies. The fear of economic loss may not be the sole reason for co-ordination in unequal market structures. Factors like the historical prominence of a leading firm, such as one of the large British liner companies, or a reputation for wisdom and fairness, might also be important. Indeed, it should be noted that all firms, irrespective of size, generally prefer stability and the *status quo*.

Another market variable is the homogeneity of product or service which can also be a factor in facilitating collusion. Price fixing and conference regulation ought to be more difficult where there is marked product differentiation, while firms selling homogenous goods need only focus on pricing decisions. The greater the number of variables affecting real or perceived differences implies greater complexity in forming a conference. MacGregor wrote:

> ...combination is much easier if there is some degree of uniformity in the products of the firms...There is also abundant evidence that the process of formation is impeded by differences in quality.[23]

Thus, while consumer goods' industries with their usual emphasis on product diversity and differentiation would seem to be poor candidates for successful cartels, minerals like coal, copper or nitrate ought in this respect to be characterised by collusion exemplified by the eighteenth-century Newcastle Vend. Shipping before 1914 was in a rather more ambivalent position. All the main liner companies and conference members exploited the contemporary techniques of product or service differentiation in terms of passenger comfort, speed of vessel, frequency of sailings, regularity, safe delivery of goods and so on in much the same way that airline companies do today. While it was in the interests of efficient cartel management to ensure standardization, shipping conferences could not prevent members from building new tonnage which

[23]D.H. MacGregor, *Industrial Combination* (London, 1906), 122-123.

incorporated all the latest refinements. However, the real differences in the quality of the services of powerful liner companies may be open to doubt.

Evidence also suggests that collusion is more likely in industries which have a low rate of technological change. Yet the shipping industry experienced rapid technological change during the nineteenth century. All companies had access to the same technology and when one firm invested in the latest tonnage, its rivals soon followed suit with a competitive programme of construction. But, once the compound engine had been refined, it might be argued that no decisive technological breakthrough came along until the development of the motor ship which was not influential before 1914. It is interesting to speculate whether the conference system held back the adoption of the motor ship by British shipowners.

Collusion is also far more likely to be attempted where demand is price inelastic since if a shipping conference is successful in raising freight rates, the merchant will continue to use its services and total revenue will be enhanced. Clearly, the conference must cover all the lines on the route or the shipper will escape the higher price by turning to outsiders. "The strength of the monopolist," explained Robinson, "lies in his power to raise prices without frightening away all his customers."[24] There is circumstantial and subjective evidence that inelastic demand for transport services was present on many of the world's trade routes from the last quarter of the nineteenth century when countries outside Europe entered international trade on a large scale. Producers in Latin America, Africa or Asia of such commodities as cocoa and tea were inextricably linked to a world market in the developed countries of North America and Europe and had no alternative but to employ foreign-owned tonnage at prevailing rates of freight to ship their crops. Moreover, the freight rate was only a small proportion of the end user value so that an increase in rates engineered by the conference lines would have far more impact on shipowners' profits than on commodity prices. Of course, it must be recognised that each trade will have its own demand elasticities.

Conference formation will also depend on the ability of member firms to be reassured that fellow members are abiding by the terms of the agreement. They must be in a position to monitor any deviations. Shipping

---

[24]E.A.G. Robinson, *Monopoly* (London, 1945), 5.

possessed strong trade associations which could provide the necessary impetus for setting up a conference and form the basis for an agreement. Trade or employers' associations like the Chamber of Shipping and the Liverpool Steamshipowners Association can gather, process and disseminate information. Most conferences established a formal administrative machinery for negotiations, published authorised charges to shippers and very often appointed a senior manager from one of the leading firms as the secretary.

The official attitude towards cartels or the failure to enforce countervailing legislation may be expected to have a marked impact on the business environment within which the conference system worked. The British government certainly maintained a lax attitude, perhaps because the success of British shipping was crucial not only to the country's prestige but also to its balance of payments. It was willing to allocate resources to the investigation of anti-competitive activities among shipowners but not to regulate them. In addition, in view of the existence of a potentially powerful rival in the world's shipping trades — Germany — it was felt that conferences could be tolerated as a means of checking the competitive might of the German mercantile marine. In addition, Dobbin has recently argued that the British government "fostered cartellisation as a way to protect smaller firms...and sustain a multitude of small-scale economic actors."[25] The stabilisation of rates through the conference system facilitated the survival of small shipowners who, under a more competitive regime, might have been driven to the wall by their more powerful rivals.

Although most economists will shy away from considering non-economic variables in the formation of a conference, they may still be important. The propensity of an oligopoly to behave monopolistically is unlikely to depend upon economic factors alone. If the participants in an agreement shared the same social background, as did many British shipowners in the nineteenth century, and were clustered in the same port, as they were at Liverpool and Glasgow, such group cohesion ensured stability. Friendships and relationships were not just professional but personal and familial. To cheat on one's social group was to run the risk of social stigmatisation as much as economic ruin. Similarly, the "personalities" of the oligopolists, the issue of whether shipowners will

---

[25]Dobbin, *Forging Industrial Policy*, 197.

follow the lead of a particular individual, may be significant in creating and sustaining a shipping conference. The presence or absence of an *esprit de corps,* or sense of group loyalty or mutual confidence and trust, may in some cases be as important as industry characteristics.[26] The British shipping industry of the late nineteenth and early twentieth century was replete with powerful individuals, men like Owen Philipps (later Lord Kylsant) and others who ran Britain's largest liner companies.

Under these conditions, the internal forces driving shipping and the broadly permissive market variables, it is not surprising that British shipowners developed the conference system in the last quarter of the nineteenth century. The first is usually reckoned to be that established in the Calcutta trade in 1875, although there is evidence to suggest that the origins go back rather further, especially in the North Atlantic and Irish trades. The conferences were generally regional leagues of shipping companies of the various European shipowning nations. The Far East conference, for example, comprised the steamship companies of the European powers with imperial possessions beyond Suez, namely Britain, France, Germany, Italy, Netherlands and Russia as well as lines from countries like Japan and Denmark.[27] Latin America was one of the last trading areas to be cartellised in this way. The Brazil and River Plate conference was not established until the 1890s, and on the west coast the main carriers did not reach an agreement until 1904. The conferences were generally stronger in the outward trades, where the volumes of cargo were small but their values were high, and outsiders like tramps were less attracted than in the homeward routes where bulk commodity imports offered traffic for everyone.

All the conferences used a variety of well-known weapons to maintain discipline among their members (fines, expulsion and so on), and to retain their customers' loyalty (matching price-cutting, fighting ships). In particular, the conferences attempted to erect effective entry barriers against outsiders behind which members could shelter to give them the time and space to prosper and solve other co-operative problems. Entry barriers are either natural and inevitably associated with the state of the industry or artificial, which could theoretically be removed. One natural barrier is the size of the market relative to the minimum efficient size of

[26]Lipczynski, "Selected Aspects of Cartel Stability," 173-179.

[27]Chamberlain, *Liner Predominance,* 24-25.

the plant in an industry, which may well deter profit-maximising entrants. The small-scale nature of the West Indian trades and the size of a company to cover calls at all the many islands deterred competitors to Royal Mail, which had long established a presence there. A widespread artificial barrier to entry was the deferred rebate which tied customers to the conference lines by offering them a five or ten percent rebate on past freight charges for uninterrupted loyalty to the established lines — which effectively tried to shut out non-members from a trade. These strategies were adopted with difficulty. In the Singapore trade the deferred rebate was only successfully imposed in 1896 after years of intermittent use once it had been accepted by the three largest shippers.[28] Pooled earnings and sailing quotas, only possible where there is a tight oligopoly, were more sophisticated conference tactics.

The Impact of Shipping Conferences

> The history of associations in the late nineteenth and early twentieth centuries indicates considerable instability. In some industries there was a procession of associations. When an association continued in existence for a number of years, periods when prices were maintained alternated with those when arrangements had to go by default partly because of backsliding on the part of members, but also because of undercutting from outsiders and by virtue of foreign competition.[29]

The literature on the impact of shipping conferences remains ambiguous. Daniel Marx argued that conferences did not secure monopoly profits for their members and Deakin's survey seems to suggest that their impact on raising rates was marginal.[30] For a later period the Rochdale Committee concluded that "it is indeed doubtful whether, in the aggregate, for any

---

[28]Chian Hai Ding, "The Early Shipping Conference System of Singapore, 1897-1911," *Journal of South East Asian History*, X (1969).

[29]Dennis Swann, *et al.*, *Competition in British Industry. Restrictive Practices Legislation in Theory and Practice* (London, 1974), 33.

[30]Marx, *International Shipping Cartels*; and Deakin, *Shipping Conferences*.

considerable period the [profits] have been at a level which would be considered adequate by any normal commercial standard."[31] Other observers have ascribed more success to the conference system. E.T.Chamberlain fairly early on noted that conferences "were more or less successful in regulating transoceanic and interoceanic passenger and freight rates."[32] Much later Oliver Westall came to more or less the same conclusion. Conferences were, he argued, "one of the most successful and long-lasting forms of collusion," while the deferred rebate was "so effective" as a loyalty agreement.[33] Is it possible to resolve this paradox?

First, we can examine the history of freight rates. A main aim of conferences was to raise long-run average prices and hence the profits of member firms above the level that would have been achieved under a competitive equilibrium. What actually happened to freight rates after 1870? They seem to have bottomed out around 1900 and slowly rose in the years immediately before the outbreak of the First World War.[34] It is true that attention paid to trampship rates, which form the major part of available indices, may be misleading since the specialised liner trades which required better facilities were relatively isolated from general trends. But the few categories of bulk cargoes, which accounted for sixty percent of the volume of Britain's shipping business, ultimately determined freights. A fall in earnings from the tramp's traditional traffic inevitably forced it into competition with cargo liners (as in the case of the Brazilian coffee trade) and the persistent presence of outsiders limited the discretion of the conference lines. Conference rates were inevitably higher than those ruling in the rough bulk trades which required the cheapest services. At all levels the service of the regular lines was superior, at a cost, but this attracted rather than lost business. Shipping as a whole has been prone to periodic overcapacity (as fixed investments in ships limit the ability of owners to exit the industry) and so the long run trend of freight

---

[31]*Committee of Inquiry into Shipping* (Rochdale Report) (London, 1970), 123.

[32]Chamberlain, *Liner Predominance*, 25.

[33]Westall, "Competitive Environment," 228.

[34]A.K. Cairncross, *Home and Foreign Investment 1870-1913. Studies in Capital Accumulation* (Cambridge, 1953), 132, 176; E.A.V. Angier, *Fifty Years Freights, 1869-1919* (London, 1920); and E.S. Gregg, "Vicissitudes in the Shipping Trades," *Quarterly Journal of Economics*, XXXV (1921), 603-617.

rates was downward. Why did shipowners continue to invest in new tonnage if freight rates were falling? An answer is, of course, that such construction gave them a (possibly temporary) commercial advantage over their rivals in the form of non-price competition, that is the *quality* of shipping services on offer.

The impressionistic evidence is that shipping conferences had but a limited impact on freight rates. "Despite some noticeable exceptions," explained Douglas North, "the ocean freight market was competitive... and the long-term secular decline in the nineteenth century reflected the operations of an impersonal market."[35] Indeed, it may be that freight rates were broadly determined by the cost of stowage and the value of the cargo so that conferences had little room for discretion. Even though freights rose after 1900 it is difficult to ascribe this to the conference system since so many factors — government action, technological change and so on — are likely to affect the course of rates. Nevertheless, conferences did have some influence over pricing if only because, as a cartel, they could indulge in price discrimination by which large shippers might receive more favourable treatment than smaller ones. Moreover, of course, it is difficult to determine counterfactually what rates would have been without conferences.

What of their impact on shipowners' profits? The theory was that by decreasing the amount of competition, shipowners were able to approach a monopoly solution and increase their profits. But, despite the fact that operating charges dropped in the last quarter of the nineteenth century as a result of greater port efficiency and declining coal prices, the gap between costs and revenues in many cases narrowed rather than widened. According to Derek Aldcroft:

> Few industries have been subject to such violent fluctuations as the shipping industries...on balance the bad years outnumbered the good. In the 45 years before 1914 the number of poor years exceeded the prosperous ones by two to one.[36]

---

[35]D. North, "Ocean Freight Rates and Economic Development, 1750-1913," *Journal of Economic History*, XVIII (1958), 539.

[36]D. Aldcroft, "The Depression in British Shipping, 1901-1911," *Journal of Transport History*, VII (1965), 14.

Between 1901 and 1911 the state of British shipping was particularly depressed and unprofitable, he argued. The worst year, 1908, was marked by "unexampled depression in all freights." Although measures of corporate profitability are notoriously difficult to handle in the late nineteenth century, it appears that rates of return for British shipowners did not markedly improve during the conference era.[37] By itself this is not irrefutable evidence of the failure of the conference system since the rates and profit margins for liner companies might have been even lower without the conferences. But the impression remains that anti-competitive behaviour by shipowners had at best limited impact on improving profitability. And, of course, it remains true that many factors besides freight rates influence the return on capital for shipowners.

Why does the conference system seem to have been unexpectedly ineffective? The lack of long-run cartel stability has characterised most, if not all, agreements in oligopolistic markets, and shipping conferences before 1914, it appears, were no exception. Writers have frequently commented on their short-run nature. Even in the case of shipping conferences, which appear to have lasted for some time, their effectiveness in overcoming market forces and in promoting joint-profit maximisation may in fact have been negligible. The reason why so many cartels fail to live up to expectations is that the "obvious" solution to oligopolistic interdependence is more complicated than it may at first appear. The bargaining strength of members is likely to change in an unpredictable way. Joint-profit maximisation requires the reduction of productive capacity (tonnage) but a shipping company which invested in new tonnage to give it a (temporary) competitive edge would want to renegotiate a conference agreement.

There are two approaches we can use to explore the short-term nature of conference durability and effectiveness: the internal pressures facing firms and the external threats to conference stability. What are the internal pressures? First, there is the question of a conference's inherent instability, in other words, the significance of the number and respective size of conference members, which may influence durability and

---

[37]For a recent discussion of the difficulties of using shipping company accounts, see A.J. Arnold, "Accounting Information and Historical Research in the Shipping Industry," *International Journal of Maritime History*, VII (June 1995), 105-115; and "Should Historians Trust late Nineteenth Century Company Financial Statements?" *Business History*, XXXVIII (April 1996), 40-54.

composition. Like all associations, shipping conferences suffered strains and stresses. A substantial number of member firms may be unsuitable for the day-to-day running of a conference. The Brazilian and River Plate conferences, forced to admit the French firms Chargeurs Réunis and Messageries Maritimes in 1897, Italian companies in 1899, and Houlder Brothers in 1906, had the difficult task of controlling the activities of more than twenty members.[38] As the number of shipowners expanded, a unanimity of goals was likely to weaken while enforcement costs rose and there was a greater likelihood of a rogue owner deliberately undercutting the conference rate. However, as the number of sellers increases, it should be recognised that the importance of each company to total output diminishes and firms are more likely to ignore the independent action of a single rival. If the fringe makes negligible inroads into the markets of existing firms they will be tolerated; if the action of outsiders has a serious impact on members' market shares retaliatory action will result. Outsiders had little to lose. Moreover, just as the initial organisation of an agreement normally required someone to take the lead and organise meetings, a strong personality against an agreement and in favour of unrestrained competition might frustrate any attempts at collusion. A good example of this process was the rate war between Elder Dempster and Royal Mail in the Caribbean after 1900 when Sir Alfred Jones won the contract to ship bananas from Jamaica.[39] As a result, skirmishes broke out from time to time and there was the problem of policing agreements to ensure an efficient collusive outcome and no cheating. Nor was it always possible to arrange costly retaliatory action through the use of fighting ships, given the opportunity cost of foregone profit.

At the same time, the lower the level of concentration the more difficult it is to detect cheating by one member and impose retribution. With a lengthy retaliation lag, the short-run gains from cheating outweigh the potential long-run losses of lower future profits. Unscrupulous

---

[38]R.G. Greenhill, "Shipping, 1850-1914," in D.C.M. Platt (ed.), *Business Imperialism 1840-1930: An Inquiry Based upon British Experience in Latin America* (Oxford, 1977), 148.

[39]R.G. Greenhill, "Bureaucrats, Businessmen and Bananas: the Colonial Office and Shipping Services in the West Indies, 1895-1925," in Lewis R. Fischer (ed.), *From Wheel House to Counting House: Essays in Maritime Business History in Honour of Peter Neville Davies*, (St. John's, 1992), 73-96.

conference members offered special discounts, "illegal" rebates and unauthorised under quotations, even "inventing" outside competition to justify their tactics. Reporting on prewar behaviour, the Booth Committee noted in 1918 that German companies "did not scruple to increase [their] advantages by the employment of unfair methods." Cases of evasion of conference commitments and subterfuge were "too numerous to be regarded as accidental."[40] Given that conference membership was locationally scattered between many countries, it was very difficult to monitor infractions. If additional profits can be obtained by cheating, the cheating will occur unless some policy of deterrence is adopted. The problem is whether there are any effective sanctions, though it is unlikely that any sanctions will be very effective if it is in the economic interests of a shipowner to break a conference agreement.

With an increasingly heterogeneous collection of firms it is more than probable that individual firms had different cost structures, which means that market sharing and pooling were unlikely to endure. They would also have had substantially different goals. What seems optimal for the group may not be optimal for each of the individual members whose interests are in fact divergent. Hence, the pay-off for each member and the levels of commitment will vary. It may be mutually beneficial for firms to collude but they each end up by breaking up a conference. Inherent internal goal conflict can rise to the surface at any time. Firms may disagree over short or long-run policies, the due regard to be paid to outside competition, and their position on likely official responses to anti-competitive behaviour. Not all firms, nor for that matter all conferences, are necessarily profit-maximising, but sales or revenue maximising, subject to a minimum profit constraint.[41] To break a conference agreement may provide great rewards for one firm with improved tonnage if it undercuts the remaining loyal members. Firms may either undercut rivals or put on additional services. Strong aggressive companies seized additional business where possible; weaker lines were on the defensive, anxious only for survival or to retain what they had. Under new management from 1903, Royal Mail became consistently more aggressive, attacking its old ally PSN at Antwerp and challenging Hamburg-Amerika

---

[40]Quoted in Greenhill, "Shipping, 1850-1914," 148.

[41]Trevor D. Heaver, "A Theory of Shipping Conference Pricing and Policies," *Maritime Studies and Management*, I (1973), 17.

in the Caribbean. In 1907 Hamburg-Amerika's attempt to increase its market share in Brazil and New York led to a year long rate war.[42]

A shipping conference will also be unstable if there are substantial possibilities for non-price competition. If the elimination of price competition leads to alternative forms such as product innovation, service quality or advertising, any co-operative solution will be undermined. An effective cartel must ensure that members do not gain an edge by non-price strategies. However, this was quite difficult in the case of shipping. A marked feature of the North Atlantic and South American trades before the First World War was the race between companies and conference partners to build modern liners evidenced in the rivalry between Royal Mail and Hamburg Sud-Amerika.[43] Pooling can delay the impact of such non-price competition since although traffic is naturally attracted to better ships (given that rates are equal) pooling protects the distribution of earnings to companies whose tonnage varies in age and efficiency. Of course, such an arrangement will not last long, as those companies which have invested will want a return on their capital rather than see it dissipated to rival lines. The distribution of profits will be bound to lead to friction eventually.

What were the external threats to a shipping conference? First, the attitudes of merchants were crucial. Shippers inside and outside Europe continued to use the conference lines which offered efficient and dependable services even when full cargoes were not available. "In the past," argues McConville, "shippers have supported the conferences because of the stability they provided."[44] Today the objectives of conferences normally include the idea of the common good of shippers and carriers. Shipowners have to strike a balance between developing a trade and earning a profit. Merchants then and now have expressed strong preferences for quality tonnage even under higher rates. More than anything else they feared damage to goods *en route*, irregular delivery and fluctuating rates which made forward planning difficult. Hard Rand,

---

[42]A.H. John, *A Liverpool Merchant House: Being the History of Alfred Booth & Company, 1863-1958* (London, 1959), 101-103.

[43]Greenhill, "Shipping 1850-1914," 149.

[44]J. McConville, "Synopsis of the General Discussion," in Molenaar and van de Voorde (eds.), *Competition Policy*, 98.

American merchants involved in the Brazilian coffee trade, did not oppose the deferred rebate, and preferred conference tonnage to cheaper outside competitors who could not guarantee reliable shipment of a valuable commodity which required careful stowage.[45] Some shippers supported a particular line through habit and convention (a brand-name effect), perhaps also on national grounds. The largest shippers enjoyed substantial incentives, including preferential terms on bulk contracts, as well as access to shipping company executives through their steamship agencies in distant ports.

But if the shipowners' tactics became unacceptable, merchants could exercise effective countervailing bargaining tactics to represent their views and organise reprisals. Concentration among shippers, the buyers of shipping services, and their market power helped to control monopolistic excesses. E. Johnston and Co., Britain's leading coffee shippers from Brazil, frequently played one line off against another. In 1902 the House abandoned its accumulated rebates with Chargeurs Réunis and loaded shipments for France instead by Royal Mail. Subsequently the partners threatened to abandon Royal Mail "to bring home to the directors that it was necessary to show some attention to their large customers."[46] Alternatively, traders like the United States Steel Corporation chartered or loaded with outsiders if conference terms were unreasonable. Edward Greene, Johnston's manager in Santos, explained in 1896 that the availability of outsiders and the current unpopularity of Lamport and Holt made shippers "determined not to ship by the combination...Knocking down freights has become the popular amusement of the hour."[47] Two years later Naumann Gepp, annoyed at the squeeze on them by the conference lines to New York, loaded with outsiders and forced Lamport to sue for peace.[48]

---

[45]United States, 63rd Congress, House of Representatives, *Report of the Committee on Merchant Marine and Fisheries on Steamship Agreements and Affiliations* (Alexander Committee) (Washington, 1914) evidence, 60-85 and report, 162-163.

[46]University College London, E. Johnston Papers, Rio to London, 3 November 1902 and 26 May 1903.

[47]*Ibid.*, Rio to New York, 4 May 1896.

[48]Naumann Gepp and Co. Ltd., London, Gepp Papers, Naumann Gepp to F. and S. Hampshire, 23 January 1898.

In a specialised trade like refrigerated shipping it was not possible for merchants to choose cheaper, non-conference tonnage which seemed to place the shipowner in a powerful position vis à vis his customers. But as a last resort shippers could operate their own tonnage. The Vestey meat-packing company operated its own Blue Star line of refrigerated ships in response to the unacceptable terms offered by Royal Mail and Furness-Withy.[49] The fact that there were such possibilities for vertical integration by merchants suggests that the power of the shipowners' oligopoly was constrained. In the very long run a merchant could even outflank the conference by seeking alternative markets or sources of supply.

For the Royal Commission on Shipping Rings, merchant associations were the "main recommendation" to restrain shipowners.[50] Critics considered that such mercantile co-operation was likely to be the exception rather than the rule since merchants were generally atomistic, unorganised and divided by genuine conflicts of interest. Meat packers had little in common with mineral exporters who required totally different shipping services. Nevertheless, H.H. Clarke formed a commercial pressure group, the British Mercantile League, in his fight against the South African conference and semi-official groups in South America united shippers.[51] Arthur Cook, secretary to the Brazilian conference, insisted to the Royal Commission on Shipping Rings, that shipowners did listen to merchants and Owen Philipps, Royal Mail's chairman, went round the textile manufacturers of Manchester in 1904 specifically to discuss freight rates from that port.[52] Fortunately, shipowning was rarely integrated vertically with trading, which would be a way in which a member could undercut the cartel by offering cut-price commodities to his retail or factory outlets while retaining the conference rate.

---

[49]Robert G. Greenhill, "British Shipping and Latin America, 1840-1930: The Royal Mail Steam Packet Company" (Unpublished PhD thesis, University of Exeter, 1970), 353.

[50]Great Britain, House of Commons, Parliamentary Papers, "Royal Commission on Shipping Rings," XLVII (1909), 85.

[51]H.H. Clarke, *The Shipping Ring and the South African Trade* (London, 1898).

[52]Greenhill, "Shipping, 1850-1914," 139.

In the long run the stability and profitability of a shipping conference will depend on the existence of outside competition and the height of any entry barriers to the trade. Easy entry for any rival will soon bring down an agreement as it charges a rate just below that of the conference, thus competing away the profits of the member lines. Ordinary market forces were therefore a powerful and continuing constraint on the conference lines and no monopoly was safe for long. Despite the artificial entry barriers raised by the conference system (rebates, fighting ships, predatory pricing, specialised services, long-term contracts) and the substantial "natural" barriers of financial requirements, outside tonnage always existed, and immediately before 1914 the Dutch, Scandinavian and Japanese became formidable competitors. Tramp shipping is a notoriously neglected area and it is difficult to be certain of its position within the so-called liner trades where the conference system largely flourished. But shipping was, and largely remains, a wholly international trade in which units are fairly easily transferable. Rising rates and profits on a trade would attract outsiders, which soon restored equilibrium. Freedom of the seas did not generally exclude shipowners from ports and the mobility of ships made freight markets contestable.

Moreover, shipping conferences had little control over the pattern of, or changes in, international demand. They had little influence, for example, over the bulk, low value trades, nitrate from Chile, grain from Argentina and outward cargoes of coal, which formed a substantial proportion of the demand for ocean shipping and for which tramps and even sailing ships were largely able to compete on equal terms. These cargoes required no specialist tonnage or handling; time was no object in shipment.

A further external control over shipowners could be exercised by government. Officials in the primary producing countries which depended on foreign tonnage to load produce generally took a dim view of the conference system. For shipping companies which had incurred official displeasure there were many ways of making life difficult — in the form of sanitary controls, berthing privileges and petty interference. In the longer run governments developed their own tonnage with subsidies and preferences to compete with the established lines. Sometimes this took the form of encouragement to locally owned coastal shipping; at other times it meant offering subsidies to one foreign company to compete with another. In the end both the Brazilian and Chilean governments raised their own ocean-going fleets in the form of Lloyd Brasileiro and

Compañía Sud-Americana de Vapores respectively, partly in response to their perceived dependence upon foreign-owned shipping companies which, it appeared, charged penal rates. The latter effectively achieved parity with PSN on the west coast of Latin America and the futility of competing with a government owned line was reinforced when the Peruvian government launched its own service in 1907. Lloyd Brasileiro, on the other hand, represented less of a threat to its east coast rivals.[53]

Legal restraint in the form of anti-trust legislation was a further weapon available to officials. In Britain, of course, the majority report of the Royal Commission on Shipping Rings recommended no action and the regulatory stance of the government, evidenced by the Mogul case in 1892, remained ambivalent, not to say permissive. It was recognised that it would be very difficult for Whitehall to deal with collusion between companies like Lamport and Holt and the Prince Line, which rarely loaded at British ports. But many officials outside Britain believed that the conference system was a problem which required a solution. The United States, which before the First World War still depended largely on foreign-owned lines, thus adopted a firmer stance. Her anti-trust legislation, the Sherman and Clayton Acts of 1890 and 1914, are well known but the actual policies directed at shipping conferences in fact amounted to little. The Alexander Committee merely recommended a closer supervision of agreements and an end to the deferred rebate, while the proceedings against the Prince Line and the Brazilian Conference, which alleged restraint of trade, ended in favour of the shipowners.[54] British Dominions and colonies, also dependent on shipping conferences, were equally suspicious. South Africa continued to threaten restraining legislation and Singapore pressed for action.[55] In Latin America, Brazil seems to have taken the lead against the conference lines, but Antony Gibbs and Sons argued that "Chilean and Peruvian law would be much more likely to be of service [to anti-trust campaigners]...These countries

---

[53]Alexander Committee, evidence, 144-145.

[54]Great Britain, Public Record Office, Board of Trade, MT9/973, M9002 (1915).

[55]Chian, "Early Shipping Conference System," 50-66.

might with more justice consider themselves prejudiced by being unable to avail themselves of the cheapest outlets available for their products."[56]

Conclusions

The pattern and development of globalization in the decades before 1914 brought many changes. Among them was the internationalization of shipping in the late nineteenth century, both in terms of a global market place and the spread of steamship technology to many operating companies, which brought both new opportunities and challenges for shipowners. Competition became fiercer on most of the world's trade routes and more persistent. As a result, shipowners, especially those in Britain, sought strategies to relieve the pressure on their revenues and their profit margins in the form of conferences, which exploited a range of devices to curb rivalry and retain customers, a solution which other businessmen also adopted from the late nineteenth century.

The impact of the conference system before 1914 has received very different interpretations, however, and its role seems, from the impressionistic evidence presented, to have been ambiguous. In some cases, notably in West Africa, the conference system did maintain a firm grip on trade; elsewhere, in South Africa, the Far East and in Latin America merchants complained at the treatment they received. Yet the observer is struck by the inherent weaknesses of the pre-1914 cartels rather than by their strength and by the failure of the shipping conferences to raise prices and profits significantly, although much of the argument here, of course, depends on whether conferences were profit maximisers or not. While incontrovertible evidence is sparse, the advantage of hindsight suggests that the tangible benefits of the conference system are hard to measure. The reality appears to have been that they were an empty shell. This may mean that shipping rates remained a product of what the market will bear and that in the final analysis anti-competitive behaviour by shipowners had very limited success in reversing market forces before the First World War.

Yet shipping conferences are one of the most long-lasting forms of international cartels and their durability, as well as the continuity of

---

[56]Guildhall Library, London, Antony Gibbs Papers, 11471/77, London to Valparaíso, 14 September 1905.

their membership, suggests that shipowners thought that they derived some benefits from joining. At least they believed it was better to be in than out. Perceptions and realities of power may differ but businessmen tend to prefer long-run stability to short-run profit maximisation. In this sense shipping conferences, irrespective of whether they raised rates and profits, seem to create the right kind of psychology crucial to confidence when cartels in many industries and services formed an essential part of the business culture before the First World War, notwithstanding textbook notions of perfect competition. Shipowners clearly believed that they were better off with conference; alternatively, the prospect of a business world without conferences would probably have seemed an unpleasant counterfactual proposition for many shipping managers.

National Alliances and Global Webs: The Internationalization of Japanese Shipping

William D. Wray

With minimal scope an account of internationalization in shipping could address a rather confined area such as transport between Britain and France across the English Channel or between Britain and the Iberian Peninsula. The latter example, of course, would cover only the "P" (Peninsular) in the P&O. To include the "O" (Oriental) the account would have to encompass Asia. These cases represent *spatial* variables of international experience. Internationalization, however, is more than just a geographic phenomenon, that is, the rapid spatial spread of shipping throughout the globe from 1850 onwards. The sub-title of this volume, "Internationalization of Sea Transport Industries since 1850," also contains certain underlying *temporal* assumptions. It suggests that internationalization was a process of becoming or of ongoing evolution, and implies that there was less of an international phenomenon before 1850 than after and that its scale subsequently increased. The process of *becoming* can be examined by asking what were the agents of internationalization, while the *evolution* can be assessed by identifying and analyzing the characteristics of its increased scale. The agents of this transition were all related to two large themes: technology and investment. This proposition occupies the first section of the present chapter.

The second section addresses the characteristics of evolving internationalization, particularly with respect to Japan and with illustrations drawn partly from the experience of the Nippon Yusen Kaisha (NYK). In late twentieth-century parlance the term "international" has come to connote the sense of "global," the other operative word in this volume's title. Indeed, the two words are often used interchangeably, as they often convey the same meaning. Yet, literally and thematically there are clearly important distinctions. The term "international" is ultimately rooted in the concept of the nation state and applies to relations between states as defined within Europe by the Westphalian system from the mid-seventeenth century or by the national aspirations of states in Asia within the framework of the Chinese tribute system.[1] The term "global," on the other hand, suggests an essentially trans-national phenomenon.

The contrast drawn here reflects two basic thematic ways of defining "international." The first, reflecting the lingering effects of mercantilism, concerns relations between networks of different nations interacting in the form of commercial diplomacy and competing for market share on a global basis. The second focuses on threads extending from the networks of each nation and together forming a global web that can be characterized as a transnational system or regime. In organizational terms, the first type gives priority to the national system, the second to connections that cross national boundaries. These two types may be viewed as occupying different locations on a continuum between which a certain blurring may occur. For example, in practical terms the regime could exist as an association of national networks that interact operationally through cross-national connections.

Besides such blurring, there are other difficulties with viewing internationalization through a simple dichotomy of two ideal types. Certain basic divides have characterized international shipping over the past century and a half. The distinction between liner and tramp is such that some shipping economists view these as essentially two separate industries. Another is the gap between competing legal regimes, with the British-Continental Europe-Japan camp tolerating conferences and the United States upholding antitrust principles. A different kind of variant from the dichotomy of national networks and global webs concerns the problem of asymmetry. Whether an international regime is characterized by an association of national networks or a web of cross-national connections, there may exist within the membership patterns of dominance or hegemony. In this case the hegemon may be considered either an extension of a national system with putative regional or global leadership or as the dominant influence over the connections that comprise the global web.

---

[1]On these systems, see Stephen D. Krasner, "Compromising Westphalia," *International Security*, XX, No. 3 (Winter 1995/1996), 115-151. The comment on p. 119, "changes in technology, especially reductions in the cost of transportation and communication, have created a more integrated global economy and made it more difficult for states to regulate the international movement of goods, capital, ideas, and labor" is relevant to this paper. See also Takeshi Hamashita, "The Intra-regional System in East Asia in Modern Times," in Peter J. Katzenstein and Takashi Shiraishi (eds.), *Network Power: Japan and Asia* (Ithaca, NY, 1997), 113-135.

Nevertheless, while bearing in mind these variants, distinctions, and qualifications, this chapter is organized around the dichotomy of national networks and international connections. Within this structure it is possible to present two contrasting narratives of the internationalization of Japanese shipping. The first is primarily a story of competition, of Japan's rise and Britain's decline, of Japanese business alliances pitted against British networks. Insofar as this narrative of competition has a national focus it also invites comparison with different national systems. This first narrative is very visible; it has dominated most of the historiography on Japan's international shipping. The second narrative is one of connections and integration. It deals with transnational strategic alliances, international coordination, and inter-system and inter-regime conflict. Unlike the first narrative, this second one is often hidden, tucked away in company and conference records that focus on daily business operations. This second narrative, however, may actually shed more light on the processes of internationalization, just as dark matter, according to most cosmologists, greatly exceeds the amount of visible matter in the universe.

These two narratives illuminate the characteristics of evolving internationalization. However, this involved the transition from a pre-modern age when trade "derived from socially-determined demand"[2] to the nineteenth and twentieth centuries when machinery created demand for distant raw materials, generated new export industries, and led to large capitalist enterprises to organize these processes. This transformation in the pattern of trade was part of a shift in economic systems from an age of mercantilism to one of industrialization in which private companies increasingly became the principal organizing agents. The links these companies established between manufacturing, communications, and distribution depended largely on technical change.

Technology

Technology generated internationalization in shipping in numerous ways. Patterns of change that affected Japan included the application of

[2]In developing a periodization of international trade K.N. Chaudhuri argued that pre-modern trade derived from "socially-determined demand," while nineteenth-century trade was "founded on the supply and production side of the world economy." K.N. Chaudhuri, "From Pre-Industrial to Colonial Trade in Asia, 1700-1850: An Essay in Interpretation," *Shakai keizai shigaku*, LI (1985), 148.

engineering to physical obstacles, development of new ship technology, advances in communications, and new technologically induced freight movements. The major example of the first of these patterns was the modification of geography through the construction of the Suez and Panama canals that shortened the travel time between distant regions of the globe. For example, to Japan the most important contribution of the Panama Canal was to bring the east coast of the Americas closer to Asia. The two technologies discussed most frequently in international expansion are the steamship and the telegraph. The steamship not only reduced the time for transport between Europe and East Asia; by eventually developing regularity of speed it provided one of the essential elements of liner shipping and the emergence of shipping conferences. Companies then had to make the investment to set up the kind of network required under conference operations. In the twentieth century ongoing innovations in technology involving iron and steel, hull design, electric welding, and turbine and then diesel engines generated new routes to the advantage of the sea as opposed to land.[3] One famous illustration of this was Japan's raw silk export to the United States. From its inception in the late nineteenth century this trade went across the Pacific to northwest ports from which it was carried by rail to New York. This route continued even after the opening of the Panama canal because the high interest charges enroute could not be offset by the cheaper freight rate of the more time-consuming sea route. However, with new engines and high speed ships developed by Japanese firms in the late 1920s and early 1930s the trade route shifted to Panama. The greater ship speed reduced interest charges enough to undermine the rail route. In effect, therefore, engine technology helped to internationalize the use of the Panama Canal.

The effect of the telegraph on internationalization is sometimes more assumed than convincingly demonstrated. Historians of empire have argued that governments could not easily change their ways and written reports tended to dominate for many decades.[4] They concede, though, that companies were more adept at utilizing the telegraph for expanded operations. As effective telegraph systems were built between Europe and

---

[3]An excellent discussion of these technologies is contained in Yukiko Fukasaku, *Technology and Industrial Development in Pre-war Japan: Mitsubishi Nagasaki Shipyard, 1884-1934* (London, 1992).

[4]Discussions with Michael Adas and Robert Kubicek.

East Asia by the 1870s, they had a major impact on the organization of business enterprise. It would be difficult to imagine the kind of network developed by the Swire and Holt firms between Britain and China without the telegraph. Administrative changes in Mitsui Bussan (the Mitsui Trading Company), one of the key constituents in Japan's shipping networks, also reflected the influence of the telegraph through its establishment of "supervisory branches." Under this system one particular branch was given authority over all company transactions in a specific commodity (the Osaka branch in the case of raw cotton).[5] This type of monitoring and coordination depended on instant communication. The same principle applied to the organization of the world charter market through an institution like the Baltic Exchange.

The telegraph did more than render information exchange instantaneous and inspire newly organized patterns of international business. It strengthened the hegemony of national British networks in the global web of trade, monetary exchange, and shipping. The denomination of freight rates in the currency of the dominant world power clearly depended upon instant communication and the transfer of funds. One intriguing example of this telegraphic connection was the fact that a good deal of the trade between China and Japan, despite their physical proximity, was actually settled in London through the buying and selling of silver and exchange bills on the Shanghai money market and telegraphic transfer to London. One result of this was that if Japan exported more to China than it imported, it ended up with a net increase in its holdings of pound sterling, which it received in London.[6]

Besides transforming the means of transport through more advanced ships and influencing business organization through new forms of communication, technology also generated new kinds of freight. These changes derived from the application of machines to the manufacture of existing products and from new products that redirected the flow of

---

[5]Seiichiro Yonekura, "The Emergence of the Prototype of Enterprise Group Capitalism: The Case of Mitsui," *Hitotsubashi Journal of Commerce and Management*, XX (December 1985), 85-89; and Japan Business History Institute (ed.), *The First Century of Mitsui O.S.K. Lines Ltd.* (Tokyo, 1985), 57-63.

[6]William D. Wray, "Japan's Big-Three Service Enterprises in China, 1896-1936," in Peter Duus, Ramon H. Myers and Mark Peattie (eds.), *The Japanese Informal Empire in China, 1895-1937* (Princeton, 1989), 45-46, taken from a description by Inoue Junnosuke.

commodities. For Japan, the principal agent in the first of these cases was the cotton textile industry. Prior to mechanization in Japan there was essentially only a single trade involving textiles and Japan. That was the import of Western manufactures. However, three new trades arose out of Japan's application of technology to this industry. These were the import of British machinery, the import of raw cotton (especially Indian raw cotton because it was considered superior to that grown in Japan), and the export of the Japanese manufactured product as it became internationally competitive. These three trades generated complex networks linking Japan with both Europe and Asia as well as America (especially as some raw cotton was imported from the United States). By the 1930s, however, Japan had domesticated one component of this trade by developing superior textile machinery that eliminated the need for imports but which also started a reverse flow of machines to Asia and the West.

A second diversified impact of technology arose from the development of the internal combustion engine and the automobile industry. This generated a new and growing trade in rubber, the transport of which became subject to route competition. Traditionally most rubber shipments had moved westward from Malaya through Suez. However, by the mid-1930s Japanese companies had switched the carriage to an eastward Pacific route, thereby illustrating how the pull of the American market changed international shipping patterns.

Investment

To take advantage of the new technologies liner shipping companies in particular had to make extensive investments in infrastructure, including port facilities and branch networks and to develop new financial and organizational strategies. This mission involved several forms of investment, which in the case of the NYK can be divided into three categories: research, ship purchasing, and infrastructure.

Research within the NYK is reasonably well documented with respect to both personnel and company organization. Perhaps the most interesting case involving the years prior to the First World War, when the network of company lines was still in the formative stage, was the activity of Ōtani Noboru. He had joined the firm in 1896 and later served as NYK president from 1935 to 1942. It was Ōtani more than any other company official who was responsible for constructing the network of NYK shipping in South and Southeast Asia during the war. Ōtani spent over fifteen years in several NYK branches between Hong Kong and Calcutta. He did extensive research in the region, compiled numerous trade reports, made recommendations for new lines, and became so involved in the rubber business that he once considered leaving the NYK to establish his own plantation. Ōtani's investigations did not simply focus on Asia. Through direct contact with NYK president Kondō Renpei, he linked Southeast Asian trade with plans for establishing round-the-world lines through the Panama Canal. There was also a connection between research activity and the targeting of reserves for route enhancement. Ultimately this research provided the underpinnings for a more organized flow of information and analysis. Structurally, a triangular system emerged characterized by reporting from branches to the board member responsible for overseas lines and analysis by the internal research office established during the First World War.

This office had two sections, one responsible for business matters such as freight and company lines, the other for technical issues. Through this latter section coordination could be carried out with research activity within Mitsubishi, from which the NYK purchased most of its ships. Between the late 1890s and the late 1920s the financing of ship purchasing can be divided into three phases. Before 1914, the NYK relied primarily on government subsidies, but after about 1910 internal company reserves became increasingly important. During the First World War enormous profits reduced reliance on existing reserves. However, the high costs of ships induced a strategy of vertical integration, as the NYK as well as several other Japanese shipping companies tried to internalize their costs by purchasing from subsidiaries.[7] Partly because much of the war-generated profits had been siphoned off in the form of high dividends, by the mid-1920s corporate bonds became the key source of financing.

Much of the cost of shipping infrastructure in Japan was borne by the government, particularly the construction of the international ports of Yokohama and Kobe. However, companies themselves also made important contributions. For example, a substantial portion of NYK

---

[7]Takao Shiba, "Succeeding Against Odds, Courting Collapse: How Mitsubishi and Kawasaki Dockyard Managed the Post-WWI Slump," *Japanese Yearbook on Business History*, II (1985), 100-118; and Hashimoto Jurō, "Kyodai sangyō no kōryū," in Nakamura Takafusa and Odaka Kōnosuke (eds.), *Nihon rekishi, vol. 6: Nijū kōzō* (Tokyo, 1989), 93-95.

investment was in bonds that financed domestic port development,[8] and also helped to fund overseas port construction, especially in Shanghai. As part of its own property acquisition it purchased wharfage facilities and access rights in numerous ports. Through this pattern of investment, involving research, ship purchasing, and infrastructure, the company created the links between new technological capabilities and an expanding business network.

Narrative I: The Rise of Japan's Networks

The initial phase of Japan's large-scale investment in shipping essentially began in the 1890s. In their Southeast Asia and China business, Europeans, especially the British, had already made investments of this kind before they reached Japanese waters in the 1860s and 1870s. In subsequent decades they were able to graft the improved telecommunications technology onto their existing business networks. By contrast, a telecommunications system already existed when Japanese firms began to put together their international networks.

Certainly, numerous kinds of business networks existed in Tokugawa Japan before the arrival of foreigners in the mid-nineteenth century. However, for Japan to compete internationally new firms had to arise and change the structure of domestic alliances. Pre-Meiji networks in Japan were primarily concerned with distribution patterns within the domestic economy, especially since foreign trade had actually played a less decisive role in Japan in the last half of the Tokugawa period than it had in the first. It took two to three decades before newly established firms or transformed units of older businesses could gain sufficient international experience and create the kind of mutual ties that generated effective business networks.

In the 1890s Japanese networks formed rapidly around shipping companies and then tended to maintain their membership. One could characterize them as multiple overlapping networks that would coalesce around the needs of a trade and the contracting patterns of trading companies. There were several constants in these networks: the shipping

---

[8]The figure was roughly thirty-seven percent in 1902; it fell to under five percent after the Russo-Japanese War of 1904-1905. See William D. Wray, *Mitsubishi and the N.Y.K., 1870-1914: Business Strategy in the Japanese Shipping Industry* (Cambridge, MA, 1984), 455.

company, such as the NYK or the OSK, a trading company (more often than not, Mitsui, but certainly many others depending on the cargo or route), and a financing institution (usually the Yokohama Specie Bank). Reasonably constant members included suppliers of fuel or ships (often oligopolistic enterprises to which the constant members had inter-firm ties). The variable members were, of course, the shippers, that is, those supplying the freight, that were both firms and industrial associations. These were not just vertical networks within Japan but horizontal combinations through the global spread of branches maintained by firms in the network. Although members in these networks were usually separate firms, their boundaries were penetrable. Inter-firm relations were characterized by long-standing business ties, personal connections, common zaibatsu links (for a few), cooperation in new trading ventures, school ties, shared experience in overseas branches, and both formal contracts and long-term common understandings.

The networks described here were not, of course, examples of what are now called *keiretsu*, or in prewar terms, *zaibatsu*. Japanese networks included firms that were members of *zaibatsu*, but representatives of industrial associations and government-related institutions were usually outside of the *zaibatsu*. The networks should be viewed as autonomous, if informal, entities. Individual members drew strength from the *zaibatsu* to which they belonged (for example, Mitsui Bussan from the Mitsui Bank that helped to finance it, and the NYK from Mitsubishi Heavy Industries, from which it purchased the majority of its ships). With additional backing from government and industry, these networks became formidable competitors.

The competitive rise of these networks in international shipping can be divided into four phases: passive participation, penetration of existing British-led networks, achievement of parity with them, and co-regimism.[9] By the term "passive participation" of stage one I mean a period when Japan's trade began to grow but when Japanese firms had little control over either its handling by trading companies or transport by shipping companies. Although there were minor, initial gains in near-seas routes, particularly to Shanghai, Hong Kong and Manila, before the 1890s

---

[9] I have chosen this particular periodization based on the rising influence within international shipping to highlight the gains by Japanese networks. My criteria for these gains are the shares and rights possessed by Japanese firms within freight conferences, the most important being the Far Eastern Freight Conference.

expansion of Japan's trading activity was disadvantaged, in comparison with European countries, by its lack of extraterritorial privileges in China. It gained these after the Sino-Japanese War of 1894-1895. Trading companies, banks, and shipping firms then rapidly established networks in China. The shipping networks that formed during the 1890s enabled the NYK to *penetrate* overseas routes, first to Bombay, then to London, that were controlled by British-dominated freight conferences. Between 1893 and 1902 discriminatory or exceptional agreements relating to its membership (such as denial of port access at London and Shanghai, and a five percent discount on rates to compensate for slow ships) were incrementally removed and the NYK achieved *parity* with other firms in these conferences. Through gains that it made during the First World War, especially its new regular stop at Liverpool, and its growing diplomatic role within the conference in restraining the entry of outsiders, by the 1920s it had attained a degree of controlling influence in the conferences along with powerful firms like P&O and Holt. In this sense it was a *co-regimist*, a status it enhanced throughout the interwar years, and then, on the basis of its good prewar reputation, quickly reestablished after 1945.

According to this periodization the breakthrough from parity to co-regimist occurred during the First World War. During those years the crucial supportive role played by the network of firms aligned with the NYK was particularly noteworthy in India. These Japanese networks, the core of which usually consisted of the NYK, Mitsui Bussan (Mitsui Trading), and the Yokohama Specie Bank, challenged P&O, BI, and Mackinnon Mackenzie as well as other powerful managing agencies in the Calcutta area. This competition between national networks invokes the theory of British imperialism that views service firms as the vanguard of Britain's overseas capitalism.[10] Like the British service firms, Japan's service enterprises constituted the "advance guard" in the overseas expansion of Japanese capitalism. Furthermore, the operations of Japan's big service firms constituted not just an interface with the world economy but an incipient challenge to the citadel of British capitalism. An interesting perspective on the broader significance of the relations between these two sets of service institutions or alliances is contained in comments

---

[10]P.J. Cain and A.G. Hopkins, *British Imperialism: Innovation and Expansion, 1688-1914;* and *British Imperialism: Crisis and Deconstruction, 1914-1990* (London, 1993).

by Janet Abu-Lughod in her study of the rise and fall of world systems in medieval times and their relevance to the present. "World systems," she writes, "rise when integration increases and they decline when connections along older pathways decay... In a system, it is the *connections* between the parts that must be studied."[11] In one sense Japan's penetration of Britain's international trading system enhanced integration within the world economy. Nevertheless, the Japanese networks could also be thought of as developing a system that operated *parallel* to Britain's and that could be utilized for more competitive purposes.

Narrative II: Alliances in the Global Web

The narrative of networks from different nations competing against one another is visible through data on market share and government programmes that support these networks, especially in the case of Japan. However, at the operational level shipping firms had to focus on issues like freight solicitation, overseas agencies, brokers, port-related tasks, inter-modal transactions, and short-term financing, among other daily matters. To assert that the confrontation of national networks constituted the exclusively valid narrative in the internationalization of shipping assumes that such networks possessed capabilities on a global scale to handle all of these "daily matters." A closer examination of the overseas expansion of Japanese shipping suggests that there was usually some foreign component in its networks. Such foreign linkages constituted many of the connections in international shipping that helped to build the global web. These connections can be found in both alliances and instances of competitive struggles. They can be broken down into at least three distinct types. The first were transnational strategic alliances (legitimately termed networks if they had sufficient longevity) in which Japanese firms would link up with foreigners mainly for freight solicitation. Second was intra-Japanese competition particularly over freight conferences. The third, also involving freight conferences, concerned inter-system or inter-regime conflict, that is, confrontations between different forms of business practice or between contrasting legal regimes. In each of these cases of conflict Japanese firms either competed against each other or acted as components within an international regime.

---

[11]Janet L. Abu-Lughod, *Before Hegemony: The World System, A.D. 1250-1350* (New York, 1989), 367-368.

Transnational Networks

Transnational alliances were common from the time Japan abandoned its policy of seclusion in the mid-nineteenth century. Even before the Meiji Restoration rising rural entrepreneurs in Japan linked up with foreign traders to bypass government controls. A similar post-Restoration alliance arose in 1876 when a remnant of Tokugawa commercial associations called the Nine Shop Union contracted with P&O to fight the government-supported Mitsubishi in coastal shipping.[12] Though this foreign alliance failed, others sprung up to support overseas expansion. During the early Meiji period Japan was heavily dependent on Chinese merchants in its Asian trade. Though this dependence had a "nationalist" narrative in that as Japanese networks arose they sometimes displaced these Chinese merchants, long-term associations were also maintained. Because of the strong position in Southeast Asian trade held by Chinese networks, even in the First World War, when Japan was rapidly gaining influence within Asian trade, Japanese firms retained close ties with these Chinese networks. In 1913 a Chinese-Japanese trade association had been formed in Batavia to promote closer links between Chinese and Japanese business in trade between East and Southeast Asia. As it rapidly expanded its regional influence during the First World War, Japan's Bank of Taiwan, one of the key components in Japanese shipping networks in Southeast Asia, strengthened its relations with the Chinese business community in Java.[13]

---

[12]For the context, see Wray, *Mitsubishi and the NYK*, 94-95.

[13]On these issues, see Noriko Kamachi, "The Chinese in Meiji Japan and their Interaction with the Japanese before the Sino-Japanese War," in Akira Iriye, (ed.), *The Chinese and the Japanese: Essays in Political and Cultural Interactions* (Princeton, 1980), 58-73; Takeshi Hamashita, "The Intra-regional System in East Asia in Modern Times," in Peter J. Katzenstein and Takashi Shiraishi (eds.), *Network Power: Japan and Asia* (Ithaca, NY, 1997), 113-135; Kagotani Naoto, "Ajia kara no 'shōgeki' to Nihon no kindai: Chūgokujin bōekishō no 'danketsuryoku' ni chūmoku shite," *Nihonshi kenkyū*, No. 344 (April 1991), 126-162; Hiroshi Shimizu, "Kobe's Overseas Chinese Merchants and Japan's Trade Expansion in Pre-war Southeast Asia: A Case Study of British Malaya," *Asian Culture*, XXI (June 1997), 1-18; and Peter Post, "Chinese Business Networks and Japanese Capital in South East Asia, 1880-1940: Some Preliminary Observations," in Rajeswary Ampalavanar Brown (ed.), *Chinese Business Enterprise in Asia* (London, 1995), 154-176, esp. 165-169.

On transoceanic routes the NYK made some of its initial gains through transnational alliances. Its initial successful challenge to the Far Eastern Freight Conference in 1896 owed much to the support of Manchester merchants. In the same year it established its Seattle line through an agreement with the Great Northern Railway. The NYK's agent in Australia, Burns, Philp and Co., not only aided in the diversification of its freight but also assisted in the extension of lines to New Zealand and cleared away potential logjams at crucial moments.[14] Within Asia, even in key ports where it had its own branch, the company often relied on British firms as its agents such as Patersons in Singapore and Dodwell in Shanghai. The most interesting such connection within Asia was that with the Andrew Yule firm in Calcutta. Andrew Yule was one of the largest British managing agencies in India with a series of diversified enterprises in Bengal. It served as the NYK's agent when it opened its Calcutta line in 1911 and later helped the NYK enter the huge jute trade in the First World War. As the NYK established its own branch in Calcutta, its personnel was able to take over some of the functions previously performed by Yule. However, business ties continued. Most illustrative of the transnational alliance were triangular contracts signed in 1918 among the NYK, Andrew Yule and Mitsui Bussan involving provision of freight, ship handling, and commission payments in Indo-Japanese trade.[15] If the NYK and Mitsui Bussan constituted the core members of Japan's most important trading network, in this case Andrew Yule was an integral component of it. This triangular alliance was of particular value in inter-regional trade during the First World War. Andrew Yule was one of the two largest managers of jute mills in eastern India, while jute constituted the largest single category in Mitsui's third-country trade between 1916 and 1918 and a key cargo for the NYK.[16]

---

[14]K. Buckley and K. Klugman, *The Australian Presence in the Pacific: Burns Philp, 1914-1946* (Sydney, 1983), 16-19, 67-68 and 87-89. I would like to thank Professor Frank Broeze for bringing this book to my attention.

[15]NYK Archives, NYK-Torishmariyaku hōkoku [Report to NYK Board of Directors], 23 January 1918.

[16]Yamamura Mutsuo, "Dai ichiji taisen igo ni okeru Mitsui Bussan Kaisha no tenkai: jūkōgyōka e no taiō o chūshin ni," *Mitsui Bunko ronsō*, XV (December 1981), 102; and Yamaguchi Kazuo, "Dai ichiji taisenki no shōhin torihiki: Mitsui Bussan to hantaishō," *Mitsui Bunko ronsō*, XXIII (1989), 138 and 140n.

These ties between Japanese shipping networks and British managing agencies in India were facilitated by the social environment among agents and branch managers in Calcutta. When the NYK established its own branch in Calcutta in December 1915 its first head was Ōtani Noboru. His diary records frequent meetings with representatives of network firms, some stationed in Calcutta, others visiting on business. From his comments on gatherings such as luncheons and parties attended by figures from banks, industrial firms, and shipping companies as well as local agents, it is possible to construct a social profile of the larger business network. Many of these contacts were informal. Ōtani established a custom of leaving the office early to play tennis with businessmen, Mitsui's representative being his most regular partner. Ōtani's ties with this Mitsui agent may have extended even to an informal type of financing. Over a period of several months in 1919 he gave Mitsui several instalments of 600,000 rupees which were repaid some months later.[17] It is well known that Mitsui's overseas branches were assigned a certain authorized capital. The discretionary money at Ōtani's disposal seems to have been part of a similar form of branch financial autonomy exercised within the NYK. It also typified the elements of trust and reputation existing between the two major firms.

The links between Japanese shipping firms and foreign agents were just one dimension of their global ties. Frank Broeze's chapter in this volume refers to the two super coalitions in contemporary container shipping, a form of concentration generated by huge capital expenses. The two major Japanese firms, NYK and Mitsui OSK Lines (MOL, postwar successor to the former OSK) belong to separate coalitions, respectively the Grand Alliance and the Global Alliance. This pattern of Japanese companies belonging to separate transnational alliances seems to go back to the early years of the century when the NYK and OSK often had different agents in overseas ports. To a degree the transnational networks to which they belonged were separate. The networks, however, had permeable boundaries. The two companies, the NYK and OSK, connected internationally at certain nodes in each's respective global web. There were several examples of such nodes. One was the freight conference. In joining it the two firms not only developed a common association but also attached to the conference their separate resource sets. Another node was

[17] Ōtani Noboru nikki [Diary].

the large trading company like Mitsui Bussan that serviced both the NYK and OSK. Other nodes that acted as cross-national linkages were agents. As one among many similar examples, the NYK's Australian agent, Burns, Philp also acted as agent for P&O.[18] One might compare the function of these agents, the nodes at the intersection of different networks, to electronic switching devices. In short, within the international shipping business there were many overlapping webs.[19] Studying these webs through the nodes that connected them may be the best way to write global business history. This point would also apply to early modern commercial networks that operated on a global scale and interacted at what might be termed "transnational nodes."

Freight Conferences and Membership

The second category of transnational alliance which can be identified is freight conferences, the membership of which had become increasingly international by 1900. Conflict over this membership exhibited "denational" characteristics, as it sometimes generated fierce intra-Japanese competition. Specifically, it created an insider-outsider split among Japanese firms. Once in, the NYK began to behave more like a British firm, helping to protect its British and continental partners against attempted entry by other Japanese firms. Such disputes often saw collisions between transnational alliances. The biggest confrontation of this kind occurred in 1919 when the OSK applied to enter the Far Eastern Freight Conference after having extended its wartime Marseilles line to London. The NYK led the battle to keep the OSK out. The OSK gained entry only after establishing a strategic alliance with the British firm, Samuel, Samuel and Co.[20] Subsequently, throughout the interwar period the NYK continued to act as a buffer between the conference and other independent Japanese firms seeking entry. This pattern of intra-Japanese

---

[18]Frank Broeze, *Island Nation: A History of Australians and the Sea* (St. Leonards, NSW, 1998), 94.

[19]These webs also acted as a precursor to the process of denationalization Broeze observes in the container consortia.

[20]William D. Wray, "NYK and the Commercial Diplomacy of the Far Eastern Freight Conference, 1896-1956," in Tsunehiko Yui and Keiichiro Nakagawa (eds.), *Business History of Shipping: Strategy and Structure* (Tokyo, 1985), 289-291.

conflict over freight conferences reached its peak in the 1950s when both the NYK and OSK desperately, but ultimately unsuccessfully, fought off the challenge to the conference from the Mitsui Shipping Co., as it sought entry.[21]

Threats to the Conference Collective

The transnational membership of freight conferences sometimes had to defend its collective procedures against external threats. These emanated from several sources including contrasting forms of business practice and laws that authorized distinctly different shipping regimes. Mitsui Bussan's relations with conferences represented the first of these threats. As a trading company with a substantial shipping operation, Mitsui had a dual interface with freight conferences. As a trading enterprise it was part of the Japanese network involving the NYK and a loyal shipper for conferences. However, as a shipping firm it could undercut the conference's rates or carry cargo usually reserved for the conference. In doing so it acted as a merchant operator, buying the cargo and carrying it on its own ships. In the most famous case of this nature, Mitsui, acting as a trading firm, purchased rubber in Malaya in the mid-1930s and then, as a shipping enterprise, carried it on its own vessels eastward across the Pacific, reversing to the detriment of the conferences the usual westward route through Suez.[22] In this instance Mitsui's dispute with the conference was an inter-system conflict in that it represented a different form of business practice, that is, Mitsui as an industrial or merchant carrier as opposed to the common-carrier style of operations practiced by the conferences.

Inter-regime conflicts, by contrast, involved the United States against the combined Japanese, British, and European networks that operated the freight conferences. There were numerous examples of this conflict involving the US government, especially in the 1930s. These, of

---

[21]William D. Wray, "The 'Mitsui Fight,' 1953-1956: Japan and the Far Eastern Freight Conference," in Lewis R. Fischer and Helge W. Nordvik (eds.) *Shipping and Trade, 1750-1950: Essays in International Maritime Economic History* (Pontefract, England, 1990), 213-234. The Mitsui Shipping Company, a spinoff from Mitsui Bussan, merged with the OSK in 1964 to become Mitsui-OSK Lines.

[22]Wray, "Commercial Diplomacy," 296-297.

course, were rooted in the US Shipping Act of 1916 that prohibited deferred rebates. In one case in 1932 the US Shipping Board tried to force Dollar Steamships into the Bombay Conference that had refused to give Dollar permission to call at Bombay. The US threatened to deny conference members access to American ports. These members, of course, were mostly British and Japanese.[23] Between 1938 and 1941 there were frequent US complaints and investigations carried out against discriminatory treatment by the Trans-Pacific Freight Conference. These protests usually concerned matters such as illegal (according to US law) rebating and mis-measurement of cargo. Japanese firms were singled out for criticism, but the conference against which the complaints were lodged included non-Japanese members such as American President Lines, A.P. Moller, and Wilhelm Wilhelmsen.[24]

In all of these cases of either transnational strategic alliances or conflict over freight conferences, Japanese firms either participated in networks that formed the global web of international shipping and trading, or fought other Japanese firms out of loyalty to their existing connections within that web and stood together with foreign partners against intervention by governments. Needless to say, this last point applied not just to actions by foreign governments. It was common in the Far Eastern Freight Conference for the NYK to advise other members of the conference on how best to handle intervention by the Japanese government.[25]

Conclusion

Neither of the two narratives presented here, one of Japanese networks gaining market share at the expense of other national networks, or the other of Japanese firms participating in transnational networks or alliances, sometimes at the expense of other Japanese firms, represents a fully valid picture. Yet neither is wholly false. They represent partial, but incomplete, pictures. They also overlap, making the distinction drawn between the two more of a typology than a full reflection of reality.

---

[23]*Ibid.*, 295-296.

[24]Material on these disputes is located in the US National Archives, particularly in consular reports from Yokohama, and in files of the US Maritime Commission.

[25]Wray, "Commercial Diplomacy," 289.

Where, for example, would freight conferences be placed within the context of this ambiguity? On the one hand, they typify the characteristics of a global web with their international membership, coordinated policies, and operational mechanisms that control the flow of freight internationally. As organizational entities their self interest transcends national priorities. On the other hand, internally there is competition among members, and that competition may be seen as a reflection of national ambition. I remain skeptical, however, of this latter perspective, for the documentary record suggests that the Japanese members of conferences placed the interest of the conference above that of Japan's perceived national interest. The national ambition was expressed more by outsiders seeking access or the Japanese government lobbying for their entry. That also reflected the hierarchy of Japanese members within the conference, with the NYK as the first entrant almost always gaining the most rights.[26]

While there may be overlaps between the national and global models I have outlined, it appears that the historiographical treatment of them displays somewhat different characteristics. I would suggest that in recent decades scholars examining the global dimension have been writing in more empirical traditions, working more closely on actual business practices, whereas those focusing on national networks have more commonly written within the framework of social or organization theory. The transnational narrative, I would argue, is in need of more attention than the national one, around which has formed something of an orthodoxy. Certainly, though, we could benefit from some synthesis of the two approaches.

One place to start reevaluating the national narrative through the transnational lens is Gordon Boyce's discussion of British networks where often core members are surrounded by either transitory or dependent partners.[27] There is certainly a functional similarity in the relationships between firms in transnational alliances to those in British networks. One question Boyce's model raises is whether the foreign bodies, such as agents, affiliated with Japanese global networks were merely in a

---

[26]See Mariko Tatsuki's chapter in this volume which asserts that the later the entry the fewer the rights received.

[27]Gordon H. Boyce, *Information, Mediation and Institutional Development: The Rise of Large-Scale Enterprise in British Shipping, 1870-1919* (Manchester, 1995), esp. 117-121, 131-152 and 176-222.

subordinate or dependent position. A recent work on Japanese production alliances in Southeast Asia characterizes Southeast Asian capitalists in these networks as fulfilling a comprador-like role for the Japanese.[28] However, in prewar shipping, although the foreign component in the network may not have occupied core positions, its role was indispensable. When a Japanese company undertook strategic planning for the opening of a new line, its timing would depend on the degree to which it could control the freight. That, in turn, depended upon the foreign presence in the projected network. Moreover, it may be argued that overseas agents, close as they were to the sources of freight, may collectively have had as much influence over the strategic direction of company lines as the head office.[29] If we look at operations on a regional basis, say between India and Japan, the national members of the Japanese network would differ according to the freight, that is, the industrial component would be variable. However, in the full membership, the foreign partner would be constant. Thus, since the foreign component would not only be indispensable but within certain spheres also constant, we could conclude that the national components of Japanese networks constituted a necessary but not sufficient factor in the scale of Japan's shipping expansion.[30] In contrast to the comprador-like role of today's Southeast Asian capitalists, it is hard to see such patterns of dominance in the transnational alliances of Japan's shipping industry. Hierarchies of power may be more common in manufacturing networks because of the proprietary concern with technology. Networks in shipping and in manufacturing, then, may have fundamentally different characteristics. There may be asymmetries in shipping networks, but the shared need for information flows seems to produce relationships of mutual benefit.

If my second narrative is a challenge to the first, then it suggests that we have to explain the strategies of Japanese shipping firms by reference to their normal business operations that constitute multiple

---

[28]Walter Hatch and Kozo Yamamura, *Asia in Japan's Embrace: Building a Regional Production Alliance* (Cambridge, 1996), 80.

[29]Frank Broeze raised this point in the conference discussion.

[30]In Wray, *Mitsubishi and the NYK*, 508-509, I emphasized the exclusively national composition of these Japanese networks (which I termed business alliances), suggesting that they functioned best when free from foreign participation. I now feel I generalized too hastily on what may have been an unusual case.

international and cross-industrial connections. Our explanations cannot fall back on interpretations rooted in purely Japanese networks or the *zaibatsu* (or postwar *keiretsu*) to which these firms belonged. This proposition leads to a slightly different emphasis than that of Geoffrey Jones in his comparison of British and Japanese trading firms. In this he attributes Mitsui Bussan's success (relative to that of British trading firms) ultimately to its membership in the Mitsui group and "the lack of a British equivalent to the Japanese enterprise group system."[31] I have, of course, stated that individual members of Japan's global networks drew support from their groups. In that sense Jones's point is consistent with my argument. However, I prefer to shift the focus toward the membership and operations of the global network to achieve a more comprehensive synthesis.

Finally, my transnational narrative encourages Gordon Boyce to go beyond the national focus he adopted in his study of British shipping and chart the transnational alliances of British shipping firms. Boyce has expanded his spatial coverage in a recent paper on the Asian business of the Holt-Scott-Swire network that includes some reference to Chinese capital ties. However, his focus remains overwhelmingly British.[32] There are, of course, empirical reasons to concentrate almost exclusively on British networks. During the mercantilist age, the British and Dutch East India companies superimposed their Asian business upon the existing networks on Islamic, Indian, and Chinese merchants.[33] By the mid-nineteenth century the structure of British Asian trade had grown out of the East India Company and evolved into a network of private firms. Meanwhile, during these changes in British institutions prior to the mid-nineteenth century, Japan remained only a passive participant in global

---

[31]Geoffrey Jones, "Diversification Strategies and Corporate Governance in Trading Companies: Anglo-Japanese Comparisons since the Late Nineteenth Century," *Business and Economic History*, XXV (1996), 115. The term "enterprise group" is a translation of *kigyō shūdan*, which is used for the postwar version of the former *zaibatsu*. *Keiretsu* is sometimes informally used for the same purpose, but it is more appropriately applied to vertical groups which form around large manufacturing firms.

[32]Gordon Boyce, "The Holt-Scott-Swire Network: Decision Support Systems and Human Resource Development" (Unpublished paper presented to the 6th North Sea History Conference, Rotterdam, August 1997).

[33]See Patricia Risso, *Merchants and Faith: Muslim Commerce and Culture in the Indian Ocean* (Boulder, CO, 1995).

trade. It was a *participant* in that commodities and goods continued to flow in and out of Japan and it exercised autonomous regulation over the trade, but it was *passive* because its maritime prohibitions prevented ships or traders from going abroad (with the minor exception of the Ryukyu Islands). Thus, it had no way of building its own overseas network. Thereafter, despite the rapid growth of trading firms like Mitsui Bussan, Japan had to establish ties with foreign firms as part of its emerging international network. The British, with a pre-existing network of their own, had less need to rely on foreigners as intermediaries.[34] Yet despite this pre-existing network, from the 1860s on, the British clearly had to establish effective ties with local agents and other merchants in Asian ports. This point, in fact, ties together both the national and international narratives of this paper. Creating links with Asian traders was part of the national competition between Britain and Japan. Insofar as Japan gained at the expense of the British it did so partly because its links became more productive. But the very existence of these Japanese connections, whether to local Asian or British agents, shows that their networks were international in scope. Some of the broader implications of this point are contained in a comment by Chris Bayly that seems to parallel my discussion of networks and nodes. "There is," he says, "an important 'analytical space' between, on the one hand, very general analyses of the growing Capitalist World System...and, on the other, the history of specific cultures and communities."[35] If it is that "analytical space" toward which we are moving, then this paper constitutes a plea to denationalize shipping historiography.

---

[34]I am not here subscribing to an interpretation of Japan based on themes of "backwardness" or "late development." My preference is for a view of Japanese history based on a pattern of anachronisms that produce dysfunctional characteristics. Upon reaching a crisis point, these generate a structural shift in the country's employment of its resources that releases latent potential.

[35]C.A. Bayly, *Imperial Meridian: The British Empire and the World, 1780-1830* (London, 1989), 14-15.

Dutch Sea Transport in Transition: The German Hinterland as Catalyst, 1850-1914[1]

Jochen Bläsing and Ton Langenhuyzen

Although the country was not well endowed with raw materials, especially those with industrial value, it occupied a strategic position astride the estuaries of major rivers and was surrounded by the large and expanding markets of Britain, Germany and France. Being inconsequential on the economic map during the fourteenth and fifteenth centuries, the Dutch nation was on its way to attaining commercial as well as cultural pre-eminence by the sixteenth century. Early in their "golden" seventeenth century, forever remembered as an era of fabulous profits, the Dutch possessed about three-quarters of Europe's mercantile tonnage and conveyed an important part of the trade in the Mediterranean and the Baltic, thus transporting the imports and exports of many countries. The United East Indies Company, the famous VOC, almost succeeded in duplicating this success in Asia; that is, it eventually obtained a sizeable share in the inter-Asian trade.

However, during the eighteenth century, the complacent colonial power faced a steady decline as other European countries developed economically and started to build up their own maritime interests. The French occupation of the country in 1795 only aggravated the downward trend of prosperity and the structural decay of the Dutch economy. Yet on the eve of the First World War, the Netherlands was once more the home of one of Europe's leading economies, with a fully developed, "modern" industrial sector. The climacteric in the economic fortunes of the Dutch occurred during the nineteenth century. This chapter explores the development of Dutch sea transport — comprising the three related branches of shipping, shipbuilding, and the port industry (chiefly Rotterdam) — to provide, *inter alia,* an insight into how and why the transformation took place.

---

[1]We would like to thank the participants at a tpre-conference for their useful remarks.

The nineteenth century was an era of contrasts for the Netherlands. The newly unified (with Belgium) kingdom stumbled into it without much luck. For decades after the Napoleonic Wars, when West European countries such as France, Belgium, and Germany were following the British model of modern industrialization, former Golden Age pioneer Holland seemed unable to do the same and drifted further back into commercial nostalgia and economic stagnation. Only during the second half of the nineteenth century, did the Netherlands modernize, leading to a remarkable reversal of fortunes.

The modernization of Dutch sea transport was particularly influenced by, if not the result of, the economic emancipation of the German hinterland. Germany's industrialization functioned as a catalyst. While the exchange of goods between Britain and Germany became increasingly important, which automatically involved the Dutch in an intermediary role,[2] Rotterdam, destined to become the principal Dutch port, was forced by competition with harbours such as Hamburg, Bremen, and Antwerp to improve its poor port facilities and vulnerable connections with the open sea. In the meantime, the hinterland's exploding need for short and cheap transportation routes to and from the sea and its massive transport requirement, completely changed the outlook of the Dutch shipbuilding and shipping industries. According to modern research, the improvement of transport technology contributed fundamentally to the renewal and re-orientation of the country's economic growth.[3]

This chapter deals with the development of Dutch sea transport into a sector of a modern industrial economy in the second half of the nineteenth century. Considering that traditionally sea transport had been dominated by the colonial trade, which had become a closed and stagnating market by 1850, one could state that the Dutch economy, characterized for long by a sort of "internal globalization," was eventually forced to modernize under the pressure of truly "external," or "global," factors. The growing importance of the German hinterland is emphasized, not only because the role of the Rhine trade and German industrialization

---

[2]J.P. Smits, *Economische groei en structuurveranderingen in de Nederlandse dienstendector 1850-1913* (Amsterdam, 1995), 162.

[3]E. Horlings, *The Economic Development of the Dutch Service Sector 1800-1850* (Amsterdam, 1995), 312.

had a critical bearing on this process but also because it has always been underestimated in the scholarly literature.[4]

Unfavourable Factors

The first question is: why did it take so long for the Dutch international transport industry to recover, make a new start after liberation from the French as well as adapt to rapidly growing international competition?

During the nineteenth century, the Dutch economy was characterized by commerce and agriculture as well as a low level of industrialization. Commercial traditions prevailed while other countries were modernizing their economies. Belgium, for instance, was one of the first countries to industrialize. The main reason the Dutch preferred to wallow in commercial nostalgia is very simple: they did not seek to industrialize because they did not see any reason to do so. Despite its economic stagnation, the country was still one of the major economic powers in Europe and surely one of the wealthiest nations in the world, surpassed only by Britain in the early nineteenth century.[5] Its transport facilities and financial institutions still generated sufficient profits. The passenger barges (*trekschuiten*) were a very stable branch of domestic transport. Because they ensured good, regular, and cheap connections between the urban markets, there was apparently little need for innovation.[6]

Dutch shipping still occupied an important place in European transport. More importantly, the Netherlands had rich colonies in the West and East Indies, the flow of goods and capital from the East Indies to the homeland exerting a particularly strong influence on the Dutch economy. Trade with the colonies meant that colonial goods dominated Dutch commerce, deterring merchants from looking for other markets or opportunities. Moreover, as trade and the sea transport industries were closely connected, shipowners and shipbuilders were denied the opportunity to exploit new markets. In addition, the Dutch themselves did not

---

[4]See J.F.E. Bläsing, *Das goldene Delta und sein eisernes Hinterland 1815-1851* (Leiden, 1997); and H.P.H. Nusteling, *De Rijnvaart in het tijdperk van stoom en steenkool 1831-1914* (Amsterdam, 1974).

[5]Horlings, *Economic Development*, 28.

[6]Bläsing, *Das goldene Delta*, 184-185; and Horlings, *Economic Development*, 268.

really produce goods that could be exported on the world market, especially after the Belgian separation in 1830, which left the Netherlands without a modern industrial sector which might have improved the country's position in the emerging global market.

Figure 1: Share of colonial remittance in the total revenues of the central government 1832-1877 and the ratio between profits and share-capital of the NHM 1830-1880 (%).

Source: E. Horlings, *The Economic Development of the Dutch Service Sector 1800-1850* (Amsterdam, 1995), 171.

Since this emphasis on colonial trade was not immediately punished by market forces, nothing changed for a while. In fact, pressure to change was often hindered as far as possible. In 1824, the transport of colonial goods was strictly regulated by the newly established Dutch Trade Company (*Nederlandse Handelsmaatschappij* [NHM]), eliminating the forces of the free market. Sea transport to and from the East Indies was assured and almost immune to supply and demand conditions in the world market. In fact, the NHM was extremely successful financially, especially after introducing the "Culture System" in 1830 which forced the colonial peasants to devote some of their cultivated land to export crops, while the NHM was charged with shipping and sales. It was at that time that the slogan was born that the Indies were "the cork on which the

Netherlands was kept afloat." As Horlings points out, at that time, the dramatic increase in colonial trade and transport became the fundamental source of Dutch economic growth. Figure 1 shows why nobody was to blame: government, the NHM, and merchants had every reason to continue earning a lot of money. The rates of return in trade and transport were simply too high to ignore.

It is true that Amsterdam was no longer the staple market for international trade that it had been in the seventeenth and eighteenth centuries, but by the 1840s, it had developed into one of the main European markets for colonial goods which resulted in an enormous inflow of capital from the Dutch East Indies to the motherland. This one-way traffic, together with the conservatism of Amsterdam merchants, meant that other forms of international commerce, such as the transit trade, were neglected.[7]

Reasons for Change

Although at the beginning of the nineteenth century only a handful of people, notably King William I and a few capable entrepreneurs, appreciated the urgent need for change, the economic standstill of subsequent decades made it necessary for a radically new approach to be adopted. Former structural advantages, such as the dependence on the staple trade, definitely turned into structural handicaps.

Pre-industrial manufacturing never recovered its traditional form after the liberation from the French. A country experiencing a severe decline while still maintaining a flourishing financial sector is not the most appropriate context for the application of revolutionary industrial processes. In fact, Dutch capitalists tended to invest their surplus money abroad rather than in technologically potent industry at home. As a result the Dutch economy started to suffer from cumulative disadvantages. In the first place, the ports were constrained by the silting up of passages to the sea, a problem that was almost entirely neglected during the first half of the century because water, wind, and small vessels were considered cheaper than large steamboats, and small vessels did not need deep water. Therefore, it sometimes took weeks to get from port to open sea. An additional disadvantage was the inadequate port facilities, even for bulk

[7]Smits, *Economische groei*, 132; and Horlings, *Economic Development*, 314-315.

goods. This was notable at Rotterdam, where the port area had not changed since the seventeenth century. Anachronistic commercial and administrative structures badly needed modifying. Only after years of discussion did the city succeed in restoring the water level in the harbour, and not with the help of modern industrial equipment, but with horses. Even the successful colonial protection overran itself in the long run.[8] For example the Indian market for textiles became saturated, there ensued an oversupply of transport capacity, and London claimed an important part of the trade in coffee and sugar, due to the poor port infrastructure in the Netherlands. Between 1840 and 1870, the growth of Amsterdam and Rotterdam lagged well behind that of most other ports in Europe.[9]

Secondly, the traditionally hostile attitude towards transit trade, which was considered at best a "necessary evil," was significant. Trade still remained the ideal, but not until 1882 did the Rotterdam Chamber of Commerce revise its negative opinion of the transit trade to and from the hinterland as a very stable source of profits. Until then trade in the German Rhine ports could not develop without Dutch participation. In fact, the most effective way for the Dutch to succeed had been simply to obstruct the transit trade as much as possible.

Rotterdam's attitude towards competition from foreign railroads was, in this context, also quite remarkable. It was argued that "our city has no need of a rail connection with the German Rhineland," for the railroad "could never compete with Rhine-navigation" and what was more, "if necessary, Rhine tolls could be removed."[10] Consequently, not long after the opening of the Antwerp-Cologne railroad in 1843, which quickly competed strongly for Dutch Rhine transport and was soon responsible for twenty-seven percent of the volume of transport to the German hinterland,[11] the Rotterdam Chamber of Commerce encouraged the Dutch government to institute a policy of duty-free trade. After decades of violent disputes between Holland and Prussia over free Rhine trade, the

---

[8]Horlings, *Economic Development*, 169.

[9]Smits, *Economische groei*, 261; and Horlings, *Economic Development*, 193.

[10]M. Callahan, *The Harbour Barons: Political and Commercial Elites and the Development of the Port of Rotterdam 1824-1892* (Princeton, 1981), 102-103 and 121.

[11]Horlings, *Economic Development*, 207-208.

Germans saw their principal liberal demands granted in the Trade and Shipment Treaty of 1851.

In the mid-nineteenth century, the Dutch government initiated a unilateral liberalization of its trade policy. With the acceptance of the new shipment laws in 1850, Holland embraced the free trade system. There was no other way; the old power was gone. The government eventually abolished all the financial measures which had made Rhine traffic unnecessarily expensive.[12] With railroad and steamship connections to German ports and to an independent Antwerp, the German hinterland could now force Rotterdam to do business on its own terms.[13] In 1877, import duties on most raw materials were abolished.[14]

All this was associated with the major political and economic force which emerged after 1813 in the hinterland. While the Dutch government was intent on protecting the old Dutch monopolies, especially those on the Rhine, the Germans, under the strong leadership of Prussia, wanted free and unhampered transit, including faster transport and lower duties. This struggle was eventually decided by the much stronger power of Prussia.[15] All traditional structures were broken down. The Act of Mainz in 1831 constituted a major watershed in the development of Rhine transport. The Netherlands was more or less forced to agree to large-scale reforms in Rhine shipping. After 1834, the formation of the German Zollverein put the Netherlands under increasing pressure to liberate Rhine transport from its last restraints. The treaties of 1837 and 1842 eliminated most of the remaining advantages of Dutch skippers and in 1850-1851 both nations granted each other the status of most-favoured nation.[16] The effects were profound. Although Dutch skippers managed initially to hold

---

[12]A. Lewe, *Invoer to lande verboden. Een verkenning van de handel over landwegen tussen Nederland en de Pruisische provincies Rheinland en Westfalen 1836-1857* (Hilversum, 1995), 50.

[13]Bläsing, *Das goldene Delta*, 121.

[14]I.J. Brugmans, *Paardenkracht en Mensenmacht. Sociaal-Economische geschiedenis van Nederland 1795-1940* (Den Haag, 1961), 387.

[15]Bläsing, *Das goldene Delta*, 182-194; and Horlings, *Economic Development*, 195-196.

[16]Nusteling, *De Rijnvaart*, 45-47; and Bläsing, *Das goldene Delta*, 56-82.

on to their share of transport, as freight rates fell, the proportion of Dutch ships in Rhine transport decreased considerably (see figure 2).

Economic pressure from the German hinterland, stimulated by its rapid industrialization and growing population, turned out to be as a blessing in disguise. In thc Rhine-Ruhr region, especially, the need for short and cheap transportation routes to and from the sea for expanding flows of grain, coal, and timber grew very quickly. Such bulk goods accounted for seventy-five percent of the business.[17] In 1913, Rotterdam had gained a dominant position in the Rhine shipment of the four main bulk goods, handling ninety-six percent of all timber, ninety-three percent of all coal, eighty-eight percent of all ores, and eighty-one percent of all grains.[18]

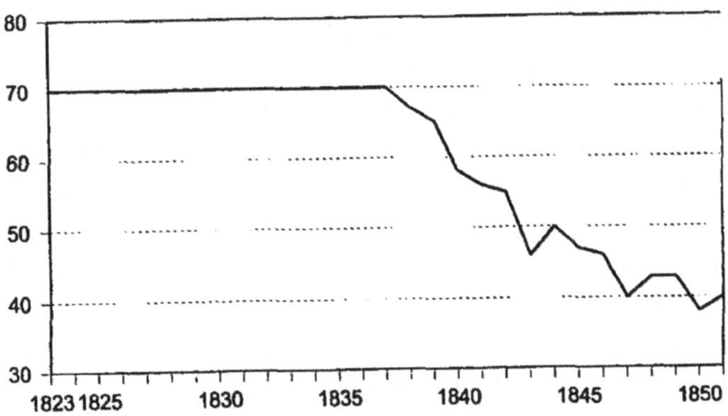

Figure 2: Share of Dutch skippers in total Rhine transport past Emmerich, 1823-1850 (percent).

Source: Horlings, *Economic Development*, 411.

In the last quarter of the nineteenth century, the development of a modern Dutch economy was also stimulated by the modernization of the domestic production of industrial and agricultural goods. At last, the Dutch themselves started to produce for the international market and began exporting domestic products instead of just trading colonial goods.

---

[17]Callahan, *Harbour Barons*, 3; and Nusteling, *De Rijnvaart*, 115, 213 and 216.

[18]P. Serton, *Rotterdam als haven voor massale goederen. Een bijdrage tot de geografie van het verkeer* (Rotterdam, 1913), 141-150.

The port of Rotterdam, situated at the mouth of the Rhine, at the nexus between Britain and the continent, occupied a vital geographical position. In satisfying its hinterland's exploding demand for the conveyance of raw materials and bulk goods — aided by the international fall of freight rates due to the growing efficiency of steamships and railways — Rotterdam laid the foundations for its current status as a major world port (see table 1).

Table 1
The Rise of Rotterdam, 1836/40-1866/70

	1836/40	1846/50	1856/60	1866/70
(1)	573	2.181	3.609	5.378
(2)	26.5	51.5	48	74.5

Notes: (1) Average bulk goods to Germany via Lobith (Rhine) (x 1000 tons); (2) percentages of total Rhine shipments.

Source: H.P.H. Nusteling, *De Rijnvaart in het tijdperk van stoom en steenkool 1831-1914* (Amsterdam, 1974), 113.

Supporting Factors

In light of all this, it is hardly surprising that the reconstruction of the Dutch economy occupied several generations. But what counts is that eventually Dutch merchants as well as the Dutch government, converted to the principles of free trade, partly from conviction and partly following the British example in the mid nineteenth century. Most authors state that commercial liberalism in Holland rose quite abruptly from a mixture of conviction and the more or less subtle "threats" of the British during the 1840s. Undoubtedly there was some British pressure. But what is much more relevant is that Britain's aims only met with open doors in the Netherlands because the Dutch could not withstand the pressure arising from German industrialization and — during the first half of the century — the very persistant Prussian demands for liberalization.

After the unilateral liberalization of the country's trade policy, the privileged position of the Dutch shipbuilding industry was no longer tenable and sailing vessels no longer dominated the ocean routes to the Dutch colonies as they had done in the absence of foreign competition. After the British repealed the Navigation Acts, and the Dutch liberalized trade, foreign-built ships could more easily sail under a Dutch flag and enter Dutch harbours. In the second half of the nineteenth century, British steamships entered into fierce competition with the old fashioned sailing vessels of the Dutch.

Since the Dutch realized that the transit trade had advantages, and that shipment to and from Germany offered enormous opportunities, Rotterdam's local government decided to improve port facilities and connections with the sea. Tolls were abolished as well as the dues on transit traffic, while Dutch pilot and navigation dues were considerably reduced. In 1856, the port of Rotterdam got its first direct railroad to Germany. In the following decades, the city became the nerve centre of a railroad network to Dutch, German and Belgian industrial and commercial centres. In 1872, the connection to the sea was considerably shortened with the completion of the New Waterway (*Nieuwe Waterweg*). New harbour basins were also dug and the port-area expanded dramatically. In 1914, Rotterdam not only had an excellent waterway which reached far into Germany, but also a better connection with the open sea than the rival harbours of Hamburg and Antwerp. Therefore, the number of clearances grew from 1940 ships in 1850 to 7268 ships in 1900 (see table 2).[19]

Table 2
Number of Clearances at Rotterdam, 1885-1913

	Ships	Tons
1885	3724	2120347
1895	5199	4177478
1905	8138	8339313
1910	9368	10658831
1913	10203	12785861

Source: P.J. Bouman, *Gedenkboek Wilton-Fijenoord* (Schiedam, 1954), 60.

[19]J. Dogwood, *et al.* (eds.), *Rotterdam, De poort van Europa. De geschiedenis van haven en handel van Rotterdam* (Rotterdam, 1946), 61.

Strong competition from other European ports was also a factor. Abroad, there were a numbers of highly competitive continental ports, while at home, Rotterdam had to meet the competition of Amsterdam, with its old colonial relationships, established markets, and well developed banking system. Such rivalry turned out to be both a disadvantage and an advantage for Rotterdam. For the first time, the Dutch had to fight for the survival of their seaports against the growing presence of foreign ports, especially after 1850. The competition of railway transport also affected the market, with trains used more and more to transport valuable goods, while Rhine shipping concentrated exclusively on bulk goods.[20] Surpassing Amsterdam in terms of quantity during this period did not mean that the position of Rotterdam was inviolable. There was intense competition from Hamburg, Bremen, Antwerp and Le Havre.[21] The crucial question, which could only be answered by competition between the West European ports, focused on the shortest and cheapest form of transportation from the sea to the German centres of industrialization.[22] Antwerp's connection to the sea was better than that of Amsterdam and Rotterdam. Furthermore, within Belgium, Antwerp had no competitors and could rely on the products of modern Belgian industry and much better railroads as well. Rotterdam, on the other hand, was the only port which could boast an excellent direct connection with the Rhine, and therefore with the rapidly expanding German hinterland. This proved decisive and Rotterdam eventually overhauled Antwerp, though the Belgian port remained a formidable rival.

"Traditional" Dutch Shipbuilding

Traditionally the Dutch shipbuilding industry was closely tied to Dutch overseas trade. Changes in the structure of Dutch foreign trade and the shipping industry was always reflected in shipbuilding. This industry is one of the oldest in the Netherlands and reached its peak during the seventeenth century when about 2000 ships a year were built, mostly to

---

[20]Nusteling, *De Rijnvaart*, 524.

[21]H. van Dijk, *Rotterdam 1810-1880. Aspekten van een stedelijke samenleving* (Schiedam, 1976), 83.

[22]Dogwood, *et al.* (eds.), *Rotterdam*, 75.

meet orders by foreigners. Exact figures do not exist. The region north of Amsterdam, the Zaan, was the area where the shipbuilding industry was concentrated. It was one of the few regions in Europe where ships could be delivered from stock.

In the eighteenth century, the Republic ceased to be the world's leading trading centre and the famous staple market of Amsterdam lost its pre-eminent position. This led to the decline of the shipbuilding industry: the number of shipyards in the famous Zaan region declined from sixty in 1707 to twenty-five in 1780.[23] After the French period, the Dutch government tried in vain to stimulate the industry. While American shipbuilders were modernizing,[24] and the British merchant fleet was gradually converting to steam, the Dutch went on constructing expensive and slow wooden sailing vessels. The Amsterdam shipyards employed 3000 workers in 1806, but only 350 by 1811. In 1816, a year after the end of the French occupation, the Amsterdam shipyards employed only 400 workers. Rotterdam witnessed a similar contraction.[25]

An important stimulus to traditional Dutch shipbuilding, however, was the founding of the Dutch Trade Company, for only Dutch-built ships were allowed to operate between the Netherlands and its colonies in the East Indies. Therefore the influence of the NHM on the building of large seagoing vessels expanded. Shipowners received much more for transporting NHM goods than they would have received if they had had to compete on the free market.[26] Indeed, the fees were about fifty to 100 percent higher than the world average.[27] The NHM trade, the demand for sea transport, and the protective measures created an overcapacity of ships

---

[23] M. Müller, *De Nederlandse scheepsbouw 1400-heden, in: Historische Bedrijfsarchieven. Basis-metaal-, metaalproduktenindustrie en scheepsbouw. Een geschiedenis en bronnenoverzicht* (Amsterdam, 1992), 155.

[24] R.W.J.M. Bos, *Brits-Nederlandse handel en scheepvaart, 1870-1914. Een analyse van machtsafbrokkeling op een markt* (Tilburg, 1978), 279.

[25] C.A. de Feyter, *Industrial Policy and Shipbuilding. Changing Economic Structures in the Low Countries 1600-1980* (Utrecht, 1982), 185.

[26] J.W. Bonebakker, *De scheepsbouwnijverheid in Nederland* (Haarlem, 1936), 4-5.

[27] Müller, *De Nederlandse scheepsbouw*, 157.

of between 400 and 800 Dutch tons. Smaller and larger ships could not profit from the NHM or government protection. Speed was not needed because of the simple fact that it did not influence payment by the NHM, nor did it influence the number of freights. The shipping companies received safe and relatively high fees from the NHM and did not need to buy modern, large, and/or fast ships.

The increase in colonial trade also resulted in the growth of the Dutch shipbuilding industry. Between 1830 and 1850, the number of Dutch ships almost doubled, while the average size of the vessels more than doubled. Most of these ships were built in the Netherlands. In 1853, the Dutch merchant fleet numbered more than 2,000 vessels, a quarter of which were intended for long-distance shipping. Expressed in tonnage, the share of this kind of seagoing vessel was even larger. In 1849, more than 6,350 people were directly employed in the industry and a couple of thousand worked in related industries.[28] Even 10,000 employees was still a relatively small number if one takes into account the fact that Dutch industry as a whole engaged a total of some 300,000 employees at that time. The total working population was 1,250,000. About half of the 10,000 shipyard workers were concerned with the construction of sea-going vessels. Of these, about 5000 worked in the dozen or so shipyards in the provinces of North and South Holland which built the larger ships, frigates and barques needed by the NHM for the Indian trade. The most important shipyards were situated in Amsterdam and Rotterdam. There were also shipyards along the main rivers which built sea-going vessels. The other 5000 workers were employed in about 500 smaller shipyards.[29]

Delay

The first steam-powered ship built in the Netherlands — a wooden river vessel with an English steam engine — was launched in 1824. In 1837, the first steel ship was built,[30] but large sailing vessels continued to dominate.

---

[28]J.A. de Jonge, *De industrialisatie in Nederland tussen 1850 en 1914* (Amsterdam, 1968), 130.

[29]De Feyter, *Industrial Policy*, 193.

[30]A.J.W. Camijn, *Een eeuw vol bedrijvigheid. De industrialisatie van Nederland 1814-1914* (Utrecht, 1987) 60-61.

The lack of initiative caused by the relative security offered by the Dutch Trade Company caused a certain backwardness in the shipbuilding industry. The transition from sailing vessels to steamships in the Netherlands in general took place gradually, as table 3 shows.[31] In 1850, less than ten seagoing steamships sailed under the Dutch flag.[32] The Dutch merchant fleet not only lagged behind numerically, but also in size, as the average tonnage of steamships increased more rapidly in other countries than in Holland.[33]

Table 3
From Sail to Steam: Shipping and Steam Tonnage, 1850-1870

	Share of World Steam-Tonnage (Percent)			Share of Steam Tonnage as Percentage of Total National Tonnage		
	1850	1860	1870	1850	1860	1870
United Kingdom	23	31.3	41.9	4.7	9.8	19.6
The Netherlands	0.4	0.7	0.7	0.9	2.3	5
France	1.9	4.7	5.8	2	6.8	14.4
United States	6.1	6.7	7.3	2.8	3.8	12.7

Source: R.W.J.M. Bos, *Brits-Nederlandse handel en scheepvaart 1879-1914* (Tilburg, 1978), 279.

[31]According to a report of a commission of the Dutch parliament in 1870, steam vessels accounted for nine percent of Dutch merchant tonnage. World tonnage as a whole, according to this report, consisted of fifteen percent steam tonnage. Although the absolute figures differ, the conclusion of the commission was that the Dutch merchant fleet lagged behind modern merchant fleets; see Netherlands, Parliament, Tweede Kamer, "Verslag der Commissie, belast met het onderzoek der enquête omtrent den toestand van de Nederlandsche koopvaardijvloot. Handelingen Staten-Generaal" (1874-1875), III, appendix.

[32]Camijn, *Een eeuw vol bedrijvigheid*, 61.

[33]Horlings, *Economic Development*, 185.

This tardy modernization was a consequence of several factors. Until their abolition in 1849, Britain's Navigation Laws restricted Dutch shipping in the trade between the Netherlands and Britain, the route on which the first Dutch steamships were mainly used. On the East Indies route, steamships were too costly[34] as supplies of coal were not readily available along this route. The ships had to carry their own coal which limited their range. A further factor in the late transition to steam was the protection afforded to sailing ships by the NHM and the government. As described above, this system of favouring Dutch ships in the trade with the East Indies was only gradually abandoned. By the end of the 1860s, it became clear that the support of the Dutch government and the Trading Company only offered an artificial protection to the Dutch shipping and shipbuilding industries. After the support came to an end, the major units of the Dutch shipbuilding industry proved very vulnerable to competition.

Although Dutch foreign trade generally grew quite rapidly during the second half of the nineteenth century,[35] and although regular shipping lines to the West and East Indies, the United States, South America and Australia were opened, the Dutch steam shipbuilding industry could not take advantage of these developments. Between 1850 and 1873, for instance, the import of goods from the Dutch East Indies (Java) rose by about fifty-four percent, but it was mainly foreign shipping which profited.[36] The old fashioned Dutch merchant fleet was not able to cope with international competition. While North Atlantic shipping, with an estimated share of world tonnage of between seventy-three and eighty-two percent, expanded in the second half of the nineteenth century, with the share of the German fleet, for instance, almost doubling, the Dutch share sharply declined (figure 3).[37]

---

[34]Smits, *Economische groei*, 146 and 151; and F.J.A. Broeze, *The International Diffusion of Ocean Steam Navigation* (Amsterdam, 1982), 79.

[35]Smits, *Economische groei*, 92-98.

[36]*Verslag der Commissie*, 10.

[37]Lewis R. Fischer and Helge W. Nordvik, "Maritime Transport and the Integration of the North Atlantic Economy, 1850-1914," in Wolfram Fischer, R. Marvin McInnis and Jürgen Schneider (eds.), *The Emergence of a World Economy 1500-1914* (Wiesbaden, 1986), 526-532.

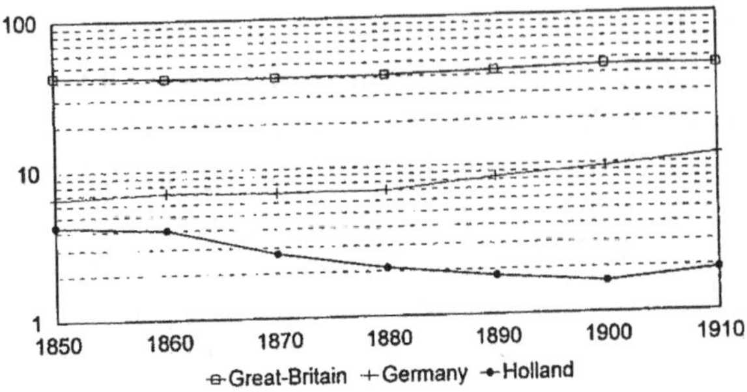

Figure 3: Percentage share of North Atlantic tonnage accounted for the fleets of Great Britain, Germany and the Netherlands, 1850-1910.

Source: Lewis R. Fischer and Helge W. Nordvik, "Maritime Transport and the Integration of the North Atlantic Economy, 1850-1914," in Wolfram Fischer, R. Marvin McInnis and Jürgen Schneider (eds.), *The Emergence of a World Economy 1500-1914* (Wiesbaden, 1986), 526.

The one-sided and strong connection between transport and colonial trade was the main reason why the Dutch sea transport industries did not react adequately to changes in world trade. When, for instance, the international coffee trade shifted from Java to Brazil, Dutch harbours lost contact with the business because Hamburg and Bremen already had regular shipping lines with South America.[38]

In 1868, the last protective measure relating to Dutch-built seagoing vessels was finally abandoned with remarkable consequences. In 1856, 204 new ships had been built in the Netherlands, but in 1875 the national output was just twenty-eight. The number of steamships remained very small. Between 1850 and 1870, only fifty-two large sailing vessels and a mere fifteen steamships were built in Dutch shipyards. Shipowners preferred to buy cheaper second-hand foreign ships. For instance, a four-year-old American-built clipper cost 150,000 guilders, while an equivalent Dutch product was priced at as much as 500,000 guilders.[39]

Yet in 1850, the Dutch merchant fleet was still the fourth largest in the world, after Britain, the United States, and France. In 1874, the

---

[38]Smits, *Economische groei*, 124.

[39]Müller, *De Nederlandse scheepsbouw*, 158.

fleet had sunk to eighth place, with Italy, Germany, Norway, and Spain having overtaken the Netherlands. In 1873, the tonnage of foreign sailing vessels allowed to sail under the Dutch flag for the first time exceeded the tonnage of Dutch-built ships. Almost the whole of the Dutch steam fleet was built outside the Netherlands. In 1874, none of the Dutch yards were able to build large steam vessels for the trade with the Indies or the United States as quickly or cheaply as foreign shipyards.[40] Only a few of the larger Dutch shipyards survived the transition to steam, though the fact that the Dutch government did not want to become dependent on foreign built navy vessels, meant that orders from the navy helped some of them to survive.

Gradually the colonial trade of the NHM lost its dominance relative to total Dutch foreign trade; steamships therefore became more important. With the rise of a modern industrial economy in Germany and the industrialization of the Netherlands, the need for good transport also became more important. Bulky industrial goods rendered mass transportation essential. This meant faster and larger steamships. The old link between shipping companies and shipbuilding was broken after about 1870, when the shipping companies which used wooden sailing vessels were overtaken by firms which used steam. These latter enterprises generally bought their ships abroad. Dutch companies preferred ships built by the British, who had acquired much experience of building large steamships. The Dutch shipyards which could build steamships did not get the chance to prove it, except for orders from the Dutch navy. It was a vicious circle: no orders for large steamships because the Dutch shipyards lacked experience, which prevented them from gaining the requisite experience to build good, cheap steamers. The Dutch government, which earlier in the century had supported and promoted Dutch shipbuilding, now followed a course of laissez-faire and free trade. These policies did nothing to promote the industry, which caused the Dutch to fall even further behind. In 1911, 69.5% of all seagoing ships worldwide were built in Britain, while the German share was 10.5%, the French 3.5%, and the Dutch 2.5%.[41]

---

[40]*Verslag der Commissie*, 5.

[41]Nusteling, *De Rijnvaart*, 411.

Modernization

The vicious circle was broken around 1880 when the shipping firms no longer neglected Dutch shipyards by ordering steamships from abroad. Even so, in 1881, a ship built on speculation in Rotterdam, while proving that Dutch shipyards were able to build modern ships, failed to sell. At the end of the nineteenth century, the growth of the international economy, and the Dutch colonies, stimulated the Dutch shipbuilding industry. The founding of the Royal Packetboat Company (*Koninklijke Paketvaart Maatschappij*) in 1888 finally helped the Dutch shipbuilding industry in its transition to steam. This company, which provided services between the islands of the Dutch East Indies, ordered its ships from Dutch shipyards as a matter of policy. In 1894, with the support of this and other shipping companies, the Dutch Shipbuilding Company in Amsterdam (*Nederlandsche Scheepsbouw Maatschappij* [NSM]) was founded. This and two other shipyards, De Schelde in Vlissingen and Fijenoord in Rotterdam, had a market share of about sixty percent by the turn of the century. Seven smaller yards built steamships. By then, the improved port facilities, railways and other infrastructural measures facilitated the use of steam.[42] The tonnage of Dutch steam and motorships grew from 307,000 tons in 1894 to almost 1.5 million tons in 1914, while sail tonnage moved in the opposite direction (see table 4). Accepting this as a cause and a symptom of globalization, the relative position of the various flags in world trade simultaneously underwent important changes. Although the United Kingdom remained the leading carrier, other nations started with remarkable success "to compete with us in our own trade with our own tools, i.e. British-built iron steamers."[43] In 1900, for instance, Holland became second among the main foreign flags in the trade of the United Kingdom, in terms of the tonnage of steam vessels (see figure 4).

After the turn of the century, the business of Dutch shipyards changed again. Because of the growing demand, a large proportion of Dutch-owned steamships were built outside the Netherlands.[44] In 1910,

---

[42]Smits, *Economische groei*, 148.

[43]John Glover, "Tonnage Statistics of the Decade 1870-80," *Journal of the Royal Statistical Society*, XLV (March 1882), 46.

[44]Bonebakker, *De scheepsbouwnijverheid*, 9.

more than 19,000 people were employed at almost 200 shipyards, half in the province of South Holland. The three large shipyards in Amsterdam, Rotterdam and Vlissingen employed 1070, 1410, and 1553 people, respectively. The companies in Rotterdam and Vlissingen still had important engineering works linked to the shipyards (see figure 5).[45]

Table 4
Dutch Merchant Fleet, 1894-1914

	Steam and Motor Ships (register tons)	Sailing Vessels (register tons)
1894	307000	130000
1899	389000	66000
1904	643500	44000
1909	904500	37500
1914	1471500	24500

Source: J.W. Bonebaker, *De scheepsbouwnijverheid in Nederland* (Haarlem, 1936), 9.

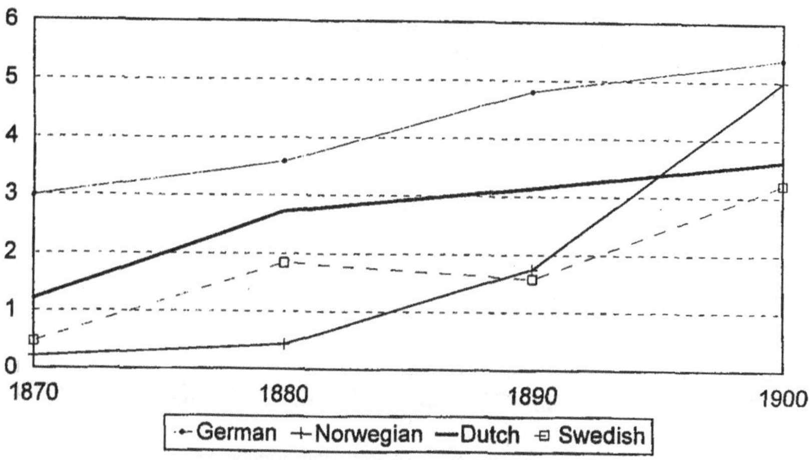

Figure 4: Share of tonnage of steam vessels of major foreign flags as percentage of the total British and foreign tonnage cleared at ports in the United Kingdom.

Source: Glover, 1902, 15.

---

[45]Camijn, *Een eeuw vol bedrijvigheid*, 62-63.

The outlook of the shipbuilding industry was also totally different. The initiative and knowledge needed to build large steamships did not come from the shipyards themselves but from the shipping companies which ordered the ships. Purchasers designed the ships, and the builders had to construct them according to the standards imposed by the companies and their technical staffs. Even the construction process was supervised by the future owners. The shipping companies were more familiar with the technical aspects of shipbuilding, due to their knowledge of vessels built outside the Netherlands, than the Dutch builders. By 1900, it was normal for the owner to provide a complete design for a ship to the shipyard which could build the ship at low cost and within the designated time frame. The shipbuilder became, in fact, a contractor.

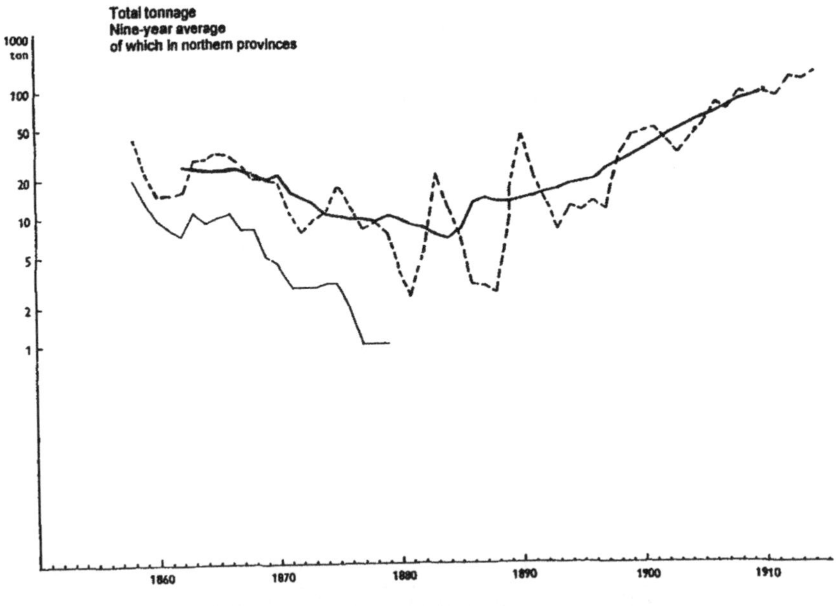

Source: J.A. de Jonge, De Industrialisatie in Nederland tussen 1850 en 1914, Amstedam, 1968, p. 137.

Figure 5: Sea-going ships under construction in Dutch shipyards, 1860-1910.

Source: J.A. de Jonge, *De Industrialisatie in Nederland tussen 1850 en 1914* (Amsterdam, 1968), 137.

Small-scale Shipbuilding

Although the importance of inland (transit) navigation and international river transport in this process of modernization has been recognized by historians, a lack of quantitative data means that it is still underrated.[46] In particular, the smaller shipyards have not been given enough attention in an historiography which focuses on the construction of larger and apparently more interesting ships.

The building of smaller ships can generally be divided into two subsectors. First, there were the vessels used for trade with North European harbours, the *kleine vaart* (small trade) ships which were mainly built in the Northern province of Groningen. Most were wooden sailing vessels. This industry was a spin off of the exploitation of peat which was cut in the northern parts of the Netherlands and transported by ship. Second, there was vessel construction for inland navigation and international river transport, the yards being concentrated along the rivers of the Dutch delta, the Zaan, and in the provinces of Groningen and Friesland.

The first of these branches declined after 1850. Dutch ships which were used in European coastal waters were built in parts of the Netherlands which were not close to the sea. Ships built in shipyards in the small towns of Groningen, for instance, had to pass through narrow canals, bridges, or sluices in order to reach larger waterways or the sea. Such ships had to be relatively small. Improvements in the infrastructure came too late. By then, the building of wooden sailing vessels was out of date, so steamships were needed. However, it was too late for the Groningen shipyards to change from sail to steamship building, which required completely different shipyards, knowledge, and capital, none of which was available. In 1857, about ten percent of total employment in Dutch shipbuilding was located at the wharves in Groningen; by 1900 this was only one percent.[47]

The second facet of the small-scale shipbuilding industry catered mostly for inland navigation and international river transport and therefore profited from the industrialization of the German hinterland. The early steamships built in the Netherlands were used by the shipping companies

---

[46]Müller, *De Nederlandse scheepsbouw*, 151.

[47]De Feyter, *Industrial Policy*, 200.

which maintained regular services between European ports and along the Rhine. For instance, Fijenoord, the Rotterdam shipyard, which was linked to the shipping company NSM, built a steamship for Rhine navigation as early as 1824.[48] Rhine navigation did not prove to be very lucrative at first. For a long time, the Dutch shipping companies dominated this route, which was resented in Germany. Trade agreements between Prussia and other members of the German Zollverein with the Netherlands ended the privileged position of the Dutch shipping companies. German companies and a railway from Antwerp to Cologne, the so-called Iron Rhine, gradually weakened the position of the Dutch on the Rhine. The NSM, for instance, suffered losses until the 1860s, a problem that persuaded the NSM to sell its navigation activities in 1859.[49] Although world trade increased in the early 1850s, the transit trade along the Rhine suffered losses. The connection between the Rhine and the sea was inadequate and large seagoing steam vessels could not reach Dutch harbours. The Netherlands also lacked a good railway system to connect the seaports with the hinterland. When this infrastructure was improved the advance of steam was unstoppable.

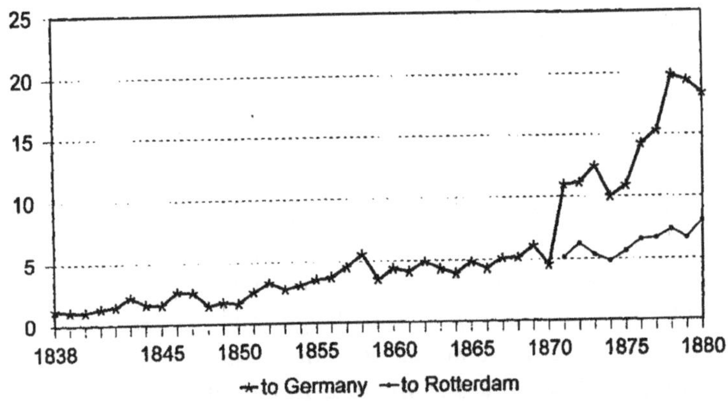

Figure 6: Rhine shipping between Rotterdam and the Hinterland, 1838-1880.

Source: H. van Dijk, *Rotterdam 1810-1880. Aspekten van een stedelijke samenleving* (Schiedam, 1976), 407 (before 1871 no Germany-Rotterdam figures available).

[48]P.J. Bouman, *Gedenkboek Wilton-Fijenoord* (Schiedam, 1954), 18-19.

[49]*Ibid.*, 30.

At first, the Rhine trade, like sea transport, was dominated by the re-export of colonial goods from Amsterdam to the hinterland. In the 1850s, Germany was the most important market for colonial products sold by the Amsterdam merchants. After that time, the close ties between trade and shipping loosened. The flow of colonial products shifted from Amsterdam to ports such as Hamburg and Bremen. The transit of semi-finished products and raw materials via Rotterdam increased sharply and became dominant in trade with the German hinterland.[50]

The Rhine trade became mainly transit traffic. In the 1850s, there were about 15,000-20,000 ships working in coastal and inland navigation. Subsequently, the number of ships grew. Accordingly, between 1860 and 1880, new tonnage delivered for inland navigation increased by thirty-six percent, while employment at smaller shipyards grew by ten percent.[51] Between 1870 and 1880, Dutch navigation on the Rhine doubled (see figure 6). As world commerce expanded, trade between Britain and the industrial areas in Germany, such as the Ruhr area, expanded, and improved access to the sea stimulated the growth of transit traffic from Rotterdam by way of the Rhine. Between 1895 and 1910, transport to Germany increased by approximately 500%. About thirty-five to forty shipyards in South Holland employed 5000 people and specialized in building iron tugboats for river transport. The importance of Rotterdam and its function as a transit harbour also affected overseas trade. Dutch sea trade became much more independent of colonial trade as the flow of goods between the hinterland, the Netherlands, and industrialized regions overseas increased. Ore and metal became the most important products passing through Rotterdam harbour en route to Germany. In contrast, the quantities of colonial products such as sugar and coffee diminished to less than one percent of traffic on the Rhine in 1913.[52]

Conclusions

The turning point in Dutch modern economic development came soon after 1850 despite some restraining factors. During the seventeenth and

---

[50]Smits, *Economische groei*, 158.

[51]Müller, *De Nederlandse scheepsbouw*, 158.

[52]Smits, *Economische groei*, 156.

part of the eighteenth centuries, when the Dutch had a virtual international trade monopoly, they could easily maintain expensive practices, but in the nineteenth century, this dominance was definitely lost. Although the Dutch initially succeeded in obstructing transit trade through their ports, and even enjoyed a revival of colonial staple trade and transport, their market shares in international trade and shipping declined considerably and steadily after about 1830. Steamships and the construction of railroads constituted major breakthroughs for most economies, for they ensured regular, large-scale, and fairly cheap transport which was exactly what the industrializing economies needed. This undermined the old power of the Low Countries. The essential change in trade patterns was clear: the profitable Dutch staples were superseded by the profitable transit trade, while the leading position of colonial goods in Dutch trade was assumed by bulk goods.

Under the persistent pressure of international competition and the economic emancipation of the German hinterland, the Dutch government eventually could do nothing else but satisfy, one by one, all German demands. It therefore chose a total liberalization of the (transit-) trade policy after 1850. The dynamic process of industrialization in Germany led to an enormous increase in the demand for the transit shipment of bulk goods, which mainly went through Rotterdam and entailed the construction of modern port facilities and the development of shipbuilding.

After 1860, the reconstruction of the Dutch economy began, based on the creation of a modern, mechanized industrial sector, the development of trade and port facilities, and the rapidly growing influence of the operations of the great seaport of Rotterdam. The nature of the Dutch service sector definitively changed from trade to transport and distribution. The shipment of goods destined for Germany and the modernization of the Dutch sea transport industries were the foundations upon which the new economic expansion of the Netherlands rested.

The Expansion of American Interests in Transatlantic Commerce and Trade, 1865-1893

William Henry Flayhart III

There is nothing unusual for an underdeveloped nation, which has experienced an industrial revolution, to seek control of the international distribution system bringing passengers and freight to its shores. This was true of the United States in the last third of the nineteenth century. The period 1865-1893 saw the rebirth of the American merchant marine following the Civil War (1861-1865). An integral part of this stage of American economic development involved transatlantic expansion as American economic ties began to stretch around the globe. Furthermore, rapid industrialization in America after 1865 made possible the construction in American shipyards of iron-hulled, ocean-going steamships. Simultaneously, the expansion of the American railroad industry provided the financial resources for investment in steamship enterprises. The Pennsylvania Railroad Company (PRR) was the largest economic enterprise in the United States and sought to expand its international trade in every way, but particularly through the port of Philadelphia.

One of the greatest rivals of the PRR was the New York Central Railroad which was admirably positioned to greet the constant stream of immigrants crossing the Atlantic to New York City and assist those passengers on their way to the hinterland of the United States. This was a challenge which simply could not go unanswered after the conclusion of the Civil War. In the Eastern United States continental rivalry fostered transatlantic competition in an effort to develop global control of the transportation of passengers and freight from European points of origin, across the North Atlantic, and to destinations throughout North America. The challenges to the Pennsylvania Railroad in attempting to achieve these goals were manifold.

The American Civil War wreaked havoc with the American merchant marine. The overall effect of the disastrous four-year struggle was the annihilation or alienation of a large percentage of the prewar American-flag fleet. Ships that remained under the American flag lost market share as cargoes went to safer flags, were laid up to rot away, or captured by Confederate raiders. The solution for a large number of owners was to leave the American flag for other flags of convenience only to find that the American Congress in a fury at such disloyalty forbade them ever to return to American registry. The American merchant marine, which was largely composed of wooden sailing vessels, would have faced operational and replacement crises anyway given the cost of new building and manning under the American flag, but the Civil War certainly precipitated an abrupt economic watershed in the American ocean-going carrying trade.

The Pennsylvania Railroad Company definitely wanted to expand its operations across the Atlantic Ocean to ensure a through service for immigrants and trade from Europe to the hinterland of the United States. It was expected that transatlantic commerce and trade would expand continuously for the remainder of the century. The desire to offer the customer one single freight bill or passenger ticket caused the PRR to turn its attention to the problem of encouraging international trade. This could be accomplished either by establishing an American-flag steamship line, or through the financing of an American-owned foreign-flag operation, or through the acquisition of a foreign-flag line. Between 1865 and 1893 all of these options would be tried in order to develop transatlantic shipping operations whose schedules and services could be dove-tailed with those of the Pennsylvania Railroad.

The Pennsylvania Railroad Company may have been chartered in 1846, but J. Edgar Thompson, Third President of the firm (1852-1874) remains the man most often credited with creating the single most powerful corporation in the nation. Thompson's presidency encompassed the unique challenges of the Civil War. Under Thompson's iron-willed leadership the PRR created a unified transportation system stretching from New York City and Philadelphia in the east to St. Louis and Chicago in the west, and from Lake Ontario in the north to Baltimore and Washington, DC, in the south. Geographically the PRR controlled an economic empire comparable to Europe west of the Urals. The Pennsylvania Railroad served the heartland of the American industrial revolution and would prosper accordingly as the United States came of age as an industrialized economy.

In 1865 everything seemed perfect for further economic experiments. The second key figure in this effort was Thomas A. Scott, Vice President of the PRR, and Fourth President of the PRR (1872-1884), who was both a highly regarded transportation magnate and a diplomat.

Thomson was respected and feared like few individuals in the Republic, and Scott was the genial public relations personality with an iron hand in a velvet glove. With Thompsons's encouragement, Scott led the way in seeking to develop Philadelphia for the PRR as a major North Atlantic terminus for trade and commerce. The first logical move was to secure a regular steamship service for Philadelphia, but this would be more difficult than expected.

In 1870 Scott tried to buy the Anchor Line of Glasgow, Scotland, and was rebuffed.[1] The international negotiations which ensued with Thomas Henderson in Glasgow reached agreement on the transfer of the American terminus of the Anchor Line from New York to Philadelphia. This would have been a great coup for the Pennsylvania Railroad. They fell apart on the demand of the Railroad that the books and total direction of the Scottish line's affairs, also cross the Atlantic and be re-established in Philadelphia. "This was too much to ask of an individualist like Thomas Henderson and the deal fell through."[2] The Anchor Line landed over 25,000 passengers in New York during 1870 and was beholden to no railroad. The Pennsylvania Railroad Company and Thomas A. Scott were after an attractive prize – and it got away.

The reversal suffered by Thomas Scott prompted him to take another course of action. Since the end of the Civil War civic forces in Philadelphia based in the Commercial Exchange had urged the founding of an American-owned steamship link with Europe. In November 1870 the Board of Directors of the PRR took the initiative and announced its willingness to provide substantial financial backing for an American-flag steamship line. The commercial interests of Philadelphia responded enthusiastically to the overture of the Railroad. The *Philadelphia Commercial List and Price Current*, a weekly journal of commerce for the Philadelphia business community, lent heavy editorial support to the project in its columns. The American Steamship Company was to be financed through a combination of $700,000 in stock and $1,500,000 in bonds. The public sale of certificates began in December 1870. In order to show public support and retain control the Pennsylvania Railroad publically purchased $400,000 of the American Steamship Company stock

---

[1]N.R.P. Bonsor, *North Atlantic Seaway* (5 vols., Jersey, CI, 1980), remains the classic reference for all the steamship lines engaged in trans-Atlantic commerce and trade.

[2]R.S. McLellan, *Anchor Line (1856-1956)* (Glasgow, 1957), 40-41.

for its investment portfolio. Early in January it was announced that all the stock in the new company had been subscribed.[3] The PRR not only subscribed to $400,000 of the stock but also guaranteed both the principal and interest on the bond issue of $1,500,000. The bonds were to run for twenty-five years at six per cent interest.[4] Hence, the commitment of the Railroad to the American Line was very substantial indeed. The title of the new enterprise was established as the "American Steamship Company of Philadelphia," but the concern would always be known as the "American Line."[5]

The Commonwealth of Pennsylvania through the General Assembly granted a Charter for the American Steamship Company on 18 April 1871. The State Charter was issued "for the purpose of establishing a line of first class steamships to run between Philadelphia and Liverpool; the steamers to be constructed in American ship building yards, and as entirely as possible of American Materials."[6]

On 5 May 1871 the Commonwealth of Pennsylvania honoured the wishes of the Pennsylvania Railroad and also issued a charter to the International Navigation Company. This occurred less than a month after the approval of the charter for the American Steamship Company. The International Navigation Company was representative of those Americans who wanted to establish transatlantic steamship lines, but who did not feel that such a business could be run successfully under the American flag. The approximately thirty percent difference in building costs between American and European yards, and the similar higher cost of American crews represented a heavy surcharge for the right to fly the American flag. These financial interests, therefore, though having their headquarters

---

[3]*Philadelphia Commercial List and Price Current*, 7 January 1871.

[4]The bonds of the American Steamship Company were issued at six percent interest. Some early accounts quote five percent, but the reality was different. Interest on the bonds guaranteed by the Pennsylvania Railroad Company would run at $45,000 semi-annually.

[5]*Philadelphia Commercial List and Price Current*, 4 February 1871.

[6]Inman Line, Red Star Line, and American Line, *Inman and International Steamship Company Limited* (New York, nd [1888?]), 49. This is an early publication of the Inman and International Line that gives a detailed background to the three steamship lines.

in the United States, would build their fleets in foreign yards, operate the vessels under foreign flags, and man their ships with foreign crews. Such was the case with the International Navigation Company (always known as the "Red Star Line" for the Red Star on the white house flag) whose foreign-flag operations were exactly the opposite of the American Steamship Company's American-flag organization.

The chief American backer and General Agent for the International Navigation Company was the shipbroking firm of Peter Wright and Sons. This concern was one of the oldest, most respected, and financially prosperous of the Philadelphia import-export houses. Automatically, as a Philadelphia enterprise, the partners in Peter Wright and Sons had close ties with the management of the PRR. Its international associates included the distinguished firm of Richardson, Spence and Company in Liverpool, England, and the firms of vender Becke and Marsily in Antwerp, Belgium. John Bernard vender Becke and William Edouard Marsily controlled prosperous Belgian firms which had dealt with Peter Wright and Sons for years. As early as 1854 J.B. vender Becke was a well known Antwerp shipowner with a fleet of five sailing vessels. During the 1860s the vender Becke firm became an important importer of petroleum products to Europe. The oil came from the newly discovered fields of Western Pennsylvania. Since one of the most active exporters of such products was Peter Wright and Sons there were numerous business connections between the Philadelphia and Antwerp concerns. The firm controlled a large fleet of sailing ships, many of which were engaged in carrying Pennsylvania petroleum, both in barrels and cases, to the European market.

While James A. Wright was the senior partner, the shipping affairs of Peter Wright and Sons were largely in the energetic and capable hands of one vigorous young man, Clement Acton Griscom (1841-1912). Griscom never forgot his Philadelphia Quaker heritage, but his adventuresome mind encompassed a much broader world. Griscom's working career spans five and a half decades from 1857 until his death in 1912. He ranks among the most important of the transportation magnates of the American industrial revolution and he played no small part in the proceedings.

James Wright recognized brilliance when he saw it and Griscom's rise in the firm of Peter Wright and Sons can only be described as "meteoric." In the five-year period 1857-1862 he rose from clerk to partner at the age of twenty-two. Peter Wright and Sons was an established import-export house specializing in china and luxury goods. Griscom was disturbed by the high cost of freight rates and broadened the interests of Peter Wright and Sons by purchasing sailing ships just as the Civil War was beginning. He filled the holds of the sailing ships with general cargo from other firms, westbound, and petroleum products, eastbound. His company prospered accordingly and profits were aided by the wartime charter market which Griscom worked to the advantage of the firm.

Simultaneously with the efforts of Thomas Scott to buy the Anchor Line in 1870, and the American backers of the American Line to found that concern with railroad backing in 1871, Clement Griscom also was given the green light by the PRR to establish a foreign-flag steamship line to develop transatlantic services to Antwerp, Belgium, and other European ports. Specifically, the Board of Directors of the PRR guaranteed the principal and interest on a $1,000,000 bond issue to underwrite the new Red Star fleet, made an offer of free wharfage at Philadelphia for Griscom's International Navigation Company (INC) and committed themselves to construct a totally new dock and grain elevator at Philadelphia with connecting rail lines for the new enterprise.[7] The remainder of the INC financing involved a $1.5 million dollar stock issue which was largely held by a small group involving executives of Peter Wright and Sons, the Pennsylvania Railroad and their associates.

Contemporaries sometimes regarded the American Line and the Red Star Line as rivals but nothing could have been further from the truth although both lines sent ships from Philadelphia to Liverpool in the early years. The PRR was represented on the board of the American Steamship Company by Herman Lombaert, Vice President and former Comptroller of the railroad, while Thomas A. Scott, Senior Vice President of the railroad, sat on the board of the Red Star Line. Almost immediately, when the initial operations of the American Steamship Company in 1873 proved extremely disappointing, the effective management of the line was contracted to Peter Wright and Sons, which meant Griscom of the International Navigation Company (1874).[8]

---

[7]Thomas R. Heinrich, *Ships for the Seven Seas: Philadelphia Shipbuilding in the Age of Industrial Capitalism* (Baltimore, 1997), 57.

[8]Temple University, Urban Archives, Pennsylvania Railroad Collection, box 89, "The Minute Books of the American Steamship Company."

Griscom's negotiations with the Belgian authorities were fruitful under the benevolent patronage of King Leopold and the necessary statutes establishing the Belgian-based concern under the name "Societe Anonyme de Navigation Belge-Americaine" (Red Star Line) were published in the *Moniteur Belge*, the Belgian government gazette, on 27 September 1872. The founding officials of the company were listed as: John B. vender Becke, President; and William E. Marsily, Administrator. Peter Wright and Sons of Philadelphia had the right to nominate three members of the Board of Directors and those individuals were: H. Houston; Clement A. Griscom; and Thomas A. Scott.

The commitment of the Pennsylvania Railroad Company to the "Societe Anonyme de Navigation Belge-Americaine" could not be underlined any more explicitly than by the presence of the senior vice-president of the railroad on the board of directors of the new steamship line. Of course this was the same railroad which was underwriting the bonds of both steamship lines. Since the PRR was vigorously pursuing a policy of eliminating competition on land as quickly as possible, it is inconceivable that the railroad, or any member of its management, would have done anything to encourage competition at sea. The simple fact of the matter was that the PRR was an active, if somewhat discrete, investor in both transatlantic steamship lines as part of its efforts to expand across the North Atlantic in order to garner more of the profitable European passenger and freight trade.

The first ships of Red Star Line were ordered from British yards before the formalization of the Belgian connection. Hence, when Griscom travelled to Europe in 1872 it was with a two-fold purpose: (1) to see if a co-sponsorship of the INC by Belgium was possible; and (2) to observe the launching of the first of his ocean liners in Britain. There was going to be a steamship line from Philadelphia to Europe but fortuitous circumstances in Belgium made its eastern terminus Antwerp. *Vaderland* sailed from Antwerp and reached Philadelphia on her maiden voyage, 17 February 1873, which prompted great celebrations on the Delaware. A local reporter wrote with unbridled civic pride of the fact that prior to this the goods imported by Philadelphia from Belgium, Holland and Germany had entered the United States via the custom house of New York, and now could come direct. It was mentioned that while the American Steamship Company was chartered first, the great energy of Clement A. Griscom and the other founders of the Red Star Line had enabled them to "open the ball."

The mail contract offered the Red Star Line by the Belgian government was not exactly what Griscom initially had bargained for but he was not upset. The Belgian government offered $100,000 a year for ten years to establish a transatlantic steamship service between Antwerp and New York with free wharfage at Antwerp for the ships worth another $30,000. Griscom accepted and the INC found itself building or chartering ships for two transatlantic services — Antwerp-Philadelphia and Antwerp-New York. The financial rewards appeared encouraging.

This was not the case with the American Steamship Company. The American Line received the right to carry the American transatlantic mails in 1874, but the return was meagre. The American-flag steamships of the PRR never earned the interest on their bonds nor paid any dividends in ten years of struggling. In a desperate effort to continue in business the management of the American Line ships was turned over to Peter Wright and Sons in 1874. By 1877 the indebtedness of the American Steamship Company to the PRR had to be resolved in some way since the steamship line owed the railroad $501,302 without hope of payment. The solution arrived at in order to resolve this outstanding problem involved the steamship line issuing the railroad an additional 5000 shares of its stock with a face value of $500,000 and paying the railroad $1502 in cash. All concerned regarded the stock as worthless since no dividends had ever been earned, nor were any likely in the foreseeable future, but at least the Pennsylvania Railroad could clean up its accounts.[9] The establishment in 1877 of a "refrigerated trade" in fresh meat and produce between Philadelphia and Liverpool was encouraging. In 1878 an offer from the Imperial Russian Navy to purchase the four ships of the American Line so that they could be converted into armed merchant cruisers for potential employment against British shipping on the North Atlantic was turned down by the Board of Directors of the American Line to the fury of the management of the PRR.

The INC did better with its foreign-flag operations, and in 1884, at the insistence of the PRR management, formally bought the American Steamship Company, which it had managed since 1874. The PRR possessed a substantial interest in the affairs of the International Navigation Company through direct stock ownership and a commitment to back

---

[9]Hagley Museum and Library, Manuscript Collection (Soda House), M85, Board No. 95, Minute, Subcommittee of the Finance Committee, Board of Directors, Pennsylvania Railroad Company, Philadelphia, 24 January 1877.

its bonds. Griscom could not afford to offend the management of the railroad but he still was capable of striking a hard bargain. The ten-year-old quartet of the American Line required immediate maintenance to strengthen their hulls at a cost of at least $25,000 per ship. The surveyors in fact indicated that the liners should not sail again without the necessary strengthening of their keels. Learning of this the PRR was so anxious to rid itself of the American Steamship Company that it gave the INC the necessary funds to buy the four American Line ships and repair them. This was accomplished by the railroad purchasing 14,500 shares of INC stock worth $725,000 which equalled the sale price for the four ships. INC also received $27,142.18 in past revenues which cancelled out about $25,000 of current debt against the ships. The American Steamship Company itself owed the Pennsylvania Railroad $778,851.65 ($690,000 principal, $88,851.65 interest), and was forced to give the railroad a Due Bill for the balance of $53,851.65 in order to close the books. The $725,000 never actually left the Treasury of the Pennsylvania Railroad, but simply was transferred between various accounts. The original stockholders of the American Steamship Company received nothing for their investment, although many of them profited in their individual business interests by virtue of being able to utilize the services of the steamship line.

The PRR absorbed $900,000 in worthless stock, and $1,500,000 in equally worthless bonds, in addition to the Due Bill of $53,851.65, as the price of venturing into the subsidy of an American-flag steamship line. The price tag for global expansion under the American flag was considerable. During the ten years that the American Steamship Company was in business the PRR apparently received payments in excess of $200,000 a year for transportation of passengers and freight to and from the ships which produced additional revenue to the railroad well in excess of $2,000,000. Even the American-flag operations, therefore, were not undertaken at a total loss if all aspects of the corporate cash-flow are considered.

Foreign-flag shipping operations were more encouraging and the late 1880s brought additional commitments and investments by the PRR. Clement A. Griscom's connections with the highest level of the management of the PRR were so well established that in 1886 he persuaded the Railroad to underwrite his efforts to gain control of the Inman Line of Liverpool, one of the premier British-flag lines on the North Atlantic.

In the 1860s and 1870s, the Liverpool, New York and Philadelphia Steam Ship Company, universally known by its nickname, the "Inman Line," was one of the premier maritime enterprises on the North Atlantic. It remains one of the most famous and celebrated of all the great nineteenth-century steamship lines engaged in the trade between Europe and America. While the primary route served was from Liverpool to Philadelphia and New York, feeder services from Europe, such as the port of Antwerp, resulted in a wider casting of the net for cargo and passengers.

The origin of the Inman Line lies with William Inman of Leicester, England (1825-1881).[10] Early in his career he joined one of the leading Liverpool shipbroking firms, Richardson Brothers and Company, joint owners with Richardson Watson and Company of Philadelphia and New York, of a regular line of sailing packets trading between Philadelphia and Liverpool. In time the firm would own steamers and be the earliest concern to carry steerage passengers on their ships.[11] Inman was one of the earliest ship managers to have a keen appreciation of the immigrant trade in steamships and the profits to be derived from it.

The death of William Inman in 1881, combined with the unsatisfactory performance of the new Inman liner *City of Rome*, produced a fiscal crisis for the concern. The vessels of Cunard and White Star were superior in size and speed, which was critical for the successful maintenance of the Royal Mail Service. With the rejection of *City of Rome*, the Inman Line fell further behind and deeper in debt. By 1886 the hour of decision had come for the Inman Steamship Company, the Line having its back to the wall financially. A stockholders's meeting was called in Liverpool on 18 October 1886, to discuss the courses of action open to the Company. Debts and obligations of the Line exceeded the value of the fleet by nearly £100,000 and were mounting steadily.[12]

---

[10]Arthur J. Maginnis, *The Atlantic Ferry: Its Ships, Men and Working* (London, 1900), 205.

[11]New York Public Library, Inman and International, *History of the Inman Line* (New York, 1887), 1. This is a company history published shortly after the acquisition of Inman by Inman and International (1886), containing descriptions of the Inman, Red Star, and American Lines and their vessels and sailing schedules for 1888.

[12]Maginnis, *Atlantic Ferry*, 68.

The critical financial straits of the Inman Steamship Company were common knowledge and became of particular interest to Clement A. Griscom and the INC through Richardson, Spence and Company, their Liverpool business associates. The Griscom shipping interests, including Peter Wright and Sons of Philadelphia, had purchased some of the debts of the Inman Line and, therefore, were primary creditors. Since the Inman Line nicely fitted into the expanding operations of the International Navigation Company, Griscom entered into negotiations for the purchase of the Line. The major stockholders of the Inman Steamship Company knew of the American move when the stockholders' meeting was called. On 18 October 1886, it was decided that the Company should go into voluntary liquidation and thus pave the way for the American purchase. The Inman owners received a sum of £250,000 for their five liners and the use of the Company name from which was deducted the large amount already owed the American purchasers.

Within two weeks a new name, The Inman and International Steamship Company Limited, replaced the Inman Line, and the transatlantic passenger lines were confronted with a rejuvenated giant whose imminent demise had been expected. An active role in the management of the new concern was assumed by Richardson, Spence and Company, Liverpool, who already were the general agents in Britain for the International Navigation Company (Red Star Line) and the American Line. Certain discussions appear to have taken place over whether the new company name should be the "International, Inman and American Line," but the final choice was Inman and International.[13] This was a wise choice for the longer name was too bulky for advertisement purposes. Furthermore, since the Inman Line was a subsidized British mail line there was no need to offend or upset the British government by stressing that American investors had just purchased one of the premier British-flag North Atlantic Lines. The situation *vis-a-vis* Her Majesty's government and the new Inman owners was to deteriorate soon enough anyway.

The first item of business for the new owners was the rebuilding of the fleet in a grand manner. Clement A. Griscom had planned and prepared some twenty years for the day when he would have a free hand to establish a truly first-class transatlantic line. He possessed a strong foundation for doing so in the two divisions of the International Naviga-

---

[13]Bonsor, *North Atlantic Seaway*, I, 235.

tion Company which he already controlled. The "Societe Anonyme de Navigation Belge-Americaine" (Red Star Line) was maintaining a prosperous Antwerp-New York trade, and the American Steamship Company (American Line) operated a growing Liverpool-Philadelphia service. Neither of these concerns was ever in a position to obtain the respect of the great British North Atlantic lines. Both Cunard and White Star had long looked down on Griscom's efforts as unworthy of attention while he built up the smaller lines. With the acquisition of the tottering Inman Line — over which Cunard and White Star had been ready to say the last rites — Griscom suddenly emerged as one of the largest steamship owners in the world. The reactions of the competing British Lines was, first, one of stunned silence, and then of a flurry of activity. Griscom, they knew, was the very essence of the fox among the chickens and he had waited years to play the part.

Upon acquiring the Inman Steamship Company, Clement A. Griscom caught the next steamer for Liverpool to discuss the future plans of the Inman Line with his British associates, James Spence and Edmund Taylor of Richardson, Spence and Company. He travelled to Britain with a commitment from the Pennsylvania Railroad to finance the construction of a single great liner for the new line. The management of the Pennsylvania Railroad was prepared to make available to Griscom the substantial sum of $1,850,000 for the new ship. In Liverpool and Glasgow, Griscom evaluated the condition of the Inman fleet and the position of the Inman and International with relation to its principal competitors and made the decision that one new ship was not enough to accomplish the desired transformation in fortunes. With great courage and determination Griscom wrote a lengthy letter to the PRR leadership in which he stated very forcefully that he needed the money to build two new liners and that he had already taken the liberty of negotiating a contract for two vessels second to none on the North Atlantic. The management of the PRR, already major stockholders in the parent INC, accepted Griscom's arguments and guaranteed him the necessary funds to build the two new ships. In the spring of 1887, before he returned, negotiations were completed with James R. Thomson of J. and G. Thomson Shipbuilding Yard, Clydebank, Scotland, for the building of the two largest, fastest, and finest commercial vessels in the world, calculated to far surpass any existing competitors.[14] Additional tonnage was needed immediately and *Ohio* was fresh from a major overhaul during which triple-expansion engines were installed with spectacular crossings at more than fourteen knots being laid down by the fourteen-year-old liner as a result. The original American Line quartet were all doing well in these years and were considered to be in sufficiently good condition to be overhauled and rejuvenated.

Griscom was determined to make the greatest possible impression upon the steamer trade with his new liners. The keel of *City of New York* was laid in June 1887. The vessels were to be as nearly unsinkable as possible — each liner was constructed with fifteen transversal bulkheads that ran from the keel all the way up to the saloon deck with no breaks in the partitions below this level. The two liners were the most perfectly subdivided transatlantic vessels ever built. The first of this famous pair was ready for launching by March 1888. A contemporary observer described the scene:

> *City of New York* stands on the ways ready to be launched, while the other steamer, the *City of Paris*, is in an advanced state. The former, as she now stands in the yard, presents a fine appearance. Her great length of 560 ft., her beam 63 ft., and her height, 44 feet, might well attract the attention of passengers on the river steamers. With the buildings on deck, she measures close to 10,500 tons, making her the largest passenger steamer in the world.[15]

Of particular note was the figurehead which graced the clipper bow of the new liner. The female figure had been carved by James Allan of Glasgow and was greatly admired. Traditionalists were particularly pleased that the new owners of the Inman line had elected to retain the clipper bow and the figurehead which had so long been associated with Inman ships.

Each vessel was outfitted with two completely separate engine rooms. The engines were of the three crank triple-expansion type, having piston valves throughout and each engine was capable of driving the ship

---

[14]Inman, Red Star and American Lines, *Inman and International*, 7.

[15]Inman and International, *Inman Line*, 8.

at four-fifths the maximum speed in the event that either set of engines should have to be stopped for any reason. Each liner was constructed with a double hull so that if the ship should strike anything which might open her interior to the sea, the second skin would be there to keep the vessel safe.

On 15 March 1888, no less a figure than Lady Randolph Churchill came north to Scotland to name the new Inman and International liner *City of New York*. Its sistership was christened *City of Paris* and launched on 23 October 1888, a little more than two months later than planned. Since the liners were constructed in a depression period along the Clyde, they were, indeed, warmly looked upon by the local populace. Their passenger accommodations surpassed anything in existence and set new standards of luxury. Of particular note were the magnificent, vaulted dining rooms of both liners complete with stained glass windows and grand organs. The vaulted ceiling of the saloon area was meant to give the impression to the first-class passengers that they were in a grand hotel or mansion instead of on a ship at sea, and this effect was fully achieved. The two liners had accommodations for 540 first, 200 second and 1000 steerage passengers.[16]

Unexpected disaster struck Griscom before the commissioning of the new ships. In 1887 the British government reviewed the arrangements for carrying the mails across the North Atlantic and decided that two sailings a week by Cunard and White Star would be adequate. Both lines were not only British built and manned, but also were British owned. Behind the scenes revenge was taken for Griscom's audacity in buying Inman. The third mail each week heretofore carried by Inman was discontinued and the subsidy cancelled. Unofficially Griscom was informed that the British government saw no reason to subsidize the new American owners of Inman and International even if it remained a British-flag steamship line.[17] This action severely affected the financial solvency of Griscom's maritime empire. It was questionable whether the two new liners could be operated profitably without some form of guaranteed income through a contract to carry the mails.

---

[16]International Navigation Company, *American Line* (New York, 1898). This is another fine publication of the firm.

[17]Bonsor, *North Atlantic Seaway*; supplement, 67.

City of New York took its maiden voyage on 1 August 1888, and was the largest passenger liner in commission at the time. *City of Paris* followed with its maiden sailing on 3 April 1889, and the two ocean greyhounds were hailed as the outstanding marine marvels of their day, with their gross tonnage of 10,500 tons, length of 560 feet, and beam of sixty-three feet. The Inman and International *Cities* also were (and are) regarded as among the most beautiful passenger ships ever constructed. *City of New York* and *City of Paris* possessed the unique Inman clipper-bow and long sleek black hulls. Each was graced with three majestic, evenly-spaced funnels and three towering masts. Oddly enough the builders deemed it necessary to outfit the liners with sails and the foremast was described as square-rigged with the other two masts being fore-and-aft rigged. It is doubtful that the sails were ever used by these twin-screw, twenty knot, passenger liners and it appears that the crossbars and sails were soon removed. Both liners carried twenty-two lifeboats as a prominent portion of their exterior equipment and it was firmly stated that "these will be capable of carrying all on board when the vessels are full."[18]

Majestic in their external appearance and most beautiful within, but would they capture the "Blue Riband?" The performance of *City of Rome* must have haunted Griscom, Spence and Taylor as the two great liners they had ordered prepared for their maiden voyages. Their fears were probably accentuated when the *City of New York* took longer than expected to work the kinks out and, while turning in a creditable performance during her first six months in service, produced no new record crossings. Its sister, *City of Paris*, made a comfortable maiden voyage (3 March 1889) which was eagerly watched but which also established no new record. *Paris* left Liverpool on its second voyage on 1 May 1889, and after the usual stop at Queenstown (Cobh) rapidly pulled away from the Irish Coast with 2855 miles of the broad North Atlantic before her. Five days, 23 hours, and 7 minutes later *City of Paris* arrived off Sandy Hook and steamed up the North River with the mythical "Blue Riband" of the Atlantic tacked to its foremast. *City of Paris* had steamed at an average speed of 19.95 knots which was .39 of a knot and two hours forty-eight minutes faster than the Cunard *Etruria* (1885, 7718 tons) over a similar distance in May of the previous year (6 days, 1 hour, 55

---

[18]Inman and International, *Inman Line*, 12.

minutes, 2855 miles, 19.56 knots). The Inman and International Steamship Company was the proud owner of the "Fastest Passenger Liner in the World." Clement A. Griscom, James Spence and Edmund Taylor in one stroke, but with PRR money, had transformed the Inman Line from a loser into a blue-blooded winner and in the process sent all their competitors to their builders. *City of Paris* was also the first passenger liner to make a westbound crossing of the North Atlantic in under six days. Later in the same month *City of Paris* arrived at Queenstown after a voyage of 5 days, 22 hrs. 10 min. and thereby completed the "double."[19] Now the Inman and International could proclaim to all the world that they had the "Fastest Liner on the Atlantic." That the first-class Inman ships continued to run to New York was no problem since by this time the PRR had bought access to New York City and could compete with the New York Central Railroad on what had been its own turf.

If Inman was the flagship line in the late 1880s, the Societe Anonyme de Navigation Belge-Americaine (Red Star Line) was also most active. Between 1883 and 1889, the Red Star Line's New York-Antwerp service steadily expanded. An average of 25,000 steerage passengers per year were landed in New York and there was a slow but relatively steady increase in the better classes, specifically from 1500 to 4000 passengers per year. The Philadelphia figures greatly exceeded these with a total of over 40,000 in 1882 alone. The Red Star Line was able to order a much bigger vessel than ever before in 1888. *Friesland*, built by Thomson's on the Clyde shortly after the Inman "*Cities*," was the only Red Star liner to be constructed with a clipper-bow. The new liner entered service late in 1889 with passenger accommodations for 226 first, 102 second, and 600 steerage class passengers. Rumours of the sale of *Vaderland* and *Zeeland* had been making the rounds for at least seven years before the construction of the *Friesland* finally made this possible in 1889. The Red Star passenger totals continued to rise and during 1891 reached over 41,000 for the port of New York. Hence, the Red Star Line was clearly prospering and carrying its weight in Griscom's International Navigation Company.

Griscom was fully aware of the need for a subsidy for his Line of first-class steamers, and therefore redoubled his efforts to obtain American recognition. Congress was pressured to change the government

[19] Bonsor, *North Atlantic Seaway*, II, 236.

policy on Federal subsidies and to alter the rigidity of the American ship registration laws. The reviving American interest in navies and maritime affairs generally aided this campaign, although it was slow to pick up speed and gain momentum. Nevertheless, Griscom and his associates (including the PRR) pushed the issue as forcefully and judiciously as possible. Griscom, in particular, must have felt that the entire survival of his multi-faceted maritime empire hung upon the need for the United States government to recognize the importance of the American merchant marine and support the Lines.[20]

Griscom took the case of his American-owned Line to the American Congress. In testimony before the Senate Commerce Committee, the President of the Inman and International Navigation Company explained that the situation of the Line was due to the maltreatment it had received from the British government. The plight of the Inman Line, with two new costly express steamers and no subsidy to defray their operating expenses, was quite obvious. The prize that Griscom was after was American registry for his liners which would permit him to apply for an American subsidy under the terms of the Postal Subsidy Act of 1891, essentially the key to the puzzle.

Two distinct shipping subsidy measures had been placed before Congress in 1890; one concerned ocean mail steamers and the other freighters and sailing ships. Both bills had been drawn up by Senator William P. Frye of Maine, the Senate's leading proponent of government aid to the American merchant marine. Senator Frye had undertaken a detailed study of the state of the American shipping industry and of the fundamental costs of marine operations. He therefore was well versed in the condition and economics of the Merchant Marine. The goals of the Mail Subsidy Bill were:

> First, to secure regular and quicker [mail service] to countries now reached. Second, to make new and direct commercial exchanges with countries not now reached. Third, to develop new and enlarge old markets in the interest of producers and consumers, under the reciprocity treaties completed and under consideration. Fourth, to

[20]United States, Congress, Senate Miscellaneous Documents No. 149, 56th Congress, 1st Session, 100-109. Testimony of Clement A. Griscom (mis-indexed "Grisco"), before the Senate Subcommittee on the "Revival of the Merchant Marine."

> Assist the promotion of a powerful naval reserve. Fifth, to establish a training school for American seamen.[21]

The various amounts stated in the bill for subsidies to the shipping industry were accepted by the Senate. Unfortunately the House of Representatives was of a different mind, and also in a frantic haste to adjourn when the measure came up for consideration. When an amendment to slash the proposed subsidy for first-class liners by one-third was brought forward, it was speedily passed to the displeasure of the bill's backers. The amended bill was immediately passed. In this manner was enacted the first significant piece of legislation to aid the American merchant marine in thirty-two years.

By the Act the Postmaster General was authorized to make contracts with American citizens for the carrying of the trans-Atlantic mail for a period of five to ten years:

> Proposals must be invited by public advertisement three months before the letting of the contract. Vessels must be American built, owned and officered. The crew of a mail steamer must be at least one-fourth American for the first two years, one-third for the next three years, and one-half, thereafter.[22]

Since it was not reasonable to lay down the same set of requirements and subsidies for all vessels, four classes of mail steamers based on tonnage and speed were established. First-class steamers had to be of at least 8000 tons and be capable of maintaining a speed of around twenty knots. Second-class liners had to be of at least 5000 tons and be capable of maintaining a speed of sixteen knots, while third-class steamers had to be of at least 2500 tons with a cruising speed of at least fourteen knots, and fourth-class vessels had to be of at least 1500 tons with a cruising speed of twelve knots. All ships in the first three categories had to be constructed of either iron or steel while the fourth-class steamers could be of iron, steel, or wood.

---

[21]Meeker, *Shipping Subsidies*, 167; and 51st Congress, 2nd Session, H.R. No. 3273.

[22]Marvin, *Merchant Marine*, 166-167.

It was intended that the major liners would serve as armed merchant cruisers (or troopships) in the event of war and all steamers in the first three classes were required to be built under the general supervision of the Navy Department. The reward forthcoming to the owners of vessels qualifying for the different classes was fixed at a maximum of four dollars per mile for the first-class liner, two dollars per mile for the second-class vessels, and one dollar per mile for the third-class steamers. All those in the fourth-class were to be compensated at a rate of 66.67 cents per mile — an accountant's headache! All subsidies were to be paid on only the outward crossings of each voyage and not for the homeward passages with a further restriction of not more than $12,000 per voyage for those liners serving between the United States and the United Kingdom.[23]

The Postal Aid Act did not result in a flood of offers to begin a first-class line of mail steamers on the North Atlantic. In fact not a single offer was forthcoming since a subsidy of only $12,000 per voyage was far from sufficient inducement to invest millions in a fleet of expensive ocean greyhounds. The offer only could look attractive to an already established line in need of a subsidy, but there was no such commercial endeavour under the American flag.

There was, however, the American owned and operated Inman and International Navigation Company that had been denied the British subsidy and was ready, willing and able to undertake a transatlantic service under the American mail contract terms. This was the moment when Clement A. Griscom ushered his two new express liners, *City of New York* and *City of Paris*, both of whom were "Blue Riband" liners, before the Senate Commerce Committee. Griscom petitioned Congress to allow his two Atlantic champions American registry. In return he offered to build two larger vessels in American yards to complete the quartet of super liners necessary for a regular weekly transatlantic service at a service speed of twenty knots.

Congress did not have to hesitate over the Inman and International Navigation Company offer for several reasons. It did not appear as though a transatlantic service would ever be taken up by an American concern.

---

[23]*Ibid.*, 419.

The Inman and International Line nearly filled this qualification since it was wholly owned and operated by American citizens. Furthermore the establishment of such a proud Line of ships under the American flag would bolster American pride and interest in the American merchant marine. At the same time the action was a slap at the British government which apparently had tried to ruin the American investors. Finally, the offer to build two consorts for the brand new and already famous *City of New York* and *City of Paris* in American shipyards promised to provide a great stimulus for the American shipbuilding industry which could use two such prestigious orders.

On 10 May 1892, Congress approved a measure giving American registry to *City of New York* and *City of Paris*, and thereby paved the way for the return of the American flag to the North Atlantic in a most spectacular manner. The Inman and International Navigation Company changed its name to the "American Line."

The Acts of Congress which created the Postal Subsidy Bill of 1891 and which gave American registry to the Inman and International Navigation Company's passenger liners *New York* and *Paris*, were the first steps in the formulation of an American Merchant Marine Policy by the United States government in the years before the First World War. These Acts represented the first major pieces of benevolent legislation towards the American shipping industry after a period of thirty years in the wilderness of statutory neglect.

The refusal of the British government to include the American-owned, but British-flag, Inman and International in the mail subsidy arrangement prompted Griscom to strike a deal with the American government. In return for the Act permitting American registry for his two new liners Griscom agreed to build two additional ships in the United States and this brought the creation of the great American Line of 1893. When the new ships were delivered in 1894-1895 the American Line possessed the best-balanced first-class service between New York and Southampton. The desire of the Clement A. Griscom and the management of the PRR over two decades for a through service from Europe to the vast American interior was achieved. The continental growth of the Pennsylvania Railroad Company between 1846 and 1870 expanded into an effort to control the movement of freight and passengers from the hinterland of Europe to the hinterland of the United States. As a result the American Steamship Company, International Navigation Company, Societe Anonyme de Navigation Belge-Americaine, and Inman and

International Navigation Company, all would be founded or reborn. The globalization of the international trade of the United States, the United Kingdom, and Belgium would result in a number of unique arrangements.

The Expansion of Japan's Shipping Interests before the Sino-Japanese War

Katayama Kunio[1]

East Asian waters were increasingly integrated into the international steamship network from the mid-nineteenth century. Before the Sino-Japanese War (June 1894-November 1895),[2] this network was in the tight grip of European — British, French, German, Dutch and Scandinavian — and American shipping firms. The entry of Japanese shipping into this business began immediately after the Sino-Japanese War, with the establishment by Japanese shipowners of major lines to Europe, Seattle, San Francisco and Australia. At the same time, once the war had ended in 1895, Japan joined the imperialist race in the Far East.

The development of Japanese shipping has often been seen as a factor in this imperialist expansion. This chapter does not argue that Japanese shipping was unrelated to imperialism.[3] However, the relationship between Japanese imperialism and shipping has been somewhat misunderstood, especially by those aware of the western historical experience. Since the Age of Discovery, Europe's maritime power had overwhelmed other countries, with empires expanding all over the world and shipping becoming an important instrument in the extension of imperial possessions and commerce. This pattern led many to assume that the growth of shipping could not be divorced from imperialism. Nevertheless, modern shipping is basically a commercial activity and we should not presuppose that strong, mutually stimulating links inevitably exist between

[1]Japanese names are given surname first in this paper.

[2]Japan waged its first modern war, the Sino-Japanese War, against Imperial China. This war broke out when both countries intervened militarily into the Korean crisis caused by the peasants' uprising in 1894.

[3]See Katayama Kunio, "The Expansion of Japanese Shipping into Southeast Asia before World War I: The Case of OSK," *The Great Circle*, VIII (April 1986); and Ang Pyongte, "Korean Shipping in the Late Lee Dynasty: The Japanese Invasion," in Horie Yasuzo (ed.), *Studies of Maritime Economic History* (Kobe, 1967).

shipping and imperialism. In describing and explaining Japan's enthusiasm for the expansion of its shipping industry before the Sino-Japanese War, this chapter emphasizes the purely commercial aspects of this form of maritime development. Thus, if international economic relations can be divided into two parts — ordinary trade and emigration on the one hand, and an incursion into the sovereignty of another state to control its economy on the other[4] — Japan's efforts to build up its shipping interests before the Sino-Japanese War clearly belong in the former category.

To understand the motives behind the establishment of Japan's first overseas lines, we need to consider the period before the 1894-1895 war, when various groups lobbied for the promotion of international shipping — notably, shipping companies, House of Representatives, government, and influential sectors of public opinion as evidenced by a series of contemporary, prize winning essays on shipping. Examination of these pro-shipping sentiments reveals that it was business rather than imperialism that provided the initial impetus to the growth of Japanese shipping.

The Background

Advocates of the inauguration of transoceanic lines owned by Japanese companies were apparent in the earliest phase of the Meiji era (1868-1912). Essentially, however, these were just paper dreams of lines to Europe, America and Australia, for the Japanese people lacked the modern technology and economic competence to participate in the modern shipping world. Although NYK (Nippon Yusen Kaisha, that is, Japan Mail) was established in 1885, its early operations were largely restricted to home waters.

William D. Wray has identified NYK as one of the big three service enterprises in Japan — the other two being Mitsui Bussan (trading firm) and the Yokohama Specie Bank (which provided foreign exchange

---

[4]W.G. Beasley, *Japanese Imperialism 1894-1945* (Oxford, 1987); and P.J. Cain and A.G. Hopkins, *British Imperialism: Innovation and Expansion 1688-1914* (London, 1993).

financing) — and analysed their role in Japan's informal empire in China.[5] No one denies that Japan was very imperialistic in East Asia. However, as Wray noted, the activities of the big three service enterprises were not limited to the East Asia, but promoted Japanese international trade in general. The Japanese government supported their establishment, a natural step in the context of the abandonment of the seclusion policy. Under the severely restricted foreign trade system before the Meiji Restoration, Japan had not gained any experience of modern international business practices. After the trial and error of the early Meiji period, these service firms were created as strategic organs for Japan's foreign trade. Moreover, the Japanese government did not ignore western shipping policies. For example, the Japanese consul in San Francisco reported on shipping subsidies provided by western countries. In his report of 1883, countries were ranked in order of the magnitude of the subsidies they gave to shipowners: thus, France ($4,750,000) was in first place, followed by Britain ($3,000,000), Italy ($1,540,000), Austria ($800,000), the Netherlands ($284,000), the United States ($200,000), Norway/Sweden ($157,000), Spain ($100,000 for Havanna; $20,000 per Manila round), Belgium ($100,000).[6]

When NYK was established in 1885, the Japanese government promised an annual grant of 880,000 yen (about $500,000) for fifteen years. This was an exceptionally large industry subsidy in Japan's small national budget at that time.[7] It must be noted, however, that the subsidy was mostly spent maintaining the line between Japan and Shanghai, which was practically a feeder service for the trunk lines operated by western companies.

In 1884, the report of an honorary consul in Germany, brought tidings of German shipping policy. He reported that the German government was preparing a bill to subsidize lines to East Asia, commenting that:

---

[5]William D. Wray, "Japan's Big-Three Services Enterprises in China, 1896-1936," in Peter Duus, Ramon H. Myers and Mark R. Peatie (eds.), *The Japanese Informal Empire in China, 1895-1937* (Princeton, 1989).

[6]Tatsuda Kaku, "Consular Report from San Francisco, 21 July 1883," in Ministry of Foreign Affairs, *Tsuho Ihen* (*Compiled Reports of Commerce*): *The Second Half Year of 1883* (Tokyo, 1884).

[7]Emi Koichi and Shionoya Yuicha, *Public Expenditure* (Tokyo, 1966).

> most German MPs traditionally have been firm free trade supporters and never agreed with such subsides to industries. However, the main opposition newspapers seem favourable in this case. Accordingly, many MPs will vote for the bill.[8]

This prediction was wrong, for in his next report, he advised that: "although the government introduced the bill to Parliament, it was not accepted in the last session."[9] Even so, in the next year, the bill was again laid before Parliament and passed.[10] As a result, the North German Lloyd company (NDL) established lines to East Asia and Australia in 1886 and was annually granted 4,000,000 marks (a little over $1,000,000) for fifteen years. Initially, this East Asian line started at Bremen and called at Singapore and Hong Kong *en route* to Shanghai.[11] Although NDL at first operated a feeder line to Japan from Hong Kong, it soon extended a main line to Japan,[12] a clear indication of the remarkable progress made by western shipping companies in East Asian waters by the 1880s.[13] Japanese consuls also related Canadian moves. Canadian Pacific (CP) built a railroad from Montréal to Vancouver, and just after its completion in June 1887, started a connecting shipping service, the Vancouver/Yokohama/Hong Kong line. This transpacific route was a notable development.[14]

---

[8]Martin Burchard, "Consular Report from Hamburg, 15 May 1884," *Tsusho Ihen: The First Half Year of 1884* (Tokyo, 1884).

[9]Martin Burchard, "Consular Report from Hamburg, 29 October 1884," *Tsusho Ihen: The Second Half Year of 1884* (Tokyo, 1885).

[10]Julius Shubert, "Consular Report from Hamburg, 26 March 1885," *Tsusho Ihen: The First Half Year of 1885* (Tokyo, 1885).

[11]*Official Gazette of Japan*, 17 August 1885 and 12 August 1886.

[12]Mitsui OSK, *Eighty Years of OSK* (Osaka, 1966), 20.

[13]In particular by P&O, Blue Funnel, NDL, O&O, CP and Scandinavian tramps.

[14]"Consular Report from London, 13 November 1885;" *Tsusho Ihen: The First Half Year of 1885* (Tokyo, 1885); "Consular Report from San Francisco," in Ministry of Foreign Affairs, *Tsusho Houkoku (Reports of Commerce)*, No. 109 (Tokyo, 1889) and No.

Thus, international shipping networks were rapidly becoming ubiquitous in the 1880s. Although Japanese people were aware of this progress, the nation's shipping interests had not grown sufficiently to follow suit in the 1880s. During the next decade, however, Japan's shipping development plans became much clearer. By this time, Japan had acquired some experience in the shipping business and its trade had grown to some extent, while there was also a concern to encourage emigration as a means of relieving the overpopulation problem. Plans for the Nicaragua Canal and the Trans-Siberian Railway, which were hot issues internationally, seemed to improve the trading opportunities facing Japan in East Asia.

The Ambitions of Japan's Shipowners

In the early 1890s, Japanese shipping companies were eager to establish lines to Europe, America and Australia. The opening of the line to Europe by Japanese ships was coveted because it was a major trunk line in world shipping, it would enable Japanese ships to carry the flag to the "centre of the universe," and Europe was then Japan's most important trading partner. This last point was important in relation to the belief of many Japanese that their ships should carry a proportion of Japan's own trade. There was some confidence in overseas shipping due to the successful opening of the Bombay line in 1893, but the existence of strong competitors and the exclusive shipping conference on the European route posed great problems for Japan.

A line to America was also deemed desirable because the United States was the friendly country that had introduced Japan to international relations and had become an important trading partner. Japan considered, too, that the opening of the line would promote Japanese emigration to North, Central, and South America. The NYK already had experience in carrying Japanese emigrants to Hawaii. Obstacles to opening such lines were the negotiations with American railways that would provide connecting services on the west coast.

The line to Australia was perhaps the most straightforward to establish, for western shipowners had not operated lines between Japan and Australia due to the distance of the route from any advanced

---

126 (Tokyo, 1889); "Consular Report from Vancouver, 8 July 1892," in *Official Gazette of Japan*, 16 July 1892.

countries. Japan had a clear geographical advantage, though the volume of trade between Japan and Australia was limited. Even so, many Japanese businessmen anticipated that economic development would progress rapidly in Australia, and naturally considered that Japanese emigrants would increase if the line was opened.

NYK was the first Japanese company to enter the international arena, making trial voyages in various waters shortly after its foundation in 1885. It is noteworthy that the firm ran tramps to Hawaii for transporting Japanese workers, while its ships also steamed several times to New Caledonia and Queensland for the same purpose.[15] As for the American line, NYK had talks with line operators such as the Mexican government and O&O (Occidental and Oriental Steamship Co.), while the Belgian government also proposed a joint operation of the European line. NYK, however, needed support from the Japanese government to establish these lines. The government refused to provide any assistance, as it did not consider the Japanese economy in general, and the shipping industry in particular, to be sufficiently developed. In short, it felt that such proposals were premature.

However, NYK made some significant strides in 1893. First, joint operation of the Bombay line, in collaboration with the Indian big business company, Tata, was successfully started as Indian raw cotton was needed by the growing Japanese spinning industry.[16] Second, negotiations for the Seattle line began. This resulted from the bankruptcy of a British shipowner, Gordon Upton, who had been engaged mainly in carrying Japanese workers to North America. Upton's agent arranged talks between NYK, Upton and the Great Northern Railroad Company, which was based in Seattle, to open the Seattle line.[17] Against this background, in 1893 NYK drew up a plan to open three major overseas lines: first, a European line, with six ships, each of 3100 grt, operating from Yokohama to London (11,980 miles); second, an American line, with two ships, each of 8500 grt, operating from Yokohama to Seattle (4200 miles); and, third,

---

[15]Ministry of Communications, *The Business Inspection of Nippon Yusen Kaisha* (Tokyo, 1894).

[16]Mikami Atsufumi, *The Business History of Indian Big Business* (Tokyo, 1993), 139-172.

[17]"Consular Report from Vancouver, 15 July 1893," in *Official Gazette of Japan*, 9 August 1893.

an Australian line, with three ships, each of 2500 grt, operating from Yokohama to Melbourne (7097 miles).[18] This scheme was designed to convince the government to subsidise the lines. It also demonstrated NYK's growing confidence and eagerness to begin overseas liner operations.

Debates in the Japanese Parliament

The first modern constitution was promulgated by the Emperor in 1889, leading to the first general election in July 1890. It was a restricted popular vote since the law required voters to have paid more than fifteen yen (about twelve US dollars at that time) in annual direct state tax. The election result was quite unfavourable to the government, as many opposition members were returned. In the first session, which opened in November 1890, the government had severe difficulty with its financial plan because the constitution required the consent of the parliament to pass the annual budget.

The development of shipping first appeared on the parliamentary agenda on 16 December 1892 during the fourth session, when Nishiyama Shizumi and eight other members of the Liberal Party introduced a shipping expansion proposal in the House of Representatives. Nishiyama argued that the existing lump sum subsidy to NYK had not led to the expansion of overseas shipping and demanded a total change in the way shipping was subsidised. His order of priority was first the Australian line and then the European line. The American line and the Vladivostok direct line were also considered, but were not regarded as urgent and were therefore postponed. Nishiyama's proposals can be summarised as follows:

a. To transform the existing subsidy system into the one that many advanced countries had taken.
b. Not to grant subsidies to domestic lines but only to overseas lines.
c. To put priority on opening the Australian and European lines.
d. To negotiate with NYK to achieve these reforms.

---

[18]NYK, *The Fifty Years of Modern Shipping: A Short History* (Tokyo, 1921).

e. To ask for the consent of the House to produce resources for the subsidy when the government should draw up the plan.[19]

Priority was placed on the Australian line simply because no regular line between Japan and Australia existed, though the Eastern and Australian Steamship Navigation Company, which was based in Australia, operated a line from Adelaide to Hong Kong and sometimes extended its voyages to Japan. The American line was not given top priority because a line to the United States required American railroad partners on the west coast to provide connecting services. As Japanese shipowners had not found partners, they were hoping to use the Nicaragua Canal that was then being planned, intending to establish a line from Japan via Hawaii, San Francisco and through the canal to New York.

There was no opposition to this proposal, though some MPs raised questions as to how Japan could cope with the counter subsidies likely to be provided by foreign governments to compete with Japanese lines. It gained widespread support because at this time the trans-Siberian railway was being built and a canal between the Americas was being planned. So the Japanese people were anticipating great changes in the transoceanic transport networks. They believed that Japan would lag far behind if they could not prepare for this. Moreover, in the 1880s, opponents of the Meiji oligarchy, political activists from various parties, and other anti-government factions launched very strong human rights campaigns. This was the high season of political activity, though political passions did calm down to some degree in the early 1890s due to the establishment of the modern parliament. As a result, MPs became increasingly interested in economic policies, and the idea of subsidizing overseas lines gained support when a financial surplus was produced in 1892.

The shipping expansion proposal was submitted to committee and amended somewhat.[20] Then it was finally adopted on 17 February 1893 in the form of a proposal of the House of Representatives that was technically a request to the government. However, ignoring the request

---

[19] *The Stenographic Records of the House of Representatives in the Imperial Parliament*, Volume 6: Fourth Session, part I, 1893 (Tokyo, 1979).

[20] The main amendment to the proposal was that the government should advance the opening of the American and Vladivostock lines according to progress on the Nicaragua Canal and the trans-Siberian Railway.

of the House was difficult for the government because the House could introduce bills and pass them. Unlike western parliaments, Japanese MPs rarely introduced bills, particularly those involving budget arrangements, for it was thought that the implementation of economic policies would be simplified if the government drew up bills.

Is it possible that this initiative of the Japanese parliament was imperialist in ambition and simply disguised as economic policy? Two things should be borne in mind when addressing this question. First, parliament rejected a naval expansion plan produced in the government's budget during this fourth session. Second, the threat to Japan at this time was the Chinese navy, which possessed much larger battleships than the Japanese navy. Though the Japanese parliament was not necessarily pacific in sentiment, plans for the development of shipping routes to Australia or Europe had nothing to do with military matters.

Informed Public Opinion

While the shipping companies and the government advocated the development of Japan's shipping interests, support for such a policy also came from academics and influential economic theorists. For instance, in 1894, Mr. Tsuboya Zenshiro published an influential work which argued that the expansion of shipping was important to Japan.[21] In the same year, the Japanese Economic Society (Nippon Keizai Kai), an organization in favour of protectionist doctrine, sponsored an essay contest on the theme "On Japanese Shipping," to be judged by a committee comprising seven leading economists and businessmen.[22] Many people entered the contest, the winning entries being published in 1894 under the title, *On Japanese Shipping.*[23] Many authorities, including the official historian of the Communications Ministry,[24] have suggested that these essays indicate the high level of public concern regarding shipping expansion in those days.

---

[21]Tsuboya Zenshiro, *On Japanese Shipping* (Tokyo, 1894).

[22]*Tokyo Economic Journal*, 20 June 1885.

[23]Yano Yoshihiro (ed.), *On Japanese Shipping* (Tokyo, 1894).

[24]Ministry of Communications (ed.), *The History of Communications Works*, Vol. 6 (Tokyo, 1941) 9 and 817-818.

The prize-winning essays, and other contemporary works, are particularly illuminating with regard to three issues: the order of priority of shipping lines to be opened; the rationale behind government subsidies; and the type of subsidy to be adopted. On the first question, there was a general consensus among informed opinion makers that Japanese shipowners should focus as soon as possible on the opening of three main lines — to Europe, America, and Australia — and that the government should subsidise these initiatives. Moreover, all those who advocated such a strategy identified emigration as a reason for establishing the transoceanic routes, whether the destination was the United States, Canada, Central and South America, or the islands of Micronesia. The order of priority afforded to each line differed from one proponent to another. For instance, while Terajima (winner of the first prize in the essay contest) emphasized the significance of the Seattle line,[25] Tokai preferred Central and South America, and Saito gave top priority to Europe, though he also recognised the potential of the Australian route.

Various reasons were put forward as to why the government should support shipping expansion. All were agreed that shipping was important to Japan's economy, though numerous reasons — national prestige, enhanced demand for the Japanese shipbuilding industry, the promotion of Japanese trade and emigration, mail carriage[26] — were advanced to support this contention. Significantly, only two authors, Terajima and Saito, mentioned military objectives and then only as marginal factors to the principal commercial rationale.The question of state subsidies for shipping was more controversial, largely because other industries were competing for government subsidies during the 1890s. Professor Tsubotani put forward the most cogent case in favour of aid for shipping, arguing that it was an infant industry worthy of nurturing, that it was vulnerable to foreign competitors and therefore needed protection,

---

[25]Terajima Narinobu was the translator of Alfred Thayer Mahan, *The Influence of Sea Power on History, 1660-1783* (1890), and later became a director of NYK. When he wrote the essay, he was a civilian employee of the Japanese Navy, engaged to translate Mahan's work.

[26]See Kokaze Hidemasa, *Japanese Maritime Transport under Imperialism* (Tokyo, 1993), 140-144.

and that it was an industry which provided useful public services, notably carriage of the mails.[27]

With regard to the methods of subsidising shipping, there were two schools of thought. First, there were protectionists, who favoured the grant of subsidies to specific operators on lines deemed by the government to be worth supporting in the national interest. Not surprisingly, those who were awarded prizes by the protectionist Japanese Economic Society tended to argue for the provision of specific line subsidies. For instance, Saito considered that tramp shipping should be promoted by the availability of shipbuilding subsidies for tramps. Terajima, winner of the first prize, was very strongly in favour of specific line subsidies, though he was the only authority to assert that ships used on subsidized lines should be built so that they could be employed for military as well as commercial purposes. Other writers cited economic factors as the sole rationale for subsidizing lines, Tokai pointedly rejecting Terajima's case on the grounds that ships designed to serve both commercial and military needs were extremely problematical to build and very difficult to operate at a profit.

Second, there were the supporters of free trade who advocated the provision of general subsidies for any overseas voyages undertaken by registered Japanese vessels in proportion to their tonnage and the length of the route. The representative journal of liberal doctrine was the *Tokyo Economic Journal*. Its owner and chief editor was Taguchi Ukichi, a supporter of laissez-faire doctrine and critic of the government's economic policies. His journal published articles supporting free trade and often discussed shipping policies from the perspective of laissez-faire doctrine. For example, in the early 1880s, a series of articles insisted that the principle of free trade should be maintained in the field of shipping, and attacked Adam Smith and J.S. Mill for approving of the navigation laws.[28] Instead, the author relied on the authority of John Ramsey McCulloch who did not see any public benefit in the navigation laws. However, the tone of the *Tokyo Economic Journal* had changed by 1894 when Ban Naonosuke remarked on shipping expansion as follows:

---

[27]Tsuboya, *On Japanese Shipping*.

[28]*Tokyo Economic Journal*, 22 July and 29 July, and 5 August 1882.

> I am a supporter of free trade. I want to emphasize the public benefit of free competition. However, as far as shipping is concerned, this principle is not always appropriate. My conclusion is that Japanese shipping has to be subsidized by the nation. The problem is how to subsidize shipping. I insist that we must assist all the qualified shipowners without any discrimination.[29]

Thus, even to the most ardent of liberal economic theorists, shipping policy was an exception to the principle of free trade.

With informed public opinion — both protectionist and free trade — running strongly in favour of the expansion of shipping, the government submitted a shipping promotion bill to the House of Representatives on 19 December 1893.[30] Not concurring with the demands of the House, the aim of the government was to pass an act to provide general subsidies for qualified shipowners operating overseas voyages. The plan to introduce specific line subsidies was retained in the fiscal budget. Accordingly, the overall system of shipping subsidies represented a compromise of different views concerning the method of subsidizing shipping. However, discussion of this first shipping promotion bill was not completed as the House began to confront the government on diplomatic affairs. Ultimately, the government dissolved the House on 29 December 1893.

Conclusion

The Sino-Japanese War of 1894-1895 was the great divide as far as Japan's international policy was concerned. Japan had entered the war without any clear idea of, or confidence in, the policy towards Korea and China, and the decisive and complete victory which ensued was not anticipated.[31] This military triumph is often considered as marking the beginning of Japanese imperialism in East Asia. However, while it might

---

[29] *Ibid.*, 28 July 1894.

[30] Japan, National Archive, "Classified Records of Government Documents," Book 17-34, 1893.

[31] Takahashi Hidenao, *The Road to the Sino-Japanese War* (Tokyo, 1995).

appear that the expansion of Japan's shipping interests was simply a product of this nascent imperialistic enthusiasm, various parties had put forward strong commercial reasons for the promotion of overseas shipping lines before the war.

The rationale behind these essentially economic arguments was clear. First, in the 1880s, western countries were improving and extending transport facilities, including transcontinental railways, canals, and shipping lines, so that Japanese policy-makers began, quite resonably, to anticipate great changes in the pattern of international shipping networks. Second, members of the Japanese parliament were becoming interested in shipping expansion. In December 1892, they demanded that the government should rationalize existing shipping subsidies so as to expand the overseas lines. As for shipping expansion, there was no parliamentary opposition to such a policy. Third, the NYK (Japan's largest shipping company) drew up plans for opening three major overseas lines — to Europe, the United States (Seattle), and Australia — and petitioned the government for subsidies for these lines in 1893. Fourth, the Japanese Economic Society (Nippon Keizai Kai), an influential supporter of protectionist doctrine, solicited essays "On Japanese Shipping" in 1893. While this in itself was an indication of public interest in the subject before the war, all of the essays insisted that major overseas lines should be opened within a few years, and should receive public subsidy. Fifth, at the same time, supporters of free trade expressed the view that shipping was significant commercially and therefore warranted the financial support of the government.

Accordingly, the broadly-based belief that major overseas shipping lines were commercially desirable was well established in Japan before the Sino-Japanese War. Because of its economic progress, Japan eagerly wanted to participate in the international shipping network which was then regarded as a vital infrastructure element in the process of economic development.

Cooperation and Reorganization on the North-South Routes from Japan in the Interwar Period

Mariko Tatsuki

The First World War triggered the reorganization of world shipping. Tonnage owned in Britain and the Commonwealth, as a proportion of world tonnage, declined steadily from forty-five percent in 1914 to thirty-five percent in 1927, while that of Japan and the US increased rapidly (see table 1). Due to reparations, Germany's ocean-going tonnage had fallen to zero by 1922, but thereafter it made a quick recovery to constitute a factor in world shipping once more. US shipping, on the other hand, was put under the control of the Shipping Board and liberalization was a slow process. Accordingly, Japan, whose tonnage had increased enormously during the war, emerged as the major growth point in the realignment of world shipping during the 1920s. As the volume of laid-up tonnage decreased significantly in 1926-1927, and world trade began to show signs of recovery, new routes were quickly developed, especially by Japanese shipping companies.[1]

The scale of the Japanese economy expanded enormously during the 1914-1918 conflict, with the cotton spinning industry leading the way in terms of exports. Taking advantage of the absence of previously dominant British textiles in areas such as South Asia, Africa, Australia and South America, the Japanese expanded from East Asia into these under-supplied markets at one fell swoop (see table 2). Japanese shipowners first entered the Australian and South Pacific routes when conferences lost control of these trades because of the war. Then, after 1918, the Japanese, in seeking outlets for their surplus tonnage, aggressively developed routes in areas where conferences control was weak or non-existent, most notably in the Pacific, to New Zealand, and the African-South American routes. Moreover, in line with the development of Japan's heavy and chemical industries, South Pacific services were

[1] O. Mance, *International Sea Transport* (London, 1945), 93, points out that the success of Japanese shipping in the interwar period was due largely to "efficiency and enterprising spirit" and "the competition's [Britain's] short-sighted policy."

energetically cultivated as supply routes for raw materials such as rubber, tin, iron ore and soda ash. On these routes it was possible to assign ships according to cargo movements uninhibited by conferences, so that Japan was able to import from a wider range of countries. For example, raw cotton was now imported from Brazil, Egypt and Uganda in addition to India and the US, and wool was brought in from Argentina, South Africa and New Zealand as well as from Australia. Shipping agreements were concluded with competitors when necessary, but in many cases they were nothing more than freight conferences or cargo transshipment agreements. Such agreements did not exert strong control and were generally short-lived.

Table 1
Owned Steamship Tonnage by Country

	000 grt (%)					
	1914		1919		1927	
Britain and Commonwealth Countries	20524	-45.2	18208	-38	21878	-34.6
USA	4287	-9.4	11933	-24.9	13606	-21.5
Japan	1708	-3.8	2325	-4.9	4033	-6.4
Italy	1430	-3.1	1238	-2.6	3396	-5.4
France	1922	-4.2	1962	-4.1	3362	-5.3
Germany	5135	-11.3	3247	-6.8	3320	-5.2
Norway	1957	-4.3	1597	-3.3	2803	-4.4
Netherlands	1472	-3.2	1574	-3.3	2645	-4.2
Total	45404	-100	47897	-100	63267	-100

Note: Tonnage given as of 30 June.

Source: *Lloyd's Register of Shipping*.

Table 2
Countries Importing Japanese Cotton Yarn and Cotton Textiles

¥ 000

1913			1920	1929	1932
Cotton Yarn		Cotton Yarn			
China	60096	China	81061	6651	257
Kwantung Province	3458	Kwantung Province	9125	682	670
Russian Asia	-	Manchuria	-	-	935
Hong Kong	5747	Hong Kong	28937	2120	1337
British India	987	British India	30253	13448	14343
		The Netherlands East India	-	771	1445
The Philippines	671	The Philippines	1586	687	250
South America	-	South America	66	-	-
Others	39	Others	1366	2397	2310
Total	70998	Total	152394	26756	21514
Cotton textiles (Total)	33606	Cotton textiles (Total)	334966	412707	288713
White Cotton/ Drill		China	130516	150116	37159
China	9101	Kwangtung Province	26593	15358	16108
Kwantung Province	5030	Russian Asia/ Munchuria	703	-	3263
British India	200	Hong Kong	9347	20785	3775
Russian Asia	107	British India	67289	109139	80654
Others	44	Strait Settlements	6949	5798	11229

			¥ 000		
1913			1920	1929	1932
Total	14483	The Netherlands East Indies	60466	42283	50229
		French Indo China	776	-	-
Raw Calico					
China	7262	The Philippines	6552	5629	2769
Kwantung Province	3118	Thailand	1362	3815	3339
Hong Kong	12	Britain	86	-	-
British India	368	Turkey	-	2210	5574
Russian Asia	435	USA	2207	124	264
Others	3	South America	4776	5232	3493
Total	11198	Egypt South Africa	3537	24410	27069
		Australia	10837	2927	4875
		New Zealand	1275	164	181
		Hawaii	545	148	169
		Others	1170	21512	33245

Source: *Dai-Nippon Gaikoku Boeki Nenpyo* (Annual Statistics for Japan's Foreign Trade), various years.

There was friction in numerous areas when British capital returned after the war. While China was the largest overseas market, Japanese cotton textiles had also made significant inroads into regions such as British India, the Dutch East Indies (modern Indonesia) and the Straits Settlements, as well as penetrating more distant markets like Australia, Egypt, the Philippines and Turkey. Japanese cotton exports to these countries continued to increase until around 1929, but exports to China decreased drastically. Commercial friction between Japan and India started surfacing in the late 1920s, resulting in trade restrictions imposed by the Indian Government Office in the 1930s which included successive increases in import duties, the enactment of a cotton industry protection law and, finally, the abrogation of the Japan-India Commercial Treaty in 1933. Japan and India negotiated an agreement in 1934, and this was followed by inconclusive Anglo-Japanese negotiations. As a result, Britain imposed import quotas on foreign cotton and rayon products in British Commonwealth countries and protectorates. In 1934, following the failure of Anglo-Japanese negotiations, talks took place between Japan and the Netherlands but these, too, broke down due to disagreements about shipping. These were eventually resolved by the Japan-Netherlands Shipping Agreement of 1936.[2]

After the Great Depression, competition in shipping intensified again, with German and Dutch companies entering routes that had been inaugurated by the Japanese. Such moves rendered the shipping agreements redundant, but with the outbreak of the Second World War, nations moved into wartime posture and the age of free shipping came to an end.

Taking Japan's north-south routes, especially those with Australia/New Zealand and Africa/South America, as a starting point, this chapter assesses the extent to which competition and cooperation influenced the realignment of international shipping during the interwar period.[3]

---

[2]For trade matters, see Japan Society for the Promotion of Science (ed.), *Tsushojoyaku to Tsushoseisaku* [Commercial Treaties and Commercial Policies] (Tokyo, 1951).

[3]Of the routes mentioned here, research has been conducted on the Indian and Indonesian routes in relation to the Japanese-Indian and Japanese-Dutch negotiations. See Shinya Sugiyama, "Nippon no Menseihin Yushutsu to Boekimasatsu" (Japan's Exports of Cotton Products and Trade Disputes); and Hidemasa Kokaze, "Nichiran Kaiun Masatsu to Nichiran Kaisho" (Japan-Netherlands Trade Disputes and Japan-Netherlands Negotiations), both in Shinya Sugiyama and Ian Brown (eds.), *Senkanki Tonan Ajia no Keizai Masatsu* (*Trade Disputes in South East Asia in the Interwar Period*) (Tokyo, 1994). In the Japanese-Dutch shipping negotiations, although agreement was reached to organize a pool, disputes regarding specific points were unresolved. A shipping agreement with the Netherlands was finally reached as a result of the intervention of the Japanese government, which obliged the four Japanese shipping companies to establish jointly a new company on an "investment in kind" basis to serve as a single entity representing Japanese interests in negotiations. In this process, Ishihara Sangyo, which had entered the route as a non-conference operator after heavy fighting, then had the largest share of the trade, but was forced to retire from the route because of political pressure exerted to promote negotiations with the Dutch shipping firms, which stuck to cargo reservation.

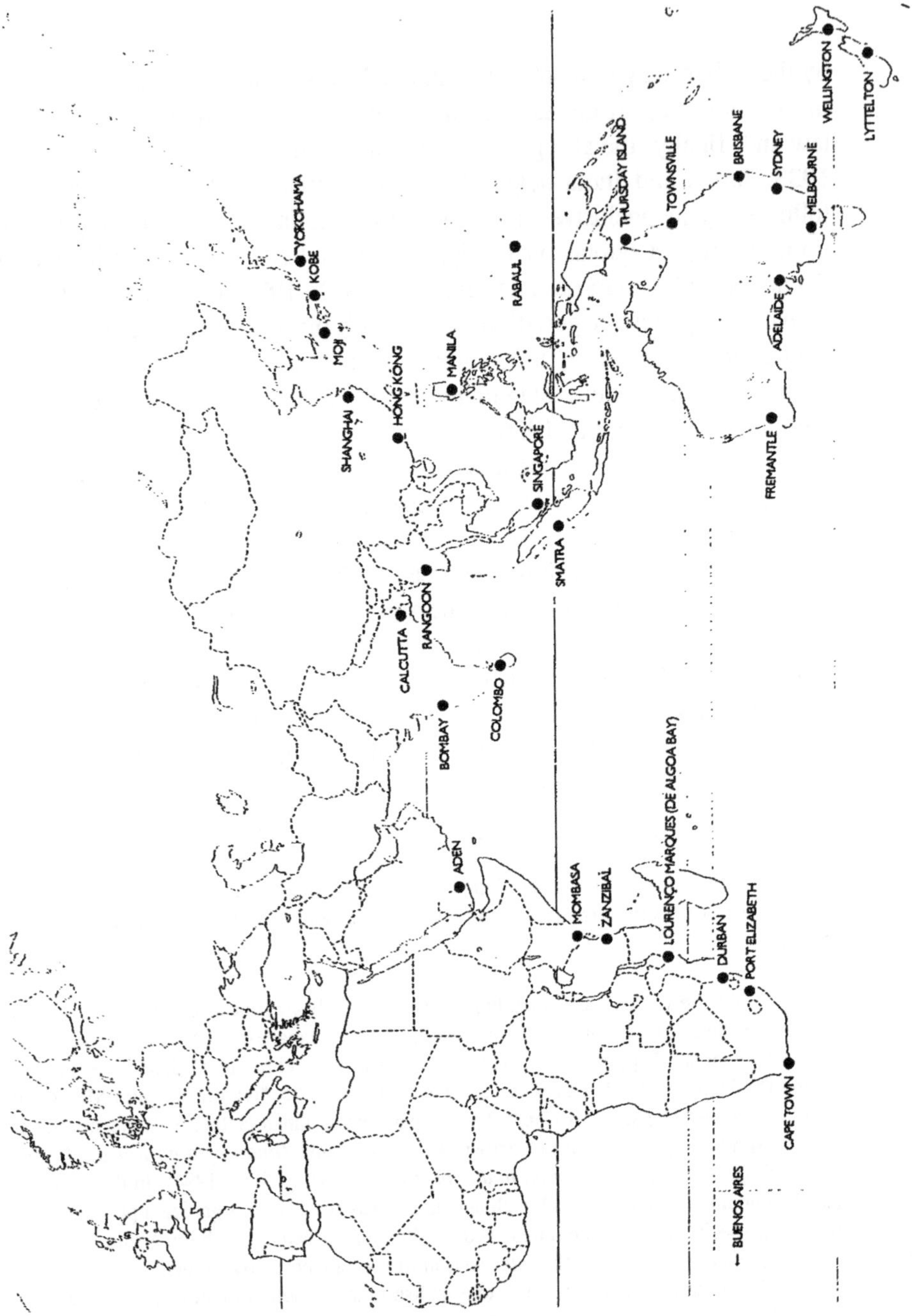

***Figure 1*:** **Indian and Western Pacific Oceans.**

***Source*:** **Courtesy of the author.**

Table 3
Operators on the Australia Routes

Opera-tors	July 1914			July 1914			December 1920			1930			December 1933		
	No. of ships	Total tonnage	Frequency	No. of ships	Total tonnage	Frequency	No. of ships	Total tonnage	Frequency	No. of ships	Total tonnage	Frequency	No. of ships	Total tonnage	Fequency
NYK	3	18109	1 per 4 weeks	3	17945	monthly	3	20821	monthly	3	18776	monthly	3	23890	monthly
OSK	-	-	-) -) -)	42	1e+08	arpprox. monthly extra									
NL	3	9659	1 per 4 weeks	-	-	-	-	-	-	-	-	-	-	-	
E&A	4	15632	1 per 3 weeks	4	14647	monthly	3	13136	monthly	3	17928	monthly	3	20881	monthly
AOL	2	4538	irregular	2	4538	bimonthly	2	4762	approx. monthly	-	-	-	-	-	-
JAL	-	-	-	-	-	-	—	-	-	3	18576	monthly	3	21703	monthly

Notes:

1) NL = Norddeutscher Lloyd (German)
E&A = Eastern & Australian S.S. (British)
AOL = Australia Orient Lines (British)
JAL - Japan Australia Line (jointly formed by Yamashita Kisen, Kokusai Kisen, and Kawasaki Kisen)

2) AOL operated between Hong Kong and Australia. B.P. and Co. and KPM operated between Singapore and Australia. In 1933, OSK's service was Japan/Australia/NeswZealand.

Source: 1930 was taken from OSK, *History of Australia and New Zealand Routes*; remainder from *Kaiun Gaikyo* (*Shipping Overview*), relevant years.

Table 4
Expansion of Japan-Australia Trade
¥000

Japan-Australia	1911	1913	1920	1925	1930	1935
Raw silk	-	-	-	1103	2783	4233
Silk fabrics	2508	1962	19703	24659	13797	6691
Cotton fabrics	166	528	10837	8297	2442	17176
Rayon fabrics	-	-	-	-	-	22306
Ceramics	204	154	2995	1032	770	2805
Toys	-	-	1243	662	350	2010
Total	8103	8638	58115	47496	25486	74793
Australia-Japan						
Wheat	212	2204	-	31243	8690	30936
Cowhide	152	17	257	0	302	2295
Wool	4024	7995	31820	96826	72336	182007
Lead	1835	2429	3029	3840	582	461
Zinc	-	138	0	6586	1983	2729
Total	7927	14943	62459	149969	94308	235149

Source: See table 2.

Competition and Cooperation on the Australia Routes

Before 1939, Australia was part of the British Empire and therefore part of a closed route network with Europe, the North American west coast and Canada. Many of the Europe-Australia routes were to Sydney and Brisbane via Cape Town and the south coast of Australia and even the routes for Melbourne and Sydney via the Suez Canal touched at Colombo and South Australia. As trade with Japan grew during and after the First World War, however, Osaka Shosen Kaisha (hereafter OSK) and other

Japanese lines entered the Australia/Japan route which had been monopolized by a conference comprising Eastern and Australian Steam Navigation Co. (hereafter E&A), Norddeutscher Lloyd (hereafter NDL) and Nippon Yusen Kaisha (hereafter NYK) (see table 3).[4] Competition was severe, but the discipline of the closed conference was maintained, largely because wool, the main inbound cargo, was controlled by the Wool Industry Association of Japan which favoured Japanese lines. E&A had to remain within the framework of the conference to maintain its revenue.

When the First World War broke out, the number of European ships assigned to the Australian waters decreased drastically, as a consequence of which the amount of trade between Japan and Australia increased rapidly, the mainstay being the inbound cargoes of wool, wheat and lead. Outbound voyages increased during the war, the principal cargoes being silk and cotton textiles, ceramic ware and timber (see table 4). It was this increase in cargo volume which tempted OSK and Taiyo Kaiun to enter the route in 1916 and 1918, respectively, and led the Australian Oriental Line to switch from the tramp services of its China Navigation days to liner services operating every two months. OSK had despatched the *Ruson Maru* on the route on a test basis to ascertain the feasibility of inaugurating a liner service in 1912, when Japan-Australia trade had begun to show a gradual increase. Four years later, influenced by the results of local market research, and taking advantage of wartime factors, notably trade expansion, the withdrawal of NDL, and E&A's disposal of vessels as it contracted to provide tramp services with just two ships, the company opened a direct route from Japan to Australia. OSK believed that a direct service, with its merit of shorter turn-around, would be to its advantage, since a number of liner and tramp ships of other companies were operating between Australia and Hong Kong. Until then, the Australian route conference had been virtually monopolized by NYK, but now keen competition started between NYK and OSK. Initially, NYK's intention was to do all in its power to prevent OSK from entering the route, the measures it took being identical to those of the traditional British conference — deferred rebates, reductions in freight rates and so

[4]NYK had entered the Australian route in October 1896 when commissioned to do so by Japan's Ministry of Communications, which paid annual subsidies to the company. At that time, E&A and China Navigation Co. (which later became Australian Oriental Line) were competing on the route. NYK complied with the freight agreement between the two companies and later joined the conference.

on.[5] However, partly due to E&A's temporary suspension of operations due to requisitioning, there was a shortage of tonnage which worked to OSK's advantage. An agreement was reached between OSK and NYK in March 1918, by which NYK had the right to sail once every two weeks and OSK once every four weeks. It was also agreed that the introduction of extra ships would be discussed when appropriate. With this agreement, OSK's membership of the Australian conference became an established fact.[6] In 1918, NYK despatched twelve liners and twenty-eight extra ships, while OSK undertook fifteen voyages, twelve by liners and three by extra ships.

After the war, rivalry again occurred, with the established conference members consisting of NYK and OSK, and Taiyo Kaiun the newcomer. Taiyo Kaiun, established in 1917, was a liner company with no ships of its own. It was a kind of NVOCC which developed liner routes exclusively on a chartering basis. One of the main shippers of Taiyo Kaiun was Masuda Gomei, a second-class *Sogo Shosha*. Noticing the rapid increase of cargo volume on the Australian route, the company established a route to Sydney and Melbourne, the first ship leaving Kobe in May 1918. At that time there was an enormous accumulation of cargoes which NYK and OSK were not able to handle, while freight charges had soared as a result of the NYK-OSK agreement.[7] When Taiyo Kaiun asked

---

[5]OSK sent a ship to Europe in 1915 and again in 1916, in line with its plan to enter European trade. NYK granted deferred rebates to its shippers to lower its freight rates to the same level as those of OSK to secure the loyalty of its shippers on the Australian route. In addition, NYK prevented OSK from obtaining cargoes by threatening shippers that it would refuse them space to Europe if they shipped cargoes with OSK. See *Osaka Shosen Hachijunenshi* (*The Eighty Years' History of Osaka Shosen*) (Osaka, 1966); and *Nippon Yusen Kaisha Nanajunenshi* (*The Seventy Years' History of Nippon Yusen Kaisha*) (Tokyo, 1956), 72-75.

[6]While it is not clear exactly when OSK joined the conference, it may be assumed that the fact of having concluded an agreement with NYK, the only liner company in the conference, would mean automatic acceptance. OSK, *Goshu-Nyujirando Koroshi* (*History of the Australia and New Zealand Routes*) (Tokyo, 1941) 46.

[7]Per ton freight rates of the outbound cargo rose from Y17.94 in January-June, 1917 to Y26.33 in July-December, 1917, ¥52.01 in January-June 1918 and ¥71.07 in July-December, 1918. However, they fell sharply to ¥22.85 in January-June, 1919, after Taiyo Kaiun's entrance to the route as a result of the termination of the war. OSK, *History of the Australian and New Zealand Routes*, 67.

NYK if it could join the conference, the approach was rejected. Early in 1919, Taiyo Kaiun challenged the two companies. As a result, while inbound tariffs were favourable, the outbound tariff never recovered from the sharp decline. In the meantime, it seemed likely that P&O would soon acquire E&A, this in fact happening in the following year. NYK and OSK judged that continued competition among Japanese ships would be to their disadvantage and, accordingly, formal approval was given for Taiyo Kaiun to join the conference in September 1919. Taiyo Kaiun, however, suspended its Australian liner operations in the summer of 1920 after the bankruptcy of Masuda Trading Co., the company's biggest charterer.[8]

Noticing that inbound voyages on the Australian route were performing well, Yamashita Kisen opened the Pacific triangle route which linked the outbound voyages of the North American route with Australia. In fact, the company had operated tramps to transport coal from Newcastle to Singapore and Penang in the preceding year to sound out the chances of opening a new route. However, the service did not prove profitable because the company was unable to obtain cargoes such as wool and general goods, which were controlled by the conference. With regard to wool, in particular, the main cargo on the Australian route, the conference had signed a shipping agreement with the Wool Industry Association of Japan in September 1922, which included a special deferred rebate arrangement. Consequently, Yamashita Kisen temporarily suspended services on the route. When reopening services in 1923, the company applied to join the conference, but its application was rejected. The company retaliated by assigning non-conference ships in concert with Kawasaki Kisen and Kokusai Kisen.[9] The conference countered this by

[8]Taiyo Kaiun, *Gojunen no Koseki* (*The Fifty Years' History*) (Kobe, 1967), 63-69 and 101-109.

[9]*Kawasaki Kisen Gojunenshi* (*The Fifty Years' History of Kawasaki Kisen*) (Kobe, 1969), 363-364 and Yamashita Shinnihon Kisen, *Shashi — Gappeiyori Jugonen* (*Company History — Fifteen Years from Merger*), (Tokyo, 1980), 419-420. It should be noted that at the request of a British shipper who was dissatisfied with the revised freight rates of the Australia/Europe Conference, Kawasaki Kisen accepted its entire cargo at twenty percent less than the conference tariff. This was a great shock for Australia and Britain. This service was discontinued after two sailings due to cancellation by the shipper, who was incurring criticism. Kawasaki Kisen also chose to avoid a clash with P&O, the parent company of E&A. But the company competed keenly with the Australia-Japan conference over a period of eighteen months.

adding a cash rebate to the deferred rebate, resulting in a sharp fall in freight rates (see table 5). After two years of fighting, the three companies were admitted to the conference in November 1925 and jointly formed the Japan Australia Line (JAL) (see table 6). However, since the shippers of Australian wool were members of the Wool Industry Association of Japan, E&A was in a disadvantageous position with regard to cargo booking and its actual loading rate was always below the pool point. As was demonstrated by the 1927 results, in which the shares were eight percent for E&A, twenty-seven percent for JAL, thirty percent for OSK and thirty-five percent for NYK,[10] E&A's account with the pool was always on the receiving side.

Table 5
Trends in Contract Freight of Japan's Wool Imports
(Greasy Wool)

Pence/Pound

Period	Freight Rates	Cash Rebate	Deferred Rebate	Total Rebate	Net Freight
Oct. 1922-Sept. 1923	1-1/4	10%	10%	30%	0.875
Oct. 1923-Sept. 1924	1-1/4	10	10	30	0.875
Oct. 1924-Sept. 1925	1-1/4	40	10	50	0.625
Oct. 1925-Sept. 1926	1-1/4	40	10	50	0.625
Oct. 1926-Sept. 1927	1-1/4	35	10	50	0.6875
Oct. 1927-Sept. 1928	1-1/4	45	0	45	0.6875
Oct. 1928-Sept. 1929	1-1/4	52	0	52	0.6
Oct. 1929-Sept. 1930	1-1/4	53	5	58	0.525
Oct. 1930-Sept. 1935	1-1/4	53	5	58	0.525
Oct. 1935-Sept. 1937	35922	15	5	20	0.5
Oct. 1937-Sept. 1940	35857	15	5	20	0.6
Oct. 1940-Sept. 1941	¥4.30		¥0.20	¥0.20	¥4.10

Source: OSK, *History of the Australia and New Zealand Routes*, 72-73.

---

[10]*The Fifty Years' History of Kawasaki Kisen*, 364.

Table 6
Trends in Wool Pool Points

Pence/Pound

Round	Period	Contribution	E&A	JAL	OSK	NYK
1st	Nov. 1925-Apr. 1926	35%	12.5	12.5	27	45
	May 1926-Oct. 1926		12.5	14.7	31.7	41.1
	Nov. 1926-Apr. 1927		12.5	18.3	29.1	40.1
	May 1927-Oct. 1927		12.5	24.3	26.4	36.8
2nd	Nov. 1927-Nov. 1929	35%	16	16	27.6	38.4
3rd	Nov. 1929-Nov. 1931	35%	15	22	30	23
4th	Nov. 1931-Nov. 1993	50%	19	27	27	27
5th	Nov. 1933-Nov. 1935	50%	20	26-2/3	26-2/3	26-2/3
	Nov. 1935-Nov. 1937	50%	21.4	Rough estimates based on results		
6th	Jul. 1938-Jun. 1940	50%	22.5	25-5/6	25-5/6	25-5/6
7th	Jul. 1940-Jun. 1942	50%	-	33-1/3	33-1/3	33-1/3

Source: OSK, *History of Australia and New Zealand Routes*, 80-81.

When the Labor Party assumed power in Australia in late 1929, it decided to raise duties on Japanese imports. Later, in May 1936, as the Australian government again imposed prohibitively high duties on Japanese imports, the Japanese government sought to prevent Australian imports by passing a law to protect Australian trade.[11] The Japan-Australia Trade Agreement was formally concluded in July 1938. Meanwhile, E&A demanded that its point level be raised, taking advantage of the complications of the Japan-Australia trade agreement. With the general goods pool, however, the Japanese companies insisted that the E&A's point level be reduced to twenty percent, resulting in a breakdown of negotiations with E&A which was insisting on equality, a claim based in part on the Australian government's intervention. With the outbreak of the Sino-Japanese War in 1937, followed by the war in Europe in 1939, the situation was becoming increasingly tense and negotiations within the conference were difficult. However, E&A stopped the operations of its liner services north of Hong Kong in February 1941, and the wool pool was discontinued in June 1940. Instead, a pool of equal shares was organized by the three Japanese shipping companies. When trade with Australia ceased due to the freezing of Japanese assets by the US and Britain, so did the liner services of the three companies, whose wool pool and general goods pool also stopped working.

During this period, there was also keen competition among Japanese operators. E&A and NYK, which possessed high pool-point levels as original members of the conference, were on the receiving side in both pools. In contrast, OSK and JAL, which entered later, were always on the deficit side in their accounts with the pools (see table 7).

Rationalization and Route Extension to New Zealand

After the First World War, Japanese trampers entered the liner routes, which were suffering from excess tonnage and declining freight rates. Though established lines tried to protect the conference and oust the interlopers, competition became severe and revenue declined. In the late 1920s OSK, which depended on cargo rather than passenger revenue, began to rationalize its ships and operations. The New Zealand route was one of the lines opened as a result of this policy.

---

[11]The loading ratio of British shipping was decreased after the First World War. In the British Commonwealth, it was eighty-five percent in 1912, and became fifty-six percent in 1929 and seventy-seven percent in 1936. Between Commonwealth and foreign countries, it was fifty-five percent in 1912 and thirty-eight percent in 1936. The total ratio of fifty-two percent in 1912 fell to forty percent in 1936. See S.G. Sturmey, *British Shipping and World Competition* (London, 1962), 89.

Table 7
Settlement of Pool Accounts

Company	Wool Pool			General Goods Pool		
	Amount Paid	Amount Received	Difference	Amount Paid	Amount Received	Difference
NYK	315952	757902	+441,949	67977	378893	+310,917
E&A	163929	752732	+588,803	33518	587396	+553,878
OSK	247649	245007	-2642	531378	4158	-527220
JAL	1144413	116303	-1028110	483164	145589	-337575

Note: Period of the wool pool for inbound voyages was from November 1925 to end of June 1940, and that of the general goods pool for outbound voyages was from December 1933 to end of June.

Source: OSK, *History of Australia and New Zealand Routes*, 83-84 and 88.

The Australian route was operated by three liner companies, NYK, E&A and NDL, before 1914. As the volume of trade at the time was not very large, they had a relatively large number of ports of call. However, during the war, when OSK and Taiyo Kaiun entered the route one after the other, the volume of direct cargo between Japan and Australia was increasing. OSK aimed at shortening the turn-around by careful selection of ports of call. It initially went direct to Brisbane from Moji, the last port of call in Japan, taking twenty-five days to sail between the two ports, roughly nine days shorter than the competition. Japan Australia Line also took a short route, calling only at Yokohama, Nagoya, Kobe, Brisbane and various minor Australian ports, and Adelaide. To counter this, NYK and E&A also made efforts to improve their speed, so that by 1930 the transit time between the Japanese ports and Brisbane was twenty-four days for NYK, twenty-nine days for E&A, and twenty-two days for JAL. While the ships assigned to the route by OSK and JAL had been built in the closing days of the war, those assigned by NYK and E&A were more than twenty years old.

This situation changed remarkably when OSK shortened the Kobe-Sydney transit time to nineteen days by putting into service three newly built, high-speed diesel ships of the *Sydney Maru* type from the end of 1929 (see appendix 1). As a result, a considerable volume of cargo on the

Japan-Australia route was absorbed by OSK.[12] Not only did OSK exceed NYK in the volume of wool it loaded, but its freight revenues had also been increasing since 1930, while those of NYK had been declining (see appendix 2). Severe competition over transit time then commenced between OSK, NYK, JAL and E&A. Naturally, companies other than OSK also took measures to cope with this situation so that the quality of ships assigned to the Australian route improved rapidly.[13] NYK's freight revenues, however, continued to be less than the growth rate of the Japan-Australia trade, and the company never recovered its previous share.

The New Zealand route changed more than the Australia route essentially because of the intensification of competition on the Australia route. This was because OSK transferred the surplus time generated by increased speeds to the New Zealand route. As for routes between New Zealand and Australia, the Union S.S. Co. of New Zealand, a subsidiary of P&O, was providing the main liner services (see table 8). The only transit ports for cargoes to and from Japan and the Far East were Honolulu and Sydney, while freight rates between Australia and New Zealand were extremely high as the Union had a monopoly on the route (see table 9). After the opening of the OSK's New Zealand route,

[12]OSK, *History of the Australia and New Zealand Routes*. Shortened turn-around not only enabled OSK to increase its loading volume of Australian wool relative to NYK but also to make up for the decrease in Australian cargoes by New Zealand cargoes, resulting in increases of thirteen percent in loading tons and twenty-five percent in freight revenues. On the other hand, assignment of diesel ships reduced sailing expenses, including cost of crew, so that the profitability of the route improved remarkably. This point has been analyzed by M. Tatsuki, "Kaiunfukyo to Teikisen no Gorika — Osaka Shosen no Kesu" (Shipping Recession and Rationalization of Liners — the Case of Osaka Shosen), *Shakai Keizaishigaku* (*Socio-Economic History*), II, No. 3 (1986).

[13]NYK put a new ship on the European route in 1930. Taking this opportunity, the company gradually converted three large, high-speed cargo-passenger vessels for the Australia route, resulting in simultaneous improvements in speed and space. See "List of Ships Acquired after the Establishment of the Company" provided in *The Seventy Years' History of NYK* , 678-686. In 1933, JAL put the 13,065-dwt *Tamon Maru* on this route. This vessel, considered to be the largest freighter in Japan at the time, was chartered from Hachiuma Kisen. See *The Fifty Years' History of Kawasaki Kisen*, 92-93. E&A also made some improvements by placing into service the 7000-dwt *Nankin* to replace the 4000-dwt *St. Alban*. These figures are the author's estimates based on the difference between the number of ships in service in 1930 according to the *History of the Australia and New Zealand Routes* and the number in service in 1933 mentioned in the *Report on Shipping and Economy*.

commodities such as timber from Hokkaido and ceramic ware, which had hitherto been exported to Australia, were now directed to New Zealand, with cargoes on the return voyage consisting of wool and dairy products (Casein). Thus, it was not until OSK extended its route to New Zealand that a fully-fledged Japan-New Zealand trade could begin.

Table 8
Operators of the Australia/New Zealand Services (1933)

Operators	Flag	No. of ships	Total GRT	No. of Sailings	Calling Ports
OSK	Japanese	3	16273	monthly	(Japanese ports/) Brisbane/Sydney/ Melbourne/Well-ington/Auckland
Union	British	4	24249	monthly	Vancouver/Auck-land/Wellington/ Lyttelton/Mel-bourne/Sydney
O&O	US	6	123761	once or twice a month	(Seattle/) Auck-land/Wellington/ Melbourne/Sydney
The Oceanic	US	2	36034	once every four weeks	(San Francisco/Los Angeles/) Auck-land/Sydney/Mel-bourne

Note: OSK = Osaka Shosen Kaisha
Union = Union S.S. Co. of New Zealand
O&O = Oceanic & Oriental N. Co.
The Oceanic = The Oceanic S.S. Co.

Source: NYK, *Report on Shipping and Economy*, latter half of 1933.

In early 1932, as a result of a fall in the exchange rate following Japan's prohibition of gold exports, together with Australia's reduced import duties, trade with Australia showed a remarkable recovery both in exports and imports, resulting in a shortage of tonnage. Trade with New Zealand likewise began to grow rapidly from 1933, while that between the Far East and New Zealand had also been increasing gradually, carried in OSK's vessels. Taking this opportunity, some companies were thought to have been planning to extend their routes to New Zealand. These included KPM, which provided services between Singapore, Batavia and Adelaide, and A&O, which operated between Hong Kong and Melbourne, as well as P&O and NDL. However, before any of them realized their plans, British India established a route between Calcutta and New Zealand ports in 1935, providing three sailings a year (March, July and November),[14] while the Japan-New Zealand route was opened by Yamashita Kisen and then by OSK before the end of 1936. Until then, Yamashita Kisen had been assigning ships to Australian waters as a member of JAL. However, in 1929 it purchased twelve 9100-ton reciprocating ships from Kokusai Kisen and developed a succession of liner routes from 1933 onward. One such was the New Zealand route which was opened in December 1935.[15] The New Zealand route had been under the control of the Australian conference, and OSK's extension to New Zealand was inaugurated with the conference's approval. However, the ships assigned by Yamashita Kisen to its direct route to New Zealand were non-conference ships. Although the majority of the conference was aware of the disadvantages of starting a fight against Yamashita Kisen, member firms did not easily agree upon granting formal permission as there were conflicts of interests between them which were also associated with the revision of the pool agreement. It was not until March 1936 that the outward voyage alone was approved on condition that JAL should withdraw its demand for an increase in the number of sailings. The conference approved wool on inbound voyages in November 1936, using the opportunity of the revision of its shipping agreement with the Japan Wool Industry Association.[16] On the other hand, OSK had already started building two large, high-speed ships in 1934 for deployment on the Australian route, and it now planned to operate a service to New Zealand via Java with three conventional ships of the *Sydney Maru* type.

---

[14]Yamashita Shinnihon Kisen, *History of the Company*, 451-453, 456-459.

[15]NYK, *Report on Shipping and Economy*, second half of 1935.

[16]OSK, *History of the Australia and New Zealand Routes*, 127-132. It should be noted that Yamashita Kisen handled all of JAL's practical business, including cargo booking, so that shippers believed that the ships on the New Zealand route were also conference ships. This is thought to be the reason why the conference found it difficult to apply sanctions against them (invalidation of deferred rebate).

Table 9
Japan-New Zealand Freight Charges
(Pound/40 cubic feet)

	1929			1932	
	Japan-Sydney	Sydney New Zealand	Total	Japan-Sydney	Japan-New Zealand
General Goods	60	47.6	107.6	72	110.6
Cotton Textiles	50	47.6	97.6	55	93.6
Ceramic Wares	45	47.6	92.6	50	70

Source: OSK, *History of Australia and New Zealand Routes*, 68, 169 and 245.

Table 10
OSK's Freight Revenue from the New Zealand Service
(¥000)

	Extension from Australia	Direct Service	Total	Freight Revenue from Conference Cargoes	
				OSK	YKK
1930	78		78		
1931	477		477		
1932	710		710		
1933	1460		1460		
1934	1901		1901		
1935	1631		1631		
1936	1812	702	2514		
1937	158	2658	2815	1701	1637
1938	271	992	1263	933	1081
1939	861	-	861	438	608
1940	506	11	11	244	261

Source: OSK, *History of the Australia and New Zealand Routes*, 234 and 248-251.

Table 11
Composition of New Zealand Trade by Country (Percent)

Destination	UK	Canada	India	Australia	Commonwealth Total	Germany	Japan	US	Netherlands East Indies
Export									
1929	73.6	6.1	0.7	4.3	85.4	2.2	0.8	6.5	0
1930	80.1	5.7	0.9	3.5	91	0.9	0.3	4.7	0
1931	88	0.7	0.2	3.3	92.9	0.9	0.8	2.7	0
1932	88	0.7	0.2	4.1	93.7	0.8	0.7	1.9	0
1933	86	1.4	0.1	3.4	91.5	0.9	0.9	2.9	0
1934	81.6	1.5	0.1	4	87.8	2	1.8	2.6	0
1935	83.6	1.4	0.1	3.8	89.8	0.4	0.9	5.3	0
1936	80.2	2	0.2	3.3	86.3	0.5	2.7	5.1	0
Import									
1929	46.2	9.8	1.6	6.7	67.8	1.9	1.3	19.1	2.4
1930	47.6	9	1.5	6.8	68.4	2.3	1.3	17.8	1.9
1931	50.1	5.1	1.6	7.8	69.5	2.4	1.3	16	3.5
1932	51	4.5	1.6	9.6	71.1	2.1	1.9	14.6	3.5
1933	51.3	4.9	2.3	10	73.4	1.8	2.6	11.6	3.9
1934	50.4	6.7	2.1	10.3	73.8	1.5	2.7	12	4.4
1935	50.4	6.8	1.6	10.9	73.3	1.5	3	12.5	4
1936	49.5	7.5	1.3	11.2	73	1.7	3	12.5	3.9

Source: United Nations, *Yearbook of International Trade Statistics* (1950).

With the opening of Japan-New Zealand routes by OSK and Yamashita Kisen, the monthly capacity amounted to 14,500 tons, comprising OSK's 5400 tons and Yamashita Kisen's 9100. This was almost a twenty-fold increase on the days of the extended route, when 9000 tons were carried annually on outbound voyages and 7000 tons on inbound voyages. Although trade between Japan and New Zealand doubled for two years in a row in 1936 and 1937, there was still an undeniable excess tonnage. In order to avoid needless competition, the two companies formed a pool for general goods and wool on the outbound and inbound voyages in January 1937. Taking into consideration the fact that Yamashita Kisen was at the time pressing hard upon OSK, the purpose of the pool was to enable the latter to restrain the former. Based on the results of the previous year when OSK was slightly ahead of its rival, the contribution was seventy percent and pool points were fifty percent each.[17] The new ship was requisitioned in July 1937 due to the outbreak of the Sino-Japanese War, which made it necessary for the *Sydney Maru* to be allocated to the Australia route. The company now had no choice but to extend from Australia in order to maintain its liner service to New Zealand. Under these circumstances, it was agreed between OSK and Yamashita Kisen that, starting from February 1938, the number of sailings should be reduced to four in three months for the two companies combined, and that operation would be on an alternate basis. In December 1937, the New Zealand government introduced an exchange/import licensing system, by which it restricted Japanese cotton and rayon fabrics, which were Japan's major export items, to a half of the previous level, while restrictions on commodities such as ceramic wares were so severe as to be almost prohibitive. This was followed by an embargo on wool exports based on the country's agreement with Britain, its suzerain, on the wool control system, which delivered a disastrous blow to trade with Japan. Consequently, the service was reduced to once every two months for the two companies combined in 1940.[18]

Trade with New Zealand was never very great in terms of absolute quantity. Although it had increased, it remained at around ten percent of trade with Australia. But cargoes carried on the direct service included many high-paying goods such as wool, cotton and rayon fabrics

[17] *Ibid.*, 224-231.

[18] *Ibid.*, 28-29, 120-127 and 132.

and general goods such as ceramic wares. In 1936, immediately after the opening of the direct route, the freight revenues rose to nearly a half of those on the Australia route. In the following year, the freight revenues on the two routes were almost equal, due to Australia's trade restrictions (see table 10 and appendix 2). However, as mentioned above, in the period that followed, in which the bloc's economy was strengthened, it was not easy to erode even a small portion of the extremely large shares that Britain and the British Empire had in the New Zealand trade (see table 11). In addition, because New Zealand was the final destination of the voyage from Japan, it was rather difficult, from the business point of view, to maintain the route's independence, although this does not apply exactly in the case of the OSK's extended Australia route. It seems that this situation was not very different for British India. That is, although it should have been less affected by the trade restriction, as it was within the British bloc, its New Zealand service was never increased to more than three voyages a year.

OSK's African East Coast Route and Competition with British and Dutch Liners

The African east coast route was a new line which contributed much to Japan's trade with Africa. Before the First World War, Japanese ships seldom called at African ports other than those in North Africa. Trade between Japan and South Africa (Cape Town) was transshipped at Singapore, Bombay or London and commodities were carried from these ports to subsequent destinations by various British shipping firms and their associates. These were: from Singapore, by Bank Line, an associate of Andrew Weir and Co.; from Bombay, by British India, an associate of P&O; from Colombo, by Andrew Weir and Co. and Buraad King (which was later acquired by the former); and from London, by Furness, Houlder Brothers and Co., an associate of the Withy and Co. and Ellerman and Bucknell, an associate of Ellerman. Such trade was characterized by long passage times and high freight rates. Naturally, there had been no significant increase in business for a long time. However, when British and German imports stopped as a result of the war, Japanese exports increased rapidly. Seizing this opportunity, OSK's ship called at Cape Town, Port Elizabeth and Durban on its voyage to South America in 1916. Subsequently, NYK opened a South American east coast route in 1917. This was just at the time when, of all Japanese import items, wool imports were showing a remarkable increase (see table 12). The main outward cargoes included rice from Hong Kong and cotton products from Japan, with wool the staple of the inbound voyage.[19] Thereafter, trade between Japan and South Africa began to grow rapidly. After the war, wool imports from South Africa almost stopped, but Japanese exports such as cotton textiles showed steady growth (see table 2).

Encouraged by local market research,[20] and with a fair prospect of obtaining route subsidies from the Ministry of Communications, OSK inaugurated the African East Coast route in March 1926. The main ports of call were Kobe, Hong Kong, Singapore, Colombo, Mombasa and various East African ports, and Durban. Initially, as it remained the custom to conduct transit transactions via Bombay, banking services for African exports were scarce, so that direct trade with Africa was slow to spread. Moreover, as Japan was taking measures to raise exchange rates for the purpose of removing the gold embargo at the previous rate, Japan's exports were sluggish in the latter half of the 1920s. As a result, there were more cargoes from intermediate ports than from Japan itself, and it was not until 1927 that direct trade between Japan and East Africa began to increase.[21]

---

[19]OSK, *Nanbei Koroshi* (*History of the South American Routes*), 23-24; and OSK, *Afurika Koroshi* (*History of the African Routes*) (inhouse material, 1941), 1-4.

[20]While staying in Calcutta to negotiate OSK's admittance to the Japan-Culcutta Conference, Sennosuke Fujisawa obtained information about Africa (numerous Indian merchants were active in there) and became aware of the importance of East Africa as the destination of a new liner service that OSK could develop independently. He noticed that Japanese cotton textiles and general goods were being re-exported to East Africa from Bombay by Indian merchants on British India ships at high freight charges. On the other hand, there were Ugandan cotton and soda ash and jute from Zaire that could be exported to Japan. OSK, *Bonbei/Karukatta Koroshi* (*History of the Bombay/Calcutta Routes*) (Tokyo, 1941).

[21]Sennosuke Fujisawa, "Chosahokoku" (Investigation Report), Mitsui OSK, *Sogyo Hyakunenshi* (*Centenary History*), 216-219 (written by the author). *Chicago Maru, Canada Maru, Mexico Maru,* and *Panama Maru* were re-assigned to the East African route from the Puget Sound route. At that time, four 9700-ton, class A-type ships completed in 1920, including *Arizona Maru*, were assigned to the Puget Sound route, but as competition intensified, two more ships of the 9500-ton class were added while the above-mentioned four ships built in 1910 for this route were re-assigned. See OSK, *Hokubeikoroshi* (*History of the North American Routes*) (Tokyo, 1925).

Table 12
Japan's Wool Imports
¥000

	Australia	Argentina	South Africa	Total
1914	8121	-	-	14784
1917	30877	2831	18593	51813
1920	31820	2515	73119	121629
1925	96826	-	536	121074
1930	72336	621	19	73610
1935	182007	612	1872	191761

Source: See table 2.

It was its agreement with KPM that helped OSK to acquire cargoes at intermediate ports such as Singapore and Colombo. OSK established a branch office in Singapore in 1918 and energetically developed routes around Java, where there was a shortage of tonnage resulting from the requisitioning of KPM ships. These new routes were the Sumatra and Java/Bangkok routes. Owing to the postwar recession, however, the income did not cover the expenses on these routes. In 1919, OSK and KPM agreed upon transshipment of each other's cargoes and issuing through bills of lading, and OSK's Sumatra route was abolished. With the existence of this agreement, OSK cargoes transshipped by KPM amounted to 1,000 tons annually, and were made up of tea and rattan for South Africa from Java, as well as sugar and tea for East Africa, and cloves from Zanzibar for Java on the inbound voyage. These cargoes contributed to the earnings of the African east coast route together with rice and machine oil from Singapore and rice from Rangoon. NYK's South American route also included Mombasa as a port of call on the outbound voyage. KPM inaugurated the Java-South East African route in 1930, thereby plunging into fully-fledged competition with OSK on all the relevant routes including that between Java and Japan. This was the beginning of the competition which culminated in the Japanese-Dutch shipping negotiations. On the South East African route, KPM accepted cargoes at a rate lower than the Singapore transshipment rate, so that OSK suffered severe losses of cargo from the intermediate ports. In addition, the Bank Line inaugurated both a Rangoon/Calcutta/ Durban/Cape Town route and a Hong Kong/Bangkok/Cape Town route to transport rice, teak and general goods. Natal Direct Line (Buraad, King and Co.), which was based in Colombo, also started to collect rice and timbers from Rangoon and Calcutta. Furthermore, from around 1929, Japan's Yamashita Kisen operated tramp ships carrying rice, timber and other goods from Saigon and Singapore to South Africa. Thus, competition on the African routes suddenly intensified (see appendix 3).[22]

Under these circumstances, an extensive route agreement, referred to as the "cooperative" agreement, was reached between NYK and OSK in April 1931 after the two companies returned unfavourable business results.[23] As a consequence, the Japan-South American East Coast route, and the Japan-South East African route came to be monopolized by OSK. In 1931, however, trade with South America became more active and the number of emigrants bound for Brazil increased, which in turn reduced cargo space in the cargo-passenger ships. Movements of cargo in the Japan-Africa trade also started to become active at the beginning of 1932. To cope with these situations, extra ships were assigned to the African route, while in the case of ships operating on the South American route, priority was given to direct cargoes between South America and Japan. In January 1934, OSK concluded an agreement with Kawasaki Kisen and Kokusai Kisen, with Yamashita Kisen joining the arrangement in May. Under this agreement, the outbound voyages of the three companies were entrusted to OSK for the transport of export cargoes, thereby enabling it to extend this route to South America.

Competition between OSK, KPM and other lines intensified in the latter half of the 1930s. Together with the South American route, OSK also took over from NYK its agreement with Rio Cape Line, an associate of Furness Withy and Co., regarding the transportation of coffee between Brazil and South Africa. In 1917, when NYK began operating ships on the South American route that sailed via South Africa on both the outbound and inbound voyages, the Rio Cape Line, which was on the point of being abolished due to financial difficulties, secured twenty-five

---

[22]OSK, *History of the African Routes*; and NYK, *Report on Shipping and Economy*, second half of 1933.

[23]OSK, *History of the South American Routes*, 256-279.

percent of coffee freight from NYK in exchange for its withdrawal from the route. The same contract was concluded by OSK in June 1931. However, when NDL (Nord Deutscher Lloyd) opened a monthly service between Buenos Aires and Durban in 1934 and began coffee transportation, and as coffee from Kenya and Java began to flow into the South African markets at around the same time, OSK's loading of Brazilian coffee decreased. OSK requested cancellation of the agreement on the occasion of its renewal in 1936, but in the end the agreement was continued with Rio's share reduced to twelve percent. The agreement between KPM and OSK was not renewed after 1931. Using JCJL's Manila-Java route, KPM started a Philippines-South Africa through service in 1931 at a lower freight rate than the Hong Kong-South Africa conference rate. It also entered the African market based on a through service agreement with NDL. OSK countered this with the cooperation of Bank Line. When KPL further extended its service to Hong Kong and Shanghai in 1935, it gave rise to heated competition with OSK. The Bank Line sent twelve or thirteen vessels to South Africa from Calcutta, Rangoon and Hong Kong, of which three or four were deployed to South America. In 1934, Andrew Weir, Bank's managing owner, acquired the Natal Line, which owned a route parallel to Bank's, and renamed it the Indian Natal Line. Bank Line and Indian Natal Line reached a service agreement by which two separate lines were established; one was the India Natal Line, which was a direct service to South Africa from Calcutta and Colombo, and the other was the India African Line for Calcutta, Rangoon, Colombo and South East Africa. Each line provided a once-a-regular monthly service, of which two to three sailings annually were extended to South Africa.

After the outbreak of war in Europe in 1939, Britain introduced a navigation certification system through which it obliged shipowners of the neutral countries to transport British necessities and to provide sailing information, and refused to issue a ship's warrant to owners who did not agree. As they belonged to countries hostile to Britain, OSK and NDL suffered disadvantages such as delays in supplies of water, oil and coal as well as in customs and clearance formalities, not only in South and East Africa but also in Colombo and Singapore. In addition, letters of credit from British banks were not issued to OSK and NDL's shippers, depressing trade. As a result, NDL was forced to suspend its services at the end of 1939, and OSK in 1941.[24] On this route, the freedom of shipping was again curtailed by war.

Conclusion

World shipping in the period before 1914 was dominated by latitudinal routes operated by British shipowners. The only non-Western shipping firms that entered these route networks were Japan's NYK and OSK. The NYK ran the national flag fleet and had made an early entrance into the business in the 1890s. With these advantages, it had established itself as a conference and developed operations more or less in the British style; thus, NYK concentrated on passenger ship operation rather than cargo transportation, was eager to protect closed conferences against other Japanese newcomers, and obtained good results. Meanwhile, the basis of OSK's operations was initially its short sea services to China and Formosa. In an effort to expand into deep sea routes as a latecomer, it fought strenuously against conferences on each of the routes it attempted to enter, and was admitted only when it had accepted more unfavourable conditions than had NYK. For this reason, after the First World War, when it had accumulated sufficient reserves, it began to expand its sailing rights through the energetic development of new routes in longitudinal directions. This situation was common to other Japanese trampers such as Kawasaki Kisen, Kokusai Kisen, Yamashita Kisen and the Shipping Department of Mitsui and Co.

Facilitating such developments was the reduction in costs accruing from the deployment of diesel-powered ships. These enabled operators to challenge the competition with lower freight rates while at the same time improving services. Diesel ships had become more numerous since the end of the First World War, and underwent a construction boom from about 1924 when there were signs of market recovery. Scandinavian shipowners began to make use of these large, high-speed motor ships, and some British companies placed them on round-the-world services.

---

[24]OSK, *History of the African Routes*; OSK, *History of the South American Routes*; and NYK, *Report on Shipping and Economy*, second halves of 1929, 1933 and 1936.

Japanese shipowners promptly followed suit, especially OSK (see table 13).[25]

Table 13
Japanese Shipping Companies' Ownership of Diesel Ships (1927)
Number of Ships and Gross Tonnage

Companies	Number of Ships	GT
OSK	12	36438
Misubishi Corp.	3	18490
NYK	2	15065
Kawasaki Shipyard	2	11795
Mitsui and Co.	3	8627
Itaya Shoten	1	5742
Suzuki Shoten	1	3834

Note: Mitsubish, Mitsui, and Suzuki Shoten are all general trading firms. Ships owned by Kawasaki Shipyard were operated by Kawasaki Kisen and Kokusai Kisen. The table covers all diesel ships of more than 1000 tons.

Source: Ministry of Communications, *Shipping Overview*.

[25]This point has previously been reported in detail by the author, citing the example of OSK's New York Express Service.

Appendix 1
List of Ships in Service on the Australia Route

1926	NYK		E&A		OSK		JAL	
Name	*Aki Maru*	6444	Unknown		*Madorasu*	3802	*Tosei Maru*	5484
	Mishima Maru	8500			*Himaraya*	5228	*China*	5870
	Tango Maru	7463			*Biruma*	4584	Not specified	
Total grt		22407		16672		13614		16380
Speed	13 knots		12 knots		10-10.5 knots	10 knots		
	15 sailings/year		12 sailings/ year		15 sailings/ year		12 sailings/ year	
1933	*Kitano Maru*	8512	*Tanda*	6956	*Sydney*	5425	*Kyokko Maru*	6783
	Atsuta Maru	8523	*Nankin*	7072	*Meruborun*	5423	*Yae Maru*	1855
	Kamo Maru	8524	*Nellore*	6853	*Burisbein*	5425	*Tamon Maru*	13065
Total gt		25559		20881		16273		21703
Speed	16 knots		12-12.5 knots		13.5 knots		10.5 knots	

Sources: NYK, *Report on Shipping and Economy*, latter half of 1926 and 1933; NYK, *The Seventy Years' History*; OSK, *The Eighty Years' History*, Yamashita Shinnihon Kisen, *The History of the Company*, and Kawasaki Kisen, *The Fifty Years' History*.

Appendix 2

Trends in Japan-Australia Trade and Performance of Australia Services of NYK and OSK

	Japan-Australia Trade	Cargo Freight Revenues (¥000)				Volume of Wool Loaded (bales)			
		NYK		OSK		NYK		OSK	
1927	100	2279	-100	2816	-100	112917	-100	88079	-100
1928	100	2067	-91	2870	-102	91857	-81	93801	-106
1929	102	2279	-100	2446	-87	100106	-89	101477	-115
1930	69	1715	-75	2757	-98	135570	-120	160319	-182
1931	76	1739	-76	3890	-138	148572	-132	165327	-188
1932	99	2053	-90	4811	-171	150269	-133	176607	-201
1933	148	2583	-113	5804	-206	138665	-123	142706	-162
1934	151	2850	-125	5964	-212	188186	-167	201594	-202
1935	179	3815	-167	6871	-244				
						253156	-112	168604	-84
1936	145	3744	-164	5450	-194				
1937	137	2235	-98	3079	-109	N.A.		N.A.	

Note: NYK also received passenger freight revenue as it operated cargo-passenger boats. However, the growth of passengers was even lower than that of cargoes. NYK's total freight revenue was ¥3.618 million in 1927 and ¥4.593 million in 1935, an increase of only fifty percent.

Sources: *Annual Statistics for Japan's Foreign Trade*; *History of Australia and New Zealand Routes*; and NYK, *Kamotsu/Kyakusen-betsu Shuyokoro-betsu Gyoseki* (*Performance of Major Routes by Cargo Revenue and Passenger Revenue*) (various years).

Appendix 3
Operators on the Far East, South East African, and South American Routes

Operator (Flag)	Main Calling Ports	1925 ships GT	Sailing	1926 ships GT	Sailing	1929 ships GT	Sailing	1933 ships GT	Sailing	1936 ships GT	Sailing
Japan/South East Africa NYK (Japanese)	Yokohama/ Cape Town	(Calls made by ships on South American Service)		(South American Service)		(South American Service)		-		-	
OSK (Japanese)	Kobe/Durban (cargo-passenger boat) (freighter)	-		4 23,174	monthly	4 23,232	monthly	(extension of South American Service) 3 21,768	monthly plus extra ships	(extension of Wouth American Service)	
Ships jointly assigned by Kawasaki Kisen, Kokusai Kisen, and Yamashita Kisen (operated by OSK) (freighter)		-		-		-		-		5 30,210	monthly plus extra ships
Far East/South East Africa											
British India (British)	Bombay/ Durban	NA	1 per 4 weeks		biweekly		biweekly	4 35,650	biweekly	4 35,650	biweekly
Bank Line (British)	1) Rangoon/Colombo/Cape Town (cargo-passenger boat)		-		biweekly		biweekly	3 12,446	biweekly	3 21,507	monthly
	2) Hongkong/Singapore/Cape Town (freighter)		-		monthly		monthly	3 14,715	monthly	NA	monthly
KPM (Dutch)	1) Manila/Batavia/Cape Town (cargo-passenger boat)		-		-		-	4 19,054	1 per 4 weeks*		
	2) Batavia/Lourenco Marques/ Monbasa (cargo-passenger boat)		-		-		-	2 6,454	monthly*	6 29,773	monthly
Tirrenia (Italian)	Aden/Magadisco/Zahzibar (cargo-passenger boat)		-		-		-	-		1 3,564	biweekly

Operator (Flag)	Main Calling Ports	1925 ships GT	Sailing	1926 ships GT	Sailing	1929 ships GT	Sailing	1933 ships GT	Sailing	1936 ships GT	Sailing
Japan-Far East/South American East Coast											
NYK (Japanese)	Yokohama/ Buenos Aires (caro-passenger boat)	3 17,672	bimonthly	5 29,537	monthly	6 35,584	monthly	-		-	
OSK (Japanese)	1) Kobe/ Buenos Aires (cargo-passenger boat)	6 42,175	10 per year	5 40,697	10 per year		-	5 47,379	monthly plus extra ships	5 47,593	monthly plus extra ships
	2) Kobe/ CapeTown/Buenos Aires/Gulf/Panama/Kobe (cargo-passenger boat)					6 50,197	11 per year	5 41,054	monthly	5 41,054	monthly
Bank Line (British)	Calcutta/Colombo/Durban/ *Buenos Aires (freighter)*					NA	monthly	3 15,384	monthly	3 15,384	monthly
Silver Java Pacific Line	Calcutta/Singapore/Java/West Coast/Gulf/Cape Town/ Calcutta (cargo-passenger boat)							5 31,927	monthly	9 58,509	biweekly
South American East Coast/South Africa											
Norddeutscher Lloyd	Buenos Aires/Durban (freighter)		-	-		-		-		2 4,893	monthly

Notes:

1) Bank Line was managed by Andrew Weir.
2) Tirrenia had been operating services such as Genoa/Suez/Dares Salaam. However, operations of African services were transferred to Lloyd Triestino as a result of Italy's shipping control in 1937.
3) Silver Java Pacific Line was jointly operated by Silver Line (US), Nederland S.N. (Dutch), and Rotterdam Lloyd (Dutch). KPM was capitalised by these two Dutch firms and was in a cooperative relation with Silver Java Pacific Line.

* Extended to Shanghai

Source: NYK, *Report on Shipping and Economy*, latter half of 1925, 1926, 1929, 1933 and 1936.

The Global Communications Industry and Its Impact on International Shipping before 1914

Lars U. Scholl

Globalization has become the buzzword of the 1990s. Beginning in the mid-1980s almost every popular or scholarly publication dealing with topics of a worldwide dimension will at one stage or the other resort to the term, taking for granted that the reader is familiar with the concept of globalization. Various definitions have been put forward and I shall not try to add a further definition of that multifaceted phenomenon. In my context it is sufficient to note that globalization is a worldwide network of economic activities transgressing the boundaries of two states. Globalization began with the expansion of European culture across the planet in the age of discovery after the so called "dark middle ages" had come to an end. It was the ship that facilitated the conquest of the globe and it was the ship that helped to create a world economy. Authors like Barraclough, Robertson and Waters emphasized the instrumental importance of the development of transportation and communication networks that physically linked together different parts of the planet, especially by railways, shipping and the telegraph.[1] A second key feature in this process was the rapid growth of trade between Western Europe and the rest of the world. This exchange of commodities and services accelerated during the industrial revolution in Britain and Continental Europe throughout mid- and late nineteenth century.

In 1972, Borchardt defined the "Industrial Revolution" as the process by which the economic emphasis shifts from old, primary sectors to new sectors, especially towards manufacturing industry. To characterize the nineteenth century and avoid the term "industrialization," Borchardt observed that it should be termed the century of "revolution in communications." While the production of commodities increased

[1]Malcolm Waters, *Globalization* (London, 1995); R. Robertson, *Globalization* (London, 1992); and Geoffrey Barraclough (ed.), *The Times Atlas of World History* (London, 1978).

enormously, the transportation of goods, people, news and capital grew even more impressively. This rise in transportation was not the outcome of the huge advances in production and productivity during the nineteenth century; rather, it was one of the pre-requisites of such growth. Mass production and bulk sales could not have taken place without railways, steamships and telecommunications.[2]

Although the label "industrial revolution" is generally used, it is commonly understood as referring to an evolutionary process consisting of various components which interacted to transform the basis of economic life, first in Britain, later in continental Europe and North America. One of these components was transport, the movement of goods, people and information between places, countries and continents by means of canals, roads, railways, steamships, telegraphs, and later, telephones and radios. One striking aspect of the individual forms of communication is that each operated most efficiently once it had developed into a network. However, roads, canals, railways, liner shipping and telegraphs did not simply develop local and regional links but also national and international connections within their own system. At the same time, much effort was deployed in attempts to link and integrate systems. For example, telegraphs often ran alongside railway lines utilising the same strip of land. Thus, the creation of national and international communication systems went hand in hand with the formation of railway networks and were therefore relatively easy to establish. Connecting the continents was obviously more difficult for the oceans had to be bridged. Nevertheless, not long after steamers began to ply the oceans, submarine cables were established. Initial failures were soon overcome as innovations such as the coating of wires with gutta-percha, together with the construction of suitable vessels, soon permitted cable laying to progress rapidly.

Headrick's seminal book on telecommunications is mainly concerned with the political aspects of information technology in modern history.[3] In contrast, this paper examines the ways in which global shipping benefitted from the telecommunication facilities that became

---

[2]Knut Borchardt, *Die Industrielle Revolution in Deutschland* (Munich, 1972), 98n.

[3]Daniel R. Headrick, *The Invisible Weapon. Telecommunications and International Politics, 1851-1945* (Oxford, 1991).

available at various stages between 1840 and 1914. As there is an abundance of general shipping histories on the one hand, and many erudite works on telegraphy, telephony and radios on the other, the paper is not concerned with general developments in shipping and telecommunications. Instead, it focuses directly on the impact that developments in telecommunication had on the business of shipping.

The Development of Telecommunications at Sea

Before the advent of telegraphy at the beginning of the nineteenth century, the only way of passing information from one part of the world to another was either verbal (by means of a messenger) or in writing (by means of letters, notices etc.). In the case of Britain, before 1661 when the Post Office started regular services on hired vessels carrying packet mail (official and business mail bound together in packets) between Harwich and Hellevoetsluys in the Netherlands, the usual way of overseas communication was by means of the shipmaster's mailbag.[4] As British trade developed, it depended increasingly on a reliable flow of information and further packet stations were established in the eighteenth century at Falmouth, London, Dover, Holyhead and Milford. These stations conveyed news to London; thus, the first network with a national capital at its centre came into being. An important improvement with regard to regularity and speed was the introduction of steam at sea in the nineteenth century. Passengers and the carriage of mail were the chief sources of profit for early steamships.

Once steamers were able to supply ocean services, the British government was prepared to spend a considerable amount of money to assure itself of regular information through subsidizing steamship companies by awarding mail contracts. The General Steam Navigation Company was given the first mail contract in 1834 for a service to Rotterdam and Hamburg, and this was followed by similar arrangements with the East India Company, P&O, Cunard, Royal Mail Line and Pacific Steam Navigation Company.[5] The American government awarded £60,000 per year to the Ocean Steam Navigation Company for a

---

[4]Ronald Hope, *A New History of British Shipping* (London, 1990), 246.

[5]Freda Harcourt, "British Oceanic Mail Contracts in the Age of Steam, 1838-1914," *Journal of Transport History,* 3rd series, IX (1988), 1-18.

fortnightly postal steamer service between New York and Bremen in 1847, the very year the Hamburg-American Packet-Actien-Gesellschaft (later Hamburg-America Line) was founded. The company carried the word "packet" in its name without receiving subsidies for mail services. Only later, in the 1880s, did the German government grant mail subsidies to North German Lloyd in order to establish regular trade links to German colonies or to those regions where imperial Germany hoped to acquire colonies.[6] While in the age of sail it took months to receive messages from the Far East and, at best, weeks from North America, the introduction of steamships was an enormous improvement. But although technical progress in many sectors helped to speed up voyages generally during the nineteenth century, there were limits to seaborne communication. Other developments which took place in a non-maritime context were far more important for providing high speed information flows over short or long distances.

Although Noah's memorable voyage in the Arc witnessed the use of doves, shipping in the early modern and modern eras made no such recourse. However, the business community and news agencies on land utilised pigeons to send messages and continued to do so in the early nineteenth century even after the introduction of the semaphore. The semaphore — the first device which allowed information to travel quicker than the fastest means of transportation — was initially monopolised by governments. During the Napoleonic Wars governments and military forces in France and Britain occupied the newly built semaphore lines for administrative and military purposes. The network of optical telegraphs in France, with Paris at its centre, served Napoleon's war needs while the Admiralty in Britain had lines built from London to Yarmouth, Deal and Plymouth (via Portsmouth) to safeguard against invasion. While most government lines were dismantled after 1815, commercial towns and businessmen built private semaphore lines in order to gain advance information of the arrival of ships. As early as 1827 the optical telegraph between Liverpool and Holyhead was established.[7]

---

[6]Arnold Kludas, *Die Geschichte der deutschen Passagierschiffahrt* (5 vols., Hamburg, 1986-1990), I, 168 ff.

[7]See Adrian Jarvis's chapter in this volume. He refers to F. Large, "The Liverpool Optical Telegraph System" (Unpublished MSc dissertation, University of Liverpool, 1996).

In Prussia a line from Berlin to Koblenz near the French border was put into operation in the 1830s but only for official business; private users were excluded. Yet because an optical telegraph network did not exist, news from London to Berlin by ship via Hamburg in 1836 still traveled faster. As in Britain, where Liverpool enjoyed a telegraph link, and the United States, where there was a semaphore line between Sandy Hook and New York City, semaphore lines were built from Cuxhaven to Hamburg on the Elbe (1837), and from Bremerhaven to Bremen on the Weser (1844-1847). Here, private business supplied the initiative. Merchants in the Hanseatic towns, like their counterparts in Liverpool and New York, were anxious to know as early as possible which ship had entered estuarial waters and would reach Bremen after sailing the last sixty kilometres up the Weser, or Hamburg after sailing 100 kilometres up the Elbe.[8] Such early information enabled shipping companies, port authorities, import and export agencies, as well as dockworkers and other personnel, to get ready for unloading ships, storing goods or preparing cargoes for the next voyage. One of the main freights was emigrants who were waiting to gain a passage to the New World. They had to wait because timetabled departures were hardly possible in the age of sail. However, the optical telegraph was short lived, peaking in the 1840s when it was quickly superseded by electrical telegraph lines.

Only a few years after land telegraphs had proved superior to the semaphores, attempts were made to lay cables in the sea. In 1850 the first submarine cable was laid from Dover to Calais. It broke within hours because a fisherman hauled it up! The second cable laid in 1851 enjoyed more permanency, lasting for several decades. Once the feasibility of cables had been proven, the French and British both rushed to lay them in the Mediterranean to ensure their respective military and administrative objectives and their trade interests in that region. For businessmen, the North Atlantic was a far more important and profitable seaway. In 1856, the Atlantic Telegraph Company was founded and, after some failures, managed to establish a line between Ireland and the United States via Newfoundland. In August 1858, President Buchanan and Queen Victoria were able to exchange greetings across the Atlantic. Before the line ceased

---

[8]Horst A. Wessel, *Die Entwicklung des elektrischen Nachrichtenwesens in Deutschland und die rheinische Industrie* (Wiesbaden, 1983); and Klaus Beyrer and Birgit-Susann Mathis (eds.), *So weit das Auge reicht. Die Geschichte der optischen Telegraphie* (Karlsruhe, 1995).

functioning in September 1858 some 400 telegrams, or 4400 words, had been transmitted. The most important message transmitted saved the British government £50,000 when an order for two regiments in Canada to return to England was canceled after the Sepoy insurrection in India had abated.[9] In Europe, businessmen and bankers were busily using existing lines as a means of exchanging commerical information about rates of exchange or price movements. Shipping companies were among the early users. They were able to act immediately on new information and redirect their ships to ports where trade opportunities emerged. Since the North Atlantic was commercially the most important international seaway the successful completion of a cable between Valentia in Ireland and Trinity in Newfoundland in August 1866 was welcomed with relief after eight frustrating years of delays and cable breakages. And then the Anglo-American Telegraph Company enjoyed a stroke of luck. The cable which broke halfway between Ireland and North America in 1865 was fished up and repaired. So within weeks two cables were available for the exchange of commercial news and messages. The influence the telegraph had on business was noted by contemporaries; thus, "the present firmness in the cotton trade is principally owing to telegraphic reports of worse accounts being received on the American yield."[10] Soon businessmen used the telegraph for short-term operations. By the 1870s, bankers and brokers could deal with financial matters and in stocks between North America and Britain within minutes, changing the face of business operations; thus,

> The telegraph put western markets in close touch with price changes in eastern centers, and the railroads facilitated delivery so that a favorable price change could be exploited. As a result, larger purchases of grain were made in markets such as Chicago and Buffalo. With the aid of telegraphic communication, a dealer in New York

---

[9]Headrick, *Invisible Weapon,* 18. The telegrams are quoted in Richard Hennig, *Überseeische Telegraphie und auswärtige Politik* (Berlin, 1919), 4.

[10]Jorma Ahvenainen, "The Role of Telegraphs in the 19th Century Revolution of Communications," in Michael North (ed.), *Kommunikationsrevolutionen. Die neuen Medien des 16. und 19. Jahrhunderts* (Köln, 1995), 73-80. The quote is from *The Economist*, 27 October 1866.

> could also purchase directly at the point of production. The degree of risk, though still large, was lessened, and the long line of individuals making advances to other individuals farther along the line was reduced.[11]

The cotton, coffee, sugar and tobacco trades immediately published lists of price currents and other market information via telegraphic transmission, thus influencing international trade and shipping to an unprecedented degree. Between 1866 and 1914 a global cable network was created that stretched to more than a half million submarine kilometres, having started with forty-six kilometres in 1852. Land lines had grown even more, to more than double the extent of submarine cables. By the beginning of the twentieth century, over 15,000 messages per day were sent via cables and wires. In Headrick's words, this was the "high technology of the late 19th century."[12]

Table 1
Submarine Cables by Nation, 1898-1913 (km)

Nation	1898	1903	1908	1913
Britain	208747	247932	253898	281828
USA	50545	75340	92288	100831
France	26157	37562	43115	43680
Germany	6186	18565	30167	43294
Denmark	13388	15316	17771	17516

Source: Richard Hennig, *Überseeische Telegraphie und auswärtige Politik* (Berlin, 1919), 47.

Significantly, from the 1860s, eighty percent or more of marine cables were controlled by private companies with Britain, the world's dominant shipbuilder and shipowner, holding the major share, its telegraphic companies owning seventy percent of the world's cables. Twenty years later they still owned about sixty-three percent and enjoyed a majority holding up to the First World War.

---

[11]Quoted in Alfred D. Chandler, Jr. *The Visible Hand: The Managerial Revolution in American Business* (Cambridge, MA, 1977), 210.

[12]Headrick, *Invisible Weapon*, 29.

Table 2

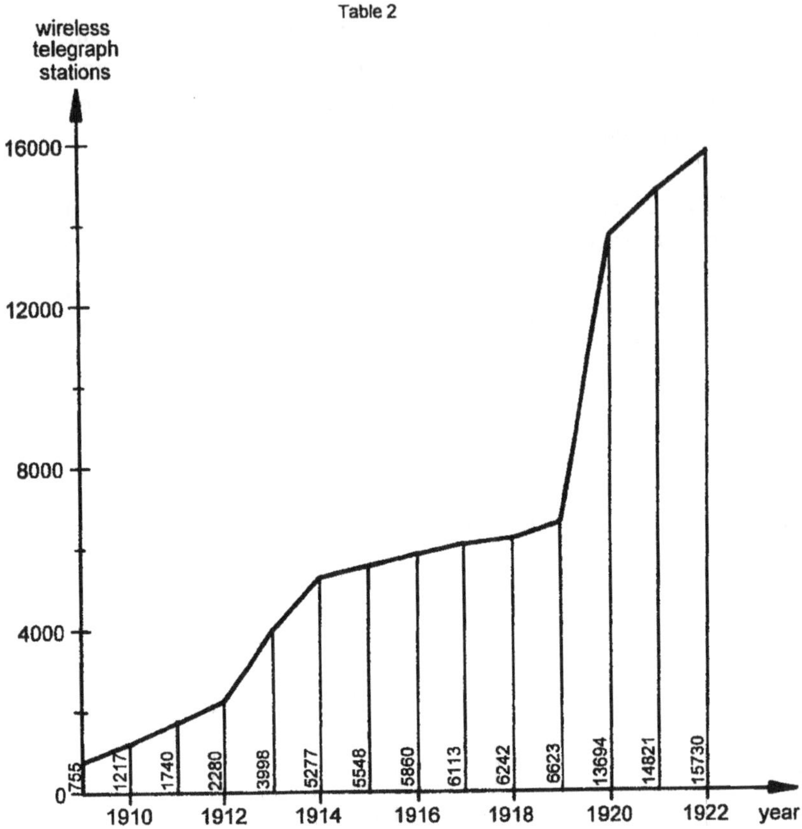

Figure 1: Wire Telegraph Stations, 1910-1922.

Source: Hennig, *Oberseeische Telegraphie*, 123.

The possession of huge parts of the international cable network strengthened Britain's position as the world's largest trading nation, contributing "decisively to the pre-eminence of the City of London as the mercantile-financial capital of the world."[13] Concern grew in France and Germany that possession of, and access to, the global cable network was so overwhelmingly in British hands. The continental powers tried to circumvent British dominance by extending their nationally controlled cables. Following the Fashoda incident in 1898, and British censorship in

[13] Robert Boyce, "Submarine Cables as a Factor in Britain's Ascendancy as a World Power, 1850-1914," in North (ed.), *Kommunikationsrevolutionen*, 81-99.

the wake of the Boer War, France and Germany strove to establish their own telegraph lines. In a bill passed by the French Parliament in 1899, the effect of British dominance of cable communication was identified:

> England owes her worldwide influence probably more to her cablenets than to the navy. Britain dominates the news for the benefit of her politics and business in a marvellous way. Telegrams from all over the world pour into London, they refer only to British trade, to British industry and to British politics...The submarine cables have helped enormously to develop British business; businessmen abroad know the London rates of exchange; Paris, Rouen, Roubaix, Lyon, Marseille, Antwerp, Amsterdam and Hamburg are places unknown to them.[14]

By 1904 the French had established cable lines between Brest and Boston, while the Germans had built a line from the isle of Borkum via the Azores to New York. With all major countries having access to the same information simultaneously, the ways in which commodities were acquired and shipped became standardized. Thus, the telegraph helped to homogenize the world economy, while the intercontinental cable network facilitated and stimulated global commerce — which was carried out mainly by means of shipping. However, cable telegraphy peaked around the turn of the century, for wireless transmission of messages was about to progress from infancy to adolescence within a few years.

Competition and Co-operation

In 1896 a young Italian came to England and applied for the world's first patent for wireless telegraphy. Since the Italian government had shown no interest in Gugliemo Marconi's apparatus he hoped to receive more attention in the country with the largest merchant marine and the most powerful navy in the world. Once it became possible to exploit wireless communication effectively, both commercial shipping and national navies would benefit because it would enable shipping companies to contact their ships at sea and it would facilitate naval manoeuvres at distances beyond

---

[14]Hennig, *Überseeische Telegraphie*, 23.

flag or lamp signals and irrespective of visibility. Marconi did not invent wireless telegraphy all by himself. Rather, he put together discoveries by James Maxwell, Heinrich Hertz, Edouard Branly, Alexander Popov, Oliver Lodge and others[15] "thereby creating a device that not only sent and received electromagnetic waves, but used them to transmit information in the Morse code."[16]

The British General Post Office [GPO] and the Royal Navy took a keen interest in Marconi's invention. A successful demonstration on Salisbury Plain in September 1896 paved the way for further tests, and with practical contributions from the GPO, Marconi's system was improved. In July 1897, The Wireless Telegraph and Signal Company Ltd. was founded in London. While Marconi's experiments received much publicity, commercial exploitation of the patent was still not feasible, for Marconi was cautious in releasing his plans to make communication between ships and coastal stations possible, undertaking further demonstrations aimed at shipping organizations. Eventually, at the request of Lloyd's of London, new trials were held on Rathlin Island, off the Irish coast, which proved that even on foggy days wireless communication between ships at sea — out of sight of shore — and coastal stations was possible. In March 1899 signals were sent across the Channel. Later that year, the Admiralty invited Marconi to demonstrate inter-ship wireless communication during naval manoeuvres, and in November, Marconi established contact with the Needles station from the ship *St Paul*, some sixty miles from the coast.

Despite these successful demonstrations, and despite orders from the Royal Navy, shipping companies in England were reluctant to buy the Marconi equipment. Further technical improvements were under way when commercial encouragement came from abroad. To Marconi's great surprise, North German Lloyd bought a wireless installation for the new transatlantic passenger liner *Kaiser Wilhelm der Grosse*, the fastest ship in the world and holder of the "Blue Riband" since 1898. Moreover, the German government ordered wireless installations for the Borkum Riff

---

[15]W.J. Baker, *A History of the Marconi Company* (London, 1970); W.P. Jolly, *Marconi* (London, 1972); Peter Rowlands and J. Patrick Wilson (eds.), *Oliver Lodge and the Invention of Radio* (Liverpool, 1994); and Ansgar Häfner (ed.), *Heinrich Hertz. Eine Funkgeschichte* (Frankfurt, 1991).

[16]Headrick, *Invisible Weapon*, 117.

lightship and the Borkum Island lighthouse. With Marconi's technical representative, George Kemp, aboard, the world's first four-funnel steamer sailed from Bremerhaven to New York in February 1900, establishing contacts with both the lightship and the lighthouse and later with Marconi stations at the Needles and Le Havre. In the words of Marconi's biographer this installation made "maritime history."[17]

In November 1900, the Belgian government had its mail packet steamer *Princesse Clementine* equipped with Marconi apparatus and this was soon followed in 1901 by the first British merchant vessels, the steamer *Lake Champlain* of the Beaver Line and the Cunard vessels *Lucania* and *Campania*. When the latter two ships met in mid-Atlantic, messages about ice and fog were exchanged amongst other news. Even a transfer of money from one ship to the other was undertaken when the two passenger liners passed each other at a distance of 100 miles. In December 1901, the *Lucania* and *Kaiser Wilhelm der Grosse* communicated continuously for three days at sea. The *New York Times*, in a lengthy article, reported on this communication at distance pointing to the fact that the operators had worked on each ship and therefore knew both wireless stations intimately. While steamers were making more tests at sea with inter-ship and ship to shore communication, signals were sent from Poldhu in Cornwall to St. John's, Newfoundland, in December 1901, bridging a distance of some 2000 miles. Although the first transmission was weak and did not last very long, nobody doubted that a steady flow of information across the Atlantic would just be a matter of time. Distances at which readable messages could be received became longer and longer as installations were improved and increased their power. In 1902 a new station was erected at Glace Bay in Nova Scotia with a considerable grant from the Canadian government. A few months later a continuous transmission of news from Poldhu to the *Lucania* during her entire voyage from New York to Liverpool was achieved. For the first time, the Cunard shipping company was in permanent contact with one of its ships.

A further important step in marketing wireless communication was an agreement by which Lloyd's of London leased wireless equipment and radio officers from the Marconi Company at specified stations both at home and abroad. These stations were not merely for reporting passing

---

[17]Baker, *History*, 58.

ships but were also available for commercial traffic to and from ships. By June 1903, Lloyd's had ordered nine signal stations to be equipped with wireless telegraphs. At this time, there existed sixteen stations on both sides of the Atlantic, while fifty-four stations were in continuous use on passenger vessels.

In order to create a global market and to get round restrictions laid down in the Telegraph Acts of 1868 and 1869 which gave the GPO a monopoly over internal communications, Marconi, in April 1900, founded a subsidiary company, the Marconi International Marine Communication Co. Ltd, with offices in Paris and Rome. As long as the Marconi Marine Company installed its apparatus and operators aboard a ship and did not charge for messages with shore stations it did not violate the GPO's monopoly. On the high seas the company could handle wireless messages and charge for them at its own discretion, avoiding restrictive clauses in the Acts. So instead of manufacturing radio sets and selling them to shipping companies, a new type of integrated business system was set up. The Marconi Marine Company offered a hire service for the wireless installations, for the operators and for the use of Marconi coastal stations. According to Hancock, the rationale for Marconi's hire-service reads somewhat different. He does not mention the Telegraph Acts at all, and claims that *service* was always the chief aim of the Marconi companies, observing that it soon became obvious that:

> no satisfactory or extensive business could be done by asking shipowners to purchase apparatus outright and to organize a public telegraph service. The company accordingly decided to adopt the bold policy of organising the service on its own account. Three things were necessary to the efficiency of the service. First, the provision of land stations adjacent to the chief trade routes; second, the equipment of vessels with wireless apparatus: and third...the working of both ship and shore stations by operators trained to observe the same rules and regulations.[18]

[18]H.E. Hancock, *Wireless at Sea. The First Fifty Years* (Chelmsford, 1950), 77.

If we take it that the truth lies somewhere in the middle, the system – with the apparatus aboard remaining the property of the company and the operators being Marconi employees – worked well and served to establish a monopoly in the hands of Marconi. Naturally, the Marconi operators worked according to uniform methods of transmitting and receiving messages with standardized Marconi apparatus. With such a strong position in the new market the Marconi Company had no interest in liaison or co-operation with any competitors and refused to allow any communication with ships or stations that were equipped with non-Marconi installations. As there were also inventors and engineers in North America and in Germany testing their apparatus aboard ships, friction was inevitable and it was just a matter of time before there was some conflict.

In February 1902, the Kaiser's brother, Prince Heinrich, travelled to the United States aboard the new passenger liner *Kronprinz Wilhelm,* the North German Lloyd's second four-funnel steamer. Equipped with a Marconi station, the Prince exchanged friendly greetings with the captains of the *Campania* and *Lucania.* On his return voyage he sailed aboard the Hamburg-America Line [HAL] steamer *Deutschland* on which the German Slaby-Arco apparatus was installed. When the Prince tried to send a courtesy message to President Theodore Roosevelt, the Marconi shore stations in New York refused to handle the message because it had come from non-Marconi apparatus. While the Germans considered this as a rebuff, which it most likely was, two biographers of Marconi subsequently insinuated that it was the Germans' fault. Jolly put forward as an explanation that the Marconi company "would have certainly communicated with *Deutschland* if they had been asked."[19] Baker, however, asks readers to believe "that on that run the *Deutschland*'s wireless was either partially or wholly out of action because of a technical fault."[20] Contrary to Headrick's verdict, this incident did not have immediate political repercussions.[21] Not long after his brother's return Kaiser Wilhelm went on a specially arranged short pleasure cruise on *Kronprinz Wilhelm* in April 1902. In his company was Professor Slaby,

---

[19]Jolly, *Marconi,* 124.

[20]Baker, *History,* 96.

[21]Headrick, *Invisible Weapon,* 117.

the driving force behind the German Slaby-Arco wireless system.[22] The Kaiser, before dinner, went to the sundeck, where "Mr. Marconi" (the radio operators were called Mr. Marconi on German ships) sent telegrams some sixty sea miles to the station in Bremerhaven (a Slaby-Arco-station).[23] Despite the advances of a German system, North German Lloyd continued to have Marconi stations installed on their ships and in 1903 HAL switched to the Marconi system because the ships of their rival in Bremen and all foreign passenger liners, as well as all relevant shore-stations in Britain and America, operated the Marconi system. A second reason for HAL's switch was Marconi's refusal to accept communications from their ships with German apparatus even though this was technically possible.

For more than fourteen months, the two German rival firms Slaby-Arco-AEG and Braun-Siemens-Halske continued to pursue separate interests before the Kaiser managed to initiate a merger. In April 1903, he wrote to the AEG-head Emil Rathenau: "The German position with regard to the Marconi company is undermined by the competition amongst the German wireless systems and it offers the British Marconi company [an opportunity] to build a world monopoly. I totally disapprove of this development because it is detrimental to German interests."[24] A few weeks later, on 27 May 1903, the "Gesellschaft für drahtlose Telegraphie" [Telefunken] was founded. The new company had difficulties in selling its installations because the North Atlantic trade, with all its passenger liners, was firmly in the hands of Marconi. Even the two big German shipping companies had succumbed to Marconi and signed long-term hire contracts so that their passengers were not excluded from wireless communication. Telefunken therefore concentrated on supplying their apparatus to vessels that sailed to South America and other parts of the world. On these less profitable routes the Marconi company again stuck to the policy of non-intercommunication.

---

[22]Karl-Heinz Manegold, "Adolf Slaby," in Wilhelm Treue and Wolfgang König (eds.), *Berlinische Lebensbilder-Techniker* (Berlin, 1990), 309-324.

[23]*Lloyd-Nachrichten*, May 1902.

[24]Hans Pieper, "Die englischen Bemühungen vor dem Ersten Weltkrieg um ein weltweites Kabel- und Funkmonopol," *Archiv für deutsche Postgeschichte* (1975), 79-95 (quote from 87).

Marconi's dominant position in this "commercial war"[25] demanded some form of response, so the German government invited representatives from Britain, France, Italy, Russia, Spain, the United States of America, Austria-Hungary and Germany to attend an International Radiotelegraphy Conference to be held in Berlin in August 1903. At this conference the Germans proposed that it should be obligatory for all shore stations to receive and transmit telegrams coming from and sent to ships, regardless of the system used.[26] Six countries which had criticized the Marconi non-intercommunication policy signed the final protocol, but Britain, Italy and the United States, the countries in which the Marconi company was most firmly based, refused to sign.

Three years later, after much preparatory work, mainly by the Germans, twenty-nine countries attended the First International Conference of Wireless Telegraphy in Berlin which decided on an International Convention based on the final protocol of the 1903 conference. The most important provision was the end of non-intercommunication. A further recommendation was that the old distress call CQD should be superseded by SOS. However, even after the Convention had come into force on 1 July 1908, Telefunken and Marconi continued their struggle behind the scenes. When, in 1905, the Marconi operators on Borkum Island refused to handle a message sent by Kaiser Wilhelm aboard the HAL steamer *Hamburg,* the Germans withdrew the licence for the Marconi station and had a Telefunken station built on the mainland at Norddeich opposite the island. Thus the North German Lloyd and the HAL, engaged in international trades, had Marconi stations aboard their ships, but at home the Telefunken stations dominated and most of the other German shipping companies had Telefunken apparatus installed on their vessels. Although both Germany and Britain had ratifed the treaty in 1906 and 1907 a very confusing situation had developed in the Channel and in the approaches to German ports. In Britain, the Wireless Telegraphy Act of 1904 undermined Marconi's dominant status since it decreed that all fixed stations had to have a GPO licence from 1905 on. Finally, the GPO bought all British shore stations in 1909. So even in Britain Marconi had to come to terms with the new situation as it

---

[25]Baker, *History,* 129.

[26]W.D. Goodwin, *One Hundred Years of Maritime Radio* (Glasgow, 1995), 15 ff.

no longer enjoyed its quasi-monopoly of the seagoing and ship to shore traffic.

When in 1910, the German government declared that in future no foreign wireless installations were to be tolerated on German vessels, the time for an agreement had come. Germany was now in a position of some strength as her merchant marine had grown to become the second largest in the world, second only to Britain. Hence, the "Compagnie de Telégraphie sans Fils" in Brussels, the licensee for Marconi patents in Germany and other European countries, was in danger of losing a major market. Eventually, Marconi and Telefunken ended their feud by founding jointly the "Deutsche Betriebsgesellschaft für drahtlose Telegraphie" [DEBEG] on 14 January 1911.[27] Telefunken held fifty-five percent of the firm's stock, while the Belgian and Marconi companies owned the remaining forty-five percent. The DEBEG's business was to organize and to run wireless stations in the German merchant marine. The new company took over all Marconi and Telefunken installations and operators on German ships. From now on intercommunication was no longer an issue. The hitherto rival systems for ship to shore and ship signaling were fully integrated, making interchangeable transmission feasible. Since there was still a problem in overcoming long distances, the Marconi system of graphic time charts was introduced by means of which it was possible to see which ship or station was nearest and could be approached. Initially, DEBEG was in charge of eighty stations. Its personnel were trained in schools in Hamburg and Bremerhaven, and were required to pass an examination supervised by the German Post Office. Once qualified, they became employees of DEBEG which, following the Marconi example, hired out wireless operators to shipping companies. Both Marconi and DEBEG conducted their business in this fashion until the 1940s.[28]

Modifications in Shipping Business

Twenty-five years after the first successful experiments on passenger liners the fascination for wireless telegraphy had not calmed down. Artur Fürst, a leading German nonfiction writer on technical subjects, wrote

---

[27]S.G. Sturmey, *The Economic Development of the Radio* (London, 1958), 49-71.

[28]*50 Jahre DEBEG. 1911-1961* (Berlin, 1961); and *75 Jahre DEBEG. 1911-1986* (Hamburg, 1986).

most enthusiastically: "Nowhere has wireless telegraphy found a greater sphere of activity than in ocean-wide shipping. Wireless telegraphy created something completely new, something hitherto totally unknown. Mankind was given a present that nobody would have dared to ask the gods for. It fell into mankind's laps all on its own as a fruit of physical knowledge."[29] Wireless telegraphy had not only proved its value in the North Atlantic passenger trade, it had also begun to make its way into other sectors, notably cargo-carrying ships and fishing vessels. The large passenger liners were the first to receive wireless telegraphy because there was enough space for relatively huge installations. On this prestigious route, with so many passengers who could be impressed by sending mostly trivial messages, but who for safety reasons were also receptive to such information as weather forecasts, the costs for the additional Marconi personnel did not matter. Before cargo vessels and other ships could be equipped with radio stations it was necessary to construct a sufficiently small and compact set. Therefore only the larger merchant vessels had been fitted with wireless telegraphy prior to August 1914.

Just before the war, following the *Titanic* disaster in 1912, the First International Safety of Life at Sea Conference (SOLAS) had been held in London and had made it mandatory for passenger vessels carrying more than fifty passengers to be equipped with wireless. Only two years later the British Government made it obligatory for all UK-registered vessels of 3000 tons or over registered in Britain to have wireless telegraphy on board. In 1917 this was extended to ships of 1600 tons or over irrespective of the number of passengers carried. In July 1914 there had been more than 4500 stations on ships and land in operation. After the war the net of coastal stations worldwide was continuously enlarged making it possible to transmit any message to any ship plying the oceans at most distant places from the European headquarters. In 1922 the first passenger liners were equipped with radio telephony thus making spoken communication at sea possible.

At the beginning of the twentieth century, the British merchant marine was the largest in the world and comprised almost fifty percent of the world's tonnage. Half of the British ships were engaged in tramp shipping. Despite severe competition and higher costs the dominating position of British tramp shipping owed much to the ability of the captains

[29]Artur Fürst, *Das Weltreich der Technik* (4 vols., Berlin, 1923-1926), I, 288.

to take advantage of market opportunities. However, the business part of a shipmaster's job was gradually reduced by means of telecommunication, and this eventually stripped him of a constituent element of his responsibilities.

Within a few years communication from one nation-state to one nation-ship was superseded by a free flow of information that may not have originally been sent from the country whose flag a ship was flying. Especially in tramp shipping the acquisition of cargo and the transport of goods were no longer dependent on the captain's acumen, but could be conducted with great flexibility from the headquarters or a branch of a shipping company or a broker's firm. Shipowners and managing agents had direct contact with their captains and could give them new instructions at any time day and night. They were constantly able to take advantage of new economic developments which might promise better profits. The whereabouts of their vessels was known in the shipping offices around the clock. The risks of shipowning, which were much larger than any other economic enterprise on shore, could be reduced considerably by permanent surveillance. The reduction of numerous uncertainties on the side of shipowners and managing agents had far reaching consequences for the captain's position on board and undermined his autocratic command over ships and crews. Captains disliked cable and wireless telegraphy because the new means of communication were seen as controlling devices that curtailed their freedom as masters of the ship. Even naval officers, who were much more used to a strict hierarchy, regarded radio technology as "a threat to their freedom of action." Quite often wireless telegraphy was not used because officers did not want to accept orders once they were at sea; thus:

> The traditional power of a commanding officer to do as he felt best with his ship or command as soon as he got out of sight of land would have been completely wiped out if someone in the Bureau of Navigation or elsewhere could give him orders. So often the instructions to the wireless room were to shut down the wireless and not acknowledge calls from shore at all.[30]

---

[30]Headrick, *Invisible Weapon,* 124.

In the pre-cable era it was almost entirely the captain's responsibility to conduct business on behalf of the shipowner and those who owned the cargo (see the chapter by Yrjö Kaukiainen in this volume). The shipowner depended to a great extent on the ability and qualification of a ship's master to complete a voyage profitably. The captain had a great responsibility and influence over the business since he had to make decisions on his own far away from offices in Liverpool, London, Amsterdam or Hamburg. "The great underlying principle in shipping business is the observance, by all parties, of good faith. Without this success is impossible."[31] Shipowners had to trust their captains and to delegate power to the shipmaster who had to be a capable seaman and a good businessman at the same time. The shipowners could, of course, lay down certain rules to which a captain had to adhere. In many cases the captain may have had an accompanying businessman versed in commercial procedures, the so-called supercargo, on board. But quite often the captain held both positions. Captains working in liner shipping on the North Atlantic were more likely to accept orders from shipping offices because their voyages were much shorter than those of their colleagues in tramp shipping who used to go anywhere to load anything at widely scattered ports. They were their own masters as long as they were away from their home port. Change began gradually with the laying of submarine cables along major routes. Shipowners told captains to call at certain ports in order to inquire whether there were new instructions waiting for them. With the advent of wireless telegraphy the captain's position underwent a considerable modification. He was told where to go according to information which had reached shipping offices from distant ports of the world. Accordingly:

> The venture system tended more and more to become a thing of the past, both import and export trade became regularised and worked along well-established lines, some of the chief uncertainties began to disappear, and regular freights, fixed commissions, organised markets with brokers and definite method, evolved. Hence there came about a very revolutionary change in shipping business,

---

[31] Adam W. Kirkaldy, *British Shipping. Its History, Organisation and Importance* (London, 1914), 152.

> not caused by any sudden upheaval, but evolving with the progress of civilisation and commerce.[32]

There were, of course, many contributory causes. But the most "definite line of demarcation between the old and new may be said to be the laying of the submarine cables to all ports of the world."[33] It can be added that wireless telegraphy abolished the last bit of freedom the captain had enjoyed as a shipmaster because the final gap in communication had been closed.

Conclusion

Wireless communication changed the operations of worldwide shipping radically. Surprisingly, maritime and economic historians seem to have paid little attention to the developments in telecommunications that took place at the beginning of the twentieth century. Once Marconi, Telefunken and other companies were able to market wireless radio communication, their main target and the main beneficiaries of the new system were shipping companies. First installed on big passenger liners sailing the North Atlantic, wireless systems were initially used almost as toys for the exchange of trivial, unimportant messages. However, their potential was soon realised by shipping companies, port authorities, shipbrokers and insurance companies. There were several major incidents in which wireless communication saved ships and passenger's lives. The most spectacular was the *Titanic* disaster in 1912. Much more could have been achieved had there been a standard method of internationally accepted warning and rescue signals. The safety aspect for passengers, property and navigation as a whole became more and more apparent to Lloyd's and other insurance companies. The potential for efficient business operation was also soon appreciated by shipping companies. Not only could they have continuous contact with their ships — and redirect them at sea in event of cargo having been sold afloat or new business opportunities having arisen during the voyage — they were also able to reorganize the management of vessels in ports and achieve much higher efficiency because they knew the exact location of their ships and could plan port

---

[32] *Ibid.*, 159.

[33] *Ibid.*, 161.

activities very precisely in advance. As soon as smaller, compact sets tailored to the requirements of cargo ships and fishing vessels (which lacked the space for major installations) became available, wireless communication became widespread and established itself as an indispensable instrument for shipowners, businessmen, underwriters, the traveling public and port authorities. Global access to any kind of information resulted in new forms in which shipping business could be conducted outside of national economies. While business opportunities multiplied the shipmaster's freedom and responsibility shrank. The captain's capabilities as a businessman were no longer required. He was reduced to his navigational duties. Wireless telegraphy was never intended to be a replacement or substitute for submarine cables but it soon came to play an important role in the global telecommunication network. Submarine cables and wireless telegraphy were important factors in imperialism before 1914. Britain, Germany, France and other countries sought to build their own networks in order to have unimpeded access to worldwide communication. One of the first actions after the outbreak of hostilities in August 1914 was to cut German submarine cables and to destroy German wireless stations on shore. Communication with German ships at sea and with German colonies was severely hampered or even impossible. For the next four years the armed forces of the belligerent countries emerged as the dominant users of wireless communication, thereby adding a new dimension to conflict on land and at sea.[34]

[34]Stefan Kaufmann, *Kommunikationstechnik und Kriegsführung, 1815-1945. Stufen telemedialer Rüstung* (Munich, 1996).

The Nineteenth-Century Roots of Globalization: Some Technological Considerations

Adrian Jarvis[1]

"Globalization" is a term with almost as many meanings as users. For the purposes of this chapter, globalization is defined simply as that situation in which a particular commodity or class of good is produced in widely different parts of the world and whose financing, marketing and sales are worldwide. Considerations of finance, marketing and sales obviously imply that certain services, as well as goods, should be at least internationally widespread, if not global. Such a state of affairs has a number of pre-requisites, some of which are partly or wholly technological, and which may be roughly divided into considerations of transport, the storage and handling of goods, and communication.

Transport is self-explanatory. Unless supply is geographically very restricted, a global market for a commodity will only exist if the cost of transport forms an insignificant part of the price it can command at its destination. It is widely recognized that technological developments in shipping, particularly the arrival of steam power and iron hull construction, had profound effects in every branch of oceanic trade. This is not new: engineers and naval architects at the time wrote in their professional papers about what they were doing *and* its importance on the wider stage. An obvious example is Alfred Holt, who was both an engineer and a shipowner: by extending the reach of the steam cargo liner to East Asia he changed, for trading purposes, the shape and size of the world. And he knew in advance that he would.[2] By the turn of the century, the transatlantic passenger traffic was being discussed by such as

[1]I would like to thank Dr. Graeme Milne for providing several references and making many helpful comments on the first draft of this paper.

[2]Alfred Holt, "Review of the Progress of Steam Shipping during the Last Quarter of a Century," *Minutes of the Proceedings of the Institution of Civil Engineers (Min Proc ICE)*, LI (1877-1878), 2-135.

Kennedy in primarily technological terms, and Kirkaldy,[3] while allotting more importance to commercial and financial factors, still stressed technological development. More recently, Hyde — primarily a business historian — emphasized the importance of Holt's innovations, and particularly his development of the ensemble of a screw-propelled iron hull with a compound steam engine.[4] In conference papers, in journals and in part-works, the transition to steam has continued to fascinate scholars.[5] In 1996, a conference at the University of Hull recognized that fascination, even exploring such novel backwaters as the development of a decisive "technology gap" based on steam and iron which eventually made piracy unprofitable on most trade routes.[6] It is almost enough to turn one into a technological determinist — but not quite.

The effects of these changes at sea on the technology of ports are particularly interesting.[7] These effects may be summarized as hinging on three changes in ships. Steamships became faster and more expensive, so time in port represented a greater proportion of their costs, cranking up

---

[3]J. Kennedy, *The History of Steam Navigation* (Liverpool, 1903); and A.W. Kirkaldy, *British Shipping* (reprint, Newton Abbot, 1970).

[4]F.E. Hyde, *Blue Funnel* (Liverpool, 1956), 165-170 and 172-175.

[5]For a useful selection of articles and extensive bibliography, see B. Greenhill (ed.), *The Advent of Steam* (London, 1993); and L.R. Fischer and G. Panting (eds.), *Change and Adaptation in Maritime History: The North Atlantic Fleets in the Nineteenth Century* (St. John's, 1985). On steamships in specific trades, see Y. Kaukiainen, "Coal and Canvas: Aspects of the Competition between Steam and Sail, c. 1870-1900," *International Journal of Maritime History*, IV (December 1992), 175-192; F. Broeze, "Distance Tamed: Steam Navigation to Australia and New Zealand from Its Beginnings to the Outbreak of the Great War," *Journal of Transport History*, Third Series, X (1989), 1-21.

[6]J. Anderson, "The Coming of Steam and the Suppression of Piracy" (Unpublished paper presented at the Steam at Sea Conference, University of Hull, 1996).

[7]Mostly incorporated or summarized in A. Jarvis, *The Liverpool Dock Engineers* (Stroud, 1996), which also has an extensive bibliography; A. Jarvis, "Steam begets Steam: The Mechanization of Ports" (Unpublished paper presented at the Steam at Sea Conference, University of Hull, 1996) goes further; see also L.R. Fischer, "The Impact of Steam on Infrastructure Development in Australian Ports" (Unpublished paper presented at the Steam at Sea Conference, University of Hull, 1996). The best succinct overview is G. Jackson, *History and Archaeology of Ports* (Tadworth, 1983). Several relevant papers are published in A. Jarvis (ed.), *Port and Harbour Engineering* (Aldershot, 1998).

the quest for speed of turn-round. They also became first much wider and then much deeper, posing fundamental problems to every dock or harbour engineer in the world.

This chapter moves behind such developments, and considers three areas of technology whose effects are less conspicuous than those fundamental problems and the responses to them. There were persistent complaints that it cost more to move cotton through Liverpool and on to Manchester than to bring it across the Atlantic.[8] It is still true today that a container does not have to go far inland before the cost equals that of bringing it from Singapore. The rising quantity of imported food entering Britain in the last third of last century clearly did not depend only on getting corn or livestock to the quays of a port: it also needed effective handling and storage methods to get them to market cheaply.

Trade requires communication between buyers and sellers, and the rapidity of developments in telecommunications over the last twenty years has surely been important. There were nineteenth-century innovations of perhaps comparable impact, such as the development of mail steamers which were significantly faster than cargo vessels, of express passenger railways and perhaps above all the telegraph, first in optical then electrical form. These all had the potential to bring into being quite new trading methods.

Refrigeration

In 1850, international trade in foodstuffs was confined to products which could withstand a long sea voyage with no more protection than careful stowage. Grain was by far the most important in tonnage terms, though dried exotic fruits and spices commanded high prices. International trade in perishable foodstuffs was time-warped in the Middle Ages. Just as fresh fish could be extremely cheap on the coast and nearly unobtainable in, say, thirteenth-century Meriden, so fresh meat in New Zealand could cost a fraction of its price in London or Liverpool in the 1850s.[9] A well-

---

[8]See, for example, the enquiries of Great Britain, Parliament, Select Committees on the Liverpool and Manchester Railway Bill, 1825, or any of the Manchester Ship Canal Bills (1883,1884,1885).

[9]Meriden claims to be "the Centre of England." For relative values of meat in London and in the Antipodes, see note 12.

developed ice trade had solved the inland fish problem and the carriage of perishables on relatively short sea passages, but importing meat across oceans meant importing livestock.

The reasons for *not* importing livestock were compelling. During the voyage some would die and all would suffer weight loss.[10] Meat from those which survived was inferior in flavour to that from animals which had not endured a voyage of some weeks. There was also the risk of importing infectious diseases, cattle from Russia having a particularly evil reputation.[11] The nastiest diseases, particularly anthrax, approached contemporary ideas of Doomsday. Finally, there was already a body of opinion which considered long-haul livestock importing an unjustifiable cruelty to animals.[12] These factors perpetuated the price differences, and were the antithesis of globalization.

This was not why people became interested in artificial refrigeration. Alexander Kirk produced a bibliography of mechanical refrigeration beginning with the Marquis of Worcester's 1663 invention for "Ffountaines of pleasure, with artificial snow or haill or thunder."[13] In 1828 Richard Trevithick thought that spirits might be more effectively produced by freezing out the excess water rather than by the traditional method of fractional distillation. Like several of his brilliant ideas, this one was laid aside.[14] A serious beginning was made by Professor Piazzi Smyth from about 1839, but for him as for other distinguished scientists

---

[10]Weight loss in cattle arriving from Argentina was estimated at twelve-fifteen percent and deaths in the whole South America trade around seven percent. S.G. Hanson, *Argentine Meat and the British Market* (Stanford, CA, 1938), 81-82.

[11]Under the Foreign Animals Order 1878, importation from Russia was completely forbidden.

[12]For example, Harold Littledale, cotton merchant and member of the Mersey Docks and Harbour Board, spoke several times at the Board against cruelty to livestock. See also S. Plimsoll, *Cattle Ships* (London, 1890), ch. 4.

[13]A.C. Kirk, "Mechanical Production of Cold," *Min Proc ICE*, XXXVII (1873-1874), 244-315. For a more recent bibliography, see the references in R. Greenhill, "Shipping and the Refrigerated Meat Trade from the River Plate 1900-1930," *International Journal of Maritime History*, IV (June 1992), 65-82.

[14]J.G.B. Hills, "Richard Trevithick and Refrigeration," *Transactions of the Newcomen Society*, XLI (1968-1969), 169-171.

including Herschel, Rankine and Joule, the primary objective was generally scientific enquiry, applicable perhaps to making ice or cooling buildings in uncomfortably hot colonies. There followed a host of treatises from authors in Britain, France, Germany and the United States. In 1860, Dr. Dullo of Konigsberg described a steam-driven ice-making plant he saw at H.M. Lawrence's works in Liverpool.[15]

In these early stages there were three basic methods in use. Harrison's ether machine, which evaporated ether *in vacuo*, abstracting the latent heat of vaporization from the vessel and then condensing the vapour by compression, was the first to succeed. It was simple — the mechanical parts were just a vacuum pump and a pressure pump, and it got down to about 0° Fahrenheit, but it had the serious disadvantage of using a highly inflammable cooling medium. Kirk advocated the cold-air machine, air being both cheap and non-flammable. This worked by compressing air — causing its temperature to rise — and cooling it to ambient temperature while compressed. Expanding it after cooling produced a marked drop in temperature, and the cold air was used directly or put through a heat exchanger to produce a supply of cold liquid. Simple in principle, these machines were complex in practice and had the disadvantage of producing large amounts of "snow." More promising was the ammonia method, which drove gaseous ammonia out of a heated solution under pressure, cooled the gas by expansion and then allowed it to redissolve at low pressure.[16]

At first these machines were chiefly used for ice-making, wort-cooling in breweries, and some limited attempts at air conditioning. In 1861, Thomas Mort established the world's first freezing works in Sydney, prompting research and development in Britain, Australia and elsewhere to unlock the obvious potential profits offered by the meat surpluses of the southern hemisphere. Freezing meat ashore could not enable international trade without a refrigerator which could go to sea. Bell and Coleman's ammonia machines seemed promising, but the pioneer voyages actually employed their cold air machines. One might expect the first target would be the USA, where meat was much cheaper and more

---

[15]Kirk, "Mechanical Production." Lawrence was a general mechanical engineer: perhaps this machine was more a demonstration model than a venture in ice supply.

[16]The alternatives are discussed in J.J. Coleman, "Air Refrigerating Machinery and its Applications," *Min Proc ICE*, LXVIII (1881-1882), 146-215.

plentiful than in Britain, because it was relatively near and did not involve passing through the tropics. Some cargoes of chilled (not frozen) meat did indeed cross the Atlantic in 1877, but they were cooled with ice or ice/salt freezing mixture – which occupied a volume one third that of the meat carried. The same year, the mechanically refrigerated *Frigorifique* arrived back in Rouen with meat from Buenos Aires, but this "double first" was marred by the poor condition of the meat on landing. In 1879, *Circassia* made the first North Atlantic voyage by a mechanically refrigerated vessel, and the following year, *Strathleven* arrived in London with thirty-four tons of frozen meat from Australia, still in good condition.[17] This ship, often claimed as the progenitor of the long-haul meat trade, had Bell and Coleman's dry air machines. But this is another case of "victor's history," for the French vessel *Paraguay* had landed a sound cargo of meat from Buenos Aires in Le Havre in May 1878. However, in Britain there was a willingness to invest in such innovations, and because investment was not forthcoming in France, the trade came to be dominated by British firms.[18]

These pioneering voyages proved that it was indeed possible to sell meat in Britain for at least three times its southern hemisphere price. Bell & Coleman faced a crowd of customers wanting entry to the new trade, which now grew rapidly.[19] Nor was the new technology confined to meat: by 1884 apples were successfully carried from Tasmania to London, and by 1895 Australia and New Zealand were significant suppliers. Other perishables, such as butter, soon followed, and even the intractable problem of chilled eggs was eventually solved.

Each of these developments presented new opportunities and tentative steps towards the day when there would be identifiable world market prices for food. The Tasmanian apples formed another pointer to the future: like the meat, fruit was carried long distances because it was cheap and plentiful in Tasmania and relatively scarce and expensive in

---

[17] While steam propulsion and refrigeration usually went together, they did not *necessarily* do so: *Strathleven* was a three-masted ship.

[18] This paragraph is based on J.T. Critchell and J. Raymond, *A History of the Frozen Meat Trade* (London, 1912), ch. 2.

[19] By 1888, there were fifty-seven vessels in the Australia/New Zealand trade; in 1891, eighty-seven; and 1898, 131, this last figure representing a capacity of 5,460,800 carcasses. *Ibid.*, 127.

Britain. But apples changed the nature of the market as well. Because they were six months "out of sync" with British apples, the antipodean product made out-of-season fruit — formerly hot-house grown for the very wealthy — available to ordinary people in ordinary shops. Thus began the process of de-seasonalization. These are far-reaching changes to arise from the invention of a reliable shipboard refrigerator. They altered trading patterns and greatly improved the standard of living of lower-middle and upper-working class people in Britain.

What was remarkable about mechanical refrigeration is less the fact of its invention, more the rapidity of its refinement, which helped bring about a steady fall in mean yearly freight rates for Australian mutton from 2d per lb in 1884 to 0.56d per lb in 1899 and a corresponding fall in the price of Australian mutton in London from 6.3d in 1883 to 2.7d in 1896.[20] Argentine meat followed suit. Part of this fall in costs arose from more efficient ammonia machines replacing fuel-hungry cold-air systems, but more came from constant minor improvements, particularly on the control side. Possibly significant, too, is that Bell & Coleman, who made the early running, was a partnership of two engineers and one scientist: the fusion of theory and practice is a fairly general characteristic of successful mechanical engineering at this period.

Bulk Cargo-Handling

In most British ports, bulk cargoes are now of enormous importance in terms of tonnage, if not of revenue,[21] and the two largest bulk trades, oil and grain, are prominent for their early price-leveling and may be seen as another forebear of globalization. The move towards bulk handling of both commodities in ports first made significant progress in the 1860s, but this case study is confined to grain.

The basic principle in most bulk handling is that all the lifting is done in a single initial stage, after which successive movements are carried out chiefly or wholly by gravity. This principle originated in brewing, and led by about 1800 to the adoption of the tower brewery.

---

[20]Figures from Hanson, *Argentine Meat,* 88-89. Mean yearly freight rates generally fell (*pace* fluctuations) over this period, but only by about fifty percent.

[21]In Liverpool at present, bulks (wet and dry together) represent roughly sixty-six percent of tonnage.

Water was pumped to a tank at the top of the tower, to be drawn by gravity to the mash tuns below. The malt had to go up there too, and the well-appointed public brewery of 1800 already elevated it by Archimedean screw.[22] These worked well, and continued in use for decades, but no systematic research as to optimum form or operating speed was undertaken. Thus, when Sir W.G. Armstrong and Co. gained the machinery contract for the first centrally-powered bulk grain warehouse in the world, at East Waterloo Dock, Liverpool, they began a careful research programme as to the most power-efficient method.[23] Many permutations of inclination, diameter, pitch and speed were tried, and they tried both male and female screws. The differences in efficiency obtained were large, but most striking was that between the best figure for any of the screws, which required 18.38 hp to carry grain at fifty tons per hour over 100 ft, and the figure of 1.02 hp to effect the same work with a conveyor belt. The total length of conveyor required was about 1.3 miles, so the importance of such a saving is easily appreciated. The aim was to increase the rate of discharge of corn from the ship's hold from the 300 tons per day which was fairly typical when the warehouse was designed, to 150 tons per hour, while at the same time employing less labour.

The original machinery never approached that figure, mainly because the tub cranes and main elevators (the first two stages of the process) proved inadequate, and after attempts at improvement, portable and floating bucket elevators were used to supplement the built-in machinery.[24] This was by no means the only poor job Armstrong's did in

---

[22]P. Mathias, *The Brewing Industry in England 1700-1830* (Cambridge, 1959), 95.

[23]Described in detail in P. Westmacott, "Description of the Hydraulic Machinery for Warehousing Grain at the Liverpool Docks," *Proceedings of the Institution of Mechanical Engineers* (1869), 208-228.

[24]The teething troubles are detailed in A. Jarvis, *Liverpool Central Docks 1799-1905* (Stroud, 1991), ch. 7.

Liverpool: perhaps they had moved their best men from hydraulics into the more profitable field of armaments.[25]

The installation was intended to handle roughly 250,000 tons per year and was geared principally to the American trade, corn from other sources tending to arrive in bag. It represented a massive investment by the Mersey Docks and Harbour Board (MD&HB) — the Waterloo Warehouses, with their associated works and their twins over in Birkenhead cost nearly £1 million — in what was seen to be the "coming technology." Bold and innovative, they paid the penalty of boldness and innovation. There were numerous teething troubles with the machinery, some clearly due to poor design detailing. The method of accounting used makes it difficult to separate out costs exactly, but the overspend was near 100 percent of the original estimate, and the schedule over-run was about eighty percent, depending on one's definition of "completion." Project and budget control were not precise sciences in nineteenth-century dock engineering, but those figures reflect little credit on Armstrong, or on G.F. Lyster, who negotiated and oversaw the contract.

Ten years after completion, the warehouses were obsolescent. It was not just that the elevators never approached their specified performance: it seemed that the fundamental operating principle was wrong. Grain was distributed by conveyor belts running along the three wings of the building at high level, and was "turned off" into "flats" (storage cells) as required, where it formed a conical heap. In the centre of each flat was a shoot communicating with the flat below, and so on to the bottom of the building. There being no other provision for grain to move downwards (apart from the dump hopper to the bottom conveyors), this meant that flats had to be filled from the bottom floor upwards, so that parts of a particular consignment would be in flats above each other, rather than alongside. Conceptually, they might as well have been in a vertical hopper, the new method which was fast taking over. It was

---

[25]In 1877, for example, a movable bridge failure occurred for which Armstrong accepted responsibility and offered to repair the girder work if the MD&HB would "place the detached portion of the structure on the site of the bridge." One wonders where it had ended up. The 100-ton crane at Langton Branch Dock (1883) proved unsatisfactory, and it was alleged that the order placed later that year for the 100-ton barge crane *Atlas* was to conceal the failure.

possible to be dismissive of their efficiency, whether in terms of labour or of power consumption.[26]

Such criticisms may not be entirely unfair, but they miss the point of changes which were in progress. When the warehouse was designed, consignees wished to be able to see their property and to check its condition, which the flat system allowed. The admittedly more efficient silo system used in America was serving a different function, owing to the practice of putting grain into silos according only to grade and not to ownership. In Liverpool the practice of consignment "to order" was growing, particularly in the bulk sector, and being able to view the goods was an advantage. The heating of grain due to germination was a process well known but less understood, so limiting the quantity of grain in each storage unit was a sensible precaution, and it also allowed, for the first time, grain which was heating to be sent round the building on the conveyors to cool down and then return to its flats. Nobody knew what size of vessel or consignment would be handled once the system was fully commissioned, because there was no precedent to draw on, and forecasts provided by the trade proved hopelessly inaccurate.[27]

The arrangements for taking in and despatching grain had, therefore, to be as versatile as possible in order to allow arrivals and departures in bag or in bulk, by road, rail or water. Some of these provisions were an almost total waste of money — railway companies, for example, were very slow to adopt bulk handling. When A.G. Lyster went on a tour of American grain handling facilities in 1880, he described bulk grain rail cars "unknown to the trade of this country" and hinted that British railway companies were reactionary.[28] This versatility had not only cost money in extra equipment but had brought into play the usual engineering rule that the more things you make a system do, the worse it

---

[26]W. Pilkington, "On the Elevation, Storage and Shipment of Grain," *Min Proc ICE*, LXXVII (1883-1884), 237-246.

[27]See Jarvis, *Liverpool Central Docks*.

[28]Lyster's draft of his report has recently been acquired by the Maritime Archives and Library (MAL), Merseyside Maritime Museum, and is provisionally listed under MD&HB, Engineer's Dept., Miscellaneous Reports; see Adrian Jarvis, "A.G. Lyster's *Report on the Several Methods of Dealing with Grain in the United States, and Also on the Elevated Railroads of New York*, 1880," *International Journal of Maritime History*, X, No. 1 (June 1998).

does all of them. On the other hand, transfer cargoes by flat or barge between Waterloo and Birkenhead became more numerous than expected, because some of the ships used in the trade soon got too deep for Waterloo and had to use Birkenhead: the division of cargo between the two installations began to be affected by the size of the ship carrying it instead of simply by its destination.[29]

But if the system were as bad as Pilkington would have us believe, how did Birkenhead become the second-largest flour-milling centre in the world, after Minneapolis? As such, it played an important part in those ongoing problems of the British agricultural industry in the last quarter of the century which occupied so many Parliamentary enquiries. While it could have been better, it did bring major savings.[30] Carrying grain in sacks was expensive: every time a sack was used it cost a penny in stitching and "rent," and large costs were incurred carrying and storing empty sacks.[31] While sacks were tolerably effective for moving grain vertically by hoists and chutes, they were very labour-intensive to move horizontally when compared with bulk grain on conveyors and even worse to stack when stored. Because they were so heavy and awkward to handle, there evolved an elite group known as corn porters who possessed the exceptional strength and stamina required — at roughly three times the pay of ordinary dock labourers.[32]

The key to this investment, and its success, lay largely in the US grain trade, where the need for up to four transhipments (farm cart to rail to Great Lakes steamer to canal boat to ship) made effective handling and short-term storage methods proportionately more important than elsewhere, even before we take into account the traditionally high cost of

---

[29]Originally Birkenhead was to serve destinations to the south and west of the river, Liverpool those to the north and east.

[30]With many vicissitudes, between 1870 and 1914 wheat imports rose from 8.6 to 27.5 million quarters, while arable acreage in production at home fell slightly, and yield/acre also fell. The price of wheat fell by about one-third.

[31]Sacks were a particular *bête noire* of Mr. Goodwin in his paper "Appliances for the Inland Transport and Manipulation of Grain in Bulk," *Journal of the Liverpool Polytechnic Society* (1878), 47-61. Much of what Lyster went to America to find was already available in this paper.

[32]This was a London practice which evolved independently in Liverpool during the 1880s.

American labour. The extension of bulk-handling to the port of destination made this tortuous transport process cheap enough to put American grain in competition with supplies from, say, the Black Sea, which was a significant step towards establishing a world market.

Telecommunications

The history of maritime telecommunication technology falls into three broad periods, overlapping as these divisions always do, but still clearly distinguishable. The first is the relatively unusual visual telegraph system, of which the most commercially (as distinct from militarily) important example is that used between Holyhead and Liverpool between 1826 and 1861.[33] It worked by means of semaphore arms mounted on a lofty frame alongside or on top of a signal house, and by careful selection of sites and sight-lines it succeeded in relaying signals over distances of up to 12.5 miles between stations. The speed of communication between stations was the speed of light, but relaying the signal to the next station was rather less rapid! It was, however, sufficiently fast and reliable to justify considerable expenditure on equipment and staff over a period of thirty-five years. Furthermore, it did not get electrified as soon as that became technically possible: the first electric telegraph under the English Channel had been in use for ten years when the optical telegraph finally succumbed. The hazards of fog and sleeping signal keepers were obviously less acute than one might imagine.

A variety of flag-based signalling systems preceded the semaphore system, and since 1763 the Dock Trustees had paid for the upkeep of such an establishment on Bidston Hill. Their effectiveness, like those of the semaphores, depended heavily on the standard of telescope available to signallers, and improvements in glass manufacture and lens-making were a pre-condition of the enhanced usefulness of the telegraph.[34] Flag

[33]For a general account of these systems, see G. Wilson, *The Old Telegraphs* (London, 1976): for a detailed treatment of the Liverpool system, see F. Large, "The Liverpool Optical Telegraph System" (Unpublished MSc thesis, University of Liverpool, 1996).

[34]Particularly important was Dollond's invention of the achromatic lens (1758) and the improvements in the manufacture of flint glass by Guinand and others at the turn of the nineteenth century. C. Singer, *et al.* (eds.), *A History of Technology* (7 vols., Oxford, 1958), III, 358-360. The Dock Trustees bought their telescopes from Dollond.

systems, however, suffered from the critical disadvantage that in unfavourable wind conditions the signal could be edge-on to the person trying to read it.

The question is not whether or not the system worked — we know it did — but whether it altered trading methods. None of the signal station logbooks survive, but two different code books do, and their vocabulary conveys an idea of the signals sent.[35] There are numerous entries for the description of cargoes, not merely their nature but also their quantity and condition. The second (1847) code book contains some 330 entries for goods and commodities, many times the number in the 1827 version, suggesting an evolution in the use of the system. Vocabulary existed for notifying sundry misfortunes, including storm or collision damage and sickness aboard. Under the Trustees' bye-laws, failure to identify an inward vessel to the telegraph station at Holyhead for pilotage purposes was punishable with the substantial fine of £5.

The telegraph was free: no charges were made for sending or receiving signals, and nearly all its expenses were met by the Trustees. Some trade associations and insurers made voluntary contributions, suggesting that their members found it an aid to business. Clearly the Trustees had an interest in enforcing their pilotage system: the Mersey approaches were treacherous and the removal of wrecks from the channels slow and costly. Probably greater benefit was gained by the Harbourmaster's department: throughout the telegraph's life, the docks were intensely crowded when the main seasonal cargoes, especially north American cotton and timber, were arriving. Knowing what vessels were arriving and when, and what they had to discharge, made the planning of berthing much easier. The telegraph also enabled the lighthouses, lightships and pilots to communicate with Liverpool. Finally, its potential usefulness as a "disaster control system" was remarked upon when it failed during the catastrophic Great Gale of 1839, and this may account for the altogether more robust nature of the buildings and equipment designed by Jesse Hartley for the re-construction of 1842.[36]

---

[35]Published (in Liverpool) by Barnard L. Watson and William Lord in 1827 and 1847, respectively.

[36]Constructional details of the Watson system are sparse, but descriptions and drawings of Hartley's work survive in MAL.

There are two reasons why the Trustees might allow the free use of the system to all comers for passing commercial information. They themselves, as individuals, were mostly engaged in occupations which would benefit from receipt of the earliest possible information on the arrival of ships and their cargoes. The less obvious reason is that they saw it as a useful "loss-leader" for the general encouragement of the trade of the port. Certainly they had ambitious plans for expansion throughout the period, and for much of it there was also concern at possible damage caused by competition from Birkenhead. There was a clear intention to win new trades for the port, and John Bramley-Moore made positive attempts to target specific new trades.[37]

The discovery of current electricity by Volta in 1800 provided the scientific and technical world with a problem. Electricity was clever stuff, but what actual *use* was it? The key to its first practical application lay in the discovery by Oersted that electricity and magnetism were related, leading to the electromagnet and the relay. Samuel Morse in America and Cooke and Wheatstone in Britain produced a workable signalling apparatus in, respectively, 1835 and 1837. The former employed the eponymous code, while the latter used deflecting pointers to spell out words letter by letter. This required one insulated wire per pointer, and was thus much more expensive than the Morse system which needed only two wires altogether: the Cooke and Wheatstone system was eventually simplified to one pointer which indicated a dot or a dash in Morse code.

It has been argued that early telegraphs were less important in the conduct of business than intuition would suggest, because they were very expensive to use.[38] That argument does not fully explain the extremely rapid growth of telegraph systems, even before their technology

---

[37]On Birkenhead's competition generally, see A. Jarvis, *The Liverpool Dock Engineers* (Stroud, 1996), ch. 4; and T. Webster, *The Port & Docks of Birkenhead 1844-52* (London, 1873), transcribes evidence given before Select Committees for the numerous Dock Acts of those years, including that of Bramley-Moore, who was Chairman of the Trustees' Dock Committee.

[38]J. Yates, "The Telegraph's Effects on Nineteenth Century Markets and Firms," *Business and Economic History*, Second series. XV (1986), 149-163; L.R. Fischer and H.W. Nordvik, "Economic Theory, Information and Management in Shipbroking: Fearnley & Eger as a Case Study," in S.P. Ville and D.M. Williams (eds.), *Management, Finance and Industrial Relations in Maritime Industries: Essays in International Maritime and Business History* (St. John's, 1994), 1-30.

approached maturity — by 1855 the Electric Telegraph Company of London owned 4500 miles of line, and while they were the biggest telegraph company in Britain, there were several others. The total for the country in 1861 has been estimated at 15,000 miles, about ten percent of the world total.

It has also been suggested that telegraph development was not an economic but a political phenomenon: the telegraph was one of the "Tentacles of Empire."[39] That the long-distance cables, submarine or overland, British or otherwise, received substantial Government encouragement in cash and in kind is undeniable, and perhaps the USA is not quite the exception it seems because it virtually constituted an empire in its own right. Yet Britain's first international cable was to France and the first oceanic cable was to North America, where lower values of colonial trade, shorter distance and faster mail steamers would suggest a low priority as compared with India or key coaling stations on the route thereto. We must take seriously the idea that the transatlantic cable was intended for business use.[40]

Britain is a relatively small country which then had the densest service of fast passenger railways in the world, enabling fast postal services and facilitating business in person. Yet its "route mileage" of telegraph lines for a time exceeded that of the USA and continued to exceed that of India, both countries where routes were an order of magnitude longer. This suggests a high density of business use, which is easily shown. John Patterson, President of the Liverpool Chamber of Commerce, gave evidence in 1868 that "many large transactions to a very large extent indeed are almost continually carried on by telegraph."[41] After nationalization it was easy to quantify telegraph use, and we find that Liverpool did indeed use it a lot — nearly 60,000 messages per week in 1872 — and that the busiest station was the Exchange, with 17,437. The

---

[39]D.R. Headrick, *The Tentacles of Progress* (Oxford, 1988). See also Lars Scholl's chapter in this volume.

[40]It is probably significant that "The £350,000 necessary [for the first Atlantic cable] was obtained largely through meetings at Liverpool, Manchester and Glasgow." J.L. Kieve. *The Electric Telegraph, A Social and Economic History* (Newton Abbot, 1973), 107.

[41]Great Britain, Parliament, *British Parliamentary Papers* [*BPP*], Select Committee on Electric Telegraphs Bill (1867-1868), XI, 333, q. 622.

Head Post Office, also in the business quarter, was second with 17,285. The total number of messages in tax year 1875-1876 was 3,520,881.[42]

It was assumed at the time that the more speculative the business, the greater the telegraph's benefits to the user, so considerable evidence was collected on one particularly speculative business, namely betting on horses. Newmarket races in 1875 generated 71,765 "public" (ie private) messages and 15,280 Press messages. Use by the Press was extensive: a list of "Special Events" — Royal visits, an accident or two, some important criminal trials — generated 49,915 messages totalling 3,226,465 words.

Press usage was very extensive and important for trade and shipping. It made up-to-date market information available in quality local newspapers throughout the country, and it allowed the whereabouts of ships anywhere in the world to be reported in *Lloyd's List* with far greater speed and accuracy. It reduced time wasted "awaiting orders." This knowledge allowed consignees to embark on a limited version of the "just in time" philosophy, reducing stocking levels and in effect using a ship at sea as a warehouse.[43] Such reports included those of piracy, giving the navies of trading nations a better chance of tracking down the malefactors. Nor did benefits to maritime safety end there. We nowadays assume that the Isle of Man ferry will not leave Liverpool if it is blowing a Force 10 in Douglas, but before the Meterological Office introduced coastal weather reporting by telegraph in the late 1860s there was much less assurance of a safe arrival.

Telegraphy did not just make it safer and faster to do business: it made it easier to obtain confidential information from around the world, bringing a qualitative change.[44] When the centre of an organisation could know rapidly what its overseas branches were doing, control could be

---

[42] These figures, together with those in the following paragraph, are from *BPP*, Select Committee on Organisation and Financial System of the Post Office Telegraph Department (1876), XIII, 1.

[43] A.J. Field, "The Magnetic Telegraph, Price and Quantity Data and the New Management of Capital," *Journal of Economic History*, LII (1992), 401-413.

[44] Privacy was much discussed by the Select Committees cited in notes 41 and 42. Customers began to use private codes which saved line time and ensured privacy. The Telegraph Code Books of firms supplying goods to overseas customers achieved considerable size. A six-letter codeword might identify, let us say, a thirty by seven foot diameter Lancashire boiler, and so on for several hundred pages.

centralised more effectively, with less reliance on "our man in Singapore." For present purposes, it had the important effect of being able to find out the state of the market for anything, anywhere in the world, quickly and accurately, and thus to make more effective decisions as to whether to buy, say, Mauritian or West Indian sugar. Those decisions could now be made in Britain rather than in Mauritius or the West Indies, bringing the two sources of supply into one market.[45]

The third phase, the wireless telegraph, is really a twentieth-century development (see Lars Scholl's chapter in this volume). Its invention is a wonderful story of bits of the solution being found by various people, an initial successful demonstration by Oliver Lodge (in 1894) and then the inspired "packaging" of the whole technology by Marconi. Because the world was already criss-crossed with submarine cables, the wireless telegraph initially had only one significant advantage: it was usable by ships. This gave an additional advantage of the type first sought by the use of visual telegraphs, of knowing where ships were, and hence allowed the continuation of change in methods of trading and operation mentioned above. It may, however, at first have been more significant in terms of its contribution to rescue and salvage than strictly to trade.

Taken in conjunction with the establishment of worldwide steam cargo liner services and the changes in the basics of port construction and operation which that necessitated, the three technologies here briefly considered may be seen to contribute to the early stages of globalization as defined at the beginning of this paper through the separate stages of transporting, handling and dealing in goods. However, with the exception of the US grain trade, every example given rests on another factor as yet unmentioned, and that is the provision of engineering expertise in Australia, Argentina, India or wherever. In general terms, Buchanan has shown how Britain produced sufficient professional engineers to be able to export them all over the world,[46] while specifically we find Liverpool-trained dock engineers turning up in all the places mentioned above and

---

[45]The "centralization" argument is advanced in R.B. du Boff, "The Telegraph in Nineteenth Century America: Technology and Monopoly," *Comparative Studies in Society and History*, XXVI (1984), 571-586.

[46]R.A. Buchanan, "The Diaspora of British Engineering," *Technology and Culture*, XXVII (1986), 501-524.

more besides.[47] It was not just a matter of building modern and efficient docks and harbours at the far end of a liner service. There was no point having excellent handling machinery if transport from the hinterland was unreliable. In the case of India, this meant exporting the entire skills of railway-building and operation, from surveying the route to working out timetables.[48] In some cases it was necessary to undertake complex harbour works simply to provide coaling stations to get the ships to their eventual destination.

Technological Determinism?

Much of the above is open to the accusation that it interprets change in terms of old-style technological determinism, long unfashionable in professional historical circles. Older works of technological history convey the idea that the history of, say, steelmaking was principally shaped by what was technically possible, and that from the ability to make large quantities of cheap steel there arose directly and almost monocausally not just steel products but also their social and economic consequences.[49]

The refutation of technological determinism in its old naive form originated with economic historians who very plausibly pointed out that engineers and inventors were, like everyone else, governed by economic and financial considerations.[50] Innovation was a response to need and if

---

[47]Jarvis, *Liverpool Dock Engineers,* ch. 5, identifies examples and gives "potted biographies" of them.

[48]It may be of passing interest to note that these "exported engineers" were often young men who took with them a livelier approach than their elders.

[49]S. Smiles, *Industrial Biography* (London, 1866) is chiefly concerned with metal makers and workers. R.A. Buchanan, *Technology and Social Progress* (Oxford, 1965), while eschewing the former excesses of technological determinism, still leans in that direction. For more recent views, see M.R. Smith and L. Marx (eds.), *Does Technology Drive History? The Dilemma of Technological Determinism* (Cambridge, MA, 1994). The work of neo-Luddites like Lewis Mumford and Jaques Ellul, deploring the cultural effects of technology, forms a powerful argument for its importance, for good or ill.

[50]Perhaps best illustrated by the choice of chapter headings in classic works like Clapham. Curiously, it also infiltrated T.K. Derry and T.I. Williams, *A Short History of Technology* (Oxford, 1960), 146-147, indicating the pervasive nature of its orthodoxy at

there was enough need, the price of innovation would rise and innovators would appear from the woodwork. Thus caricatured, the argument appears nearly as ridiculous as the interpretation it supplanted, which it was not, but it was less than complete. In the first place, it was not always correctly based in fact: the development of iron-smelting by coke was portrayed as the result of R&D processes forced into being by acute shortage of charcoal, occasioned by a shortage of oak. As Rackham has shown, there was no real timber shortage.[51] More importantly the argument rests on ignorance of the practice of charcoal-burning: the conflict between shipwrights and charcoal burners is entirely imaginary. Charcoal burners being intelligent men desirous of continued employment, they harvested coppiced wood as a renewable resource. Increased demand for large timber would, if it had any effect, cause a glut of wood of the size the charcoal burners sought, and hence a rise, not a fall, in the supply of charcoal.

Early economic determinists had to undermine the "Hero as Engineer" culture built by Smiles and others, so underlying economic determinism we normally find the anti-heroic assumption that anyone can invent things: if James Watt had not improved the steam engine, someone else would have done. That is not necessarily how things happen in real life. There are some devices which men have been trying to make for centuries and which have proved either impossible or ineffective. A classic example is the rotary-piston engine, whose history stretches back to Watt himself.[52] It offers perfect dynamic balance, a near-complete absence of stress reversal, an extremely even turning moment and a phenomenal power-to-weight ratio. A few designs of rotary steam engine and the Wankel rotary petrol engine achieved those *desiderata*, but they were more than outweighed by high manufacturing cost, poor long-term reliability and abysmal thermal efficiency. In less extreme cases, solutions have been found, but only after a century or more. To take another "prime mover" example, Sir Samuel Morland designed a high-pressure steam

---

that date.

[51] O. Rackham, *The History of the Countryside* (London, 1986), 90-97.

[52] An entire class of the *Abridgement of Patents* is devoted to this perennial pipe-dream. For early rotaries, see E. Galloway, *The Steam Engine: Second Edition with an Appendix by Luke Hebert* (London, 1834).

engine in 1682, but the nineteenth century had dawned before Richard Trevithick built the first effective.[53] Morland failed because of the inadequacy of contemporary boiler making and machining. One reason Trevithick succeeded was that these constraints had been removed.

On the one hand we have successful collaborations like that between Professor W.J.M. Rankine and F.J. Rowan, marine engine builder, which brought impressive improvements in thermal efficiency.[54] Those branches of the profession which retained a "greasy-hands and none of your fancy theories" approach, as did some leading railway locomotive engineers, ossified.[55] We may wonder whether the purchase of some key patents by a firm of the latter school might not have arrested technical progress and inhibited investment in refrigerated vessels, the freezing works for consignment and the cold stores for receipt of the goods. Certainly Kirkaldy's claim that in refrigeration "an ounce of practice was worth more than many hundredweights of theory"[56] was dangerous nonsense which might justify the speculation. Refrigeration was a branch of applied thermo-dynamics in which, as in high-tech steam engines of the period, theory and practice had to march in step.[57]

In the case-studies above, we find that refrigerated shipping and bulk grain handling developed in response to known opportunities for profit and further we find that the early technological lead of the French in shipboard refrigeration was lost through lack of investment. The case of the three generations of telegraph is less clear: in each case the invention preceded its application and it may be that we can identify

---

[53]H.W. Dickinson, *Sir Samuel Morland, Diplomat and Inventor, 1625-1695* (London, 1970), 75-81. For Trevithick, see D. Cardwell, *From Watt to Clausius* (Ames, IA, 1989), 83-84 and 154-156.

[54]F.J. Rowan, "On the Introduction of the Compound Steam Engine," *Transactions of the Institution of Engineers & Shipbuilders in Scotland*, XXIII (1880), 59.

[55]For adverse comparisons between British and foreign (especially American) locomotive design, see M.C. Duffy, "Technomorphology and the Stephenson Traction System," *Transactions of the Newcomen Society,* LIV (1982-1983), 55-78.

[56]Kirkaldy, *British Shipping*, 115. It must be admitted that such statements were sometimes made to justify an author's incomprehension of the theory involved.

[57]This is a main theme of Cardwell, *From Watt to Clausius*, which provides many further references.

technological push predominating over economic pull. It is not, however, at that direct level of contact that a conclusive case may be made either way.

We need not revert to hero-worship of great engineers to acknowledge that the role of technology in changing the way that trade and markets worked was of at least some significance, even at this second remove, below the movers and shakers making their great changes in ships and in dock and harbour construction. Within this smaller field there is a lower level as well: technology is cumulative. The construction of mechanical refrigerators stood on a foundation of pumping technology, so that when an engineer wanted a pressure or a vacuum pump or a small steam engine to drive it, no design work was necessary: pumps could be bought off the shelf. When Armstrong's team designed the hydraulic equipment for Waterloo Dock, most of what they needed and all the means of manufacture, already existed. Barnard L. Watson did not need to begin work on his telegraph by inventing an achromatic telescope.

This accumulated know-how is the background to the background, but it also fed directly into the foreground innovations. When Alfred Holt started to design a compound engine, the theory and practice of construction and manufacture were already in place. Like many other important and successful engineers, he succeeded by synthesizing the right *ensemble* of existing technology. In that sense, the existence of a background technological culture, technological determinism seems sound enough that we cannot reject it out of hand, and therefore we may see the technological developments outlined above as having some importance in the beginnings of globalization.

The Global Fish Market: Internationalization and Globalization, 1880-1997

Poul Holm

The development of the world's fisheries and fish market over the last century provides a significant example of the roles of politics and economics in the international market. This chapter distinguishes between the forces of internationalization, which have characterized the fisheries throughout the period, and the forces of globalization, which have marked their development during the last twenty or thirty years.

The Concepts of Internationalization and Globalization

At the threshold of the twenty-first century, the nation state is no longer the uncontested centre of economic life. Now the main economic, political and social contrasts are increasingly between the "forces of globalization and the territorial-based forces of local resistance seeking to preserve and to redefine community."[1] The process of globalization is the subject of a rapidly growing body of literature. While there seems to be substantial agreement on the diminishing role of the national market as the central unit of economic life,[2] there is less agreement on the potential counter-balancing role of the nation state[3] and even less on the territorial basis of multinational companies.[4]

---

[1]R.J. Barnett and J.A. Cavanaugh, "A Globalizing Economy: Some Implications and Consequences," in B. Mazlish and R. Buultjens (eds.), *Conceptualizing Global History* (Boulder, CO, 1993), 171.

[2]R. Reich, *The Work of Nations* (New York, 1991).

[3]P. Kennedy, *Preparing for the Twenty-First Century* (New York, 1993).

[4]M. Carnoy, "Multinationals in a Changing World Economy: Whither the Nation State?" in M. Carnoy, *et al.*, *The New Global Economy in the Information Age: Reflections on our Changing World* (Basingstoke, 1993).

A distinction should be made between "internationalization" and "globalization." Internationalization by definition implies a system of companies or states which to an increasing degree interact and negotiate, but are based in a national framework. Globalization, on the other hand, denotes the process since the late 1960s whereby nation states and international organisations, including multinational companies, are superposed and transformed by non-territorial economic, informational and political networks. Globalization is an ongoing process that radically changes and undermines national and international structures as it sets free the flow of capital and jobs. Globalization goes hand in hand with territorialization, *i.e.*, localized responses and resistance to global challenges.

Globalization may be viewed as disruptive to society and culture, but it may also be seen as liberating industry from local constraints and parochial mind sets. The state of the fisheries in the age of globalization has been deplored by writers who point to overfishing, the scrapping of ships, the decay of harbours and the loss of jobs. While these observations are true, they are only part of the global picture. Deploring local decay does the observer little service if the object is to understand what has taken, and is taking, place. This chapter points to some long-term trends. It does so by first examining global figures of production and consumption, and then by tracing the development of some major national fleets. Finally, it considers the growth of the fish market.

Literature and Sources

The globalization of fisheries is a vast research field, which has so far not really been taken on by historians. In spite of a vast body of local, national and international studies of the fishing industry published in recent years, there is no full analysis of the period in a global context. Historians tend to cover only the trawling industry or the inshore sector, in a national or European/American context, while economists, geographers and biologists have produced valuable work only on the period after 1950.

Figures for world catches and trade in the nineteenth century are only available for a limited number of fisheries. Statistics on the Northeast Atlantic fisheries have been produced since 1903 by the International Council for the Exploration of the Seas. Worldwide figures for 1938 and from 1950 onwards are available in The United Nations Food and

Agricultural Organisation (FAO) Yearbooks on Fisheries.[5] As a rule, statistics are better for catches than for trade; indeed, inshore and pond fisheries for domestic consumption are probably still underestimated. In recent decades, Western figures are flawed by systematic fraud to evade catch quota regulations. Soviet figures were, on the other hand, inflated to cheat in the other direction. Figures of fish catches and trade in this paper should therefore be taken as approximations only.

Long-term Trends in Production and Markets, 1880-1995

World catches have risen dramatically over the last century (see table 1). The doubling of production in the second half of the nineteenth century was mainly due to the increased catching effort effected by the expansion of manpower and the number of vessels in Europe, particularly in Britain, related to the development and diffusion of the modern steam trawler after 1878. Even more rapid growth occurred in the first decade of the twentieth century and in the 1950s and 1960s. The decades of rapid growth followed the introduction of steam and motor-powered vessels and new fish-finding technologies in distant-water operations. Growth was slow in the 1970s, only to pick up somewhat in the 1980s. Since the 1970s, global landings of pelagic fish have continued an upward trend while landings of demersal fish have stagnated. These trends reflect the state of overfishing in high-priced demersal stocks which is not fully compensated by the relatively low-priced pelagic stocks. In recent years, aquaculture has emerged as one of the fastest growing food production activities in the world with annual growth rates in weight and value since the mid-1980s of around ten percent. More than eighty percent of the global catch is taken by only twenty countries. The growth is concentrated in East and Southeast Asia, specifically in China which replaced Japan as the world's largest fish producing country in 1988. In coming years catches are likely to stagnate as global marine resources seem to have

[5]Full data sets of the United Nations Food and Agricultural Organization (hereafter FAO) Yearbooks of Fishery Statistics are available on request from FIDI-Inquiries@FAO.org [FAO FISHSTAT PC covers Catches and Landings, 1950-1994, and FAO FISHCOMM PC covers Markets, 1976-1994]. For full details, the printed *FAO Yearbooks on Fisheries, 1950-1993* (Rome, 1952-1995) are indispensable. References in this paper to FAO reports are to publications available from www.fao.org on its Rome server.

been exploited almost to the full, while the production of aquaculture may double.[6]

Table 1
World Fish Production, 1850-1995 (million metric tonnes)

Year	Catches	Aquaculture	Total
1850	1.5 - 2		
1900	4		
1913	9.5		
1938	22		
1950	17	2	19
1960	31	4	35
1970	59	6	65
1980	62	10	72
1990	86	12	98
1995	91	21	112

Sources: FAO SOFIA, 1850-1938; J. Coull, *World Fisheries Resources* (London, 1993); FAO 1950-1990: FAO FISHSTAT, 1995.

Most of the production is consumed nationally, and extremely localized and ineffectual markets still abound. In these markets the barter economy is prevalent and the fish reaches the consumer in a decayed state due to poor infrastructure.[7] However, an increasing proportion of high-value fish is distributed on the world market, mainly for Western customers. Although total fish landings are likely to stagnate, more fish may be expected to reach the world market as infrastructure is improved and fish is transferred from the barter to the money economy. The transfer will tend to redistribute fish from the poor to the rich world.

Fish consumption patterns change slowly. Generally, Western fish consumption increased with improved transportation in the late nineteenth century. There is no overall historical study of fish consumption levels but Continental European figures indicate that fish was still a marginal consumer good on the eve of the Second World War when consumption

---

[6]FAO SOFIA, FAO 920.

[7]J. Coull, *World Fisheries Resources* (London, 1993), 235-242.

rarely exceeded ten kg per capita. In recent decades, however, fish consumption in the Western world has risen to the present level of twenty-two kg per capita. Politically motivated efforts in Europe to enhance fish consumption prior to the First World War met with little success,[8] while the recent rise in Western per capita demand for fish seems to be associated with the recognition of fish as a health food. On the other hand, Russian fish consumption declined dramatically from twenty-nine to nine kg per capita between 1989 and 1993 due to the demise of the distant-water fleet and the ensuing lack of cheap supplies. In Asia, especially Japan with a per capita consumption of seventy-one kg, fish consumption was and still is very high as fish represents the major source of non-vegetable protein. In most of the countries of the world, fish constitutes a very small proportion of the diet.[9] In the long term, demand will rise faster than supply, and there is good reason to expect increased competition for fishing rights and market supplies.

National Fleets: The Trawling and Transport Revolution, 1880-1939

By the mid-nineteenth century, fresh fish was a low-priced commodity which often reached the consumer in a decayed state. Markets were not integrated and global production was therefore extremely localized. Only a few large cities like Boston, New York, London and Copenhagen had regular fresh fish provisions from nearby riverine or estuarial fishing grounds.

The main exception was the Atlantic fish market in dried and heavily salted goods which had existed since the High Middle Ages. Salt-fish prices rose in real terms between 1825 and 1875 compared to general food prices in the period.[10] These favourable conditions prompted French, American and British deep-sea smacksmen to compete with inshore North Norwegian, Faroese and Icelandic fishermen for the demersal species, mainly cod. At the end of the century, however, salt-fish prices fell

---

[8]J. Sarrazin and comments by P. Holm, in "War, Public Intervention and Structural Changes in the Fishing Industries, 1914-1930," in R. Skotheim, P. Holm and D.J. Starkey (eds.), *Maritime Industries and Public Intervention* (Stavanger, 1998), forthcoming.

[9]FAO SOFIA.

[10]T. Solhaug, *De norske fiskeriers historie* (Oslo, 1976), 585-587.

relative to other food commodities, while fresh fish prices improved.[11] After the Second World War, the salt-fish market contracted, and sales are today virtually restricted to a few Mediterranean countries.

The fishing industry profited greatly from the transport revolution embodied in the advent of railways and steamships. Improved transport changed the market profoundly. On the one hand, fresh fish could be sent inland and arrive at markets which developed a taste for high-quality, high-value fish. On the other hand, iced fish could be transported in bulk and be marketed for the urban population as cheap, low-quality but nutritious food. These two markets were well defined, both in Europe and North America by the 1890s.

Fast transport was the prerequisite for highly specialised markets and producers. Generally, the inshore fisheries became characterised by self-ownership and market-orientation, either for nearby city populations or for export. The artisanal fleet served the high-quality market; the fleet consisted of tens of thousands of small skipper-owned vessels which responded very quickly to changing demand. Markets could influence local fisheries over long distances. Thus, high-priced specialities, like smoked mackerel for New York's bar customers or iced whitefish for Berlin's middle classes, were the foundation for the breakthrough of Scandinavian fisheries around 1900. Inshore fishermen earned enough money to buy decked motor-powered vessels and the fishing sector fostered an important export trade.[12]

In the distant-water fisheries, on the other hand, steam was put to the service of a quantity-oriented business. British steam trawlers served the large domestic market providing some twenty thousand fish 'n' chip shops with cheap food for the urban working classes. The fleet consisted of a few thousand very expensive steam trawlers. Ownership was organized in limited liability companies, which wielded much political influence on the scale and character of railway and port investments. The trawling industry concentrated on a narrow product segment (the whitefish

---

[11]P. Holm, *Kystfolk* (Esbjerg, 1991); and W. O'Leary, *Maine Sea Fisheries: The Rise and Fall of a Native Industry, 1830-1890* (Boston, 1996).

[12]Holm, *Kystfolk*.

industry) and soon needed to explore new fishing grounds off the Faroes and Iceland as overutilisation of the fish stocks occurred.[13]

The British model for the trawl fisheries was copied by most of the major European fishing countries who perceived high-seas fisheries not only as an economic option but as a marker of national political presence on the world scene. Germany, in particular, developed a state-subsidized distant-water fleet in a drive to feed the fast-growing domestic population while at the same time developing a maritime labour force. The German government nurtured hopes that the fishing fleet would be a "nursery for seamen" for the new German navy, a belief that was also current in the UK.[14]

In the First World War, the European fish market was a target for both German and British buyers. While neutral fishermen profited initially, from 1916 the British prohibition of the trade in fish with Germany disrupted the fisheries, with serious and adverse financial consequences for Norwegian and Dutch fishermen. The British ban did not hit the Danes who therefore enjoyed very high profits from the German market in the later stages of the war.

Disruption of the market in wartime, and the ensuing depression of the early 1920s, had very different effects on the leading North European fishing nations. British companies used war reparations to rebuild a fleet of even larger trawlers which were working all the North Atlantic and Arctic grounds by 1930. There were no direct state subsidies to British trawling, but government seems from this time to have perceived the trawler owners as constituting the fishing sector in general. Government pursued a policy which indicated that distant-water fishing was the key to success, while the inshore fisheries were ignored. German fleet rebuilding after the war followed the British model with the significant exception that heavy state subsidies were involved.[15] Policy was largely directed at national food needs and therefore a large and very modern distant-water fleet was financed. Uniquely for the larger fishing

---

[13]R. Robinson, *Trawling: The Rise and Fall of the British Trawl Fishery* (Exeter, 1996).

[14]Sarrazin, "War, Public Intervention."

[15]*Ibid.*

countries, the German fish trade was, nevertheless, predominantly export-oriented as domestic consumption remained low.

Norwegian fishermen were badly hit by the war, so the government introduced immense subsidies. Strategic social and cultural values were attributed to the inshore fisheries. Such values were later of crucial importance to Norwegian regional policies and subsidies for North Norwegian fringe settlement.[16] Dutch fishermen, who were as badly hit by the war, did not receive any subsidies, and their fisheries were in slump during most of the interwar period with very slow technological change.[17] Denmark's fisheries did relatively well in the same period without subsidies, probably because of the immense profits which had been earned at the end of the war. They built a thoroughly modern motor-powered fleet which benefited from the lack of British interest in nearby resources in the North Sea. The Danish seiners specialised in small landings of quality fish for the British market to supplement British landings of frozen fish from Icelandic and Arctic waters.

The American fisheries stagnated in the interwar period. There was not a large home market for fish, and consequently the trade volume was not sufficient to stimulate investment in large trawlers. Many jobs were connected with the traditional pattern of fishing on the Grand Banks and supplying salt-fish for consumers in the Mediterranean and the Caribbean. Canada's fisheries were still dominated by open dorries, line fishing and salt-fish production until the Second World War, but production was run at a deficit and therefore heavily dependent on state subsidies. As in Norway, the role of fishing in dispersed settlements was the key political factor governing the state's willingness to pay. The traditional salt-fish ports of the United States, which did not receive the same support, succumbed to international competition and declining

[16]H. Hamre, in "War, Public Intervention and Structural Changes in the Fishing Industries, 1914-1930," in Skotheim, Holm and Strakey (eds.), *Maritime Industries*; and B-P. Finstad, "Modernizing the Fishing: Regional Fisheries Policy in Northern Norway, 1945-1970," in P. Holm and D.J. Starkey (eds.), *Studia Atlantica 2* (Esbjerg, 1998) 179-190.

[17]F. Loomeijer in "War, Public Intervention and Structural Changes in the Fishing Industries, 1914-1930" in Skotheim, Holm and Starkey (eds.), *Maritime Industries*.

demand for salt-fish. In return, both east and west coast inshore landings increased as city demand for fresh fish rose.[18]

In the Pacific, the Japanese developed a deep-sea salmon fishery in order to feed a domestic market which could no longer be fed by the traditional inshore artisanal fisheries. A massive investment programme brought Japan's landings on a par with the British by 1910, and by 1938 Japan was the world's leading fishing nation with a catch of three million tonnes, three times the quantity of British landings.[19]

All in all, from the late nineteenth century, especially after the First World War, national fisheries developed along individual lines with regard to the fishing fleet and state involvement. State subsidies played a decisive role in shaping the world market for fish when the governments in continental Europe, and then Japan and Russia, encouraged the building of distant-water fishing fleets. While a partial objective was to feed the urban masses, politicians were often more concerned with furthering the fisheries as a "nursery for seamen" for the navy and carving out a national share of the world's marine resources. While these political ambitions were often frustrated, they are not the concern of this chapter. What matters here is that the distant-water fisheries found a secure backing in political circles, which did not necessarily reflect their true economic importance. Some fleets went farther and farther to sea to secure large enough catches to pay for ever more expensive ships, while other fleets concentrated on inshore resources. However, it was just a question of time before the sea would no longer be able to provide enough fish.

Internationalization: The Volume Years, 1945-1975

While the North Atlantic and North Pacific fish stocks were heavily exploited by the 1930s, the Second World War served as a moratorium on fishing. Actual stock depletion does not seem to have occurred before the 1950s when the fishing fleets were rapidly rebuilt. The sonar — developed from the wartime asdic system — detected the shoals beneath the surface and improved productivity immensely.

By 1950, North Atlantic catches dominated the world's fish supplies. Soon, however, the Pacific Ocean was to be the world's most

---

[18]O'Leary, *Maine Sea Fisheries*, 252-292.

[19]F. Bartz, *Die Grossen Fischereiräume der Welt* (Wiesbaden, 1964), 39.

important source of fish. The Japanese fleet was rebuilt with government support, and its rapid growth ensured the primacy of the Pacific Ocean during the 1950s and 1960s (see table 2). By 1959, fourteen factory ships and 407 fishing vessels operated in the Bering Sea.

The Soviet Union had built a considerable steam trawler fleet in the 1930s and set up large combines to process the fish. From the early 1950s, the Soviet state launched an ambitious plan for the exploitation of distant-water resources. Soviet economists argued that fewer man-hours were needed to produce one unit of fish protein than one unit of meat, and a massive change from inshore artisanal fisheries to large-scale fisheries ensued.[20] Due to large subsidies, by 1975 the fleet consisted of 831 fishing vessels of over 1000 grt and 547 floating factories, in addition to transport vessels, fuel and water carriers. This fleet had an exceptional range of up to 8000 miles from home.[21] The factory ships made trips of between six and eighteen months duration, and Russian trawlers reached well-known banks in the North Atlantic as well as virgin grounds off the coasts of third world countries.

Table 2
World Catches by Oceans, 1950-1990 (million metric tonnes)

Year	Pacific	Atlantic	Indian	Southern
1950	6	10	1	0
1960	15	14	2	0
1970	33	23	3	0.4
1980	35	25	4	0.6
1990	53	23	6	0.4

Source: FAO FISHSTAT. The Southern Ocean is the FAO term for waters largely between Australia and the Antarctic.

Another remarkable addition to the global fisheries in the 1950s was the Peruvian anchovy fishery. Demand for cheap protein for agricultural use, mainly in the rearing of pigs and chickens, was the driving force behind the new large-scale pelagic trawling operations. Industrial reduction of low-value fish for meal and oil was a well-known

---

[20]FAO SOFA.

[21]J. Nicolson, *Food from the Sea* (London, 1979), 86-87 and 187.

technical process, but it only took on large-scale proportions with the discovery of immense pelagic resources off the South American coast. Production went from 59,000 tonnes in 1955 to 3 million tonnes in 1960, peaking in 1970 with 13.1 million tonnes, making it the world's largest fishery. Three years later the fishery collapsed with only 1.7 million tonnes landed as the combined result of overfishing and the recurrent climatic change known as the El Niño.[22]

The postwar years were characterized by world-wide operations and ruthless exploitation of marine resources, some of which – like the North Atlantic cod – were showing clear signs of overexploitation by the end of the period. Most of the distant-water fisheries were driven by domestic demand and subsidies and therefore little of the catch was traded internationally, the most notable exception being fish meal. For the same reason the increasing political conflicts over the protection of marine resources took on a nationalist character, most notoriously in the British-Icelandic "Cod Wars" from 1960 to 1976.[23]

In the 1950s, the British government, hitherto opposed to state subsidies, introduced financial support for the medium-range Icelandic trawlers, and later even for the largest and most modern trawlers. Distant-water fisheries were simply not profitable relative to the high operational costs but were supported perhaps because the government associated significant British qualities with a large fishery. Similarly the Japanese fisheries became ever more subsidised. When other coastal states began to claim nearby resources for themselves and bar foreign distant-water fishermen from access, these actions were not only a question of fish but a signal of new rules on the international scene. The keywords were territorialization and globalization.

Territorialization, 1975-1995

Iceland's unilateral declaration in 1975 of an Exclusive Economic Zone (EEZ) of 200 nautical miles had a domino effect.[24] Within a few years almost all coastal states claimed an exclusive economic zone. Thus, the

---

[22]R. Lawson, *Economics of Fisheries Development* (London, 1984), 149-151.

[23]J. Thór, *British Trawlers and Iceland 1919-1976* (Esbjerg, 1995).

[24]*Ibid.*

fisheries had been territorialized and the free movement of distant-water operators was severely challenged. The impact on distant-water operations was immediate. Total non-local catches by all states rose from 7.5 to nine million tonnes from 1970 to 1990 but dropped as a percentage of global marine catches from thirteen to eleven percent.[25]

Britain and Germany scrapped or sold the remains of their North Atlantic fishing fleets, while the European Union's (EU) own territorial waters were a poor compensation for lost resources in distant waters. With the admission of Spain as a member of the EU in 1986 distant-water interests gained renewed attention, and the EU bought licenses to fish in third world countries, particularly off the coast of West Africa. Recent developments indicate that the EU and other European fishing nations want to obtain more fishing licenses in third-world countries.

By 1980, Japan was also feeling the brunt of EEZs in the Pacific and diminished returns on fishing operations led to a real contraction of the Japanese high-seas fisheries from 2.1 million tonnes in 1970 to 0.9 million tonnes in 1993. The USSR's distant-water fleet continued operations through the 1980s by obtaining fishing rights within the EEZs of third-world countries, mainly in West Africa. With the dissolution of the Soviet Union and the abrupt cut of state subsidies, the distant-water fleet was either scrapped or privatised. The output of the fisheries of the Russian Federation declined dramatically from ten million tonnes in 1989 to four million in 1994. While forty percent of its total catches originated from distant-water fisheries in 1983, the proportion was down to twenty percent ten years later.

Outside the major economic blocs, Norway and Iceland have benefited from the collapse of the old European distant-water companies. Thus, one Icelandic company, the Samherji Group, operates seventeen large German, Scottish and Faroese trawlers and has obtained quotas on both sides of the Atlantic and in the Arctic.[26] This and other companies benefit from the collapse of the traditional European distant-water firms in the short run, while it remains to be seen if they can reverse the tide running against the distant-water fisheries in the long run.

Generally the output of distant-water operations have declined since 1980, largely due to the demise of the Soviet, East European and

---

[25]FAO SOFA.

[26]*Dansk Fiskeritidende,* 30 January 1997.

Japanese fleets, while West European fishing capacity has been redistributed but largely maintained. Part of the background to the continuation of the European distant-water fishery is the early overfishing of the North Atlantic. While catches in most oceans only culminated in the 1990s, FAO estimates that North Atlantic catches reached their peak in the early 1980s and have been stagnating or falling since then.[27] A considerable reduction in fishing capacity would therefore be necessary to achieve a long-term improvement in fishing prospects in the near- and middle-water European fishing banks, and there is consequently a strong incentive to send the larger ships into distant waters.

Heavy state subsidies support the world's excess fishing capacity. In 1989, FAO estimated that total world revenues from fishing of around $70 billion were returned by the world's fishing fleet which operated at an aggregate cost of $92 billion. Including capital costs the deficit was calculated to be about $54 billion. The Soviet fleet alone accounted for a deficit of $5 to $8 billion, while at the same time the Japan Fisheries Association estimated that the credit balance extended to fisheries from both commercial and government sectors was around $19 billion. Direct European Community support rose from $80 million in 1983 to $580 million in 1990. Indirect subsidies, including protectionist measures, loans and payment by government for distant-water fishing licenses, etc. continue to distort fleet size and encourage wasteful fishing practices.[28]

Nevertheless, territorialization has had a heavy countervailing power on state subsidies. The main beneficiaries of the EEZs were coastal nation states close to the continental shelves, largely developing countries, mainly in East and South East Asia and in South America. Countries like Thailand and Indonesia had obtained a leading position among the world's fishing nations by the 1990s, as they expanded their catches, especially of tuna. Biological surveys indicate that there is still some potential for increased catches. China is now the world's chief fish producer, her growth being mostly related to aquaculture, although a policy change in the early 1980s entailed the development of distant-water fisheries in the North Pacific and the export of fish, mainly to the large Hong Kong market.

---

[27]FAO 920.

[28]FAO SOFA 1992.

Asian aquaculture is rapidly emerging as a major source of fish. In 1994, five Asian countries accounted for eighty percent of global fresh-water and salt-water aquaculture production, China alone accounting for 60.4% (15.4 million tonnes). India produced 6.3% (1.6 million tonnes) of production, followed by Japan (5.6%; 1.4 million tonnes), the Republic of Korea (4.3%; 1.1 million tonnes) and Philippines (3.1%; 0.8 million tonnes). Only ten percent of aquaculture products originate from outside Asia.[29] Unfortunately, many aquacultural enterprises are heavy pollutants, and future development can only take place at the cost of a strong environmental effort. The financial breakdown of East Asia in 1997 does not bode well for this urgent need.

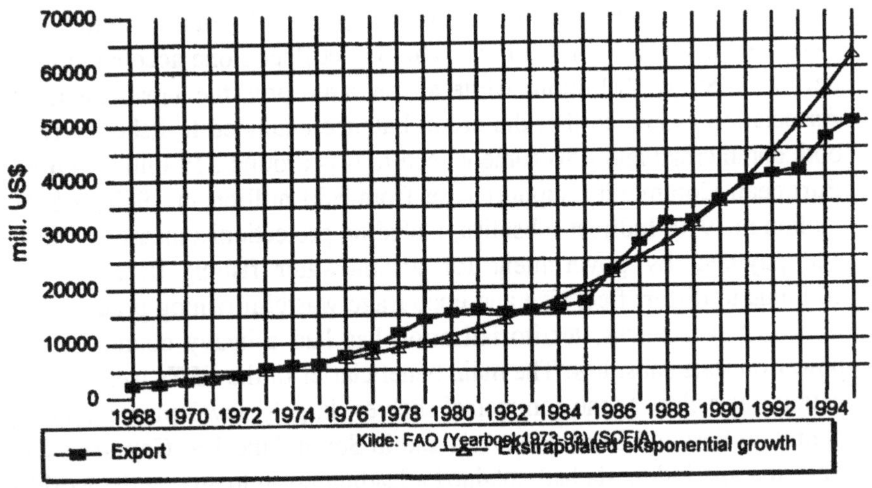

Figure 1: World Fish Trade, 1968-1995.

Source: FAO Yearbook on Fisheries, 1968-1993 (Rome, 1969-1995) and FAO SOFIA and FAO Yearbook on Fisheries, 1976-1993 (Rome, 1977-1995).

The North American fisheries have also grown considerably in recent decades, benefitting both from the exclusion of European and Japanese fleets and rising prices on the national fresh fish market. Canadian fishermen also benefited initially, while they suffered from the

---

[29]FAO Aquaculture 1994.

collapse of the Grand Banks fisheries in the early 1990s and have little prospect of immediate improvement. In spite of the growing fishing effort, North America is a net importer of fish, especially of some high quality species. Peru and Chile have also expanded their fisheries, especially the resurrected fish meal industry, which experienced some good years in the early 1990s, until a new collapse occurred in connection with the El Niño effect of 1997. Furthermore, aquaculture is still expanding in these countries.

By the 1990s, the FAO consensus is that the majority of the world's ocean resources have been used to the full — many indeed are over exploited. Apart from a few marginal resources, only the potential of the Indian Ocean has not yet been fully utilised. On the other hand, there is a potential for a doubling of the world's aquacultural output provided the environmental problems are solved.

From Internationalization to Globalization

Territorialization is one facet of a development which leads to globalization — as the fisheries have become more localized, there has been a tremendous growth in world trade. The success of territorial claims boosted world trade as the major Western fish consuming nations had to rely on imports for their home markets. World fish exports have grown exponentially from 1970 through the 1980s and early 1990s (see figure 1). As distant-water landings have fallen relative to inshore landings and the production of aquaculture, trade volume claims an increasing percentage of landed catches (see table 3). The trade balance shows that some developing countries have earned vital foreign currency with the globalization of the fish trade (see figure 2). Developing countries' net earnings of foreign exchange have risen from \$5.2 billion in 1985 to \$20.9 billion in 1995.[30]

Between 1981 and 1993, eighty percent of total fish imports in the world went to only fifteen countries, while more than sixty percent of all fish exports originated from only fifteen countries (see table 4). Eight countries appear on both lists (USA, Spain, France, UK, Denmark, Thailand, Canada and Netherlands). The list conceals the tremendous export growth in East Asia in recent years, as a result of which Thailand has emerged as the world's leading exporter, while Indonesia has jumped

[30]FAO, *Commodity Market Review 1996*, 8.

within five years from almost no exports to a position as the world's ninth biggest exporter. The developed countries accounted for eighty-eight percent of total imported value in 1970 and eighty-six percent in 1989. In the same period, Japan's share of total imports has risen from eight to twenty-eight percent, reflecting stagnating national catches around ten million tonnes, while the United States has reduced its relative share of world imports from twenty-five to sixteen percent, reflecting increased national catches from 2.8 million tonnes in the mid-1970s to almost six million tonnes by 1990.

Table 3
World Fish Trade, 1960-1995
(catches and aquaculture)

Year	Trade Volume as % of Catch
1960	20
1970	36.6
1980	33.1
1990	37.5
1993	40.9

Notes: Peru's fish meal exports explain the high in 1970; 1993 is the latest year available.

Source: FAO *Yearbooks*, SOFIA

Frozen fish blocks have become the basic currency unit in the fishing industry worldwide and turned hitherto segregated markets for Alaskan pollock and North Atlantic cod into a highly competitive whitefish market. Vertical integration has meant that a handful of supermarket chains and fish processing plants serves North European and North American fish consumers. The Unilever company, for example, handles an estimated ten percent of the world whitefish market.

European and American fisheries have been deeply affected by this development. The decline of the distant-water fleets quickly benefited inshore and middle-distance skipper-owned vessels, but recent trends have eroded this. World trade in whitefish and a vast increase in the production of Alaskan pollock levelled out the lucrative cod market. In the last few years, East European and Russian trawling companies have marketed cheap fish blocks in Europe as privatization has forced them to cater to the higher-paying Western market rather than the cheap home market.

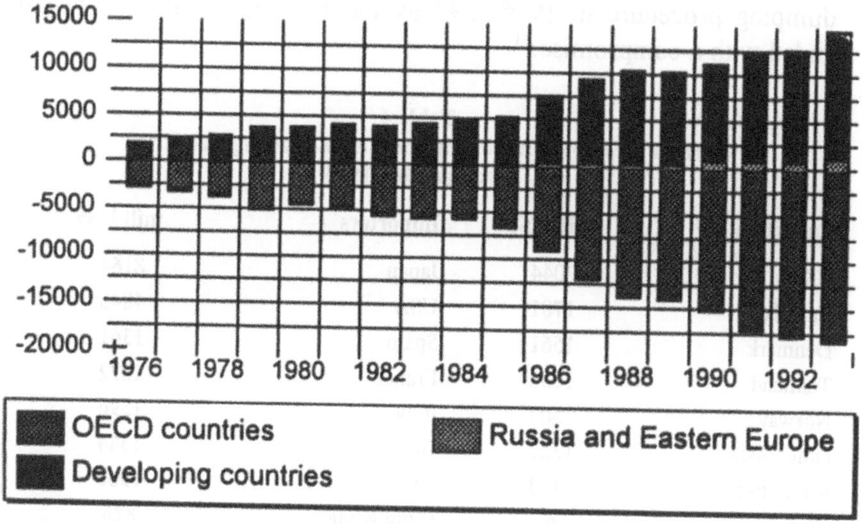

Figure 2: World Fish Trade Balance

Source: See figure 1.

Animosities against globalization run high among Western fishermen, and European politicians have felt the need to impose or prolong customs barriers while pursuing a long-term commitment to abolishing customs and developing trade with third countries. The luxury fish market likewise follows the globalization trend. In the past ten to fifteen years, air freight has increased the possibility of marketing high-quality fish like lobster, shrimp, salmon and tuna to European and American customers. The Norwegian farmed salmon industry is a case in point, both as regards worldwide trade, state intervention and the rise of developing countries. While the Norwegian industry profited in the 1980s when salmon aquaculture was first introduced, it suffered a severe blow as international competition led prices to fall throughout the 1990s. State subsidies have enabled Norwegian producers to secure a worldwide market share of fifty-four percent. The main markets for farmed salmon are Japan, Europe and the United States. In spite of protectionist measures, the EU has so far failed to close the market. In recent years, however, Chilean producers have enjoyed a feast on the American market, which was closed to the Norwegians in 1991. A similar antidumping procedure in 1996-1997 by the EU against the Norwegians ended with a compromise.[31]

Table 4
Top Fifteen Fish-Importing and Fish-Exporting Countries
(average 1981-1993)

Exporters	mill US$	Importers	mill US$
USA	2044	Japan	8164
Canada	1781	USA	4845
Denmark	1561	Spain	1341
Thailand	1558	France	1872
Norway	1507	Italy	1596
Other Asia	1320	Germany	1344
Korea Rep	1193	UK	1368
China	961	Hong Kong	826
Indonesia	949	Denmark	717
Iceland	910	Thailand	442
Netherlands	899	Canada	511
Chile	704	Netherlands	560
UK	660	Belgium	525
Russian Fed	637	Portugal	391
Spain	616	China	313
France	607	Singapore	324

Source: FAO *Yearbooks*, 1982-1993.

At the same time, East Asian aquaculture has grown rapidly, serving both the global market for luxury fish and crustaceans and the ever larger domestic market. The future expansion of this industry, however, relies on an increased import of expensive fish-meal as feed, because the best quality feed brings the best prices and minimizes waste which has become a serious threat to the industry as large coastal stretches have become polluted. European fish-meal producers are the main suppliers of quality meal, and Asian growth therefore increases the globalization trend in both exports and imports.

---

[31]Stefan Stippi, "Norwegian Salmon in Brussels," *Fish International,* No. 4 (1996), 12-18.

From 1948 to 1989, the share of total food dollars in the US spent away from home increased from twenty-four to forty-six percent. While most of the growth has occurred in the fast food industry, full service restaurants have also expanded, not least in the market for specialised fish menus. High income families spend more on fish than low income families.[32] The fish demand in Europe and Japan probably follows the same trend, albeit on a slower pace. While real prices of fish were seventy-five percent higher in the United States in 1988 compared to the base year of 1971, they were twenty percent higher in Japan and thirty-five percent higher in the United Kingdom.[33]

The collapse of the East European distant-water fleet has meant that the West African fish market has suffered in the short run. Previously the Russians paid for the licenses with supplies of fish, while payment today is in cash. If the income from the sale of fish quotas to the EU were invested in local shipbuilding and service industries there would be a potential for a future West African fishery, but it is doubtful if this possibility is being seized. The FAO therefore expresses concern over the lack of supplies of cheap and nourishing pelagic fish for the African market.[34] This negative development is as much a result of local politics as of globalization itself.

Conclusion

The growth of the fishing industry in the nineteenth century was mainly determined by an increase in the real price of fish relative to other foodstuffs. In the twentieth century, European and Japanese distant-water fisheries developed as an economic and political means of carving up the world's marine resources. The strong link between nation states, fleets and home markets inhibited world trade until the 1970s. Fishing overcapacity and depletion of fish stocks were the results of heavy state subsidies both in the Western and Soviet economic systems. By the 1970s

[32]C.R. Handy and Alden C. Manchester, "Structure and Performance of the Food System Beyond the Farm Gate," Commodity Economics Division White Paper for the US Department of Agriculture Economic Research Service Planning Retreat, 24-27 April 1990.

[33]FAO SOFA.

[34]FAO 884.

overfishing and political resentment in coastal states threatened distant-water operations, while the soaring costs of running the operations eroded the political will to maintain state subsidies. The distant-water fishing regime collapsed when coastal states extended their EEZs to 200 nautical miles. In recent years, the international law on EEZs and the rise of aquaculture in some developing countries, especially in East and South-East Asia, have made the global fish market grow exponentially.

In the Western world, globalization in the fisheries has meant fewer fishermen, diminished catches, more state control and more state subsidies. In a few developing countries, mainly in Asia, globalization has meant more fishermen, rapidly growing catches and a boom in aquaculture with relatively little state control and subsidies. Markets are still ineffectual in many developing countries, but overall fishermen in the developing world and consumers in the developed world have profited from the dissolution of the old national distant-water fishing regimes. Western fish traders and Asian fishing industrialists have profited from globalization, while the losers have been distant-water fishing operators, especially in the former Soviet bloc and Japan. Western inshore fishermen have become exposed to global competition as markets are less protected. Most third world countries have been little affected by the change. Immense problems of resource management of the oceans and environmental protection remain.

Convergence or National Styles? The Japanese Challenge to British-Norwegian Hegemony in the Twentieth-Century Whaling Industry

Bjørn L. Basberg[1]

"Modern" whaling had its origins in Norway in the late nineteenth century. This entailed innovative operational techniques which soon spread to other countries. Some nations were successful in applying the new methods, some were not. Britain and Norway emerged as the most important whaling nations in the early twentieth century, and both in economic and technological terms it is possible to talk of a British-Norwegian hegemony. The development of the industry clearly involved increased internationalization as well as globalization. While the leading nations expanded their businesses to whaling grounds all over the world (Arctic, Antarctica, North and South Pacific, North and South Atlantic, Australia), the number of nations which adopted "modern" whaling techniques on local whaling grounds also increased. Accordingly, the technology spread worldwide, the labour market, especially for skilled workers, became to a large extent global, and the market for whale oil became truly international.

As this maritime industry developed along global lines, the only challenge to the British-Norwegian hegemony came from Japan. The nature of this challenge, and the relationship between the rival states, are the subjects of this chapter. Whaling had been an important activity in Japan for centuries, and it is possible to distinguish between several

[1]A substantial part of the research and writing for this chapter was done during a term as scholar-in-residence at the Kendall Whaling Museum, Sharon, MA, in 1997. I would like to thank the staff of the museum for providing an excellent environment for research. In particular, I owe debts of gratitude to Stuart M. Frank, Michael P. Dyer and Jennifer O'Neill for their assistance with, and comments on, an earlier draft of the work. The initial version of the paper was presented at the pre-conference to the XII International Congress of Economic History, held in Piraeus, 12-14 September 1997. My thanks are due to the participants at this seminar, especially the commentator, Lewis R. Fischer, for their many valuable comments on my work. I have also received useful comments from Mikael Hård.

phases according to techniques and styles. When the country embraced "modern" whaling, the new technology was called the "Norwegian method," in deference to Svend Foyn's innovative steam whale catcher and grenade harpoon gun. The period considered is c.1890-1970, from the time the Japanese took up this method of whaling to the time the Norwegians themselves (and most other nations) withdrew from the business. During this time, Japan gradually developed into a modern industrial society and became world leader in many industries and a top ranking growth nation.[2] The process has been described by economists as one of "catching-up" especially in relation to the US. Many nations, of course, have experienced such development, although none of them to the same degree as Japan. After the Second World War, many nations experienced the process, which has been described as a "convergence" in productivity and growth.[3] The chapter will place the development of the whaling industry in the context of Japanese economic development, and will also apply the concepts of "caching-up" and "convergence" to the whaling industry.

Various explanations of the Japanese economic miracle and convergent development, especially in the post-1945 period, have been put forward. The importance of special institutions and economic planning and policy is probably cited most often.[4] Another set of explanations relates to the special character of Japanese work organization and the structure of Japanese enterprises.[5] A third set of explanations, which does

---

[2]M.G. Blackford, *The Rise of Modern Business in Great Britain, The United States, and Japan* (Chapel Hill, NC, 1988): and D.B. Smith, *Japan since 1945. The Rise of an Economic Superpower* (London, 1995).

[3]M. Abramovitz, "Catch-up and Convergence in the Postwar Boom and After," in W.J. Baumol, R.R. Nelson and E.N. Wolff (eds.), *Convergence of Productivity. Cross-National Studies and Historical Evidence* (Oxford, 1994); A. Maddison, "Explaining the Economic Performance of Nations, 1820-1989," in Baumol, Nelson and Wolff (eds.), *Convergence of Productivity;* and G. Silverberg and L. Soete (eds.), *The Economics of Growth and Technical Change. Technologies, Nations, Agents* (London, 1994).

[4]C. Johnson, *MITI and the Japanese Miracle. The Growth of Industrial Policy, 1925-1975* (Stanford, 1982); and J.E. Vestal, *Planning for Change. Industrial Policy and Japanese Economic Development, 1945-1990* (Oxford, 1993).

[5]W. Lazonick, "Social Organization and Technological Leadership," in Baumol, Nelson and Wolff (eds.), *Convergence of Productivity.*

not necessarily exclude the others, emphasizes the importance of learning, adaptation, imitation and borrowing technology.[6] These and other possible causes of Japanese economic development, will be compared to the development of the Japanese whaling industry. Emphasis will be placed on the process of technology transfer, an important factor in the emergence of a global whaling industry, in stimulating the process of convergence and also in underpinning a shift in technological and economic leadership. The Japanese case will be analysed using the Hayami-Ruttan taxonomy on phases of international technology transfer, distinguishing between so-called material, pattern and capacity transfers.[7]

From a Norwegian perspective, at least in the late nineteenth and early twentieth century, the direction of technology transfer was exceptional. Norway was herself an importer and borrower of technology in most industries. The "Norwegian method" in whaling spread to the world in a period when even Norwegian shipping was backward.[8] In explaining the results of the technology transfer and adoption process, it is also important to identify genuine national styles. What was adopted from the European pioneers and what traditions continued from earlier Japanese whaling? In which areas did the Japanese style differ from the Norwegian method that was adopted? To what extent was globalization really a convergent process, and how important were national styles?

---

[6]A.H. Amsden and T. Hikino, "Borrowing Technology or Innovating: An Exploration of the Two Paths to Industrial Development," in R. Thomson (ed.), *Learning and Technological Change* (London, 1993); and T. Hikino and A.H. Amsden, "Staying Behind, Stumbling Back, Sneaking Up, Soaring Ahead: Late Industrialization in Historical Perspective," in Baumol, Nelson and Wolff (eds.), *Convergence of Productivity*.

[7]Y. Hayami and V.W. Ruttan, *Agricultural Development: An International Perspective* (Baltimore, 1971).

[8]A number of studies of technology transfer in Norwegian industrialization may be found in K. Bruland (ed.), *Technology Transfer and Scandinavian Industrialisation* (Oxford, 1991). The chapter by F. Hodne, "Transfer Patterns of Technology: Theory and Evidence," is an explicit analysis of the Norwegian case in the context of the Hayami-Ruttan theory. He also reviews (p. 181) the few industries, including whaling, where the direction of technology transfer was *from* Norway.

The Long-Run Development of Japanese Whaling

In assessing Japanese involvement in twentieth-century whaling, it is important to note the particular development of the nation's whaling interests before 1900.[9] Japan, like many other coastal nations, had been involved in "passive whaling" from ancient times, in that drifting or beached whales were taken.[10] "Active whaling," in which harpoons were used, is believed to have started in the sixteenth century. At the end of the seventeenth century this was followed by a third and very important stage, net whaling. This method dominated Japanese whaling throughout the nineteenth century. Some Japanese whalers adopted American whaling techniques in the nineteenth century, though not very successfully and net whaling was never replaced. The real challenge to net whaling came from the "Norwegian method" in the 1890s, and it was this technique that gradually changed the entire structure of the Japanese whaling business. As well as these five stages, the literature on Japanese whaling history distinguishes between three different types of whaling: small-scale coastal whaling, large-scale coastal whaling, and pelagic whaling.[11] The "Norwegian method" was first adopted in large-scale coastal whaling – the shore station whaling – and later in pelagic whaling. Consequently, this chapter will focus on these two types.

---

[9]For general accounts of Japanese whaling, see A. Kalland and B. Moeran, *Japanese Whaling. End of an Era?* (Copenhagen, 1992), which while primarily an anthropological study of Japanese whaling communities, whaling culture and work organization is also an account of the stages of development that Japanese whaling has experienced since ancient times. See also J.N. Tønnessen and A.O. Johnsen, *Den moderne hvalfangsts historie (DMHH)* (4 vols., Sandefjord, 1959-1970), especially II, 194 ff.; III, 455 ff.; and IV, 248, 335, 428, 462, 485, 503 ff., which is the authoritative history of twentieth-century whaling, with detailed accounts of the development of Japanese "modern" whaling. Tønnessen and Johnsen's one-volume English edition, *The History of Modern Whaling* (London, 1982), also covers Japan in detail (128, 415, 514, 529 and 573 ff.). R. Ellis, *Men and Whales* (New York, 1991) offers an account of Japanese whaling and is especially good on the recent international controversies surrounding Japanese whaling (488 ff.). For a short historical account, see "The Japanese Whaling Industry," *Norwegian Whaling Gazette*, No. 11 (1954); and T. Akimichi, *et al.*, *Small-type Coastal Whaling in Japan. Report of an International Workshop* (Edmonton, 1988).

[10]Kallan and Moeran, *Japanese Whaling*, 65 ff.

[11]*Ibid.*, 79 ff.

Figure 1 shows the relative position in the world whaling industry of Norway, Britain and Japan in the period from 1910 to 1969. The relative position is calculated as the number of whales killed by a single nation in a year as a percentage of the total number of whales killed in that year. This is a crude measure, since it does not tell us anything about the types and sizes of the whales which were caught. They could be anything from the largest Blue Whales to the small Minke Whales. However, to get an impression of relative strengths, calculations based on the number of whales killed provide a sufficiently accurate picture of long run trends.[12] Accordingly, when comparing the three whaling nations, the long run development is quite clear. Norway was the pioneer in the twentieth century whaling industry and was solely responsible for sixty percent and more of world catches in the pre-1914 era. Even Britain lagged then. The war caused a decline in Norway's position while Britain took a jump upwards, relatively speaking. Throughout the 1920s, Norway's whaling industry was responsible for about fifty percent of the world whaling catch, while Britain was the other dominant nation with around thirty. The Great Depression of the early 1930s also influenced the whaling industry and caused a major change in the relative positions of Norway and Britain. The infamous lay-up season (1931-1932) affected Norwegian companies much more than British companies, as can be seen clearly in figure 1. Many companies went permanently out of business, and most of them were Norwegian. So, in the late 1930s, Britain and Norway were of equal importance. That was also the case after the Second World War, with both countries dominating the industry in 1945-1946, each taking about forty percent of the world catch. However, that was never to be surpassed. From the late 1940s, the relative importance of both nations in world whaling declined. By the late 1960s they were both out of business.

---

[12] A possible solution to this problem is to use the theoretical concept measuring an "average" whale; the so-called "Blue Whale Unit" (BWU). The concept was first used by the International Whaling Commission in the 1930s for analytical purposes, and became an important measure in comparing the efficiency of different whaling expeditions. Unfortunately, data on BWU do not exist for the entire period under consideration. Evidence on output is another alternative. Data on the annual value of the whaling of different nations have never been available. The most commonly reported output data is the annual production of whale oil (in tons or barrels). The long-run shifts between nations in relative strengths will, however, be very similar to the picture revealed in figure 1.

The Japanese pattern of development was rather different. Although a nation with a long whaling tradition, Japan's catches could not compare with those of the new dynamic Antarctic whaling industry. But no other nation could. Japan was number three in the world in terms of catches thoughout the entire interwar period. Argentina and the United Stated were of equal importance in some years, but they were generally far behind. They also had a declining relative share, and this is where Japan's development contrasted with that of other countries. From the 1934-1935 season, when Japan entered into Antarctic whaling, her relative importance increased dramatically, so much so that on the outbreak of the Second World War Japan had almost reached the levels of Norway and Britain. After the setback of the war, the Japanese had again to start from scratch in Antarctic whaling, but this time the expansion proceeded, and Britain and Norway increasingly lost their dominant position during the 1950s while Japan became the leading nation in world whaling, accounting for around forty percent of the world catch.

Figure 1
Norwegian, British and Japanese Shares of World Whaling, 1910-1969
(Percentage of the total number of whales killed)

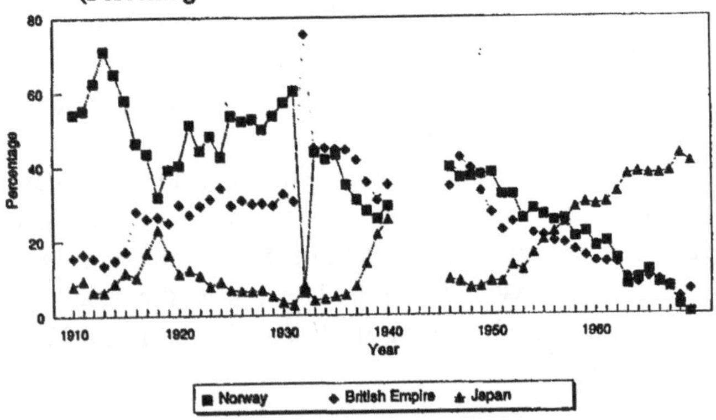

Note: Before 1939, *International Whaling Statistics* recorded data for the "British Empire," which included whaling by companies registered in the UK (the dominant nation), Canada, New Zealand and South Africa. After the Second World War, these countries were reported separately. I have aggregated them to make data comparable for the period 1910-1969.

Sources: *International Whaling Statistics*, XVI (1942), table h; LI (1964), table e; and LXI (1970), table e.

Japanese growth was first and foremost a consequence of expansion into Antarctic pelagic operations. Shore station whaling was not really an option. At the time the Japanese started Antarctic whaling, shore station whaling was a much less profitable business than pelagic whaling. But as the Antarctic whaling grounds gradually became exhausted, the Japanese, instead of winding up their business entirely, looked for new grounds. In 1957 a Japanese whaling shore station was established in Chile, although not without opposition from the Chilean whaling community. Three years later a shore station was built south of Rio de Janeiro in Brazil,[13] and when, a few years later, the whaling stations on South Georgia were evacuated by British and Argentine companies, Japanese whaling firms were ready to take their places and moved in for a short period — just to learn, as had their predecessors, that South Georgia was a whaling ground of the past.[14]

With few exceptions, other Antarctic whaling nations were of moderate importance compared to Britain, Norway and later Japan. Argentina took part from the beginning through one pioneering company; the "Compañia Argentina de Pesca" at South Georgia. Germany had a short "career" in the 1930s. After the Second World War, the Netherlands participated, and so did the Soviet Union. Together with Japan, the Soviet Union became the leading whaling nation after 1945. When Norway and Britain went out of business, both Japan and Soviet Union were each responsible for about forty percent of world whaling, and they were left alone to harvest the Antarctic whaling grounds for a number of years.[15]

Adoption of the Norwegian Method

Svend Foyn's revolutionary whaling methods, first put into use in the 1870s on the coast of Finnmark, spread to other whaling grounds in the 1880s and 1890s. The Russian Pacific coast was one of them. In 1890 a Norwegian catcher boat with a Norwegian crew arrived in Vladivostok,

---

[13] *Norwegian Whaling Gazette*, No. 7 (1957), 394; and No. 3 (1960), 133.

[14] A.B. Dickinson, "Some Aspects of Japanese Whaling and Sealing in South Georgia," in B.L. Basberg, J.E. Ringstad and E. Wexelsen (eds.), *Whaling and History. Perspectives on the Evolution of the Industry* (Sandefjord, 1993).

[15] If the focus of this chapter was on the development of world whaling as such, we would have had to deal with Soviet whaling in detail. But the focus is on describing and analysing the relationship between the Norwegian-British and Japanese development in the context of shifts in economic and technological strength.

and soon local whaling companies were started and more equipment was brought in from Norway.[16] The Japanese were introduced to the new methods of whaling through these Russian operations. Some Japanese whalers were in Russian service, but the Russians also brought their catches to Japan for sale. The Japanese whaling community, especially in the Nagasaki and Yamaguchi districts, naturally became interested in the new methods, and soon several attempts were made to adopt the new technology. From 1896 onwards companies were started. The first was founded by a Japanese whaleman with experience in Russia. He bought equipment from Norway and put it to use onboard a small wooden vessel. It was not a success. The second attempt involved a Norwegian gunner who had also been working for the Russians. A catcher boat was built in Japan, and once again it was equipped with modern whaling gear from Norway. Again the attempt failed. Several companies were then established in 1898 and 1899 which proved more successful, and the beginning of "modern" whaling in Japan has been dated to these years. A catcher boat, whaling equipment, gunners and seamen were brought in from Norway, typically via employment in Russian whaling. However, as early as 1899 the first catcher of a truly Norwegian design, the *Daiichi Chōshu Maru*, was built at the Ishikawajima yard in Tokyo. The whaling company responsible for this was the Nihon Enyō Gyoguyō K.K. of Yamaguchi, founded in 1899, a company which in many respects pioneered modern Japanese whaling, and was also more successful than most of its predecessors. The establishment of this company was sponsored by the Japanese government which wanted to stimulate the Japanese economic growth and independence from Russia: indeed, this was the first of many instances of state support for the Japanese whaling industry. One of the founders of the firm, Jurō Oka, went to Norway to study the whaling industry and establish contacts. The trip was initiated by the government, and shows that a very traditional mechanism of technology and knowledge transfer was indeed at work right from the beginning.[17]

---

[16]Tønnessen and Johnsen, *DMHH,* II; and Kalland and Moeran, *Japanese Whaling,* 75 ff.

[17]Jurō Oka is responsible for a valuable source of information on the history of the company Nihon Enyō Gyogoyō K.K (which became Tōyō Gyoguyō K.K. in 1904, Tōyō Hogei K.K. in 1909 and in 1945, after a number of changes of names, Nihon Suisan K.K., one of the leading post-war whaling companies). For the introduction of the Norwegian method of whaling into Japan, see Oka's contribution to the company history

Henceforth, the industry expanded. New companies were founded, especially in the wake of the Russo-Japanese War (1904-1905). The years from 1906 to 1909 were a boom period. In 1908 there were twelve companies operating according to the newly adopted Norwegian method and the Japanese whaling association (Nihon Hogeigyõ Suisan Kumiai) was founded. Several distinct characteristics of Japanese whaling can be discerned during these early years. The skills and technology required for the new catching methods were adopted from Norway. Some catchers were locally built according to Norwegian design, but most of them came from Norway. They were not, however, employed by Norwegian whaling companies that set up shore stations — as was the typical Norwegian way of expansion around the globe. Foreign companies were *not* allowed to start whaling in Japan, so instead the Norwegian shipowners chartered the catchers to Japanese whaling companies.[18] As the industry expanded, however, more and more catchers were built in Japan.

Another distinctive feature of the industry was that while the catching technology was adopted from Norway, processing continued according to the Japanese style. While Norwegian whaling (and the former European and American whaling as well) was largely focused on oil-processing, Japan's prime interest was meat and other parts of the whale for human consumption. The Japanese did not need to learn how to deal with the whale once it had been brought ashore.

Yet another particular feature was a strong merger movement which started during the years of expansion following the Russo-Japanese war. Over a ten-year period the industry was completely restructured, as the pioneer company Nihon Enyõ Gyogyõ K.K. (from 1909 Tõyõ Hogei K.K.) took over a number of smaller enterprises, and developed into the largest whaling firm in the world.[19] From 1916 there were only three large

---

Honpõ No Norway-shiki Hogeishi, published in 1910 by Tõyõ Hogei K.K. The book was translated into Norwegian by Masahiko Inadomi as "Hvalfangst etter norsk metode i Japan" (original typewritten copy at Com. Chr. Christensen's Whaling Museum, Sandefjord, Norway).

[18]This somewhat unusual arrangement in the international whaling business has been labeled the "chartering period." See Tønnesen and Johnsen, *DMHH,* II, 203-206.

[19]In terms of capital and equipment, and not catches (production); the company could not compete in catches with the companies operating at South Georgia, where the whale stock at that time was abundant; *Ibid.*, II, 216.

independent companies left. Later on, a few new firms entered the business, but they were soon taken over so that the number of whaling companies was never more than a handful.[20] This was indeed a different pattern of development than that evident in Norway and other European whaling nations where there were very few mergers, and the gradual reduction of the number of active companies over the years took place because firms went out of business. In Japan, business concentration was the rule from the turn of the century, and the whaling industry is a very telling example.[21]

During the 1920s the Japanese whaling industry gradually loosened its ties with the Norwegians, though dependence was still apparent in many ways. Catchers of high quality were built in Japan, but a large number were also bought second hand especially from Norwegian and British companies. Expansion into Antarctica demanded larger vessels, and Japan — where the whaling took place in more sheltered waters — was one possible recipient of obsolete technology. Another element of the core technology was without exception imported from Norway throughout the whole interwar period; guns, harpoons and the "forerunners" (a special lightweight rope attached to the harpoon). The people who manned them also continued to come from Norway. At the outbreak of the First World War, approximately sixty percent of gunners were Norwegians, and though the number declined, Norwegian gunners were employed right down to 1939.[22]

Antarctic Debut (1934-1940)

In 1934 Japanese whalers moved into Antarctic waters. This was thirty years after the Norwegians had started whaling at South Georgia and the

---

[20]*Ibid.*, II, 210. Tønnessen based much of his writing on Japanese whaling on information provided in English by Hideo Omura at the Whale Research Institute in Tokyo. Extensive correspondence, tables and statistics can be found in Com. Chr. Christensen's Whaling Museum, Tønnessen's Archive, box 4, "Korrespondanse og bilag angående hvalfangstens historie. One of Omura's tables, "Historical List of Whaling Companies in Japan," shows all Japanese whaling companies and the merger pattern from 1898 to 1950.

[21]Blackford, *Rise of Modern Business,* 80.

[22]See Com. Chr. Christensen's Whaling Museum, Tønnessen Archive, H. Omuro, "A Note on Japanese Pre-war Whaling."

South Shetlands. An extraordinary expansion had taken place. At first whaling activity was concentrated on shore stations and factory ships anchored in the sheltered waters around the Antarctic and sub-Antarctic islands. Then attention shifted to pelagic whaling, with the floating factory ships moving offshore from the mid 1920s. In the late 1920s, an "all-time-high" was reached in terms of catches and profits.

Why did Japan not take part in this prosperous business earlier? The Japanese had obviously acquired the necessary catching technology in terms of catcher boats and skilled men. But they did not need to go all the way to the Antarctica to take whales, as Japanese waters and the North Pacific provided sufficient stocks. The proximity of these grounds was important for another reason. Since the most important product of Japanese whaling was meat for consumption, distance to the market was crucial. It took time before freezing technology was sufficiently developed to allow for the long voyage from Antarctica. But in the late 1920s the desire to take part in profitable pelagic whaling became too strong, and in 1930 Tōyō Hogei K.K. bought a vessel in England for conversion into a floating factory ship, not for the Antarctica, but for whaling in the Bering Strait. But before work started, the economic crises of 1931 brought the whole whaling business to a halt, and the ship was never completed. The crises had, on the other hand, a positive effect on the Japanese whaling business. Both the British and the Norwegians had been very sceptical about Japanese plans to start whaling in Antarctica, and had been reluctant to sell any factory ships. But after the 1931-1932 lay-up season, the Norwegian-British whaling business was restructured and a number of the oldest factory ships were taken out of business. Suddenly there were vessels offered for sale, and so in 1934 the twenty-eight-year-old Norwegian *Antarctic* (along with five catcher boats) was sold to Nihon Sangyo K.K. (former Tōyō Hogei which had gone through yet another change of name) and renamed *Tōnan Maru*.

After *Tōnan Maru*'s first season in 1934-1935, a remarkable expansion in Japanese whaling in Antarctica took place, an expansion which coincided with a period of general economic growth in Japan.[23] Taiyō Hogei put two factory ships into operation in 1936 and 1937 (*Nisshin Maru* and *Nisshin Maru 2*), while the owners of *Tōnan Maru* built two ships in 1937 and 1938 (*Tōnan Maru 2* and *Tōnan Maru 3*).

---

[23]Smith, *Japan since 1945*, 11.

Finally, Kyokuyõ Hogei built *Kyokuyõ Maru* in 1938. Thus, only three companies were involved, showing clearly how concentrated the industry had become.

The direction and pattern of technology transfer once more involved the Norwegians. *Tõnan Maru* was an old ship and represented an obsolete technology at the time she was sold to the Japanese. The other five vessels, however, were modern. They were not, as was the rule in those days, built in a British shipyard. Instead the Japanese managed to buy blueprints of two of the British built factory ships, plans for *Sir James Clark Ross* (built in 1930 for Norwegian owners) being sold by Furness Shipbuilding Co. Ltd. for £7,000; as a consequence, *Nisshin Maru* and *Nisshin Maru 2* were built. The plans for *Svend Foyn* (also built in 1930 for Norwegian owners) were the next acquisition, resulting in the construction of *Tõnan Maru 2* and *3*. Both *Sir James Clark Ross* and *Svend Foyn* represented state-of-the-art floating factory design, based on a concept developed in the late 1920s.[24] So by way of another classic method of technology transfer, well known to the Japanese in a number of other industries, they had, in Tønnessen's words, the key to expansion in Antarctica.[25]

The Japanese entry into Antarctic whaling represented a new direction in several ways. While it took place in a different region, the floating factories were new, and so was the market served. While the output of the coastal whaling had been a variety of products, with food for human consumption the most important, the Japanese now followed the Europeans and focused on oil. There were several reasons for this. For one thing, the transportation of meat over such long distances was a problem. Before the freezing technology was developed, whale meat had to be salted, an operation that required seperate plants in the floating factories. The Norwegian-British designs did not contain such plants. The first Japanese built factory ship, *Nisshin Maru*, could not deal with the meat, and so most of it was thrown overboard. But when *Tõnan Maru 2* was built in the following year, the design was modified, with an extra deck being installed for the storage of salted meat. Japanese shipbuilders

[24]B.L. Basberg, "The Floating Factory: Dominant Designs and Technological Development of the Twentieth-Century Whaling Factory Ships," *The Northern Mariner/Le Marin de nord*, I, No. 1 (January 1998).

[25]Tønnessen and Johnsen, *DMHH*, III, 460.

were highly skilled and could without any problems make local adaptions to the imported technology for different purposes. Experiments with meat-freezing took place at the same time, and the first refrigerator vessel accompanied the *Nisshin Maru* in 1937,[26] though it was not until after the war that meat freezing became significant in Japanese Antarctic whaling expeditions.

The main reason why the Japanese focussed primarily on oil in the prewar Antarctic whaling seasons was not, however, because they lacked methods for preservation of the whale meat. It had more to do with income, foreign currency and war preparations. Whale oil was in great demand on the world market. It was sold largely in Europe and generated a valuable inflow of foreign currency which could then be used for the import of goods used for war preparation.[27]

By purchasing the blueprints from British shipyards, the Japanese had obtained the core technology for pelagic whaling. The skills to build catcher boats had been adopted earlier, and in 1937, during the first years of Antarctic expansion, the Japanese made an important contribution to catcher-boat design by introducing the diesel engine.[28] Special equipment, like harpoon guns, was still imported from Norway. The same was true for some of the specialized oil cookers. While the Japanese built traditional pressure cookers, the more sophisticated Hartmann and Kvaerner cookers were bought from Germany and Norway. However, when the last prewar factory ships were fitted out (*Tõnan Maru 3* and *Kyukuyõ Maru*), even these kinds of cookers were made in Japan.[29]

What about the manpower? Since the Norwegian method had been adopted around the turn of the century, the skills to operate the catcher boats had been gradually transferred. When whaling moved to the Antarctic, the Japanese again needed the skills of the Norwegians, and a

---

[26]*Ibid.*, IV, 580.

[27]*Ibid.*, III, 460.

[28]J.D. Harland, *Catchers and Corvettes. The Steam Whale Catcher in Peace and War 1860-1960* (Rotherfield, England, 1992).

[29]Details on the numbers and origin (types, manufacturing countries) of different cookers on board the prewar Japanese factory ships are to be found in Com. Chr. Christensen's Whaling Museum, Tønnessen Archive, H. Omuro, "A Note on Japanese Prewar Whaling."

number of gunners were hired from Norway. In the first Antarctic season, 1934-1935, *Tõnan Maru* also employed a few skilled factory ship workers (flensers). But that was not repeated,[30] as the Japanese knew how to process the catch. Taking the 1938-1939 season as an example, the Japanese Antarctic whaling fleet employed 2,793 Japanese and fourteen Norwegians. The relative proportions of Norwegians employed in the fleets of any other major whaling nations were much higher.[31]

As figure 1 shows, Japanese output increased dramatically in these years because more capital equipment was deployed. But the process of catching up — and convergence — also implies that productivity improves in absolute and relative terms. How did productivity gains arise during these early years of Japanese Antarctic whaling? There are a number of ways productivity may be calculated, depending on the aspect of the whaling operation under consideration.[32] Table 1 shows three possible approaches; productivity in labour, in catching, and in processing.

In the case of labour productivity (A), Britain and Norway were way ahead, but the improvement in the Japanese figures was dramatic. However, they never reached the level of British and Norwegian expeditions during the interwar seasons. One obvious reason for this is that Japanese expeditions employed several crew members who worked in meat processing (salting, freezing). This specialization required more men and left less meat for oil production, and consequently affected the ratio. From 1937-1938, when the Japanese began to focus on meat freezing, the output of oil per crew member declined. This is to be expected. The productivity in catching (B) and processing (C) show the same trends, with Japan lagging initially, but soon catching up, and reaching the level of the British and Norwegian Antarctic whalers.

Norwegian and British whaling communities were increasingly worried about the possible outcome of the Japanese expansion. They tried to stop it by several means. Laws were passed which restricted the export of second-hand factory-ships and the movement of skilled labour. But the

---

[30]*Ibid.*

[31]*International Whaling Statistics*, XVI (1942), table s.

[32]Several possible approaches — and many pitfalls — are analysed in B.L. Basberg, "Productivity in the 20th Century Antarctic Pelagic and Shore Station Whaling," *The Great Circle*, XX (1998), forthcoming.

expansion seemed impossible to stop when someone always saw possibilities for a quick profit, for example by selling blueprints of floating factory ships, or equipment to put into them. It is also important to note that Japan did not participate in the International Whaling Agreement of 1937, and consequently did not put restrictions on catches or equipment. Though an analysis of politics and regulations is beyond the scope of this chapter (Tønnessen and Johnsen may be consulted for more details), it seems quite clear that there were no legal constraints which could hinder or even slow down the process of technology transfer from the Norwegian and British whaling industries to the Japanese.

Table 1
Productivity in Norwegian, British and Japanese Antarctic Pelagic Whaling 1934-1939

(A) Labour productivity; output (barrels of whale oil) per crew member:

	1934/35	1935/36	1936/37	1937/38	1938/39	1939/40
Norway	384	334	309	366	233	-
Britain	420	367	294	311	264	-
Japan	63	119	187	210	172	-

(B) Productivity in catching; number of whales caught per catcher boat:

	1934/35	1935/36	1936/37	1937/38	1938/39	1939/40
Norway	198	176	183	180	128	140
Britain	234	186	179	184	142	144
Japan	71	128	150	186	153	137

(C) Productivity in processing; output (barrels of oil) per whale:

	1934/35	1935/36	1936/37	1937/38	1938/39	1939/40
Norway	76.5	77.4	77	77.4	73.1	82.4
Britain	78.6	79.3	79.1	71.6	79.7	78.6
Japan	60.1	69.1	79.9	69.3	64.1	77.1

Note: - indicates no data.

Source: Calculations based on the annual *International Whaling Statistics*.

When the Second World War interrupted Antarctic whaling, the structure of the business had changed dramatically during the previous five or six years. Norway and Britain, the dominant whaling nations for so long, now had a rival of almost the same size.

Challenge and Dominance, 1946-1970

The Japanese pelagic whaling industry was in ruins when the war ended in 1945. Together with a substantial part of the merchant fleet, all the six prewar factory ships had been sunk in war actions, and it was not obvious that there was going to be a new start. However, General MacArthur, Supreme Commander for the Allied Powers (SCAP), initiated a gradual return to normalcy during the years of American occupation (1945-1952), and whaling was among the dedicated industries.[33] The Japanese people needed food, and the Americans wanted the oil. So in August 1946 the Americans allowed two expeditions for the coming season. There was no time to build new ships, so two tankers were converted into *Hashidate Maru* (10,794 grt.) and *Nisshin Maru 1* (11,781 grt.). Conversions from tankers to factory ships had for years been quite common in the whaling industry and made functional ships, but these conversions were obviously done in a hurry, and the vessels were in many respects far behind the state-of-the-art prewar floating factories.[34]

There was no further expansion before 1951, the last year of American occupation. *Hashidate Maru* was removed from business, and two other factory ships were brought in (*Nisshin Maru* and *Tōnan Maru*). The real expansion, however, occurred from 1956. In that year two more factory ships went into business (*Matsushima Maru* and *Kyokuyō Maru 2*).

---

[33]The whaling operations were managed by the Natural Resource Section of SCAP. Material on the activity of this office may be consulted at the Kendall Whaling Museum in the Papers of Benjamin Goldberg, who worked with the Natural Resource Section and was also an inspector on one of the Japanese factory ships in the 1950-1951 season. The papers also contain reports from inspectors on the 1949-1950 season, as well as a detailed historical survey of Japanese whaling by one of the inspectors; W.M. Terry, *Japanese Whaling Industry Prior to 1946* (Tokyo, 1950). The American inspector on board the first Japanese Antarctic whaling voyage in 1946 was D. R. McCracken, who wrote a book about his special whaling experience: *Four Months on a Jap Whaler* (New York, 1948).

[34]McCracken, *Four Months*, 109 ff.

In 1957 yet another followed (*Nisshin Maru 2*), and then three more in 1960 (*Kyokuyō Maru 3*), 1961 (*Nisshin Maru 3*) and 1962 (*Nitto Maru*). In these years, Japanese whaling in Antarctica reached its zenith, with seven expeditions employed in one season.

There were altogether thirteen factory ships employed (but not at the same time) in Japanese whaling after the Second World War. One was very small and never used in Antarctica. Another was somewhat larger, and used for just one season down south. A third, *Kyokuyō Maru,* was of a traditional design (rebuilt 1955, 11,448 grt.), but was only used in the North Pacific. That leaves us with ten factory ships which (under different names) were employed in Antarctic whaling between 1946 and 1970. As in the interwar years, when the ships were either second-hand Norwegian ships or were built in Japan according to foreign blueprints, the expansion after 1945 was made possible by the same patterns of technology transfer. The two ships which went to the Antarctica in 1946 were moderately converted tankers, and were not as sophisticated as the last prewar purpose-built vessels of British-Norwegian design. With the exception of *Nisshin Maru* (16,811 grt.), which was built in Japan in 1951 according to a conventional design, the rest of the Japanese postwar factory ships were converted tankers or taken over as second-hand ships from the European whaling nations.[35] While the Panamanian-registered Onassis factory ship, *Olympic Challenger,* became *Kyokuyo Maru* in 1956, the South African (former British, former German) *Abraham Larsen* became a new *Nisshin Maru 2* in 1957, the British *Balaena* became *Kyokuyō Maru 3* in 1960, the Norwegian *Kosmos III* became *Nisshin Maru 3* in 1961, and, finally, the Dutch *Willhelm Barendsz I* became *Nitto Maru* in 1962. They were all slightly rebuilt and modified when they were taken over, and a few of them were also rebuilt later to cater for the Japan's concentration on frozen meat. But the main concepts of the dominant design, as developed in Norway and Britain, were never altered by the Japanese. As regards the floating factories, the Japanese whaling industry continued to adopt technology. It was the typical pattern of the era. The remarkable expansion took place during a period in which the economic growth rate

---

[35]One exception should be mentioned. *Tonan Maru 3,* built by the Osaka Iron Works Ltd. in 1938, was sunk in 1944, but was lifted in 1950 and put back into business. It continued to operate through the 1967-1968 season, and thus became the longest-serving Japanese factory ship.

was high in Japan, and a substantial part of investment capital went into the acquisition of foreign technology.[36]

When it came to the smaller catcher boats, the development was different. The basic design was in all respects developed by the Norwegians (this was indeed the core of the "Norwegian method") and most catchers had been built in Norwegian and British yards. The Japanese did, as we have seen, begin to build catchers themselves from the early twentieth century. After the Second World War, another stage was reached when catchers were built in Japan for European owners. Japanese vessels were now considered superior: the direction of technology transfer had been reversed. Two catchers were delivered to Norwegian whaling companies for the 1948-1949 season, while six were built for the next season, and more were to come.[37] The decision of the European whaling companies to purchase Japanese-built catchers had much to do with their price, but the vessels were of the largest and most modern design — very similar in design to vessels built in Norwegian and British yards. But there was one major difference between Japanese and Norwegian-British catcher boats; the engine. As we have seen, the diesel engine was used in catcher boats by the Japanese in the 1930s, and after the war it became the standard engine in Japanese catchers. The British and the Norwegians were reluctant to follow this lead, and steam engines were never really replaced as the "normal" way of powering their catchers. Attitudes, of course, varied from one company to another, but the majority stayed with steam. For example, the major Norwegian whaling company, Anders Jahre, bought its one and only diesel catcher in 1964 — from Japan.[38]

In maritime industries, a slow transfer from steam to diesel is generally viewed as a sign of conservatism and backwardness. In whaling, however, it is not that simple. There were several obvious technological and economic reasons which favoured steam engines in whale catchers. Both Tønnessen and Johnsen, and Harland, are probably right when they conclude that *this* difference between the Japanese and the Anglo-

---

[36]Smith, *Japan since 1945*, 110.

[37]*Hvalfangstliv*, IV (1949), 15.

[38]Harland, *Catchers and Corvettes*, 150.

Norwegian style is not an indication of the backwardness of the latter whalers, or an example of the disadvantage of an early start.[39]

There were a number of less significant areas, in which technological development took place and where there were differences in style and opinion between the Japanese and the Norwegian-British whalers, and their respective whaling research communities. Both in Norway and Japan there were research institutes dedicated to improvements in whaling methods and to improving knowledge of whale biology. Much of this research seems to have taken place quite independently in the two countries.[40]

What was the character of a Japanese whaling expedition in these years? How was the work organized on board? Kalland and Moeran's account of work organization in pelagic whaling (based on interviews and Japanese sources) suggests that the structure of the whaling operation and the work process had few unique Japanese features.[41] It was similar to the Norwegian-British model. The "core" of the whaling operation, the actual catching and the first stages of processing on the factory ship (hauling up, flensing), seems to have been little different to the way in which the Norwegians and the British operated. This was also true of the oil making process, in which cookers of European design were used. McCracken's account of his season (1946-1947) aboard *Hashidate Maru* confirms this picture.[42] He was not a whaler man, but a military who was appointed inspector, and consequently knew little about the trade. However, his description of most of the operations on board the Japanese factory ship and catchers could have been an account of any Norwegian or British whaling voyage.

---

[39]*Ibid.*; and Tønnessen and Johnsen, *DMHH,* IV.

[40]Two examples of this independent development are the research and experiments in using electricity in killing whales and the improvements in grenade design (from pointed to flattened head); Tønnessen and Johnsen, *DMHH,* IV, 511 ff. and 541ff. The latter is analysed by M. Hirata; "Experimental Investigation on Flattened Head Harpoon. An Attempt for Restraining Ricochet," *Scientific Reports of The Whale Research Institute* (Tokyo), VI (1951), which describes a very similar technology that at the same time was being developed in Norway, but without any references to that development or the Norwegian patents from before the Second World War.

[41]Kalland and Moeran, *Japanese Whaling,* 101 ff.

[42]McCracken, *Four Months.*

But there were differences. McCracken's successor in the 1949-1950 season, William Terry, wrote: "Japanese whalers did alter operating methods which they had learned from Norwegian whalers. Although catching technique remained much the same, dismembering and processing methods were modified to fit the physical and mental peculiarities of the Japanese laborer."[43] And, of course, there was one major difference from the Norwegian-British style of whaling; the concentration on frozen meat. This did not affect catching methods, hauling-up, and the flensing of blubber, but the way the carcass was handled and processed. As we have seen, freezing and refrigerator vessels were introduced in the late 1930s, but such development took place on a wider scale after the war, and made a Japanese Antarctic whaling expedition look somewhat different from a typical Norwegian-British voyage. In addition to the catchers and the floating factory ship, a Japanese venture included an oil-tanker (as did those of other countries), a stand-by freezing ship, a fleet of smaller vessels to ferry the meat from the factory ship to the freezing ship, and finally refrigerator ships to return frozen and salted meat back to the home market as fast as possible.[44]

Quantitative evidence of this specialization is exhibited in table 2, which shows the output of whale meat from Norwegian, British and Japanese Antarctic whaling. Because of this specialization in meat processing, the number of men employed in a Japanese expedition was usually more than 1000, while in a typical Norwegian-British expedition there were about 500-600. The Norwegian journal *Hvalfangstliv* commented that the labour force of 1115 employed on the *Hashidate Maru* and seven catchers in the 1947-1948 season was "incredibly high."[45] The author was probably unaware that the Japanese figure included more than just the crew of the catchers and the factory ship. Still, experienced Norwegian and British whalers felt that the Japanese used considerably more labour to do the same operations, especially in the seasons immediately following the end of the Second World War. Although we cannot rely too much on McCracken's account, his observation is worth noting: "[O]ften they worked needlessly. One day I counted seventeen men

---

[43]Terry, *Japanese Whaling*, 17.

[44]Tønnessen and Johnsen, *DMHH*, IV, 581.

[45]*Hvalfangstliv*, IV (1949), 4.

manning a rope with which they were hoisting stuff from a hold, while the winch which ordinarily would have been used for the purpose was idle. Three men could have done the job just as well by using the winch."[46] But he was also impressed by their willingness to work, and to work in teams — an important characteristic of the Japanese workforce that over the years contributed to success in whaling as well as in most other industries.

Table 2
Output of Whale Meat (tons) from Norwegian, British and Japanese Antarctic Whaling, 1949-1965

	1949/50	1954/55	1959/60	1964/65
Norway	17	73	2159	7142
UK	9346	5660	6080	-
Japan	37461	36381	82953	147721

Sources: Calculations based on the annual *International Whaling Statistics*.

Table 3
Productivity in Norwegian, British and Japanese Antarctic Whaling, 1949-1965

(A) Productivity in catching; number of whales caught per catcher boat:

	1949/50	1954/55	1959/60	1964/65
Norway	130	132	152	207
UK	160	166	142	-
Japan	132	165	179	218

(B) Productivity in processing; output (barrels of oil) per whale:

	1949/50	1954/55	1959/60	1964/65
Norway	67.4	60.3	61.5	30.3
UK	71.3	60.2	58.1	-
Japan	79.8	61.6	49.9	30.1

Sources: Calculations based on the annual *International Whaling Statistics*.

---

[46]McCracken, *Four Months*, 175.

Productivity figures offer a more accurate picture of the efficiency of Japanese whaling operations relative to those of the Norwegians and the British. While it has not been possible to obtain comparable data on crew sizes, and therefore labour productivity,[47] there is sufficient information to chart the development of productivity in catching and processing during the 1950s and 1960s (see table 3).

The productivity figures relating to both catching (A) and processing (B) clearly show that by the 1949-1950 season Japan had caught up with the Norwegians and the British in terms of efficiency. Productivity in catching improved from one year to the other, so that by the 1960s, Japan was in the lead. As to the productivity in processing, Japan was already in the lead during the 1949-1950 season, which was, in fact, remarkable in terms of processing results, the Natural Resource Section of SCAP reporting that: "The Japanese Antarctic whaling expedition of 1949-50 surpassed all expectations of production and set new records of efficiency of operation in the Japanese whaling industry...The efficiency of whale oil production was the highest in history of Japanese whaling."[48]
was declining. This was the case for the three whaling nations, although Japan reached a very low level at an earlier point (1959-1960). There are two particular reasons for this decline. The whales were smaller (fewer Blue whales, more Sei whales, etc.), thus generating fewer barrels of oil per whale. Consequently, productivity, calculated in this way, decreased. The decline also reflects the shifting emphasis towards products other than oil (meat, by-products), to the detriment of oil processing. Japan led this development, as the productivity figures indicate, but whaling companies of other nations started generating a wider variety of products, especially in the 1950s and 1960s.

---

[47]The *International Whaling Statistics* record the total employment of different nationalities, but not for which country they worked. This is a particular problem for Norwegian crew data, since large numbers were employed in whaling fleets registered in other countries, especially the UK, Panama and South Africa. Consequently, the number of British whalers does not give a good indication of the extent of British whaling. The figures for Japanese whaling crews include those aboard freezer and refrigerator ships and are therefore difficult to use in comparative productivity calculations.

[48]Kendall Whaling Museum, Benjamin Goldberg Papers, Natural Resource Section/Supreme Commander for the Allied Powers, Weekly Summary 235, 9-15 April 1950.

In considering catching-up and convergence, the relevant point is not so much whether the trends went up or down, but how the whaling nations developed in relation to each other. We may conclude that Japan followed the trends and kept up with her European rivals. This was apparent before the Second World War, when the catching-up process made a big leap forward. Such success was also due in part to the overall policy of rationalization adopted by Japanese industries in the 1950s and 1960s. An important agent of economic planning in Japan in this period was the Ministry of International Trade and Industry (MITI), established in 1949. Rationalization of industries, including whaling, was one of its main priorities. Accordingly, when the MITI introduced the law to promote the rationalization of firms (*Kigyō Gōrika Sokushin Hō*) in 1952, whaling was one of the thirty-two industries selected.[49]

The gradual shift in power and the sale of factory ships to Japan, did not go unnoticed, especially in Norway, where the whaling community felt that the industry was being eroded — which, of course, was true. While the whaler men saw their living gradually disappearing overseas, companies, on the other hand, knew (at least by the mid-1950s) that there was no future in the business, and were eager to sell. So there seems to have been a real buyers' market in the late 1950s, with the Japanese dictating conditions and prices. There were more factory ships on sale than were bought by the Japanese.[50]

Only one Norwegian-registered factory ship actually ended up in Japan, although several others were under consideration, possibly due to the Norwegian authorities' reluctance to grant the necessary export licence. Thus, according to one report on the sale of *Kosmos III* and five

---

[49]Vestal, *Planning for Change*, 34.

[50]A telling example is the negotiations which took place in Sandefjord, Norway, in October 1956 between Japanese agents and representatives of the two whaling companies, Union Whaling of Durban and Anders Jahre of Sandefjord. Both companies had ships for sale (*Abraham Larsen* and *Kosmos IV*). They were laid-up for repair between seasons in Sandefjord, and each potential seller did his utmost to convince the Japanese of the superiority of his vessel. See University of South Africa, Pretoria, Union Whaling Company Archives, De Jong Collection, N.E. Olsen to Union Whaling Company, 21 October 1956; and E. Cook to Union Whaling Company, 26 October 1956. Union Whaling was lucky, and *Abraham Larsen* and eight catchers were sold to Taiyo Gyogyo K.K., Tokyo. At the same time the British Salvesen company negotiated with Nichiro Gyogyo K.K. concerning *Southern Venturer* and seven catchers, but without result. *Norwegian Whaling Gazette*, No. 1 (1957), 23.

catchers: "... it was stressed by the Norwegian authorities that the grant must not be taken to form any precedent for future transactions. The grant of a licence in this case must be regarded as a once-for-all event which was connected with the desire to pave the way for a certain readjustment of the Norwegian whaling industry."[51] A "readjustment" was definitely under way. While British Antarctic whaling was in its final season, the Norwegians had only a few more whaling seasons left.

Conclusion

The development of "modern" whaling in Japan during the twentieth century displayed many of the hallmarks of Japanese economic development in general. Thus, mergers occurred from the turn of the century; the government played an active role in promoting development; growth was based on technology import: American policy during the years of occupation assisted in the rebuild of the whaling industry; and rapid growth in the 1950s and 1960s was based on technology import and an active government policy of rationalization. Significantly, in the long run, catch-up and convergence took place.

The process of technology diffusion progressed through distinct phases — a developmental pattern very similar to that evident in other industries and between other countries — between centres and peripheries. The adoption of the so-called "Norwegian method" of whaling implied the most basic form of technology transfer, with both physical equipment (catcher boats, harpoon guns) and skilled workers (gunners, mates) being imported. A shipbuilding capability was obviously present in Japan, and gradually the Norwegian type of catcher was locally built. Skills in processing the whales were also well established, but gradually skills required for the new hunting methods were built up. Japan's interests in Antarctic whaling began in the same way. The country again imported the necessary technology with the purchase of a second-hand Norwegian floating factory ship. Very soon, and typically, the transfer went into a second phase; instead of the physical equipment, plans were transferred, as Japan bought the blueprints of the state-of-the-art Norwegian-British factory ships.

---

[51] *Norwegian Whaling Gazette*, No. 8 (1961).

After the Second World War, the Japanese again relied on the import of second-hand floating factory ships. The Norwegian-British design was to some extent modified and domesticated to cater for Japan's specialization in frozen meat. But the major elements of the original design — the hauling-up and flensing arrangements, the main lay-out of the deck and superstructure, and the factory — were largely unchanged by the Japanese. This was also true of the catcher boats. The "Norwegian method" (the grenade harpoon gun used on board a powerful boat) was never abandoned, though the Japanese made significant contributions to technological development especially in introducing the diesel powered catcher. More and more catchers were built in Japan and many were purchased by the European whaling companies.

Thus, throughout the twentieth century, Japanese whalers relied heavily on the transfer of technology from the European pioneer whaling nations. At the same time a distinct national style was developed which was reflected in equipment design, but especially in work organization. However, despite such national variations, the development of the twentieth-century whaling industry was one of increasing internationalization and globalization. This chapter has focussed on the process of catching-up and convergence as demonstrated by the case of the whaling industry in which a British-Norwegian hegemony was challenged and then superseded by the Japanese, who ultimately became the world leaders in whaling. But the emergence of industrialized large-scale whaling in other countries could have been discussed from a similar perspective. A fairly open market existed in which both technology and labour could be transferred with alacrity. Indeed, during the twentieth century, the whaling industry not only became highly integrated but also global in scope.

International Trends and Greek Shipping: The Business Strategy of Demetrios Moraitis, 1893-1908

Vassilis Kardasis

By the early twentieth century, competition in the international transport markets had become fierce. It was particularly intense in the passenger business, with British and German companies vying with each other for supremacy on the North American routes. Germany was also competing strongly with the British in the Mediterranean. The bedrock of German liner shipping was the immigrant trade to North America, its hallmark being the high quality of the services provided, which gave the Germans a great advantage over their British competitors.[1] While the transport of immigrants emerged as the focal point of Anglo-German shipping competition, it also enabled the Germans to penetrate the international sea transport industries.[2]

In 1907 a Greek passenger company attempted to connect the Eastern Mediterranean to New York, the first "formal" attempt by Greek shipowners to enter this highly competitive segment of transoceanic shipping. It was a "great leap forward" for the Greek shipping industry, because it marked the departure of Greek passenger steamers from narrow national boundaries to the open waters of the international sea lanes. This shift was undertaken by the greatest Greek shipowner of his time, Demetrios Moraitis, an entrepreneur who had made his money in tramp trades and bulk cargoes — the classic Greek pattern — a decade before he diversified into the passenger field. This paper is concerned with Moraitis' efforts to emulate his North European counterparts by establishing the

---

[1]R.H. Thornton, *British Shipping* (Berkeley, 1945), 88-89.

[2]The issue of Anglo-German competition has been discussed extensively. See, for instance, the contemporary view of A.W. Kirkaldy, *British Shipping* (2nd ed., New York, 1970), 433; German imperialism was directly connected with the dynamic expansion of German shipping. For a recent account, see Alan Cafruny, *Ruling the Waves. The Political Economy of International Shipping* (Berkeley, 1987), 153. See also Ronald Hope, *A New History of British Shipping* (London, 1990), 309 and 333-334.

Transoceanic Greek Steam Navigation Company, focussing on the "new" fund raising techniques he deployed to launch this pioneering transatlantic venture.

Demetrios Moraitis and the Greek Shipping Industry, 1880-1900

Greek shipping was ready for expansion by 1900. The process of readjusting the mercantile fleet to the new technology of steam had been underway for the last twenty years. Greek tramp steamers, although bought second-hand from Britain, had cornered a large proportion of Mediterranean trade, especially in bulk cargoes. Wheat grown in the coastal regions of the Danube delta and southern Russia, and then exported from the Black Sea not only made Greek shipowners wealthy, but also provided the foundation stone for the development of Greek steam shipping. It was here that Greek shipping capital was generated and here that a new breed of Greek shipowner emerged. Bold entrepreneurs familiar with the business world, with contacts in the major commercial houses, originated from places with a long pedigree in the business of sea transport. From the Ionian and the Aegean Sea, the islands of Cephalonia, Ithaca, Andros, Syros, Chios and Kasos, the new shipowners had built up a significant fleet of tramp steamers by the beginning of the twentieth century.

One of their number was Demetrios Moraitis. His father had left Peloponnese to settle on the Aegean island of Andros sometime after 1770, his descendants being nicknamed "Moraitis," after the Morea, i.e. the Peloponnese. Moraitis was born on Andros in 1866. His schooling was limited but his maritime experience was great, since he spent many years at sea alongside his father, who was captain of a sailing ship. It was customary in those days for nautical families to intermarry and he duly wed Marika Embiricos, daughter of the Andriot shipowner Nikolaos Embiricos. In 1893 Moraitis bought his first steamship with funding from the shipping and banking house owned by the Greek Vagliano Brothers in London, an important source of capital for Greek investment in shipping.[3] For this reason the Andriot entrepreneur's first steamship was called the *Panaghis Vagliano*. By 1900 Moraitis was the seventh biggest Greek

---

[3]See G. Harlaftis, *A History of Greek-Owned Shipping: The Making of an International Tramp Fleet, 1830 to the Present Day* (London, 1996), 93 and 100.

shipowner with three steamships aggregating 4345 net registered tons (nrt); five years later, he was in the top position with seven steamships of 13,881 nrt.[4] One of his great achievements, which brought him fame in his home island, was the chartering of vessels to ply routes in the Atlantic and beyond. For instance, one contemporary journal informed its readers that on its maiden voyage, Mr. Moraitis' "great steamship," *Corinthia*, was to transport petroleum from New York to Bombay,[5] though the carriage of grain from South America to Europe, with coal as a return cargo, emerged as the most important route for Moraitis' steamships. It is also evident that the Andriot shipowner had strong connections in the Americas, particularly in New York, at a time when few Greek steamships visited North American ports.

Though just one of many shipowners, and active in the business for a relatively short period of time, Moraitis' impact on the course of Greek merchant shipping and shipowning was highly significant. His investment behaviour, the innovations he made to the system of co-ownership, and his vision of the future of Greek steamship navigation constitute an enormous contribution. The real extent of this contribution can only be perceived if the state of the Greek shipping industry in the last two decades of the nineteenth century is appreciated. At this time, the industry's principal problem was a shortage of capital. Firms were small, their organization old-fashioned and their field of activity restricted to the eastern Mediterranean. This orientation was not just a function of the comparative advantage ensuing from the presence of Greeks in the commercial centres of the East (Constantinople, Smyrna, Alexandria, the Danube, Odessa, the sea of Azov). It was also unavoidable, as shipowning companies were unable to operate in more distant seas where highly competitive terms prevailed. It was precisely this prospect which required ample capital, strong organization and, above all, the immediate adoption of the new shipping technology developed in Western Europe.

A further key weakness of Greek shipowners on the eve of the twentieth century was the lack of financial organizations at home, that is the absence of a banking sector to direct loan capital to shipping firms. The input of capital by Greek businessmen abroad was, of course, still important and remained common practice. However, it was no real

---

[4]*Lloyd's Register of Shipping*, 1900 and 1905.

[5]*Naftiki Ellas*, 1 December 1903.

substitute for the lack of cheap ship loans. Proof of this is evident in the early twentieth century, when the Bank of Athens first turned its attention to lending to shipowners, investment in new technology ships increased considerably.[6] The problem, of course, arose because Greek shipowners lacked their own capital. And how else could it be? However profitable sailing ships had been in the past, they could not possibly generate the high investment funds that the purchase of steamships from abroad required. The general inability of shipowners to meet the high cost of steamships was the main reason why many turned to the merchants and bankers of Constantinople and London.

Moraitis tried to overcome this obstacle by applying the system of the multi-participant company. Co-ownership was a device well known to Greek shipowners at the beginning of the twentieth century, and was to constitute the prime instrument for the development of the Greek merchant fleet during the next few decades.[7] However, Moraitis' entrepreneurial behaviour was distinctive in the extent to which he broadened the circle of shareholders in his ships. His primary purpose was to attract funds in any conceivable way from small-scale savers. According to Moraitis, even the meagre savings of the lower classes were absolutely necessary if he was to dominate Greek shipowning circles. Accordingly, he bought second-hand and new built steamships from England with capital supplied by large numbers of contributors. By offering returns greater than the bank interest rate, he persuaded ordinary people from Andros to invest their small savings in his ships. What appeared tempting to the public was the apparent guarantee of high capital returns. Moraitis seemed to offer an annual return of fifteen percent, a prospect that at times of low freight rates raised a lot of questions as to the credibility of the guarantee and gave rise to heated controversies amongst his colleagues. Some of their accusations were justified up to a point, because during periods of economic crisis, when freight rates were at a low ebb, the search for new investors was rather problematic, with the prospective rate of return on

---

[6]Harlaftis, *History of Greek-Owned Shipping*, 132. On page 140, there is a discussion of the reasons why the state was reluctant to institute maritime mortgage laws which would have allowed the banks to make large shipping loans.

[7]G. Harlaftis, "The Greek Shipping Enterprise: Investment Strategies, 1900-1939," in M. Dritsas and T. Gourvish (eds.), *European Enterprise. Strategies of Adaptation and Renewal in the Twentieth Century* (Athens, 1997), 144.

the capital invested emerging as a decisive factor in the decision-making process.

On the other hand, the petty capitalists who became co-owners were only interested in profit. Their only motive in participating in a Moraitis venture was the guaranteed profit, and thus dowries, inheritances, and small savings were all converted into lucrative investments.[8] It is clear that the co-owners had absolutely no idea either about the finances of the company or about the voyage, freight rates or cargo of the ship. A letter sent to Naftiki Ellas by an anonymous shareholder is quite characteristic: "*It is true that none of us has ever thought to act for the checking of the accounts, nor did we think to call the directors to provide for us an analytical budget, while the government remains silent and never interferes in the clearing of the accounts.*"[9] Under normal circumstances such complaints were not taken seriously; when, however, turbulent times arrived, they came to the surface.

If nothing else, Moraitis' investment strategy underlines his deep conviction that the future of Greek shipping was dependent upon the development of a steamship fleet, as well as his confidence in the superiority of the new means of transport over traditional sailing ships. At the same time, however, it emphasizes the Andriot shipowner's paucity of capital. The entries in the Andros ship register are revealing with regard to Moraitis' modus operandi. The cost of the ship was defined as share capital which was divided into 100 shares and the small investors (sailors, civil servants, labourers, even housemaids)[10] were invited to buy shares from the Moraitis offices in Andros. Moraitis himself was named as the owner of the steamship, and it was he who determined her voyages and manning, and it was he who had the first and last word on her

---

[8]See Ralph Davis, *The Rise of the English Shipping Industry in the 17th and 18th Centuries* (London, 1962), 178.

[9]*Naftiki Ellas*, 15 February 1904.

[10]The same variety of professions characterized the lists of shareholders in Spanish ships. See Jesús Valdaliso, "Spanish Shipowners in the British Mirror: Patterns of Investment, Ownership and Finance in the Bilbao Shipping Industry, 1879-1913," *International Journal of Maritime History*, V (December 1993). Similarities with the Greek case are quite clear; see also Harlaftis, *History of Greek-Owned Shipping*, 141.

operation.[11] As in the British case, real control lay in the hands of the managing owner, the shareholder that had purchased the ship and who had offered shares to friends and acquaintances.[12] Moraitis' own small shareholding in no way diminished this sovereign presence. Indeed, in some cases Moraitis actually had a smaller share in the capital of the vessel than other shareholders. For example, he possessed only 1.25% of the share capital in the SS *Corinthia* (registered in 1904),[13] whereas other capitalists such as Otto Tetenes or the Athens Bank owned sixteen percent and fourteen percent, respectively. The number of shareholders was invariably large, generally well over fifty, indicating a wide dispersal of shares. The SS *Hellas*, registered in 1903, in which Moraitis owned 3.25% of the shares, was divided amongst seventy-seven shareholders, while, there were eighty capitalists engaged in the SS *Boiotia*, registered in 1902, several with shares of less than one percent. In other words, Moraitis' ownership of the vessel was fictitious as far as extent and substance were concerned, but was very real at the level of directing her operation.

The similarities in the practice developed by Moraitis to that of the British system is obvious, not only in the large number of shares (sixty-four in the case of Britain) but also in the shipowner's access to the

[11]He was not exactly like the managers of Spanish shipping companies that J. Valdaliso describes in "Explaining the Structure and the Boundaries of Spanish Shipping Firms (1860-1935)" (London School of Economics and Political Science, Business History Unit Occasional Paper, 1996), 9, in referring to the structure of Spanish shipping companies at the end of the nineteenth century. The sources do not indicate that Moraitis was reimbursed with a certain percentage on the freights.

[12]Davis, *English Shipping*, 172.

[13]*Naftiki Ellas*, 1 December 1903, reported that the "great steamship" *Corinthia* of Mr. Moraitis was chartered for her first voyage to carry petroleum from New York to Bombay. But the transport of grain from South America to Europe with coal as a return cargo was also a typical voyage of Moraitis' steamships. It is evident that the Andriot shipowner had powerful connections in the Americas, particularly in New York, at a time when few Greek steamships visited North American ports.

local capital market, through which he secured the necessary funds.[14] Such a strategy was well known. It had been used by merchants and shipowners from the island of Hydra in the pre-revolutionary Greece,[15] and the shipowners of London and Bristol in the seventeenth and eighteenth centuries. In each case, an appeal to a wider market of small capital holders proved necessary to attract adequate funds. However, it is notable that the Greek experience came rather later than the British. At the beginning of the twentieth century, when Moraitis was tapping a wider circle of petty capital holders in Andros, Owen and John Philipps had transformed their business from that of a personal and family firm with twenty-two shareholders, the single ship venture entitled the King Alfred Steamship Co., into the Royal Mail giant.[16] It is certain that Moraitis knew all about the British example when he decided to implement his own system. This, in a way, is proved indirectly by the fact that some London and Newcastle Houses purchased shares in his ships. The Andriot shipowner, however, went much beyond the British paradigm.[17] The sources of capital were not confined to a narrow circle of relatives and friends as the Philipps brothers had been in the first phase of their entrepreneurial activities.[18] Networks of sponsors — as identified by Boyce

---

[14]Analyses of 64thers have been attempted by Kirkaldy, *British Shipping*, 165; and Davis, *English Shipping*, 171-179. The practice of shareholding probably dates back to the twelfth century. The 1854 Shipping Act in Britain defined the 64th as the shipowning unit in British ships. G. Boyce, "64thers, Syndicates, and Stock Promotions: Information Flows and Fund-raising Techniques of British Shipowners Before 1914," *Journal of Economic History*, LII (1992), 181-205, refers to the function of multi-participant shipping companies in Britain.

[15]Greek merchants and shipowners from the island of Hydra had developed long-distance trade between Eastern and Western Mediterranean from the late eighteenth and early nineteenth centuries.

[16]E. Green and M. Moss, *A Business of National Importance: The Royal Mail Shipping Group, 1902-1937* (London, 1982), 11.

[17]*Ibid.*, 8-18. The information on family shipping companies in Hull by David J. Starkey, "Ownership Structures in the British Industry: The Case of Hull, 1820-1916," *International Journal of Maritime History*, VIII (December, 1996), 9-16, is illuminating.

[18]Green and Moss, *Business of National Importance*, 8-18. The Spanish experience of multi-participant enterprises at the end of the nineteenth century, as recorded by Valdaliso, "Spanish Shipowners," 7, indicates that the entrepreneur drew his funds from

– extended to the entire community, many of whose members had nothing to do with maritime enterprises, embracing everybody who could accumulate small savings from their income. It was a world fascinated by rumours of the success of the new transport modes, peopled by many who trusted their whole life's savings to the care of a persuasive Andriot businessman.

At this point the usual practice of buying and selling shares after the purchase of the ship, even after its entry in the ship register, should be stressed. This was also copied from the British model.[19] With a simple signed agreement between the two parties, the share was transferred to the new owner. Moraitis was the epicentre of this process, the shipowner buying and selling shares with remarkable frequency, to such an extent that a cursory glance at the Andros Ship Register suffices for one to ascertain the labyrinthine structure of Moraitis' shipping companies. It is clear that anticipated profits, the means of attracting new small shareholders, the prospect of buying a new ship, and even the inability to discharge current profits, were factors that stimulated the frequent purchase and disposal of shares by the Andriot shipowner. In any case, Moraitis' reputation for honesty, and above all the just, pro rata sharing of the profits, was the most reliable guarantee of the good management of the invested money. Moraitis personally assured the shareholders who trusted him with their capital of his "assiduous and indefatigable vigilance."[20] Even so, it was said that Moraitis' office did not keep even basic analytical accounts of the investors and their contributions, an allegation that was confirmed so painfully later.

In 1904, a heated polemic broke out against Moraitis in the columns of the distinguished magazine *Naftiki Ellas*, though none of the authors referred to Moraitis by name. The timing of the attack was not accidental, as the decline of freights in the Mediterranean after 1900 was

---

a narrow and limited circle of capitalists.

[19]Davis, *English Shipping*, 203.

[20]*Patris*, 7 February 1904. Moraitis sent a letter thanking the shareholders who entrusted him with their capital. The trust between the asset holders and the shipowner in multi-participant companies is fundamental, as Valdaliso points out in "Spanish Shipowners," 19.

especially intense during 1903-1904,[21] leading to a fall in shipping profits. The capital returns on the shares in Moraitis' ships were the subject of much debate. Here is the view of one of his colleagues:[22]

> I offer 6-10% and I can't find shareholders, because they tell me that others gurantee them 15% and if they change their mind during the next two years refund of their capital is assured. But when the surveyor from Lloyd's comes he finds the ships in bad need of repair and then the shareholders' problems begin. They are asked for money for repairs, so they either do not receive any return or they pay from their own capital.

Another shipowner added: "they give dividend from the capital with the result that a share bought two years ago for 10,000 francs providing a dividend of 2000 francs, is worth today no more than 6000 francs."[23] And a small capitalist commented: "We deposit our money and ignore their management and we take blindly whatever is offered to us regardless of whether this is a dividend or our capital offered as a dividend."[24]

The accusations became more direct and began to focus on one person, Demetrios Moraitos. The sin of which he was accused was clear: the high dividend he paid came from the ship's own capital. The Andriot shipowner hastened to reply through the pages of the Athenian press, thereby exposing himself, for the accusations had not mentioned any names. He invoked the testimonies of other co-owners, referring in detail to some of the voyages of his ships. This was all in vain as he failed to convince the readers of the magazine, especially as *Naftiki Ellas* proceeded to publish detailed records of the real returns of the chartering of Moraitis' ships. According to these the shipowner was presenting

---

[21]Harlaftis, *History of Greek-Owned Shipping*, 123, shows the evolution of freights during the period 1870-1910.

[22]*Naftiki Ellas*, 4 March 1904. It was not the first time that Moraitis' practice occupied the press columns; see also *ibid.*, 25 November 1901.

[23]*Ibid.*, 14 March 1904.

[24]*Ibid.*, 15 February 1904.

fictitiously higher profits and deliberately distorting reality. For example, his estimate of the length of the voyage of the cargo ship *Attiki* from Odessa to Cardiff and then to Piraeus, was much shorter than the records of *Lloyd's Register* revealed. Naturally, this reduced fuel costs, wages and the victualling of the crew. Moraitis' intentions can be clearly discerned. False, but high dividends were distributed to shareholders in order to attract new ones. In the short-term this policy of the distribution of fictitiously high returns brought the results that Moraitis needed, but in the long run it just proved to be a reckless venture.

Moraitis Enters the Transatlantic Trade

In 1907 Moraitis decided to set up a company to engage in the trans-atlantic trade, linking Greece and the eastern Mediterranean directly with America. Essentially, his objective was to exploit the wave of emigration to the United States that was sweeping through this region, and much of Europe, at this time. Indeed, the movement of Greeks was so intense that foreign companies were engaged in systematically ferrying emigrants from the southern Peloponnese, and the islands, to Marseilles, and thence to the New World.[25] In particular, the German companies Hamburg-America and North German Lloyd, as well as the Italian Florio and Veloce,[26] dominated the carriage of passengers from Greece to America.[27] According to an official report of the Minister of Home Affairs, published in 1912, more than 80,000 Greeks emigrated to the America between 1899 and 1906 (see table 1). This exodus included people coming from

---

[25]E. Repoulis, *Study for the Proposal of a Law Concerning Emigration* (Athens, 1912). There is also important information on emigration to America in the report by the Greek Consul in Chicago for 1911; see *Bulletin of the Ministry of Foreign Affairs: Reports on Greek Emigration to America* (Athens, 1912). On the causes of emigration, see the epigrammatic *Dependence and Reproduction* (Athens, 1978), 148. On the preparation for departure, the steamship voyage, as well as the working conditions of emigrants in America, see the disturbing narrative of an emigrant from Peloponese in Th. Valtinos, *Synaxari of Andrea Kordopati* (Athens, 1990).

[26]The development of Italian — as well as German shipping — was based on emigrant transportation to the USA. 157,000 Italian emigrants were conveyed annually to North America in the 1895-1914 period. See Hope, *New History*, 335.

[27]*Naftika Chronika*, 15 August 1932.

the Ottoman Empire, as well as the neighbouring Balkan states. Emigration from Greece to America began in the early 1880s. The tide of departure increased tremendously after 1902, a fact which presumably persuaded Moraitis to found the "Transoceanic Greek Steam Navigation Company." Some historians attribute the mass exodus to the currant crisis that affected parts of the Peloponnese in the period 1895-1910. This view is corroborated by information available to us from the press of the day. Moreover, regional tables published by the Minister of Home Affairs, E. Repoulis, indicate that the main bulk of emigrants did indeed leave from the provinces of the Peloponnese.

Table 1
Emigration from Greece

Year	Emigrants	Total Immigration to USA
1899	2395	311715
1900	3775	448572
1901	5919	487918
1902	8115	648743
1903	14376	857046
1904	12625	812870
1905	12144	1026499
1906	23127	1100735
1907	46283	1285349
1908	28808	782870
1909	20262	751786
1910	39135	1041570

Source: E. Repoulis, *Study for the proposal of a Law Concerning Emigration* (Athens, 1912), 11 and 31.

Moraitis intervened in the emigrant trade in anticipation of high profits: this was neither erroneous nor misguided. Some of his fellow shipowners also believed that this venture would generate considerable returns and underpin the development of the Greek mercantile marine.[28]

[28]S. Katakouzinos, *The Commerce, Shipping and the Emigration of the Greeks* (Athens, 1908). The author confidently asserts that the steamship *Moraitis* will benefit to the maximum from carrying emigrants and merchandise to America. Katakouzinos called

After all, Moraitis was only imitating the successful policies pursued by large-scale foreign shipping companies – growth built on the transportation of immigrants to North America. The continuous flow of immigrants to the east coast of the USA was, in a way, a guarantee of success. In the event, the first phase of Moraitis' transatlantic venture vindicated his decision. But not long after, the favourable conjuncture of circumstances changed.

Moraitis bought a Sunderland-built steamship of 6000 grt. It was 130 metres long, fifteen metres wide, with two triple-expansion engines, a maximum speed of sixteen miles per hour and accommodation for 1650 passengers.[29] According to other sources[30] the vessel provided beds for 100 first class passengers and two decks in which 1000 immigrants could be lodged. The ship had a hospital, a pharmacy, bathtubs and a sterilizer; she was valued at £85,000, and her first master was the shipowner's brother, Nikoklis Moraitis. On 19 June, SS *Moraitis* embarked on its maiden voyage to the United States,[31] steaming from Smyrna to Piraeus, Kalamata, Patras, Naples and New York in thirteen days, with thirty-one first class passengers and 708 third class passengers on board. The call at Naples was obligatory, since the port was a focal point for channeling emigrants to North America. Apart from carrying passengers, *Moraitis* also carried cargoes to and from the USA. The inauguration of the line was a major event greeted with some surprise by Moraitis' contemporaries because the Andriot shipowner had done nothing to presage this ambitious investment. Enthusiasm among promoters of Greek shipping was unbounded, as the establishment of a steamship company with a regular route to the USA was a major advance for Greek steam navigation.

It is plausible that Moraitis' attempt to penetrate the Atlantic passenger trade was not designed to compete with the powerful and established foreign companies. The Andriot shipowner could not rival the

---

Moraitis "a genius in steamship navigation" and proposed that he should collaboratewith expatriate Greek shipowners.

[29] *Sfaira*, 8 June 1906. The ship was entered in the Andros ship register as number 99 on 13 June 1907.

[30] N.R.P. Bonsor, *North Atlantic Seaway* (5 vols., Jersey, CI, 1979), III, 1370.

[31] *Ibid.*

British or the Germans, nor could the comfortable and relatively spacious *Moraitis* be compared with giants like Cunarder's *Mauritania* or White Star's *Celtic* in which comfort had been replaced by luxury. He could, however, guarantee a core of Greek immigrants for his ships, partially competing with the Italian lines in this way. Indicative is the view of the British Consul in Piraeus, who characterized the founding of the company as the most important event of the year.[32] The venture assumed the status of a joint-stock company, with Moraitis as Managing Director.[33] This was a step forward in Greek entrepreneurial practice. The formation of "Societes Anonymes," or joint stock-companies with appointed directors, was a completely new phenomenon in Greek shipping. It remained to be seen how successful the experiment would be, particularly as Moraitis was burdened with negative rumours about his capital mismanagement. After his bankruptcy, Moraitis was to be accused of having drafted the articles of association in such a way that he had the powers of a Tsar. The truth is that the ordinances (articles 10-23) granted significant authority for a period of seven years (article 47) to the managing director who had to be a member of the board and was appointed after a vote. It is obvious that since Moraitis controlled the board his position as a director was secure.

A company with few shareholders, as listed in the articles of association (see table 2), certainly was a departure from Moraitis' prior investment behaviour. Never before had he included such a limited number of shareholders in the share capital of his ships. It is equally certain, however, that a large proportion of his personal shares was resold to small capitalists, as events in the wake of the company's bankruptcy suggest. Notable among the shareholders was Georgios Mandakas, a shipowner who applied the same practice as Moraitis of buying and selling shares in Andriot tramp steamers, and Nikoklis Moraitis, brother of the main shareholder and captain of *Moraitis*. As the owner of a large percentage of the shares, Demetrios Moraitis had immense power in the decision-making process.

---

[32]The Consul wondered whether the propitious circumstances of the increased wave of emigration will last or will be to the company's detriment. Great Britain, Foreign Office, *Annual Series*, 4228 (1908), 2.

[33]*Government Gazette*, No. 58 (2 April 1907), 214, articles of association of the company.

Table 2
Founders of the Transoceanic Greek Steam Navigation Company

Shareholders	Value in Gold Francs
Moraitis, Demetrios G.	2590000
Mandakas, Georgios B.	200000
Moraitis, Nikoklis	60000
Dallaportas, Ioannis S.	50000
Karystinakis, Georgios Ant.	2,590,000
Embiricos, Alexandros L.	30,000
Dambassis Demetrios, Ath.	20000
TOTAL	3,000,000

Source: *Government Gazette*, No. 58 (2 April 1907), 213

The profits in the first six months of the steamship's operation exceeded the expectations of the company's owner; in just three voyages, the Moraitis made a net profit of 322,234 drachmas, which was distributed to the shareholders.[34] The dividends came to ten percent of the nominal value of the shares. These very positive operating results were due to the sharp rise in emigration during 1907, when the number of emigrants doubled in comparison with the previous year; no less than 46,283 Greeks emigrated, 36,580 of whom came from the Kingdom of the Hellenes.[35] The increasing number of passengers meant that Moraitis had to extend the third class accommodation area.

Foolhardy and over optimistic, Demetrios Moraitis in early 1908 ordered another new and larger transoceanic steamer. The move was to cost him dearly. Soon, the Transoceanic Greek Steam Navigation Company ran into difficulties as the number of emigrants in 1908 fell to a half of the level of the previous year (see table 1). The crisis did not only hit Transoceanic; all companies working the Atlantic routes encountered great difficulties in 1908 as emigration to the USA plum-

---

[34]*Oikonomiki Ellas*, vol. 1, 1907, 77, where the balance sheet for the second half of 1907 was published.

[35]See Repoulis, *Law Concerning Emigration*, 8-10

meted and freight rates plunged to very low levels.[36] In August 1908, the Athens Appeal Court declared Moraitis bankrupt following his inability to fulfill loan obligations to the Bank of Athens.[37] Greeks and foreigners have attributed the failure of Moraitis both to the decline in freight rates and to his haste in ordering a second transoceanic.[38]

The overall pressure on Moraitis' enterprises should also be taken into account. In March 1908 his tramp steamer *Hellas* sunk off Cape Malea.[39] The captain, the owner's nephew and the crew were saved, but the circumstances of the accident were extraordinary and the newspapers of the day spoke openly of a fraudulent wreck. This incident irreparably damaged Moraitis' reputation as a businessman. It destroyed the "atmosphere of trust" that had been created by the positive results of the voyages to the United States. Unfortunately, statistical data on the operation of his cargo steamers is not available. However, in 1908 there was also a fall in freight rates in the Mediterranean, the main source of employment for the Greek fleet, and hence for Moraitis. According to C. Knick Harley, grain freights from the Black Sea to British ports, and equally coal freights on the return trip, decreased by a whole shilling per ton, a significant amount that served to depress the profits of cargo steamships.[40] In the case of Moraitis, whose business was based on high rates of return, this decline had multiple effects. The man who adopted byzantine methods to administer his ventures was to be crushed at the first negative conjuncture. Companies without any rational administration, developed on their ability to attract small capital investors with the reward

---

[36]For the general problems that the shipping companies faced in the north Atlantic transport, see Bonsor, *North Atlantic*, III, 1371. See the diagrammatic representation of Isserlis' data in Harlaftis, *History of Greek-Owned Shipping*, 123.

[37]The Bank of Athens had acquired shares in his ships and in pursuing its interests asked for the dissolution of the company.

[38]See A.I. Tzamatis, *The Greek Transoceanics*, 1907-1917 (Athens, 1996), 38; and Bonsor, *North Atlantic*, III, 1371.

[39]Ioannis Zografos, "Remembering the Past," *Andriaka Chronika*, part 3 (1759-1941), 15 (1963), 212. The author uses information drawn from the newspaper *Acropolis*.

[40]C. Knick Harley, "Coal Exports and British Shipping, 1850-1913," *Explorations in Economic History*, XXVI (1989), 311-338.

of fake rates of return, managed by an able but also ambitious entrepreneur, were liable to collapse when difficulties arose. The two steamships, *Moraitis* and *Athenai*,[41] passed to a new board of management imposed by the Bank of Athens, which continued the company's transatlantic run.[42] Despite various scattered publications that characterised him a crook and a swindler most — without denying his responsibility for the loss of property of small shareholders — believed that Moraitis was a victim of his own choices.[43]

It is evident that Moraitis tried to bypass the traditional model of the Greek family business, a model that had been applied extensively in Greek shipping since the late eighteenth century. Appealing to the capital contribution of hundreds of small capitalists he attempted an opening to the international practice, a new experience for the Greek status quo. The failure of his deed that brought the financial ruin of many small capital owners and the outcry of the public opinion and of the press of the day, almost became the landmark for the end of the system of the multi-participant company in Greek shipping.

---

[41]It should be noted that Moraitis never received the *Athenai*, the new transoceanic that he ordered. The bankruptcy of the company came before its completion and the ship passed directly into the hands of the new management. On the dissolution of Moraitis' company see *Naftika Chronika*, 15 August 1932, where the adventures of the steamship *Athenai* are described: it risked being impounded in America because of deceiving the American authorities. See Zografos, "Remembering the Past," 215.

[42]The company did not last long under the new management. Voyages continued without much success. It is evident that ownership by the Bank of Athens was not the best solution. In 1912 in order to ensure higher profits, the illegal transport of emigrants to the USA was attempted, but this was discovered by the US authorities. The result was a loss of 70,000 dollars. Finally the company was purchased by the National Steam Navigation of the Embiricos Brothers. See Tzamtzis, *Greek Transoceanics*, 43.

[43]On the problems created for the shareholders see *Metochos*, 25 October 1908. Questions are asked as to the real reasons for the bankruptcy and the extent of Moraitis' fraud, since all the evidence tends to show that the Andriot shipowner had himself been financially ruined. A. Andreades, "La Marine Marchande Grecque," *Journal des Economistes* (1913), is particularly harsh towards Moraitis. In referring to the founding of the company he writes: "The founder of the company, Moraitis, was alas a rogue, but his plan was sound and outlived him." And he adds in a footnote: "in contrast to the lack of honesty, he had ideas and knew how to realise them. Some was ruined on account of his megalomania. In any case he managed to escape prison by escaping abroad."

Moraitis was a pioneer in Greek shipowning. This was not only because he inaugurated scheduled trans-Atlantic service; or because he was among the first to see the need for Greeks to transfer the bulk of their ships to the Atlantic; or even because he introduced innovative methods of investment into Greek shipowning. Instead, Moraitis was a pioneer because he was the first to establish a model of the "risk-taking entrepreneur," who by his actions attracted the many other capitalists, both large and small, to the maritime arena. He was an entrepreneur for a new era who managed to break with the investment practices of his time. This was surely an unprecedented achievement in traditional, risk-averse Greek business circles.

Organizational and Managerial Patterns of Greek-Owned Shipping Enterprises and the Internationalization Process from the Interwar Period to 1990[1]

John Theotokas

During the twentieth century, Greek-owned shipping firms have grown into large scale companies and participated successfully in the global shipping market as internationalized enterprises. This process did not affect their organizational and managerial structures which remained substantially the same from the interwar years to 1990.

This unorthodox pattern may be attributed to three main factors: first, it owes much to the lifespan of Greek shipping firms, which in the majority of cases did not exceed one generation; second, Greek shipowners consider shipping to be a profession and not simply an activity that brings in an income; and, third, the family-oriented nature of Greek shipping firms is a key influence on the pattern of development. Their competitive advantage, however, was mainly gained during the post-1945 period, largely due to the positive interaction between their organizational structures and the environment in which they operated.

Organizational and Managerial Models

As enterprises pass through the different stages of development, various characteristics, primarily in the manner of their management, are transformed. In the initial stages the managerial tasks are simple and easily undertaken by the owner of the firm, especially if he has previous experience. At this juncture the owner is the firm's sole managerial agent. As the firm develops and grows in size, so the managerial tasks become more complex and an organizational hierarchy evolves. It then becomes

[1]I wish to thank Dr. Gelina Harlaftis for the many helpful discussions and advice and for her continuous support during the last five years, and Dr. Jesús Valdaliso for his comments on the first version of this paper.

necessary to employ personnel charged with supervising other workers.[2] When the size and activities of the firm increase to a significant extent, the owner's ability to supervise is limited and essential managerial duties are entrusted to personnel at different levels in the hierarchy.[3] The owner relinquishes responsibility for operational management of the business and the distinction between ownership and management becomes obvious. The owner maintains the role of the firm's leader, but the top managerial personnel assume responsibility for the company's operation.

In essence, firms undergo a transition from the entrepreneurial-familial or financing stage, in which they are managed either by their owner or his family or by their financiers, to the managerial stage (managerial enterprise) in which salaried managers are responsible for their stability and long-term development.[4] This procedure is used to define the evolution of contemporary business during the second industrial revolution. The modern industrial firm "was a collection of operating units each with its own specific facilities and personnel, whose combined resources and activities are coordinated, monitored, and allocated by a hierarchy of middle and top managers."[5] According to this theory, the business that invested in production facilities to achieve cost advantages of scale and scope, developed product-specific marketing and purchasing networks, and at the same time recruited and organized managers who were needed to supervise functional activities to co-ordinate the flow of goods through the processes and to allocate resources, became first

[2]Only the very smallest of enterprises can be successfully managed by a single individual. Once the firm expands and employs more than ten workers, success depends on developing a management team. Kevin Keasey and Robert Watson, *Small Firm Management. Ownership, Finance and Performance* (Oxford, 1993), 12, 196.

[3]As the firm develops, new people enter. Their initial role is to support the owner in particular areas of business and, in time, they might supplant the owner's skill. When this happens, the owner must spend less time doing and more time managing, which means delegating. See Neil C. Churchill and Virginia L. Lewis, "The Five Stages of Small Business Growth," *Harvard Business Review*, LXI (May-June 1983), 31-42.

[4]A.D. Chandler, Jr., "Managerial Hierarchies," in D.S. Pugh (ed.), *Organization Theory. Selected Readings* (London, 1990), 96-100.

[5]A.D. Chandler, Jr., *Scale and Scope: The Dynamics of Industrial Capitalism* (Cambridge, MA, 1991), 15.

movers.[6] Businesses that did not follow this path continued to be managed by founders or family members, whose main goal was to provide themselves with a large and stable income rather than the long-term growth of the firm. Britain was a country whose businesses did not follow the three steps towards "modernization," and this is considered to be a reason for its failure.[7]

At the same time it is contended that the business can remain personally or family managed while its size and activities expand. Indeed, it has been argued that, as the cases of Japan and Germany have shown, "family ownership and control could be a source of strength even in large diversified business organizations."[8] The question that then arises is: why do family firms prove to be successful in these cases, while in Britain they were a source of failure? As Roy Church points out, "greater attention should be paid to the cultural differences which produced contrasting behaviour and performance regardless of the major characteristics of corporate structures.[9]

However, national culture is not the sole factor that determines the structural evolution of the firm. The "contingency" approach suggests that there is no perfect way to organize and to manage an organization, for these features depend upon the particular environmental and contextual factors that every organization faces.[10] Apart from the national culture and social milieu in which business evolves, the firm's environment and context include factors such as its size, its lifespan, the market in which it participates as well as the particular culture of its owners. All of these factors contribute to the shaping of organizational and managerial models.

Size also has an important bearing on the competitiveness of enterprises, especially when they operate in internationalized industries. While small- and medium-sized companies account for a substantial

---

[6]*Ibid.*, 31 and 35.

[7]*Ibid.*, 390-392.

[8]Roy Church, "The Family Firm in Industrial Capitalism: International Perspectives on Hypotheses and History," *Business History*, XXXV, No. 4 (1993), 26.

[9]*Ibid.*, 39.

[10]F.E. Kast and J.E. Rosenzweig, *Organization and Management: A System and Contingency Approach* (New York, 1985), 115-116.

portion of international trade, they often focus on narrow segments or compete in relatively limited markets.[11] Only rarely do such companies compete directly with large-scale enterprises.

In the case of the shipping industry, and of bulk shipping in particular, the developmental pattern differs from that evident in land-based industries. Whereas in a large, globalized land-based industry size is usually a pre-condition for competitive participation in the international market, this is not the case in shipping.[12] Size is a factor that can add competitiveness, since it contributes to cost formation through exploiting economies of scale, but it is not, at least for the present, the key determinant of a firm's participation in the market. Bulk shipping enterprises, irrespective of their size, are able to exploit the advantages of the globalized market and to obtain benefits corresponding to those of land-based multinational companies. These benefits mainly accrue from exploiting the mobility of factors of production on an international basis, avoiding economic and political obstacles to their activity, and participating in the world market.[13] This trait permits the coexistence of small-, medium- and large-scale companies that compete directly with each other. This singularity of bulk shipping is crucial to an analysis of the organizational and managerial patterns of Greek-owned shipping companies, especially in the postwar period.

Although the bulk shipping sector did not offer sophisticated systems of corporate governance, this did not mean that the systems adopted were uniform. Since the strategies which shipping firms adopted were by no means identical, there were key differences between the systems deployed. Consequently, the creation of competitive advantage

---

[11]Michael E. Porter, *The Competitive Advantage of Nations* (London, 1990), 62.

[12]This can happen in segments of shipping, like liners, in which size is a precondition for competitive participation in the market. For example, the small-scale, Greek-owned company Sarlis Container Services, which operates a containership fleet, participates in an internationalized market, serving domestic or regional demand, without competing directly with large-scale companies like Hapag Lloyd or Maersk. On the contrary, a small, single-ship company which operates a handy-sized bulk carrier is able to compete directly with all other companies that operate similar ships in the same area.

[13]Ch. Carvounis, "Efficiency and Contradictions of Multinational Activity: The Case of Greek Shipping" (Unpublished PhD thesis, New School for Social Research, 1979), 94.

depended to some extent on the nature and efficiency of the systems which emerged or were implemented.

Greek-owned Shipping Enterprises During the Interwar Years

Greek-owned shipping during the interwar years developed at an impressive rate. The gross registered tonnage (grt) of the fleet increased by approximately 125 percent between 1914 and 1936 (see table 1). As a rule Greek-owned shipping enterprises at this time were small. Their average size in 1914 was 2388 grt, which had almost doubled by 1934-1935 to 4458 grt (see table 2).[14] The majority of these businesses belonged to shipowners of the first generation, that is their lifespan was short. Although the Greek fleet expanded to markets outside the Mediterranean and the Black Sea during the interwar years, in 1938 these still constituted forty-four percent of the ships' ports of call.[15] On the basis of the geographical areas of activity, as well as the fact that labour on board and on land came almost exclusively from Greece, and that the connection with the Greek state, mainly through its flag, was total, Greek-owned shipping enterprises cannot be considered as internationalized businesses in this period.

The small average size of firms conformed to the model of newly-established shipping enterprises entering the market. The combination of individuals with limited capital, who were connected either by ties of affinity or relations of common origin, in order to purchase a ship, with the help and support of a Greek office in London, which also assumed the commercial management of the vessel, was the norm.[16] Accordingly,

---

[14]The size of a shipping company is measured by the gross registered tonnage of its fleet.

[15]Gelina Harlaftis, *A History of Greek-Owned Shipping. The Making of an International Tramp Fleet, 1830 to the Present Day* (London, 1996), 187.

[16]"The master-owner of a sailing ship was concentrating his savings, adding together the present value of his ship, and when this capital did not capture the advances for the purchase of a ship and for working capital — a case that was the norm for these years — he turned to traditional affinity to form co-ownership, and he was traveling to London, not only because London was the biggest ship market of the world, but also because there were specialized fellow countrymen whose intervention to the purchase of a ship was necessary." Andrea G. Laimou, *Modern Greek Seamen* (Athens, 1971), 47.

during the interwar years, the relatively few Greek offices in London functioned as intermediaries, and very often as partners, for the large number of single-ship businesses in Greece.[17] It was a mutually beneficial cooperation that contributed to the development of both parties.

Table 1
Greek Owned Fleet as Percentage of World Fleet

Year	A. Greek-Owned Fleet*	B. World Fleet*	A/B
1914	0.8	49.1	1.7
1936	1.8	65.1	2.8
1948	2.3	80.3	2.8
1958	11.9	118	10.1
1975	48.3	342.2	14.1
1990	52	423.6	12.3

Note: Million grt.

Sources: C. Chlomoudis, "The Greek Merchant Marine, 1910-1939. The Coexistence of Different Modes of Production" (Unpublished PhD thesis, University of Macedonia, 1991), table 46; *Naftika Chronika* (Piraeus, 1991).

Affinity and common roots constituted the basis for the development of both the small, single-ship companies in Greece and Greek shipping offices in London. With regard to the latter, one should speak of established companies, while in respect of the former one should speak of companies in a protracted stage of creation.[18] And if for the London firms

---

[17]C. Chlomoudis, "The Greek Merchant Marine, 1910-1939. The Co-existence of Different Modes of Production" (Unpublished PhD thesis, University of Macedonia, 1991 [in Greek]), 112-113 and 129-135.

[18]Any new organization faces two general problems: getting off the ground and institutionalization. These represent distinct stages in the business' life-cycle. Once off the ground, organizations must develop strategies for longer run survival and growth. See John R. Kimberly, "Issues in the Creation of Organizations: Initiation, Innovation and Institutionalization," *Academy of Management Journal*, XXII, No. 3 (1979), 441 and 455.

their capitalist character and inherent goal of profit maximization was the rule, for the single-ship companies, with broadly-based ownership structures, survival, even with prolonged periods of loss, was the prime objective.[19]

For much of the interwar period, single-ship companies comprised around seventy-five percent of the Greek fleet.[20] In 1935, twenty-two percent of these firms were represented by a London office.[21] It is possible that some of the single-ship companies in this category did not maintain a management infrastructure on land, and the technical management of the ship took place on board. However, even for firms that kept their management infrastructure in Greece, their size and lifespan indicate that this was based mainly on the shipowner and members of his family.

Thus in the interwar period, the majority of Greek enterprises were small, family-oriented partnerships of short duration. Moreover, they were barely internationalized, while shipowners normally managed their own concerns.

Greek-owned Shipping Enterprises During the Postwar Period

The Greek merchant marine and Greek shipping enterprises developed rapidly during the postwar period. In terms of grt, the fleet expanded from 2.3 million in 1948 to fifty-two million in 1990, the latter figure amounting to 12.3% of the world tonnage (see table 1). However, the deployment of the fleet remained substantially the same. In 1990, when Greek shipowners were increasingly investing in more specialized vessels, general cargo ships, bulk carriers and tankers still constituted 85.5% of

---

The volatile character of shipping markets may lengthen the creation stage of shipping enterprises.

[19]"Single ship companies were distinguished by two important characteristics that gave them the ability to decrease costs during the crisis. First, the presence of so many owners on board as masters or chief engineers enabled them to keep costs under control and to keep up maintenance. Moreover, profit maximization was not always the main point; survival even at loss was not an unusual goal in these troubled times." Harlaftis, *History*, 204-205.

[20]Chlomoudis, "Greek Merchant Marine," 110-111.

[21]Harlaftis, *History*, 205.

the grt owned by Greeks. The small firms of the interwar period gave way to larger internationalized businesses, most of which were established in centres outside Greece. Their average size in 1958 was 53,759 grt, increasing to 70,814 grt in 1970, and 94,966 grt in 1990 (see table 2). The increase in average size resulted from the need to reduce cost through economies of scale, and the need to respond to technical progress and market conditions. The permanent place of the Greek-owned fleet at the top of world shipping league since the 1970s is a clear indication of the successful adaptation of Greek-owned shipping enterprises to technological and market changes.

Table 2
Number and Size of Greek-owned Shipping Enterprises

Year	No. of enterprises	Average size of enterprises
1914-1915	309	2.388
1934-1935	293	4458
1958	201	53759
1975	641	70814
1990	548	94966

Note: Includes ships over 1000 grt only.

Sources: Chlomoudis, "Greek Merchant Marine," tables 14 and 42; Gelina Harlaftis, *Greek Shipowners and Greece 1945-1975. From Separate Development to Mutual Interdependence* (London, 1993), table 2.4; Ioannis Theotokas, "The Greek-owned Shipping Companies of Piraeus. Organizational and Managerial Methods, 1969-1990" (Unpublished PhD thesis, Department of Maritime Studies, University of Piraeus, 1997).

Enterprises of various sizes have invested in Greek-owned shipping since the war, though, the majority were relatively small scale, as table 3 shows. Although the proportion of diminutive Greek-owned shipping firms declined, it was still high in 1990. Furthermore, this reduction seems very minor in the context of structural changes that have marked world shipping since 1958.

The internationalization of almost all Greek shipping firms occurred during this period. Postwar Greek-owned shipping enterprises can be described as internationalized multinational enterprises, since they exploited the mobility of factors of production (capital, labour, technology) on an international basis and tried to avoid political and economic obstacles to their operation through flags of convenience.[22] This development did not affect the internal articulation of the firms, however, for the central characteristics of their organization and management remained unchanged. While ownership and management continued to be one and the same, shipowners and their families played an active role in the operation of companies. These two traits determined their organization. This should be attributed to three interconnected structural features of Greek-owned shipping enterprises: their tendency towards fragmentation; the entrepreneurial philosophy of the Greek shipowners; and the familial nature of the firms.

Table 3
Percentage of Small, Medium and Large Greek-owned Shipping Companies

Year	up to 50,000 grt	50,001-200,000	more than 200,000 grt
1958	75	18	7
1975	72.6	21.1	6.3
1990	65.9	23.9	10.2

Source: Theotokas, "Greek-owned Shipping Companies of Piraeus."

Two classes of shipowner can be distinguished in Greek-owned shipping, depending on the length of their participation in the market. The traditional owners, whose families were at least second-generation shipowners after the Second World War, and the non-traditional owners, first-generation shipowners who were involved in another profession before becoming shipowners.[23] Whereas a significant number of traditional shipowners exists, there is no corresponding number of traditional enterprises, that is firms surviving longer than the lifespan of their founders. During this period, with the exception of a small percentage of firms that kept the same name and the same organizational structure for more than one generation, the bulk of firms which belonged to traditional

---

[22] Carvounis, "Efficiency and Contradictions," 94-111.

[23] Gelina Harlaftis, *Greek Shipowners and Greece 1945-1975. From Separate Development to Mutual Interdependence* (London, 1993), 10.

shipowners had been hived off existing concerns by members of traditional shipowning families.[24] Examples of the former are companies like S. Livanos Hellas and Andriaki Shipping, while examples of the latter are the various companies controlled by members of families like Laimos, Pateras, Peratikos and Xylas.

The phenomenon of the fragmentation of firms not only typified traditional enterprises and traditional shipowning families, but also non-traditional ones. Companies that are controlled by one family usually split a few years after their founding.[25] Several family firms divided while their founders were still active, a fact which supports the argument that conflicts and clashes over business management occur at the time of transition from the first to the second generation of owners.[26] It is estimated that only three in ten family businesses make the transition to the second generation successfully and only one in ten to the third generation.[27] This tendency is apparent in non-traditional Greek-owned companies too. Descendants of first-generation shipowners hive off from the family company and establish their own firm, even in cases when the founders of the companies are still active.[28]

There were analogous tendencies in enterprises controlled by more than one family. From firms that began as co-ownerships, new firms

---

[24]Ioannis Theotokas, "The Greek-Owned Shipping Companies of Piraeus. Organizational and Managerial Methods, 1969-1990" (Unpublished PhD thesis, University of Piraeus, 1997, [in Greek]), chapter 7.

[25]Usually this phenomenon concerns companies that are controlled by brothers who are first-generation shipowners. Shipowning families like Comninos, Lignos, Petrakis, Prokopiou Gianniotis, and Agoudimos provide examples.

[26]L.B. Barnes and S.A. Hershon, "Transferring Power in the Family Business," *Harvard Business Review*, LIV (July-August 1976), 105.

[27]M.F.R. Kets de Vries, "The Dynamics of Family Controlled Firms: The Good and the Bad News," *Organizational Dynamics*, XXI (Winter 1993), 60.

[28]Companies like Ermis Maritime, Seaways Shipping Enterprises and Stelmar Tankers were established by descendants of non-traditional shipowners, who are still managing their own companies.

emerged a few years after their founding.[29] In a sample of fifty shipping companies it was found that thirteen were either founded as co-ownerships and belonged to one shipowner by 1990, or were founded by shipowners who had left the companies they co-owned until then. The reasons behind the hiving off are various. However, in each case, a conflict of interests and authority, and the domination of one side over the other, had a decisive impact.[30]

The fragmentation of shipping firms had positive as well as negative effects on the Greek-owned fleet. On the positive side, there was an increase in the total number of enterprises, renewal in the shipowning profession, and, as a consequence, general development in Greece's shipping interests. The inability of the fragmented business to expand its size and to exploit further scale economies were the principal negative factors. According to which tendency was prevalent, the organizational and managerial patterns of fragmented companies might assume very different forms.

One basic characteristic of Greek shipowners, which contributed to the fragmentation of shipping enterprises, was their attitude to maritime activities. They did not operate as investors but as entrepreneurs, and they did not perceive shipping exclusively as a source of income but as a profession. This trait owes much to the previous professional experience of the vast majority of Greek shipowners. In a sample of fifty shipping companies, it was found that twenty-eight (fifty-six percent) were created either by former officers or by entrepreneurs who had worked in shipping and related industries (brokers, naval architects, shipping company employees etc.).[31] Such men maintained, or sought to maintain, absolute

---

[29]This tendency was prevalent in Greek-owned shipping throughout the twentieth century. Shipowner K. Hadjipateras in an autobiographical letter to his grandsons, describes his entrepreneurial life: "My brothers and I, K.D. Pateras and his brothers and P.D. Laimos and his brothers, we bought the steamship *Marietta Ralli*, which was the first ship that has been bought by the three families, each of whom owned 1/3 of the ship...In May 1907 (two years later) our co-owners of *Marietta Ralli* bought our shares and our family operated only the steamship *Leandros*...Our co-ownership contained my brothers and my sons. At the end of 1917 we dissolved our co-ownership." Konstantinou I. Hadjipatera, *Letters to his Children* (Athens, 1994), 55 and 61.

[30]Theotokas, "Greek-Owned Shipping Companies of Piraeus," chapter 7.

[31]*Ibid.*

control of their firm and it was they who made both the strategic and operational decisions. When this was not possible, they left the business to create new firms.[32] The conflicts and clashes that led to the break up of family firms — and in general of firms with more than one owner — can be overcome by recruiting professional managers to supervise operations. This presupposes limiting the power of the family members who own the firm on issues of business strategy and policy.[33] Consequently, this is a move towards the creation of an hierarchy of middle and top managers, one of the stages in the Chandlerian model of company development.

In Greek-owned shipping enterprises during the postwar period, salaried managers responsible for running the firm were employed in only a few, mainly large-scale, enterprises.[34] In most of these firms, shipowners and managers did not enjoy a simple, conventional relationship. The managers were either relatives of the shipowners or minor shareholders in the company. On the contrary, in medium- and small-scale enterprises, in which the size of the organizational structure was limited and management tasks less complex, shipowners were responsible for the entire managerial operation of the firm. This was especially so with shipowners who had previous professional experience relevant to shipping; in these cases, the ownership and the management were identical. This was the dominant characteristic of Greek enterprises throughout the period.[35]

The third basic trait of Greek-owned shipping enterprises that conditioned their organizational and managerial forms reflects the fact that they belonged to one or more families, whether connected by ties of affinity or not, whose members participated in the company's management, usually in critical managerial posts. Such familial structure gave shipowners flexibility and allowed them to respond immediately to market

---

[32] *Ibid.*

[33] H. Levinson, "Conflicts that Plague Family Business," *Harvard Business Review*, XLIX (March-April 1971), 90-98.

[34] Salaried managers were also employed by a small percentage of firms that were parts of diversified or vertically-integrated companies with differentiated organizational and managerial patterns.

[35] S. Makridakis, L. Papayiannakis and I. Kalogirou, *Greek Management. Developments, Tensions, Prospects* (Athens, 1996 [in Greek]), 47.

fluctuations and opportunities.[36] Furthermore, it formed the dominant culture within the business, which was based on the shipowner's power and directly influenced its managerial operation.[37] In the power culture, the structure of organizations is pictured as a web. This culture depends on a central power source with rays of power and influence spreading out from the centre. Organizations based on this culture have the ability to move quickly and to react well to threat or danger.[38] As one Greek shipowner has observed: "in Greek shipowning business there is no place for the democratic but time-consuming processes of decision making in Boards and General Meetings. Dictatorship of one or oligarchy of the able ones in the family, who are guided by experience and intuition at sea, chart the course of the firm."[39]

The familial nature of enterprises meant that members of the shipowner's family participated actively in the management of the firm. This was true in the vast majority of cases, regardless of the scale of the firm.[40] The managerial contributions of family members brought competitive advantages to the business, largely because it fostered knowledge of shipowning and ship management, a resource that was passed on to successors whether they remained in the company or set up their own firm. This explains why those members who disengaged themselves from family firms continued to be active in shipping. In addition, recruiting family members as managers reduced the dependence of the firm on the labour market.

The importance of corporate culture is apparent both within the firm, and between firms in the same sector. One of the most important aspects of this culture is the extent to which it promotes trust and, as a

---

[36]As traditional shipowner I.M. Karras stated about the familial nature of business and its advantages: "if you make a mistake, it isn't necessary to appear to the shareholders in order to explain why did you make it. The person to whom you might explain the matter is just your father in law." *Argo* (December 1974 [in Greek]), 58.

[37]Theotokas, "Greek-Owned Shipping Companies of Piraeus," chapter 7.

[38]Charles Handy, *Understanding Organizations* (New York, 1993), 183-184.

[39]D. Los, *Shipping 1980-1990. Crisis and Responses of a Stormy Decade* (Athens, 1990 [in Greek]), 64.

[40]*Ibid.*, chapter 7.

consequence, reduces the cost of transactions. In a high trust culture, complex interdependencies between firms can be sustained by "arm's length" contracts, while within each firm the owner can rely on the loyalty and integrity of employees.[41]

In the case of Greek shipping firms, the high trust culture spawned competitive advantage in two principal ways. First, it allowed the implementation of strategies that contributed to the increase and renewal of Greek shipowners as a class. It has been proved that Greek-owned shipping companies implemented to some extent alternative investment strategies that led to the minimization of entry barriers to newcomers to the shipping market. These strategies included the provision of capital necessary for the acquisition of the first ship to the buyer from the seller, not only in the interwar years but also during the postwar period. Between 1969 and 1990 this alternative investment strategy was implemented by eight shipping companies either as sellers or buyers, out of a sample of fifty.[42]

Second, the high trust culture allowed shipowners to base their management style on the willingness of employees to remain faithful to the owner and the company. Most shipping companies were therefore able to impose decisions on their workforce, while the recruitment of employees was based on traditional methods such as the use of an internal labour market, with loyal ships' officers being promoted to fill positions ashore, and the employment of people known to the owner. Affinity and common origin continued to play an important role. It is notable that of fifty shipping companies, thirty-six (seventy-two percent) used these methods, while only fourteen (twenty-eight percent) used them in conjunction with the mechanism of the external labour market to recruit employees.[43] These policies allowed shipowners to exert moral pressure which proved to be a useful complement to supervision.[44]

---

[41]Mark Casson, "Entrepreneurship and Business Culture," in J. Brown and M.B. Rose (eds.), *Entrepreneurship Networks and Modern Business* (Manchester, 1993), 42.

[42]Theotokas, "Greek-Owned Shipping Companies of Piraeus," chapter 6.

[43]*Ibid*, chapter 7.

[44]Casson, "Entrepreneurship," 44.

It has been argued that the strength of the culture and its suitability to the environment, govern long-run corporate performance.[45] The environment embraces all the factors that affect firms — the market and its characteristics, competitors, technology, etc. Greek owned shipping companies throughout the period, especially in the postwar years, based their competitiveness on three basic traits that are connected directly or indirectly with business culture. However, while the Greek-owned fleet expanded at an unprecedented rate in the postwar period, it did not grow to the same degree during the interwar period. This implies that the basic characteristics of Greek-owned shipping companies functioned in different ways when they were applied in different environments. In the postwar period, they functioned in a positive way because they were combined with the factors that constituted the specific environment. For example, it has been proved that the use of flags of convenience (FoC) after 1973 by the traditional maritime countries did not yield the same results for all of them. While for Greece and Japan the use of FoC contributed to the preservation of their shares in the world shipping, this was not true for countries like Britain and Norway.[46] Various factors contributed to this, and certainly the organizational and managerial models of the business are amongst them. In addition, during the 1980s, Greek-owned shipping companies implemented strategies that allowed them to strengthen their position, like the asset play. Other nation's shipping companies did not follow the same strategy. Again, the advantage gained by Greek firms in this respect can be attributed to their organizational and managerial structures, and the entrepreneurial philosophy of their owners.

Of course, the environment that any firm or shipping nation faces can vary, which means that there are some factors that are useful only to particular players. In the case of Greek-owned shipping companies, the shipping policy of the Greek State is one of the factors that distinguishes their environment.

The competitive advantage that organizational and managerial patterns created in Greek-owned enterprises does not mean that the same results would accrue elsewhere. In Greece they have functioned in a positive way, while in other environments similar structures may have

---

[45]*Ibid.*, 44-45.

[46]H. Thanopoulou, *Greek and World Shipping* (Athens, 1994 [in Greek]), 220-221.

proved detrimental to company growth and profitability. As one analysis of the organizational patterns of British shipping companies from 1870 to 1919 — which were similar to those of Greek-owned companies — contends: "networks as well as hierarchical frameworks or unfettered market mechanisms can serve as an institutional basis for winning or relinquishing international competitive advantage. What is best in any context depends upon how economic actors interact dynamically with the full range of environmental conditions."[47]

Conclusion

While the course followed by Greek-owned shipping enterprises during the twentieth century should have led to changes in their organization and management, their structural features meant that the opposite occurred. The enterprises increased in number and size, responded successfully to technological progress and market conditions, and completed the path to internationalization. However, their organizational and managerial models remained unchanged during the twentieth century. They continued to function as family businesses, over which the founders and owners retained absolute responsibility for management.

This was due to three basic features of Greek-owned shipping enterprises and Greek shipowners. The first is the frequency of fragmentation, which reflected the culture in which the organizational and managerial structures developed. The second is the Greek shipowners' belief that shipping is not simply a profit-making activity but a profession, a philosophy which has led to the absolute domination of the organization and management of firms by their owners. The third is the familial nature of the firms, which on the one hand gave the shipowners flexibility, and on the other added competitive advantage to the firm.

These features created a competitive advantage which allowed the Greek-owned fleet to stay at the top of the "world shipping league." But this evolution was discontinuous. While the organizational and managerial patterns remained stable from the interwar period to 1990, a marked competitive advantage emerged in the postwar period. This was because these patterns functioned positively in the context of the largely favourable environment in which Greek-owned shipping companies operated.

---

[47]Gordon H. Boyce, "Institutional Development in Maritime and Business History," *International Journal of Maritime History*, IX (June 1997), 257.

Internationalization and the Collapse of British Shipbuilding, 1945-1973

Lewis Johnman

Globalization and the Limits of Definition

There are strong reasons for doubting the analytical validity of the term "globalization." Indeed, one of the main features of the term is the wide diversity of its use in explaining a range of modern economic phenomena. There is no doubt that the term's midwife was in the period between 1973 and 1979, with the collapse of the Bretton Woods system and the two oil-price shocks. This destroyed well-established price, supply and demand schedules and completely undermined political and economic policy processes which had been based upon them. Uncertainty and inflationary pressure became the main policy problems and finance and industry struggled to overcome this by seeking wider outlets for investment and goods. This, in its turn, resulted in higher bank lending abroad, culminating in the debt crisis, the growth of the Eurodollar market and an increase in the foreign trade to Gross Domestic Product (GDP) ratios of the advanced capitalist countries (ACCs). This was to some extent codified in policy terms by the widespread deregulation of financial markets, notably exchange controls, and implicitly, their increased internationalization in the late 1970s and 1980s. Concomitant with this was the observed increase in the de-industrialization of the ACCs, with growing long-term unemployment, and the rise of a number of newly industrializing countries in the Third World and their penetration of ACC markets. This last phenomenon provoked a debate on the role of standardized mass production — epitomised by the use of the term "post-Fordism" — wherein the large, nationally-centred oligopolistic corporation, operating as the principal economic agent, was challenged by flexible production systems operated by less tightly structured firms, usually multinational enterprises, but including smaller-scale companies, functioning in a world environment of hitherto unimagined complexity.

It is not the intention here, to analyse the "long boom" of 1945-1973; suffice it so say that the period's recently acquired sobriquet as the

"Golden Age" attests to its significance in modern economic history.[1] A few points are, however, worth reiterating. The boom's dominant feature was the growth in production. Between 1950 and 1973, output in the advanced capitalist economies grew by 180 percent and the growth records in the second phase of the internationalization of the world economy easily eclipsed anything which had occurred previously, as table 1 illustrates.

Table 1
Long Term Growth, 1870-1973 (average annual percentage growth rates)

	Output	Output per head of population	Stock of Fixed Capital	Exports
1870-1913	2.5	1.4	2.9	3.9
1913-1950	1.9	1.2	1.7	1.0
1950-1973	4.9	3.8	5.5	8.6

Note: Arithmetic averages of individual country figures.

Source: A. Maddison, *Phases of Capitalist Development* (Oxford, 1982), 91.

Gross world production grew in the order of 5.5% per annum between 1960 and 1973, with Japan achieving an historically unprecedented rate of over ten percent per annum in the same period. The factors underpinning the boom were: technological dynamism, cheap energy, a widely-shared, quasi-Keynesian policy regime which promoted growth and kept inflation within tolerable boundaries, increasing interdependence and a huge growth in world trade. Between 1951-1953 and 1969-1971, the volume of world trade in manufactures grew at the unprecedented rate of 349 percent, whereas the volume of output grew by 194 percent. The ACCs' exports of manufactures grew by 480 percent between 1950 and 1971, with the fastest growing part being in the form of trade between theACCs themselves.[2]

---

[1]See, for example, F. Cairncross and A. Cairncross, *The Legacy of the Golden Age* (London, 1992).

[2]P. Armstrong, A. Glyn and J. Harrison, *Capitalism Since 1945* (Oxford, 1991), 155. See also A. Maddison, *Dynamic Forces in Capitalist Development* (Oxford, 1991).

Doubtless the trauma unleashed by the collapse of expectations schooled by the long boom was profound. The increase of uncertainty and unpredictability in economic markets and the occasional rapid institutional change were dominant forces. It is one thing, however, to observe them, quite another to state that they are all features of globalization. Indeed there may be strong grounds for believing that what is occurring is merely a third phase in the internationalization of the world economy, the earlier phases having been 1870-1914 and 1950-1973. The features usually cited as characterizing globalization are the growth in foreign trade and the huge increase in global capital flows, but these were also facets of the two earlier phases. The increased use of technology is also cited, but here again, earlier phases were both substantially marked and enabled by what might be termed "real-time information." Further, the growth of transnational corporations, genuine stateless entities, pursuing strategies of "global localization," it is held will become dominant. The evidence for this, however, is marginal, and whilst this does not deny the increased importance of foreign direct investment (FDI) and branch plants, there is a marked reluctance to relocate core functions, such as high value-added production processes and research and development, overseas. The best that can be said is that large companies remain nationally-based and internationally orientated; a phenomenon which marked both of the earlier phases. The final argument usually employed in support of globalization is the absence of a hegemonic power; Britain in the period 1870-1914 is held to have underpinned the *pax Britannica*, whereas the USA policed the *pax Americana* of the post-1945 period. This, however, is radically overdone. The influence of US monetary policy may not have the resonance that it once had, but the US remains the largest single economy and the motor of world demand, while the dollar remains the key currency in world trade. Militarily, the US remains hegemonic, being the only possible guarantor of the world trading system and the openness of world markets.[3]

The aim of this chapter is to analyse why it was, in the context of the Long Boom, a generation of unparalleled economic expansion in which the maritime industries both shared and helped sustain, that the British shipbuilding industry failed to hold or expand market share internationally, and indeed, witnessed what had been a traditionally

---

[3]For an overview, see P. Hirst and G. Thompson, *Globalisation in Question* (Oxford, 1996).

bespoke national market in the UK, became subject to severe import penetration throughout the period of the boom.[4] It is remarkable that neither established shipbuilding nations, nor new entrants, suffered anything akin to the fate of the British shipbuilding industry in this period of expansion. It is the contention of this paper that the underlying causes of this competitive and comparative failure reside largely in the attitudes of British shipyard owners and managers to the international market. At almost all levels the attitude of British shipbuilders to the international market was one of thinly disguised hostility; the booming market itself was consistently viewed as "abnormal," with a "next slump is bound to come" mentality prevailing. Moreover, on the issues of ship type, ship size, construction methods, propulsion systems, marketing, research and development and foreign competition, British shipbuilders struck attitudes which were, at best conservative, at worst, positively antediluvian. Before examining such attitudes in detail, it is necessary to detail exactly the scale of the expansionary market within which British shipbuilders were operating between 1945 and the late 1960s.

The world merchant fleet doubled from just over eighty million gross registered tons (mgrt) to 160.4 mgrt between 1948 and 1965. This reflected the absolute growth of nearly all mercantile marines in the period. Table 2 illustrates the major trends.

A number of points are worth making. Firstly, between them, fourteen countries held over eighty-six per cent of the world merchant fleet in 1948 and that the same fourteen, with the addition of Liberia, held over eighty-three percent of world merchant fleet in 1965. The second obvious feature is the share of growth rates for almost all individual nations. In some cases — Liberia, Japan, Norway and Greece — this growth was spectacular and resulted in substantial increases in market share; in others the growth was less spectacular, if just as marked, but the only countries to lose significant market share were the USA and Britain.

---

[4]Space prohibits any treatment of the general issue of British industrial decline, but see M. Dintenfass, *The Decline of Industrial Britain, 1870-1980* (London, 1992); D. Coates, *The Question of UK Decline* (Hemel Hempstead, 1994); D. Coates and J. Hillard (eds.), *UK Economic Decline* (Hemel Hempstead, 1995); and the extensive bibliographies which all three volumes provide.

Table 2
Merchant Fleet Growth, 1948-1965 (000 grt)
Percentage shares of world fleet in brackets

	1948		1965	
World	80,292	(100)	160,392	(100)
Denmark	1,223	(1.4)	2,562	(1.6)
France	2,786	(3.5)	5,198	(3.2)
FRG	300	(0.4)	5,279	(3.3)
Greece	1,286	(1.6)	7,137	(4.4)
Italy	2,100	(2.6)	5,701	(3.6)
Japan	1,024	(1.3)	11,971	(7.5)
Liberia	-	-	17,539	(10.9)
Netherlands	2,737	(3.4)	4,891	(3.0)
Norway	4,261	(5.3)	15,641	(9.8)
Panama	2,716	(3.4)	4,465	(2.8)
Spain	1,147	(1.4)	2,132	(1.3)
Sweden	1,973	(2.5)	4,290	(2.7)
USSR	2,097	(2.6)	8,258	(5.1)
UK	18,025	(22.4)	21,530	(13.4)
USA	29,165	(36.3)	21,527	(13.4)

Source: *Lloyd's Register of Shipping*.

Table 3
Shipbuilding Launches: World and Main Countries, 1950 and 1967 (000 grt)
Country Percentage of World Output in Brackets

	1950		1967	
World	3,489	(100)	15,780	(100)
Belgium	66	(1.8)	121	(0.8)
Denmark	125	(3.5)	488	(3.1)
France	181	(5.1)	553	(3.5)
FRG	155	(4.4)	1,002	(6.5)
Italy	107	(3.1)	507	(3.2)
Japan	348	(9.9)	7,497	(47.5)
Netherlands	228	(6.5)	339	(2.1)
Norway	51	(1.4)	522	(3.3)
Spain	27	(0.7)	406	(2.6)
Sweden	348	(9.9)	1,308	(8.2)
UK	1,325	(37.9)	1,298	(8.2)

Source: See table 2.

The phenomenal growth of international shipping is reflected in the substantial rise in world shipbuilding output. World shipbuilding launches grew from 2.3 mgrt in 1948 to 15.8 mgrt in 1967.[5] The main trends are illustrated in table 3.

Table 4

Tonnage Launched in Principal Shipbuilding Countries Showing Proportion for Home and Overseas Registration, Averages, 1948-1956 and 1957-65

		Total (mgrt)	Home (000's grt)	Export (000's grt)	Export as % of total
UK	1948-56	1.3	865	467	35
	1957-65	1.2	994	208	18
Japan	1948-56	0.6	287	278	32
	1957-65	2.6	1,154	1,485	55
Sweden	1948-56	0.4	145	279	68
	1957-65	0.9	246	603	70
FRG	1948-56	0.5	274	248	31
	1957-65	1.1	381	708	65
France	1948-56	0.2	186	40	14
	1957-65	0.4	272	199	42
Italy	1948-56	0.2	137	37	31
	1957-65	0.5	318	122	26
Netherlands	1948-56	0.3	169	142	44
	1957-65	0.4	232	215	50
Norway	1948-56	0.1	99	1	1
	1957-65	0.3	295	27	7

Note: All figures rounded up.

Source: See table 2.

As with the statistics on merchant fleets, some trends are obvious. In 1950, eleven countries launched just over eighty-four percent of the world's ships, whereas in 1967, the same eleven countries accounted for nearly eighty-nine percent of launchings. The most obvious feature is the breathtaking rise of Japan, paralleled by the decline of the UK. Every

[5]Unless otherwise stated, all figures in the text are either from or calculated from *Lloyd's Register of Shipping*.

other major shipbuilding nation expanded its output, and with the exception of Belgium and the Netherlands, all countries did so substantially, even if this did not automatically bestow an increased market share; Sweden, for example, expanded its output by almost one million grt and still lost market share. The figures are testimony to a fiercely competitive international environment but also to the staggering growth rates engendered by the long boom. The extent of the internationalization of the shipbuilding market is best exemplified by the struggle for export markets, as table 4 demonstrates.

All countries increased their absolute output for their home markets and all countries, with the exceptions of Britain and Italy, increased their shares of exports as a percentage of their total output. What the figures relating to the maritime industries illustrate is the considerable dynamism of shipbuilding and shipping within the context of the long boom and they stand as a testament to the internationalization of the maritime industries.

British Shipbuilding And the Second Phase of the Internationalization of The World Economy

From the foregoing analysis two trends become immediately apparent: Britain's struggle to retain a substantial share of the foreign market; and a consistent drift towards overseas builders on the part of British owners. The struggle in the foreign market is best exemplified by British building for the Norwegian market, the most important overseas outlet for British shipbuilding in the postwar period.

The Norwegian Market

Throughout the early 1950s Norway constituted over thirty percent of the market for British ship exports. Indications that Norway would provide a substantial market for shipbuilders came before the Second World War ended. The Norwegian broking firm A/S Securitas Ltd., wrote to a number of British shipbuilders, admittedly attempting to sell their services as agents, but portraying the likely level of future demand as high. With a small-scale shipbuilding sector, renewal of the Norwegian fleet could only come through imported tonnage, "therefore in the coming years large building orders for Norwegian account will be placed with foreign shipyards."[6] Referring to the ten years before the war the Norwegians observed that some two million grt had been built for the Norwegian account in thirty five yards in six different countries. The leading countries were: Sweden, Germany, Britain and Denmark, with Britain supplying some 440,000 grt, or twenty-two percent of the total tonnage. It was further observed, however, that the percentage had fallen throughout the decade from sixty-five percent in 1930 to only ten percent in 1938. Unsurprisingly, given the pitch of the letter, one reason ascribed for this fall was the lack of representation in Norway of British shipbuilders.[7]

Table 5
Vessels Launched for Norway in UK, 1948-1956

Year	No of ships	GRT	UK share of Total Norwegian tonnage (%)
1948	37	133,474	31.6
1949	39	255,864	44.0
1950	20	139,212	27.8
1951	30	308,787	48.4
1952	17	151,699	32.4
1953	18	135,992	23.4
1954	22	237,334	31.1
1955	19	234,043	30.3
1956	12	144,114	16.4

Source: See table 2.

Such was the importance of the mercantile marine to the country's balance of payments — "out of all proportion to Norway's population," as the British consul commented — that the Government and shipowners had made the restoration of the fleet a national priority.[8] As the Norwegian fleet almost doubled in tonnage terms, from 4.2 million grt to eight million grt, between 1948 and 1956, British shipbuilders had a significant

[6]Great Britain, National Maritime Museum (NMM), Shipbuilders and Repairers National Association (SRNA), 8/S47, Norway, A/S Securitas Ltd. to Fairfield Shipbuilding and Engineering Co. Ltd., 11 May 1945.

[7]*Ibid.*

[8]*Ibid.*, J.C. Aird, "Norwegian Shipping in 1947," 15 December 1947.

share in this rapidly expanding market. Between 1948 and 1956 ships for the Norwegian account constituted some thirty percent of all British launchings for overseas registration and Norway was the industry's most important foreign customer. Table 5 illustrates the position.

Britain, therefore, held over thirty percent of the total Norwegian market between 1948 and 1956. It was not long, however, before complaints began to be aired. Thomas Falck, the Chairman of a Bergen shipping company observed that British yards had "lost" over a quarter of a million tons of potential orders between 1953 and 1954 because "British shipyards were not competitive today."[9] Rising prices and late deliveries were becoming almost endemic complaints with respect to British shipbuilding. Sir William Souter, the chairman of the Sheaf Steam Shipping Company, for example, stated that an 18,600 dwt oil tanker, ordered in February 1950 at an estimated cost of £735,000, had been delivered in November 1953, seven months late at a cost of £949,817.[10] As the tanker boom continued post-Suez, the trade press commented that this "emphasised the capacity of yards abroad to build to modern requirements and sizes...[and that]... owners generally are less inclined to be impressed...by the superiority of British workmanship and design."[11] The industry, however, had an ingenious answer to such criticisms. The "conservative policy" regarding modernization and productive capacity, opined *Shipbuilder and Marine Engine Builder*, would prove to be "wise," as with the passing of the boom, any disadvantage accruing from late delivery dates would soon disappear.[12] The boom, however, did not pass.

British shipbuilding's reluctance to increase its capacity and take marketing seriously were central factors in losing market share at home and abroad. As Mr. Rae of the Shipbuilding Conference commented:

> We say that one of the headaches for the shipbuilding industry in the future is likely to be the very considerable excess world capacity in relation to any foreseeable future

---

[9]Quoted in *Shipbuilder and Marine Engine Builder*, November 1954.

[10]Quoted in *ibid.*, December 1954.

[11]*Ibid.*, February 1957.

[12]*Ibid.*, December 1958.

> demand. In my recent visit to Denmark, Sweden and Norway I found not only an apparent lack of concern about this but a good deal of what one might call expansion mindedness. New berths, new shipyards, as well as modernizations designed to increase output, were all current talk and seemed to be allied to an almost naive faith in the likelihood of substantial demand in future — and for big ships.[13]

The impact of such attitudes is illustrated in table 6.

Table 6
Vessels launched for Norway in the UK, 1957-1965

Year	No. of ships	GRT	UK share of Total Norwegian Tonnage (%)
1957	2	18968	2.1
1958	10	113,045	8.5
1959	3	28,270	2.7
1960	5	71,526	8.1
1961	8	121,873	10.5
1962	7	94,994	7.2
1963	6	204,500	13.8
1964	0	0	0.0
1965	1	51,972	2.8

Source: See table 2.

Britain's share of the Norwegian market, which had averaged thirty percent between 1948 and 1956, collapsed after 1956 to an average of just over six percent between 1957 and 1965. The scale is dramatically illustrated by the fact that in every year, with the exceptions of 1957 and 1964, Norway remained Britain's most important export market: even the one ship launched for Norway in 1965 was the year's best export performance. This was especially poor in that the Norwegian mercantile marine expanded from just over eight million grt in 1956 to over 15.5 million grt in 1965. Competition from Sweden, Germany, Norway, and latterly Japan, hammered the British market in Norway (see table 7).

---

[13]NMM, SRNA, 8/S49, Norway, Mr. Rae, "Shipbuilding Capacity: Scandinavia," 21 April 1959.

Table 7
Shipbuilding for the Norwegian Account

Year	Sweden			Norway			FRG			Japan		
	A	B	C	A	B	C	A	B	C	A	B	C
1956	30	288,377	32.8	78	166,946	19.0	33	175,479	19.9	1	12,500	1.4
1957	31	326,658	35.9	79	236,653	26.0	23	162,423	17.7	5	57,857	6.3
1958	30	324,917	24.4	72	255,239	19.2	43	403,890	30.3	1	9,350	0.7
1959	26	335,408	32.0	56	305,476	29.1	23	224,316	21.4	1	20,310	1.7
1960	22	290,933	32.8	43	187,095	21.0	18	236,386	26.7	1	30,250	3.4
1961	20	276,025	23.9	56	330,911	28.6	20	222,698	19.3	6	95,187	8.2
1962	28	404,588	30.6	74	355,753	26.9	23	291,142	21.9	1	28,391	2.1
1963	24	458,663	30.9	51	328,604	22.1	13	261,536	17.7	1	36,000	2.4
1964	24	608,417	36.2	72	334,301	19.9	8	249,764	14.9	11	398,713	23.7
1965	24	771,728	41.6	82	328,594	17.7	19	298,434	16.0	10	331,129	17.8

Notes: A denotes number of ships; B denotes grt; and C denotes percentage of Norwegian market.

Source: See table 2.

Sweden was traditionally a major builder for Norway and like Britain had over thirty percent of the market, but significantly did not lose market share between 1957 and 1965. Norway averaged just under twenty percent of its own market in these years, and the strong entry of Japan in 1963, where building for Norway, had hitherto been insignificant, reflects the trend towards VLCCs and ULCCs.[14]

By the 1960s the newly established organisation, British Shipbuilding Exports (BSE), a belated attempt by the Shipbuilders and Repairers National Association (SRNA) to arm itself with marketing information, was commenting that Norway was "the second most important and the steadiest growth market for ships in the world."[15] Whilst the report went into considerable analytical detail on the Norwegian market it could not avoid criticisms of British shipbuilders. As R.B. Shepheard, the Director of the SRNA commented, the report disclosed:

> a widely held, disturbing and, for us, a very damaging state of opinion of the British Shipbuilding Industry among potential Norwegian customers...they have voiced a series of complaints, the principal of which...is that in addition to regarding us as unreliable over delivery, many are now saying that we cannot be trusted to honour contracts.[16]

Indeed, the report was coruscating as to the attitudes of British shipbuilders who, despite building for the Norwegian market over many years, and with Norway as their largest and most important overseas market,

---

[14]For the growth of shipbuilding industries in Sweden and Japan, see K. Olsson, "Big Business in Sweden: The Golden Age of the Great Swedish Shipyards, 1945-1974," *Scandinavian Economic History Review*, XLIII (1995); T. Chida and P.N. Davies, *The Japanese Shipping and Shipbuilding Industries. A History of Their Modern Growth* (London, 1990); and Y. Yamashita, "Responding to the Global Market in Boom and Recession: Japanese Shipping and Shipbuilding Industries, 1945-1980," in S.P. Ville and D.M. Williams (eds.), *Management, Finance and Industrial Relations in the Maritime Industries: Essays in International Maritime and Business History* (St. John's, 1994), 185-202.

[15]NMM, SRNA 8/S49, Norway, L.S. Holt, "British Shipbuilding Exports. The Norwegian Market," 28 September 1967.

[16]*Ibid.*, R.B. Shepheard to Principals of Certain Member Firms, 24 July 1967.

understood neither the market nor the Norwegian shipowner. Shipowning, the report commented, was the "most important single factor in the Norwegian economy...[and]...because of this the fortune and experience of one owner automatically becomes the concern of all the others."[17] Problems, therefore, with one contract in one British shipyard automatically became the preserve of all Norwegian shipowners with all the consequences which this entailed.

British builders regularly made the mistake of treating Norwegian shipowners in the same manner that they did British owners, but this approach failed to recognize two key differences. British owners were, and had traditionally been, operators of sophisticated liner tonnage operating within conferences. Tramping was not a predominant activity for the British owner whereas for Norwegian owners it was the staple fare of the industry. The second difference was that Britain was a major importing and exporting economy whereas Norway was not. The British mercantile marine was largely tied to trade with the UK, but the Norwegian fleet was mostly concerned with trade outside of Norway and was consequently exposed to world-wide economic and trading factors. The Norwegian owner, therefore, was a sophisticated tramp operator functioning in a world market with all of the stresses and strains that this imposed. This global operation had led to a form of business which British shipbuilders most commonly misunderstood — although they had been given ample warning of the problem in the 1945 letter from A/S Securitas Ltd. — the relationship between shipowners and brokers:

> No shipowner in Norway operates without the services of brokers. Selling ships therefore to Norwegian owners requires a close relationship with and knowledge of Norwegian shipbrokers. The Norwegian broker combines the activities of a freight and ship-broker. His activities and connections are world-wide. He arranges the freight contract, nurses the owner and the builder; establishes contact with the user of the space, and is the vital link in the purchase of a new ship.[18]

---

[17]Holt, "British Shipbuilding Exports."

[18]*Ibid.*

This relationship placed a premium on delivery dates as the new vessel was often tied to a charter and failure to deliver on time was possibly the single most damning feature of British shipbuilding.

The report commented that the British shipbuilding industry had two inbuilt advantages with respect to Norway; the British were well-liked and the Norwegians would rather build in Britain "provided we are competitive." However, "the disadvantage of this...lies in the fact that rightly or wrongly the damage done to our image is all the greater when we default."[19] Thus:

> our first task should be to do everything possible to meet reasonable Norwegian demands for damages on current contracts which have gone sour. Some of the owners concerned have lost badly on charters fixed at the time of concluding the contracts. This is of course the way much of Norway's shipping works. The Japanese, the Danes, the Swedes, and West Germans know this and recognise it — they meet it by delivering on time. We have not delivered on time and so should meet it by as flexible and generous an approach as possible. Such an attitude will do more than anything else at this time to improve our image.[20]

Over the years, however, the image of British shipbuilding had been battered. The report's author, Stopford Holt, commented that he had been asked "time and time again" why the British went to such apparent lengths to "emphasize ...woes and tribulations and...inability to cope effectively with those troubles."[21] Every reported speech by a British shipbuilder in the Norwegian press, Holt claimed, usually comprised a list of excuses for poor performance, ranging from official or unofficial stoppages, shortage of labour, failings on the part of sub-contractors, modernization schemes not producing the anticipated savings, to recently completed contracts having entailed substantial losses. The impression gained by the Norwe-

---

[19]*Ibid.*

[20]*Ibid.*

[21]*Ibid.*

gians, according to Holt, was of an industry where the shipbuilders had no control or responsibility over problems, and worse, had no ideas as to how to address the problems.

Surveying the Norwegian market in detail, Holt was both pessimistic and optimistic about Britain's prospects. He went into painstaking detail as to the volume of reference material on shipping published in Norway, usually by brokers, and suggested that at the very basic level, British builders should acquaint themselves with this material and make connections with brokers, otherwise they stood little chance of gaining orders. The report stressed the importance of tankers in the Norwegian market and emphasised that whilst this market was buoyant, ordering would be "all for very large ships." In terms of combined bulk carriers, the Norwegians had "been in the forefront of this development" and interest in them had been "pronounced." Whilst the Norwegian market for this type of vessel was "important," they had "established satisfactory relationships...with Swedish and Japanese yards and wonder why British shipyards have devoted so little attention to them." In the liner trades, which constituted some twelve percent of the Norwegian fleet, Holt forecast that this market would be altered beyond recognition by the "container revolution." He predicted two likely trends as a consequence: first, owners combining to raise the finance to enter the container market; and second, liner operators switching to other trades, probably involving specialist ships. Detailing individual owners, Holt noted that Wilhelm Wilhelsen was at an advanced stage with a design for a container vessel, but he held "very strong views on British shipbuilding...[and]...to get him to order British is going to require a major selling effort." Olsen and Larson, on the other hand, were probably "worth talking to" as neither held "such very strong views against British shipbuilders." Thus, although there were substantial opportunities for British yards in Norway, at all levels "competition from Norwegian and continental yards will be severe." Holt concluded his survey, somewhat plaintively, by observing that British yards should immediately and urgently address their problems in the Norwegian market. His suggestions for improvement were the results of months of research and interviews with over 150 Norwegian shipowners, whose views had been given "with a genuine desire to assist an Industry to regain its position as Norway's natural supplier of ships."[22] Despite the

---

[22]*Ibid.*

thoroughness of the report, it was too little and too late. Britain's hold on the Norwegian market was decisively broken in the mid-1950s and the increased competition from industries with radically different outlooks in terms of production and marketing and the lack of, or uncertainty of, the response from British shipbuilders combined to ensure that there would be no way back into the Norwegian market once it was lost. Therefore, in its most important and rapidly expanding overseas market, the rise of international competition and Britain's inability to meet it led to comparative and competitive failure.

British Shipbuilding: Failure in International And Domestic Markets[23]

The figures in terms of the decline of British shipbuilding are well known and somewhat stark. Between 1948 and 1967, British shipbuilding output maintained a steady state. Total output in 1948 was 1.2 mgrt and was slightly lower in 1965. Indeed, the highest figures for output occurred in the 1950s when in four individual years output reached over 1.4 mgrt, with the highest level of output being in 1955 when output reached a postwar record of 1,474,000 grt. Yet in the context of a vibrantly expansionary market, this was hardly a recipe for success. Table 8 shows the relative failure of the British shipbuilding industry in the international market.

Perhaps one should be wary of making too much of this particular set of statistics, but a declining national share of an internationally traded product, such as ships, even where the absolute level of national production is not falling, can usually be taken as an indicator of declining national competitiveness. In some senses, a declining national volume with

---

[23]In the extensive literature on the history of British shipbuilding, the two main analytical paradigms can be described as "institutional" and "entrepreneurial failure." These are best represented in the work of E.H. Lorenz, *Economic Decline in Britain: The Shipbuilding Industry, 1890-1970* (Oxford, 1991); and E.H. Lorenz and F. Wilkinson, "The Shipbuilding Industry, 1880-1965," in B. Elbaum and W. Lazonick (eds.), *The Decline of the British Economy* (Oxford, 1986), 109-134, for the institutional approach. The "entrepreneurial failure" argument is best characterised in A. Slaven "Marketing Opportunities and Marketing Practices: The Eclipse of British Shipbuilding, 1957-1976," in L.R. Fischer (ed.), *From Wheel House to Counting House: Essays in Maritime Business History in Honour of Professor Peter Neville Davies* (St. John's, 1992), 125-151; and D. Thomas, "Shipbuilding — Demand Linkage and Industrial Decline," in K. Williams, J. Williams and D. Thomas, *Why Are The British Bad at Manufacturing*? (London, 1983), 179-216.

an increasing international market share is preferable to an increasing national volume and declining market share which, usually, portends serious problems at the next downturn in the trade cycle. Arguably, the experience of British shipbuilding broadly follows this latter pattern. Whereas absolute levels of output can be sustained for some time if world demand rises faster than new capacity, if either world demand falls or new capacity outstrips it, an uncompetitive industry, or shipyard, will be the first to feel the impact, and probably the last to recover, given that orders will go to the more competitive sectors first. The only way in which such a situation can be avoided is through increased competitiveness.[24]

Table 8
World and UK Output of Merchant Ships, 1947-1967 (000 grt)

Year	World	UK	UK Share as % of World
1947	2,093	1193	57
1948	2,303	1,176	51.1
1949	3,126	1,267	40.5
1950	3,489	1,325	38.0
1951	3,639	1,341	36.9
1952	4,394	1,303	29.6
1953	5,095	1,317	25.9
1954	5,251	1,409	26.8
1955	5,315	1,474	27.7
1956	6,670	1,383	20.7
1957	8,501	1,414	16.6
1958	9,270	1,402	15.1
1959	8,746	1,373	15.7
1960	8,356	1,331	15.9
1961	7,940	1,192	15.0
1962	8,375	1,073	12.8
1963	8,539	928	10.9
1964	10,264	1,043	10.1
1965	12,216	1,073	8.8
1966	14,307	1,084	7.6
1967	15,780	1,297	8.2

Source: See table 2.

[24]B.W. Hogwood, *Government and Shipbuilding: The Politics of Industrial Change* (Farnborough, 1979), 22-24.

Table 9
UK Shipbuilding Output for Domestic and Overseas Registration and Total Imports, 1948-1971 (000 grt)

Year	Total	Domestic	Overseas	Imports	A	B
1948	1,176	766	410	0	0	0
1949	1,267	745	522	0	0	0
1950	1,325	884	441	0	0	0
1951	1,341	739	602	0	0	0
1952	1,303	888	415	21	2.4	1.6
1953	1,317	953	365	49	5.1	3.7
1954	1,409	927	482	54	5.8	3.8
1955	1,474	935	539	37	4.0	2.5
1956	1,383	949	435	119	12.5	8.6
1957	1,414	1,152	261	158	13.7	11.2
1958	1,402	1,064	338	285	26.8	20.3
1959	1,373	1,257	115	449	35.7	32.7
1960	1,331	1,185	146	465	39.2	34.9
1961	1,192	911	281	509	55.1	42.7
1962	1,073	908	165	569	62.7	53.0
1963	928	644	284	438	68.0	47.2
1964	1,043	894	149	233	26.1	22.3
1965	1,073	937	136	244	26.0	22.7
1966	1,084	777	306	479	61.6	44.2

Notes: A denotes percentage of home market taken by imports; B denotes percentage of total output taken by imports.

Source: See table 2.

In this respect the figures for Britain make comparatively poor reading as table 9 demonstrates. If the figures for total, domestic and overseas output are worrying, then those on import penetration are truly alarming. From 1952, when foreign builders took 2.4% of the UK domestic market for ships, the loss of market share was dramatic. By 1961, imports were over fifty percent of ships produced for domestic registration and by 1967, the UK was a net importer of tonnage. In the same year UK output for UK registration fell below fifty percent for the first time. Competition in the British market was genuinely international; in the first four years of import penetration, orders were concentrated on German, Japanese, Dutch and Commonwealth yards, but from 1956 onwards British orders were spread throughout the major shipbuilding countries. The most serious damage was done by Japanese, German and Swedish yards which, with modernized shipyards and a strong commitment to meeting delivery dates, could meet the growing demand for larger ships. Even more worryingly Dutch yards consistently ate away at the market for smaller ships.

At face value the statistics do not corroborate one of the oft advanced reasons for the failings of the British industry, the failure to take advantage of the tanker market and the trend towards larger ships. As table 10 demonstrates, Britain was not radically out of kilter proportionately with other main builders of tanker tonnage.

Table 10
Proportion of Tonnage Launched as Tankers (%)

Year	World	UK	FRG	Japan	Sweden	Norway
1950	45	46	6	33	62	-
1951	42	62	8	16	77	46
1952	45	49	32	45	79	31
1953	56	58	40	58	76	66
1954	55	50	46	32	67	47
1955	45	44	26	47	61	66
1956	34	37	7	44	40	40
1957	45	37	20	57	58	69
1958	51	41	34	57	68	69
1959	50	38	28	53	66	60
1960	44	46	36	34	61	18
1961	35	33	23	36	56	48
1962	36	37	38	39	57	48
1963	43	40	43	55	57	45
1964	54	40	44	67	77	63
1965	44	39	27	51	75	33
1966	37	23	36	39	62	52
1967	31	20	20	36	40	42
1968	39	9	36	46	35	60
1969	46	30	37	48	76	50

Source: See table 2.

If there is an observable failure, it lies in the inability of Britain to participate in the two post-Suez ordering booms of 1957-1958 and 1968-1969. Perhaps, more worryingly, the erosion of the British market for tankers provides a better indication of the main trends than for figures for proportion of output. Table 11 illustrates the sudden and dramatic loss of market share.

Once again, the significance of the 1957-1958 post-Suez boom is marked. Market penetration is barely discernible before 1957, but from that date Britain becomes a heavy importer of tanker tonnage, becoming a net importer in terms of tonnage launched for the domestic market in 1961 and a net importer in terms of tanker tonnage launched in 1962. By the time of the second Suez boom Britain was a net importer of all tonnage. Failure in the tanker market, therefore, particularly in the late 1950s, does explain, in part, the difficulties of the British shipbuilding industry.

Table 11
Tanker Launches UK, 1950-1967 (000 grt) and Percentage of Tonnage Imported as % of Total Launched

Year	Total	Domestic Registration	Overseas Registration	Imported
1950	614	367	247	0
1951	834	340	494	0
1952	643	353	290	2.8
1953	762	527	235	4.9
1954	714	424	290	2.8
1955	648	354	294	0
1956	518	333	185	4.6
1957	535	474	61	22.2
1958	577	396	181	35.2
1959	529	479	50	72.9
1960	618	534	87	51.8
1961	393	320	74	87.8
1962	403	372	31	106.7
1963	369	233	136	92.4
1964	420	367	52	47.4
1965	421	365	56	162.5
1966	244	192	52	132.4
1967	260	68	192	178.5

Source: See table 2.

The lack of modernization of the plant and layouts of British shipyards have also been blamed for the comparative and competitive failure of British shipbuilding, particularly with regard to the construction of large ships. Once again, however, the statistics are contradictory. The average size of ships launched in the UK remained larger than the world average between 1950 and 1970. But only in 1950 and 1959 did Britain launch the largest vessel in the world, and from 1957 onwards the largest vessels launched in the UK were consistently smaller than those launched in Western Europe and Japan. Indeed, in 1966 and 1967, when Japan and Western Europe launched their first 100,000-grt vessels, the largest vessels launched in the UK were 62,000 and 60,000 grt, respectively. As the report of the Committee of Inquiry into Shipping noted in 1970, the two closures of the Suez Canal had "hastened the speed of development of larger tankers."[25] The normal measure of the output of tankers used in the tanker market was a measure of comparison with that of the standard T.2 tanker built in the Second World War.[26] This measured the deadweight tonnage of the vessel and its sailing speed. For time series figures, however, the measure is less than satisfactory, as although it does measure tonnage and capacity, it takes no account of the increase in the normal sailing speed of tankers. In terms of T.2 equivalents, the deadweight tonnage of tankers increased by 129 percent and the carrying capacity increased by 148 percent. The economies of scale of large vessels therefore conditioned the growing size of tankers. Even by 1963, when 100,000 deadweight ton vessels first entered service they could, transiting the Suez Canal in ballast and via the Cape when full, deliver oil more cheaply to Western Europe than could a smaller tanker passing through the Canal in both directions The cost per ton-mile of carrying oil in a tanker of over 200,000 dwt — thirty-seven of which were in service in 1969, with a further 169 on order — was less than one-third that of carrying it in a 20,000-dwt vessel. The larger vessel did not require a larger crew and had a capital cost of about £30 per deadweight ton as compared with £90 per deadweight ton for one a tenth that size. Although

---

[25]Great Britain, Board of Trade, Committee of Inquiry into Shipping, *Report* (London, 1970), 155.

[26]A T.2 equivalent is defined as a vessel of 16,765 dwt with a service speed of 14.5 knots. A tanker's T.2 equivalent is thus:

$$\frac{\text{service speed in knots} \times \text{deadweight tonnage}}{14.5 \times 16{,}765}$$

analysis of the size range of tanker fleets does not show the UK register as being much different from that of the world register — 79.5 percent of British register was in the under 50,000 dwt class, with 20.4% in the 50,000+ class, the equivalent figures for the world register being 79.5 and 20.7% — what is certain is that British orders were increasingly going abroad on grounds of ability to build, delivery dates and prices.[27] The trend, therefore, was to build larger ships, but of the twenty-seven shipyards examined by the Shipbuilding Inquiry Committee (SIC or Geddes Committee) in 1965, only nine had the capacity to build ships of over 40,000 grt and only five could build over 65,000 grt. The capacity of the other eighteen yards ranged from 4776 grt to 38,996 grt.[28] Thus the lack of attention by British shipbuilders to the main market trends in tankers and the size of vessels can be interpreted as a major contributory factor in the industry's decline.

The loss of both overseas and the home market was a cause of considerable concern to the Geddes Committee.[29] As the Board of Trade defined the issue in a memorandum to the Committee, "shipping and shipbuilding are 'international' industries whose prosperity depends on their ability to compete in an international market."[30] The paper noted that "since 1962 imports have exceeded exports by a substantial margin" and that tankers and bulk carriers formed a much larger proportion of tonnage ordered overseas for UK registration than of export orders in the UK. The Board of Trade analysed orders for British owners placed abroad in 1964 with worrying conclusions. The position of tankers and bulk carriers was conceded with foreign yards offering "more attractive prices, delivery terms and credit facilities...public statements by the shipowners concerned have emphasised that prices in Sweden and Japan, particularly for bulk carriers and tankers, have been much lower than in the United

---

[27]Committee of Inquiry into Shipping, *Report* (1970), 153-155.

[28]Great Britain, Board of Trade (BT), Shipbuilding Inquiry Committee (SIC), *Report* (London, 1966), appendix D.

[29]No attempt has been made to analyse the role of the state in this chapter. On this issue see L. Johnman, *The State and British Shipbuilding, 1945-1965* (Glasgow, 1998); and Hogwood, *Government and Shipbuilding*.

[30]Public Record Office (PRO), BT 186/11, SIC, "Shipbuilding Imports and Exports," Note by the Board of Trade, 8 February 1965.

Kingdom."[31] More worrying still, an Alfred Holt order for two expensive high speed cargo liners in Japan, was considered "especially significant, not only because just four vessels in their existing fleet of 51 ships were built abroad, but because it had hitherto been assumed that British shipyards were competitive for specialised vessels of this type."[32] The Board of Trade paper conceded that the main reasons for the decline of British shipbuilding, in both the export and domestic markets, was the increased internationalization of the maritime industries and was "primarily due to the emergence of Japan and Sweden as major suppliers in the world export market." Despite the erosion of British markets, the value of British exports of ships totalled over £243 million between 1958 and 1964, although the annual figure had fallen from £55 million in 1961 to £16 million in 1964. Any further erosion of British markets would turn a positive contribution from shipbuilding to the balance of trade into a negative one.[33] In terms of shipping, the position was rather more complicated. The Chamber of Shipping calculated a range of examples based on a 10,000 grt cargo liner of £1.2 million, bought for twenty percent cash with repayments over ten years at 5.5% interest. If sold to a foreign owner, the total benefit to the balance of payments over ten years would be £1.5 million. The same vessel built for a British owner, would provide an annual cash flow to the UK of £303,000 of which £101,000 would be foreign currency earnings. As the Chamber remarked, "the benefit of building for UK account is even more apparent since the annual cash inflow of £303,000 might be expected to operate in reverse if the ship were foreign owned."[34] In similar vein, whilst earnings from British-owned ships built abroad still contributed to the balance of payments, what had to be discounted was the cost of the ship. The Chamber of Shipping's conclusion was that unless credit terms in Britain were eased and made comparable to those in Germany and Japan, then

---

[31]*Ibid.*

[32]*Ibid.*

[33]*Ibid.*

[34]PRO, BT 186/11, "Shipping and the Balance of Payments," Memorandum by the Chamber of Shipping of the United Kingdom, October 1965.

there would be an increasing erosion of both the domestic and overseas markets for British ships.[35]

What underpinned this decline of British shipbuilding and the erosion of British markets at home and abroad, is partly explicable by the attitudes of British shipbuilders to the market situation of the postwar period. British shipbuilders themselves seem to have shown remarkably little concern over their market position in the 1950s. Indeed, over many years, most British shipbuilding companies had sought to stabilize their market positions by forming alliances with buyers and a bespoke builder-client relationship had developed, largely based upon the personal relationships between the chairmen and managing directors of the building firms and shipping companies.[36] The striking feature of this situation, however, was not its strength but rather its weakness, in that the shipbuilders had little power to manipulate the market which was driven by the owners, and the best that could be said was that the shipbuilders knew, with some degree of accuracy, what the preferences of their customers were. Thus the domestic order book tended to replicate the pattern of overseas ordering; the concentration of activity in a few well established market areas. Heavily conditioned by the interwar period, few British shipbuilders saw the need to change their minds in the post Second World War period. What was unique about the post-1945 period, however, was the Long Boom and the near thirty year expansion of the international economy and the maritime industries.

Such expansion, if not exactly antipathetic to British shipbuilders, certainly did not accord with their mind-set which, if not driven by a slump mentality, was certainly heavily conditioned by a cyclical mentality. A perfect example of such attitudes comes from the 1948 AGM of the Wearside yard of Joseph L. Thompson, where the Chairman, Cyril Thompson, commented on the yard's order book, which comprised cargo liners and tankers, that "in order to build these vessels, which are practically all-welded, we have been forced to put on order...capital equipment...costing £28,500." Here the language is instructive; "forced" to spend £28,500 over two years, which was little more than double the

---

[35]*Ibid.*

[36]A. Slaven, "British Shipbuilders: Market Trends and Order Book Patterns between the Wars," *Journal of Transport History*, III (1981-1982), 37-62.

directors' fees for the same period, against profits of over £160,000 for the year ending in March 1948. But Thompson continued:

> you will appreciate that while we have a very good order book we must face the fact that this expenditure is necessary to hold our own in a highly competitive market which calls for the building of mainly welded ships. The Shipbuilding Industry is notorious for seven lean years following seven fat ones and bearing this in mind, we hope to establish substantial reserves including a dividend equalisation reserve.[37]

Such an attitude was entirely typical of those existing among British shipbuilders; respond piecemeal to the prevailing market conditions, never forget that the next slump is bound to come, therefore, stiffen the reserves to get through it, and at all costs protect the dividend.

As the market continued to boom in the 1950s, British shipbuilders gave little serious consideration to issues such as technology, organisation and marketing. The response to the tanker boom, for example, was treated not as an opportunity but rather as an intrusion. As G.W. Barr, the managing director of Fairfield and past president of the Clyde Shipbuilders Association (CSA), complained, there was a "complete lack of enquiry for the highest classes of passenger and cargo liners, for coasters and smaller craft generally." The heavy ordering of tanker tonnage merely served to conceal what Barr termed those "disturbing features," which were "clear enough to those who appreciate the importance of balance as well as volume in the shipbuilding order book." Tankers, therefore, were useful enough for ensuring continuity of work but somehow did not represent "real" shipbuilding.[38] The then current President of the CSA, Charles Connell agreed, commenting that:

> Many yards have never built and are not designed or equipped to build tankers, although in the face of the

---

[37]Great Britain, Tyne and Wear Archives, 1811/216/9/1-3, J.L.Thompson and Sons Ltd., 54th Annual General Meeting, 31 August 1948, Chairman's Notes.

[38]G.W. Barr, "Handicaps on Shipbuilding Industry," *Glasgow Herald Trade Review, 1950.*

> great tanker demand some yards have undertaken this class of work for the first time. Obviously the tanker boom brings no comfort or orders to the many builders of small craft, coasters, colliers and specialised river and estuary vessels. Tankers provide, proportionately to other types, less work for the finishing trades, which are so important in the building of high-class passenger vessels.[39]

Tankers were simply not "class" vessels. Even in 1951, with the industry satiated by the Korean War boom, having an order book comprising one thousand ships, of 6.25 million tons, worth £550 million and representing four years work, the President of the Shipbuilding Conference could still complain that it was "an abnormal and artificial order book."[40] As Lester Goldsmith, of the Gulf Oil Refinery Company, commented in terms of ordering in Britain, British shipbuilders were always ready with the "brush off" that "our order-books are filled."[41]

By the onset of the mild recession in 1958, with a record amount of tonnage being built overseas for British owners and more being built than Britain was building for foreign owners, the recession only served to vindicate the views of the shipbuilders that the lean years were bound to come. As the President of the Shipbuilding Conference noted in 1958, in the face of the recession, "soundly based British shipowners...[were]...less likely to cancel their orders than some overseas customers."[42] The same theme was taken up by the managing director of Lithgow's, A.H. White, who extolled Britain's conservatism and confidently predicted that "the nations have overbuilt and some shipyards will go out of business...it will be a case of last in, first out, and that Britain's policy of modernising her

---

[39]C. Connell, "Declining Shipbuilding Order Books," *ibid*.

[40]J. Ramsay Gebbie, "The Shipyards: An Unprecedented Order Book," *Lloyds List Annual Review 1951*.

[41]PRO, Admiralty (ADM) 205/106, "Present Weakness of the Marine Engineering Industry and Its Consequences," appendix 4, extract from a private letter by Lester Goldsmith, 15 May 1953.

[42]J.A. Milne, "Shipbuilding: Outlook Uncertain," *Lloyds List Annual Review, 1958.*

shipyards without any great expansion of their capacity will pay dividends in her future competition with the 'mushroom' yards."[43] This, however, was something of a counsel of despair, as what it did was simply re-assert the strength of the order book, maintained the fiction that no increase in British capacity was required and that the market would come back to the British. As *Shipbuilder and Marine Engine Builder* commented in 1960, "while British owners...[were]...more universal in their outlook in the placing of orders, it is reasonable to assume that ordering abroad in such volume was abnormal and it is not likely to be sustained as and when the flow of orders resumes a healthier trend."[44] At all levels this analysis was wrong; by 1962 *Fairplay* was examining the second quarter returns from *Lloyd's Register* and concluding that "Great Britain and Northern Ireland now has the smallest share of world construction in all her history."[45] As the glutted order books of the mid-1950s thinned in the recession so the grounds for confidence crumbled and the attitudinal problems of British shipbuilders were fully revealed.

British Shipbuilding: A Problem of Attitude

The problems of attitude within the shipbuilding industry were comprehensively exposed in the course of the SIC in 1965. Through the Chamber of Shipping of the UK, the Geddes Committee circulated a questionnaire to British shipping companies. The final report of the Committee, whilst succinct in its summation of the views of British shipping, especially on issues such as credit, price and delivery dates, was perhaps less critical than it could have been in terms of the material submitted in evidence.[46] The questionnaire brought replies from twenty-seven shipping companies, ranging from single sentence replies to the thirteen questions in one or two cases, to twenty-plus page replies in others. On the main issues of price and delivery date, fourteen companies expressed the view that prices abroad were lower and delivery dates both quicker and firmer than in

---

[43]Quoted in *Fairplay*, 15 September 1960.

[44]*Shipbuilder and Marine Engine Builder*, December 1960.

[45]*Fairplay*, 26 July 1962.

[46]SIC, *Report*, 22-26, 27-31, 132-133 and 141-142.

British yards. Of the other thirteen firms replying, four did not build abroad as a matter of policy and nine stated that the evidence on prices was at best mixed. At least three — Shaw Saville and Albion, Ben Line and Cunard — were stridently patriotic in their support of British builders, but of the other ten at least some reservation was held in terms of delivery dates and the British marine engineering industry.

Support for home shipbuilders by British shipping firms was strongest among those companies which had well-established bespoke relationships. The Ben Line's relationship with the Clyde yard of Charles Connell, for example, had evolved since the Second World War based upon a developing vessel design which was subject to incremental improvement. Similarly, Clan Line, which was a subsidiary of British and Commonwealth Shipping Co. Ltd. (B&C), favoured Greenock Dockyard for its building, the Greenock yard also being wholly owned by B&C. Furness Withy also owned its own yard, Furness Shipbuilding, as well as another very pro-British shipping line, Shaw Saville and Albion, and did not tender abroad. The "root of all our industrial troubles affecting delivery of home requirements and exports alike," according to Shaw Saville was late delivery by sub-contractors and the failure of sub-contractors to honour contracts.[47] Indeed, this was a criticism which was widespread throughout the replies to the questionnaire — a major failing with British shipbuilding was inadequate control exerted by shipyards over sub-contractors, leading to late delivery and higher prices.

When the SIC turned to the issue of sub-contractors, however, a dramatically different picture appeared. The major problem emerging from replies from sub-contractors and ship management companies, was "the failure by some sections of this industry to appreciate that a modern ship is a complex engineering problem," and there was no longer any room in the industry for shipyards which were in fact "a metal box builder" which sub-contracted "all engineering work, both mechanical and electrical, to outside firms."[48] The shipbuilder of the future "must become

---

[47]PRO, BT 186/32, SIC, Replies to Questionnaire from the Ben Line, British and Commonwealth Shipping, Furness Withy, and Shaw, Saville and Albion; 3 and 22 August, and 1 October 1965.

[48]*Ibid.*, "Factors Affecting the Competitiveness of the British Shipbuilding Industry," Evidence by Captain H. White, Technical Director of J. and J. Denholm (Management) Ltd., Glasgow, 29 July 1965.

a co-ordinating organization for all the specialised equipment going into the ship," although the traditional attitude by which the "shipbuilder built everything and was well able to understand everything fitted on board, dies hard."[49] Not only did the industry require an increase in the number and quality of engineering staff at all levels, the problem was most acute at top management levels. The shipbuilding firm had to take full responsibility for all engineering work going into the ship and not sub-contract to outside firms.[50] A more caustic view came from the Director of P.A. Management Consultants, Alan Beaton, who had offered in 1960 to formulate, free of charge, a Labour Charter for the industry, but had his proposal rejected by the Shipbuilding Employers Federation. Beaton's conclusion was that :

> With some notable exceptions, who could not act independently while still members of the Federation, the calibre of the majority of Shipyard Management was below what one meets in other industries. Backward looking rather than progressive, they are as much responsible as the Unions for the poor state of the industry. Their appreciation of labour relations is poor and conditioned by the past rather than the future. Furthermore, the skill and spirit to bring about the changes that must take place if the industry is not to succumb altogether is lacking.[51]

The problems of sub-contracting, therefore, could not be solved unless the problems of British shipbuilding management were resolved first.

Shipbrokers and consultants may have had one view of the problems, but whilst the brokers attempted to have more shipbuilding work done in-house, the sub-contractors themselves appealed that they should exert more control over components as the shipyards simply did not possess the engineering skills concomitant with modern shipbuilding.

---

[49]*Ibid.*

[50]*Ibid.*, Statement by Mr. Alan Beaton, Director, P.A. Management Consultants Ltd., 20 September 1965.

[51]*Ibid.*

Elliott Marine, for example, had been formed with express intent of providing complete control systems for main and auxiliary machinery, but had "encountered considerable resistance from United Kingdom Shipbuilders." Elliott Marine's view was that control engineering companies should take full responsibility for the engineering, supply, installation, commissioning and servicing of equipment which required "skills not normally available in UK shipyards." The small scale of most UK shipyards meant that it was prohibitively expensive for individual yards to attempt to build up or maintain such technical expertise. The Glasgow manufacturer of pumps and cranes, J.H. Carruthers and Co. Ltd., took much the same line, arguing that historically the shipyard had offered all of the technical knowledge which was involved in the design, construction and operation of all types of ships. But, as in all branches of engineering: "ships...are becoming increasingly sophisticated and we believe that the time has been reached now when shipyards should be prepared to pass on to contractors the technical responsibility for large elements of the whole complex, which is a marine cargo vessel." With ships as amalgams of sub-contracted packages, the only way in which a yard could exert more control over the ultimate cost of a ship was through the placement of technical responsibility with firms possessing expert knowledge. The experience of Carruthers in "dealing with a number of shipyards outside Britain" was that yards "which subscribe to this policy...today are successful yards."[52] Despite, therefore, the unanimity of the criticism over sub-contracting, the position seemed far from easily treatable with polar opposite solutions being offered to the SIC.

More worrying than the sub-contracting position, however, was the attitude of a number of shipping companies which had traditionally built in Britain. Alfred Holt and Co., which operated the Blue Funnel Line, and had not ordered outside of the UK prior to 1964, ordered two specialist cargo liners in Japan in that year and submitted a lengthy memorandum in support of their decision, which stated that the position of the British industry seemed "to be in a state of flux and to be deteriorating rapidly;" although UK prices were generally competitive with most European yards, they were higher than Sweden and twenty percent "above the Japanese." The position with regard to delivery dates was termed "deplorable" with completion times in Japan being at least half

[52]*Ibid.*, Memorandum by Elliott Marine Automation Ltd., September 1965, and letter from J.H. Carruthers and Co. Ltd., 6 October 1965.

of those in the UK. Although it was "manifestly more convenient to build in the UK," Holt's could "conceive of virtually no circumstances in which we would place an order with a British yard."[53] As if Holt's corporate view was not bad enough, the company's Chairman, Sir Stewart MacTier, advanced the view that the major problem in British shipbuilding was the "grave deficiency" in the top and middle management of the industry. There had to be more interest in production engineering and production planning and this could only be achieved by an influx of graduates into the industry and possibly by introducing top management from outside.[54]

Another prominent British shipping company, P&O, had also begun ordering abroad in the early 1960s. P&O outlined thirteen quotations for a 62,000 dwt oil/bulk/ore carrier, four from British yards, five from European yards and four from Japanese yards. British tenders ranged from £3.38 to £3.77 million, the European tenders ranged from £3.32 million in Sweden to £3.62 million in Germany, whereas the Japanese quotations ranged from £2.90 to £3.24 million. The highest Japanese tender, therefore, was below the lowest British and European tenders. Quotations for an 82,000 dwt revealed an even poorer position for British yards, in that the lowest UK quotation was well above Japanese, Danish and Swedish quotations. The issue of delivery dates was also of concern to P&O and here the issue of delivery was brought sharply into focus. P&O analysed twelve orders placed in six British shipyards in the late 1950s, of which only two had been delivered on time, with the others between one and nine months late. Only one vessel had been delivered at or below the contract price, the overrun on the other vessels totalled £1,766,050, at an average cost of £160,550 per vessel. The position had not been changed with the move to fixed price contracting, in that of four tankers ordered in British yards in November 1962, none had achieved their contracted delivery dates. As P&O commented, British yards had "little confidence in their ability to maintain forecast dates," whereas they had "no reason to doubt...[that]...the anticipated delivery dates offered by the Japanese will be maintained," a fact supported by "heavy penalties accepted by the Japanese for late delivery." At almost all

---

[53]*Ibid.*, "Notes by Alfred Holt and Co., Liverpool," 11 August 1965.

[54]*Ibid.*, "Note on Meeting with Sir Stewart MacTier of Alfred Holt and Co.," 6 July 1965.

levels, price, delivery dates, technical ability and after sales service P&O preferred Japanese shipbuilders to British.[55]

As with P&O, BP had normally built in the UK but had started ordering abroad in 1963. BP analyzed seventeen quotations for a 19,000 dwt tanker, thirteen from UK yards and four from Swedish yards. The Swedish quotations ranged from £1.21 million to £1.38 million, whereas the British quotations ranged from £1.49 to £1.91 million, and as with P&O's experience as the size of the vessel rose to the 75,000 dwt range so the price differential between British and Swedish prices increased. Delivery dates were also of concern for BP and they analysed eleven orders placed between April 1963 and January 1964, three in Sweden and eight in the UK. The Swedish orders were all delivered on time, whereas the British orders were between one and ten months late. The British yards took between twelve and sixteen months to construct a 19,000 dwt tanker, whereas Swedish yards took between six and seven months. As BP commented, "construction periods from placing a contract to delivery are too long and delivery is frequently, if not invariably, late...this is deplorable." Like P&O, BP would have preferred to have built in Britain, which as they noted, was justified by them only having ordered abroad when no reasonable delivery dates were obtainable in Britain. More worryingly, however, "with the increasing competition in international shipping and the importance of ensuring competitive costs in oil transport, it is doubtful whether tanker operators...[would]...be able to afford to buy in any except the best (price/quality) market." As with other commentators, BP had wide ranging criticisms of the shipbuilding industry, including the "paucity of higher grade technical staff in the higher echelons of management, but even more particularly at the middle level, where the sheer numbers abroad ensure the attention to detail which is essential to high quality at low cost." This time it was Sweden, rather than Japan, that had the advantages on price, delivery dates and technical ability.[56]

The Geddes Report conjectured three potential outcomes on the basis of action or inaction by the industry with respect to their recommen-

---

[55]*Ibid.*, "Peninsular and Oriental Steam Navigation Company, Evidence for Shipbuilding Inquiry Committee," August 1965.

[56]*Ibid.*, "BP Tanker Company. Completed Questionnaire to SIC," undated, but probably August-September 1965.

dations. On the basis of full acceptance and implementation, the authors believed that the industry's output could reach 2.25 mgrt, thereby "justifying the support of the Government." This growth strategy envisaged the UK industry achieving and holding over twelve per cent of world output. A "holding on" scenario envisaged some changes in attitudes, practices and resource deployment but essentially a defensive stance with the industry neither renewing nor attracting additional resources. In this scenario market share was envisioned as ten per cent with annual output at 1.75mgrt. The decline scenario posited "gradual evolution on recent trend," with no gain in competitiveness, no improvement in turnover, falling profitability and cash resources rapidly becoming inadequate. On this basis, market share would fall to 7.5% and would be marked by "sporadic appeals for government aid to ease the decline."[57] But even the SIC could not have been prepared for the extent of competitive failure that would ensue in the wake of their report. After a massive injection of public money into the industry — £160 million in six years — output had not increased and market share continued to be lost. As world launches increased from 12.2 mgrt in 1965 to 31.5 mgrt in 1973, British output continued to hover around the 1 mgrt mark. The result was a further erosion of world market share from 8.8% in 1965 to 3.2% in 1973. The industry had underperformed to an extent that not even the SIC had considered possible. The situation was bad enough to encourage yet another full scale government sponsored inquiry into the industry.

The consultants, Booz-Allen and Hamilton had the singular misfortune of delivering their report in 1973, the year which marked the end of the long boom; it did, however, make familiar reading in its criticisms of British shipbuilding. In terms of the view of shipowners the comments were much as they had been in 1966; late delivery performance and high prices were considered endemic, with shipbuilding managements blamed for deficiencies in marketing effort, labour control and production planning. As the report noted, "consistent sustained improvement in yard performance is required to alter shipowners' attitudes substantially.... Certain owners have dismissed the possibility of improvement sufficient to attract them back to UK yards." Marketing also came in for familiar criticisms; little direct selling was undertaken, marketing policies were loosely defined and poorly researched, little advance planning was

---

[57]SIC, *Report,* 152.

undertaken and the main burden of generating orders was borne by senior executives, with contract tendering and administration being seen as support functions. Design remained an inherent part of the production process, with little thought being given to longer-term design developments, but even so, the co-ordination of drawing office work and production schedules was poorly integrated and often resulted in delays in construction. Purchasing and stockholding policies were viewed as underdeveloped management services. Planning remained nebulous, with managements neither understanding its role nor recognising its need, and there was little co-ordination, with informal approaches to both progress reporting and problem solving remaining the norm. Despite the huge scale of state support since 1967, the extent of technical modernization was criticized, there being a continuing reliance on "traditional methods and old facilities" and "no evidence of significant improvement in the last five years." The industry had also failed to develop "comprehensive personnel and labour relations policies and procedures," and financial planning and control systems were underdeveloped with "few changes in prospect."[58] The criticisms in 1973 therefore, remained much the same as those that had become cumulative by the time of the Geddes Report.

What is revealed during the second phase of internationalization, within the maritime industries, is that in a period of vibrant expansion of the shipbuilding and shipping industries, the British industries, especially shipbuilding, underwent a period of comparative and competitive decline. British shipbuilders neither modernized adequately, nor taken adequate readings of market trends in the post-war period. As Shaw, Saville and Albion commented the "historical aspect of previous happy connections between Shipowner and Builder" remained very strong, but with increased internationalization of the maritime industries and price, quality and delivery dates increasingly at a premium, the traditional linkages and bespoke relationships which had for a long time sustained the base load of the shipbuilding industry were beginning to unravel.[59] Firstly, the foreign market declined, as European and Japanese yards modernised their equipment, layouts and organisation and took serious market

[58]Booz-Allen and Hamilton, *British Shipbuilding* (London, 1972), 75, 102, 116-120, 139-144, 145-158 and 159-186.

[59]PRO, BT 186/32, SIC, "Replies to Questionnaire by Shaw, Saville and Albion Co. Ltd.," 1 October 1965.

readings of the likely nature of demand for the types and sizes of vessels required. With British order books glutted in the 1950s, the failure of the industry to increase its output and productivity in a booming market told heavily on its fortunes following the mild recession of 1958-1961. By the time of the Geddes Inquiry, a number of companies which had been in bespoke relationships with British shipbuilders were increasingly placing their orders overseas. The difference, for example, between British and Commonwealth's submission to the SIC and the personal statement of Sir Nicholas Cayzer, the company's chairman, to the Committee is notable. He registered a strong complaint in terms of delivery dates, and while B&C had had no "occasion to get a quotation from Japan" he stated "that he thought that it would not be long before they came into competition in this field."[60] The internationalization of the maritime industries in the post Second World War period, and in particular the lack of response in the British shipbuilding industry, was a major reason for the cumulative failure of British shipbuilding in the context of the long boom.

---

[60] *Ibid.*, BT 186/20, "Note on Meeting at British and Commonwealth Shipping Co. Ltd.," 20 July 1965.

Globalization and International Competitiveness: The Experience of the Japanese Shipping Industry since the 1960s

Shin Goto

While ocean-going shipping has always been international in character, the management of the resources it utilizes — especially in terms of the registration of vessels and the origins of employees afloat and ashore — have generally been organized on a national basis. The Japanese shipping industry typified this pattern after the Second World War. However, since the mid-1960s a process of globalization — defined for present purposes as the cross-border procurement and utilization of productive resources — has occurred, leading to the multi-nationalization of fleet assets, seamen and the management resources employed by shipping companies. This chapter examines the causes and consequences of this process.

Globalization has become an urgent concern in advanced shipping countries because the cross-border procurement of resources invariably entails a decrease of domestic investment and employment, and impedes the development of a reservoir of skilled seafaring labour: this process is known as the "hollowing out"of an industry. In this respect, the Japanese Ministry of Transport (MoT) stated in a White Paper on shipping in 1996 that Japan's ocean-going shipping industry is characterized by the greatly advanced state of the hollowing out process, compared with manufacturing industries. According to this report, only eleven percent of the ships of 2000 grt and over operated by the five largest Japanese shipping companies were registered in the country, while Japanese citizens accounted for only twelve percent of the labour force engaged in these vessels.[1] The government thus identified as urgent the need to arrest the hollowing out of shipping, and has recently established a Japanese international ship system. However, Japan's experience begs two important questions: does globalization in shipping inevitably lead to the hollowing out of the industry in the countries concerned? and while the

[1]The Ministry of Transport [MoT], *Nippon Kaiun no Genkyo 1996* [*The Current Situation of Japanese Ocean-going Shipping in 1996*] (Tokyo, 1996), 53.

phenomenon of hollowing out implies that there will be a loss of international competitive advantages, has this been true in the case of the Japanese shipping industry?

In the first part of this chapter, the impact of the globalization process on Japan's ocean-going shipping is outlined, the emphasis being placed on how ocean-going shipping firms, the seamen's union and the MoT coped with the circumstances and causal factors of globalization. An attempt is made to identify the key features of the globalization of Japan's shipping industry, and to view the process from an historical perspective. Secondly, the chapter assesses whether globalization has eroded the competitive advantages of Japanese shipping in the international market. The chapter focuses on the thirty years between the mid-1960s and the mid-1990s, the period being divided according to the three chronological phases through which the process of globalization in Japanese shipping has passed. In the concluding part of the chapter, the question of international competitiveness is examined.

The Onset of Globalization in the Late 1960s and Early 1970s

This period witnessed the final era of rapid economic growth in Japan. It was also a time when the government's maritime policy was largely designed to enlarge the Japanese fleet. But the capacity to add new tonnage could not keep pace with the rapidly growing demand for shipping because of two restrictions on the supply side. First, major shipping operators had weakened their ability to raise funds for new tonnage under the terms of the five-year reconstruction programme which followed the reorganization of the Japanese shipping industry in 1964. Second, the government's Sponsored Shipbuilding Scheme was basically funded for a single fiscal year, so that the scale of newly-built tonnage could, and did, fluctuate annually according to the state of fiscal revenue; it also had an upper limit. In addition, after the reorganization, only participating firms were eligible to build vessels under the Programmed Shipbuilding Scheme. These constraints meant that operators had to rely on chartered tonnage to meet shipping demand. In this period of rapid economic growth, the long-term provision of tonnage was particularly important for the maintenance and expansion of the transactional relationship with shippers.[2] At first, Japanese shipping firms exclusively relied on chartering Japanese vessels, but from the late 1960s, they became increasingly dependent on chartered foreign vessels for the procurement of tonnage.[3] In 1969, some 236 foreign ships of 2000 grt and over, aggregating 6,557,000 deadweight tons (dwt), were chartered, a total that comprised seventeen percent of Japan's merchant fleet (which consists of Japanese-flag vessels plus chartered foreign vessels) by tonnage. In 1970, foreign vessels exceeded 10,000,000 dwt, and in mid-1975 they accounted for approximately forty-six percent of Japan's merchant fleet (see appendix 1). Most of these foreign vessels were medium- and small-sized cargo ships chartered on long terms. In mid-1975, for instance, over ninety-five percent of the chartered foreign vessels were engaged for periods exceeding six months, while eighty-five percent of these long-term charters related to vessels of 50,000 dwt or less.[4] As their tonnage suggests, foreign vessels chartered in this era were mainly deployed in the near sea market.[5]

In this market, the main outward cargoes were steel, fertilizer, cement, and general cargoes, with wood and lumber, iron ore, and coal being carried inward to Japan. The principal bulk cargo was lumber (*lauan*) from the South Seas. The restricted discharging capacity of port facilities in this business meant that medium- and small-sized ships below 10,000 dwt tons were usually deployed. These ships were largely provided by Ehime shipowners (Ehime is one of the prefectures in west Japan), who had shifted the focus of their business from coastal to ocean-going shipping during the 1950s by chartering out their own ships to

---

[2]Yamashita Shinnihon Kisen, *Shashi* [*History of Yamashita Shinnihon Lines*] (Tokyo, 1980), 117.

[3]Yasunori Doi, "Kinkai Kaiun to Shikumisen" [Near-Sea Shipping and a Tie-in Ship], *Sen'in*, XXVII (May 1975), 4-5. The chartering of a foreign vessel, in particular on a long-term charter, was regulated by government agencies set up to save foreign currency, but this regulatory policy was abolished when Japan joined the OECD in 1964.

[4]MoT, *Nippon Kaiun no Genkyo 1976* (Tokyo, 1976), 50.

[5]The "near seas" comprise the Greater Coasting Area, which is bounded by the Kamchatatka Peninsula to the north, Papua New Guinea to the south, the Marshall Islands to the east, and Indonesia to the west.

larger operating firms.[6] The near-sea market had been monopolized by Japanese shipowners, so Japanese-flag vessels were overwhelmingly dominant. But the competitiveness of Japanese-flag vessels in this market declined rapidly from the end of the 1960s. Analyses of the charter cost differentials between vessels built within the Programmed Shipbuilding Scheme and foreign vessels in 1974, indicated that if the cost of a foreign vessel was 100, the Japanese cost was 151 in the case of a general cargo vessel of 10,000 dwt, 128 in respect of a vessel of 30,000 dwt, and 112 in terms of a tanker of 90,000 dwt.[7] Although large, specialized vessels maintained their competitiveness well, medium- and small-tonnage general cargo vessels operated at a great disadvantage in relation to foreign vessels.

This was caused, in part, by the rapid rise in Japanese seamen's wage levels. According to a report into the labour costs of ocean-going vessels owned by firms belonging to the Japanese Shipowners' Association, in the 1965 fiscal year, the cost of seamen per ship was 57.49 million yen, rising to 283.36 million yen in fiscal year 1976, a five-fold increase over the decade.[8] This largely reflected the escalation in wage levels from a base of 100 in 1965 to 440 in 1976. This rapid rise was itself caused by the price inflation precipitated by the first oil shock in 1973. However, seamen's wages rose more steeply than did consumer prices.[9] Moreover, it should be noted that Japanese seafaring labour costs

---

[6]Nippon Senshu Kyokai [Japanese Shipowners' Association], *Kinkai Kaiun no Mondaiten* [*The Problems in Near-Sea Shipping*] (Tokyo, 1975), 38.

[7]Compared to the charter base necessary to earn operating profits equivalent to the total value of a ship within a decade. The figures are calculated on the premise that a vessel would be built under the conditions of the Programmed Shipbuilding Scheme in fiscal year 1974, including a ship's value, costs of repair and insurance, and crew cost. MoT, *Nippon Kaiun no Genkyo 1975* (Tokyo, 1975), 26.

[8]Nippon Senshu Kyokai, *Henbo suru Nippon Kaiun* [*Japanese Shipping Undergoing a Remarkable Change*] (Tokyo, 1977), 72-73.

[9]Whereas rising consumer prices in Japan between fiscal years 1973 and 1975 were 16.1%, 21.8% and 10.4%, respectively, those of ocean-going seamen's wages were 21.1%, 41.5% and 17.3% during the same period. Zen Nippon Kai'in Kumiai [All Japan Seamen's Union], *Zen Nippon Kai'in Kumiai 40 nen shi* [*Forty-year History of the All Japan Seamen's Union*] (Tokyo, 1986), 430. Such large wage gains were attributed to the union's triumph after a prolonged ninety-one-day strike in 1972. Thereafter the union also

included not just the wages paid to seamen aboard, but also those paid to seamen ashore. Significantly, in principle, Japanese seamen were guaranteed lifetime employment, so that wages were paid during leave from a ship and were therefore included in the vessel's operating costs. The ratio of seamen ashore, but remaining on the register, to seamen aboard is called the reserve ratio. If this reaches fifty percent, it means that when a crew of, say, thirty seafarers is engaged, the number of reserved seamen is fifteen (thirty persons × 0.5), so that the total number of seamen on the register per ship is forty-five.[10] Multiplying the number of seamen on the register by the cost per person yields the total labour costs per ship. The rise in seamen's wages pushed up labour costs more sharply than in other countries, because this system of reserve seamen was peculiar to Japan's shipping. Accordingly, with the fiscal year 1965 as standard, the cost per seamen on the register was 499 in the 1975 fiscal year, while the cost per seamen on board, including reserve seamen, which was the actual cost of labour per ship, jumped to 648 during the same period.[11]

The smaller the vessel, the stronger is the impact of the rising cost of seamen. Thus, the move towards the de-Japanization of the fleet emerged in the near-sea market which was dominated by medium- and small-sized vessels. The larger shipping companies withdrew their own ships from this market, transferring them to newly established affiliates, and chartered foreign ships rather than Japanese-flag vessels.[12] A report on the problems of near-sea shipping, compiled in March 1975 by the Japanese Shipowners' Association, admitted that: "as a result of multifarious investigations into the future of Japan-flag vessels in the near sea...we are in its final stage to decide a full-scale withdrawal from this

---

wrested concessions from employers' associations regarding institutional conditions, such as standard wages and paid holidays. The union's victory, however, accelerated the process of de-Japanization by Japanese shipowners. See, for example, the leap in vessels sold abroad in 1972 in column 7 of appendix 1.

[10]Given the lifetime employment system, the reserve ratio of seamen never fell to zero because of paid vacations, sickness, injuries, etc.

[11]Nippon Senshu Kyokai, *Henbo suru Nippon Kaiun*, 72-73.

[12]Doi, "Kinkai Kaiun," 4-5.

market."[13] This was a clear recognition of the withdrawal of Japanese-flag vessels, but not Japanese shipowners, from the near-sea market, which was not surrendered to foreign shipowners. In fact, Japanese shipowners devised various means to maintain their control over this business. These devices entailed the deployment of tie-in ships, charter-back ships, and *maru*-ships, all of which were designed to retain market share by diminishing the burdens of rising labour costs.

In essence, these devices represented the first step towards the globalization of Japanese shipping. But what were they? According to the MoT White Paper published in 1976, a tie-in ship is a new vessel built for a foreign shipowner (usually in Hong Kong) in a Japanese shipyard, with a Japanese shipping company not only acting as intermediary between owner and builder but also as long-term charterer of the vessel.[14] It was called a tie-in ship because building berth, building funds, and cargoes to be loaded were pre-determined by the various interested parties before the keel was laid down. There was another factor in the emergence of this practice. The Bank for Japanese Exports and Imports, which financed the export of vessels, began, in the mid-1960s, to seek long-term, often eight-year, charter contracts with first-rate charterers as a necessary condition for lending. Thus, foreign shipowners, in particular in Hong Kong, endeavoured to enter into contracts with influential Japanese operators, and after making such charter parties, signed building contracts with a Japanese shipbuilder. However, as soon as the shipyards had full order books, Japanese shipowners starting reserving berths on their credit, and thus acted as intermediaries between foreign shipowners and Japanese builders. The newly built vessels, were, of course, chartered for a long term by the shipowners, and were therefore called tie-in ships.[15] In this case, the relationship between Japanese shipping companies and foreign shipowners is simply contractual, and thus these early tie-in ships were called "simple" tie-in ships.

Since the late 1960s, however, a new type of tie-in ship has emerged. This is dubbed the "complete," or "joint," tie-in ship, in which a Japanese shipowner has formed an overseas subsidiary solely (a

---

[13]Nippon Senshu Kyokai, *Kinkai Kaiun no Mondaiten*, 48.

[14]MoT, *Nippon Kaiun no Genkyo 1976*, 50.

[15]Yamashita Shinnihon Kisen, *Shasi*, 152-153.

complete tie-in ship), or jointly with a foreign shipowner (a joint tie-in ship), to order a vessel from a Japanese shipyard, with the subsidiary owning the new ship, and then chartering it for a long term, with foreign seamen on board.[16] Japan's major shipping companies utilized such ships from 1969,[17] establishing their overseas subsidiaries in quick succession at that time.[18] The tonnage built by the six major shipping companies during this first period is shown in table 1.

Table 1
Tie-In Ships Built by Six Major Shipping Companies
1969-1975

Year built	Cargo Vessels Nos.	Cargo Vessels 000G/T	Tankers Nos.	Tankers 000 G/T	Total Nos.	Total 000 G/T
1969	2	33	0	0	2	33
1970	5	56	0	0	5	56
1971	8	152	0	0	8	152
1972	10	140	2	171	12	311
1973	18	376	2	184	20	560
1974	12	200	5	487	17	687
1975	20	391	9	862	29	1253

Notes: The six major companies were Nippon Yusen, Mitsui-OSK, Kawasaki, Yamashito-Shin Nippon, Japan Line, and Showa.

Source: Ministry of Transport, *Nippon Kaiun no Genkyo 1976* (Tokyo, 1976), 52.

While a tie-in ship is a newly-built vessel with a foreign registry, a charter-back ship is a former Japanese vessel registered abroad. It is a

---

[16]*Ibid.*, 154.

[17]Tomohei Chida, *Nippon Kaiun no Koudo Seicho* [*High Growth in Japanese Shipping*] (Tokyo, 1993), 259.

[18]Y. Yamamoto, "Kaiun Gorika to Shikumisen" [Rationalization in Shipping and a Tie-in Ship], *Sen'in*, XXVII (May 1975), 2.

vessel which a Japanese shipowner sells to a foreign shipowner and charters anew with seamen from the developing countries on board.[19] This device, designed to overcome the disadvantages of high-cost Japanese labour, was first adopted by medium- and small-scale shipowners in 1965 and by major companies in 1969.[20] It increased at a rapid rate from 1972, with most of the ships sold to open registry countries. For example, out of 306 ships of 1000 gross registered tons (grt) and larger, totalling 2.34 million tons, sold abroad in 1972, 162 ships (1.21 million tons) were sold to Panama, forty-seven ships (0.76 million tons) to Liberia, fourteen ships (70,000 tons) to Singapore, and eleven ships (60,000 tons) to Hong Kong. In aggregate, some 234 vessels, amounting to 2.1 million tons, were re-registered in these states, about ninety percent of the total tonnage sold abroad. Moreover, 243 of these ships were 10,000 tons and under, about eighty percent of those sold abroad,[21] a proportion which indicates that medium- and small-sized ships became uneconomic earlier. Many of these foreign vessels were chartered and deployed in the Japanese near seas again — over sixty percent of chartered foreign vessels in 1975 comprised so-called flag of convenience (FOC) tonnage, including the Liberian and Panamanian flags.[22] In 1974, the proportion of tie-in ships and charter-back ships to chartered foreign ships, operated by the six major shipping companies, is shown in table 2.

While the tie-in ship and the charter-back ship are registered foreign, the maru-ship is designed to gain the same advantages, namely savings in labour costs, while remaining in Japanese registry. A *maru*-ship is a Japanese-flag ship which is chartered out overseas. That is, a Japanese shipowner devises his ship to a foreigner on bare-boat charter, and re-charters it from the foreigner who makes arrangements to man it with labour drawn mainly from developing countries.[23] In Japan, at least until the ratification of the International Convention on Standards of Training

---

[19]MoT, *Nippon Kiun no Genkyo 1976*, 50.

[20]Chida, *Nippon Kaiun*, 252.

[21]MoT, *Nippon Kiun no Genkyo 1976*, 17.

[22]Nippon Senshu Kyokai, *Henbo suru Nippon Kaiun*, 43-44.

[23]Zen Nippon Kai'in Kumiai, *Gaiko Kaiun to Nippon Sen'in* [*Ocean-Going Shipping and Japanese Seamen*] (Tokyo, 1985), 39.

Certification and Watch Keeping for Seafarers (STCW) in 1982, the recruitment of seamen depended not upon the registry of a ship, but on the nationality of the operator or manning agency. It was, therefore, legally possible for a foreign operator or agency to make arrangements for manning a Japanese-flag vessel. However, three factors prevented the utilization of foreign seamen on ocean-going vessels in Japan until the appearance of the so-called maru-ship.[24] First, the government advised shipowners not to employ foreign seamen on Japanese ships, based upon the Cabinet's understanding of the problem of accepting foreign workers in domestic employment on land. Second, the provisions of the Law for Ship's Officers provided that only certificated officers could work aboard Japanese vessels, but as foreigners found it difficult to acquire certificates due to the language requirement, almost all serving officers were Japanese citizens.[25] And, third, an agreement, implementing a closed shop system, concluded between the Shipowners' Association and the All Japan Seamen's Union, prohibited shipowners employing foreign seamen.

Table 2
Tie-in Ships and Charter-Back Ships Under the Control of Six Major Shipping Companies, March 1974

	Cargo Vessels Nos.	Cargo Vessels G/T	Tankers Nos.	Tankers G/T	Total Nos.	Total G/T
Chartered foreign tonnage (A)	462	8990	43	2603	505	11593
Tie-in ships (B)	47	723	8	719	55	1442
Charter-back ships(C)	55	622	15	523	70	1145
(B) + (C)	102	1345	23	1242	125	2587
(B+C)/(A) %	22.1	15	53.5	47.7	24.8	22.3

Source: S. Idemoto, "The Actual Situations of a Tie-in Ship," *Kai'in* (Seamen), XXVII, No. 5 (May 1975), 13.

---

[24] T. Sugiyama, "Gaiko Kaiun-gyo no Kokusaika to Kudoka" [Internationalization and Hollowing-up of the Ocean-going Shipping Industry], in H. Yamagishi and I. Terada (eds.), *Kaiun no Konnichi-teki Sho Mondai* (Tokyo, 1995), 163.

[25] Zen Nippon Kai'in Kumiai, *Yendakaka no Gaikokaiun to Nippon Sen-in [Ocean-going Shipping under the Pressure of Rising Yen and Japanese Seamen]* (Tokyo, 1989), 5.

If the manning agency was a Japanese ocean-going shipping firm, it was difficult to employ foreign seamen due to the first two of these constraints, but such restrictive factors were not at work if the manning agency was a foreigner who chartered a vessel from a Japanese shipowner.[26] This is why the maru-ship came into being, probably in 1970 when a Japanese shipping company sold a ship to the Indonesian government on a deferred payment basis, and then operated it with Indonesian seamen even though it remained a Japanese-flag vessel until the date of last payment.[27] Thereafter, mixed manning with both Japanese and foreign seamen developed into a common practice in near-sea ships by the mutual consent of management and labour.[28] The near-sea shipowners (in Ehime), whose medium- and small-sized ships were losing their cost-competitiveness, were thus the first users of such *maru*-ships.[29]

Moreover, when the Act of Marine Transport was amended in 1970, regulations relating to chartering out abroad were relaxed, so that notification rather than permission was required for a ship with a charter period of less than two years. With this relaxation, the ships chartered-out abroad increased from 138 vessels (1.19 million tons) in 1969 to 183 vessels (2.38 million tons) in 1974.[30] Not all of these ships were utilized as *maru*-ships, but the de-Japanization of labour proceeded as Japanese shipowners devised their ships abroad on bare-boat charters and re-chartered them with low-paid foreign seamen to reduce operational costs.[31]

---

[26]After the adoption of the Convention on STCW by IMCO in 1978 and its ratification, the Law of Ship's Officers in Japan was revised in May 1982 (in force in April 1983). The criterion of manning has thereby changed from the nationality of an operator or a manning agency to the registry of a ship. It also became obligatory on a *maru*-ship for Japanese licence-holders to comprise at least nine of the officers. MoT, *Nippon Kaiun no Genkyo 1989* (Tokyo, 1989), 104.

[27]Chida, *Nippon Kaiun*, 49-50.

[28]Working Group on the Problem of Flagging-out, *A Countermeasure Against Flagging-out* (Tokyo, 1988), 9-10.

[29]Chida, *Nippon Kaiun*, 251.

[30]*Ibid.*, 250.

[31]Zen Nippon Kai'in Kumiai, *40 nen shi*, 473.

The globalization of human resources has thus been a pronounced feature of the Japanese shipping industry since the early 1970s. How did the government respond to the accelerating de-Japanization of fleet assets and human resources by Japanese shipowners? In this first period, the MoT's fundamental policy was that a merchant fleet consisting of Japanese-flag vessels should be the main instrument in the transport of Japan's seaborne trade. The enlargement of the Japanese fleet, mainly by the Programmed Shipbuilding Scheme, was seen as pivotal for this purpose. The MoT therefore adopted policies to ensure indirectly that chartered foreign vessels would not infringe upon Japanese-flag vessels. For example, in December 1964, the MoT made it a policy not to approve of the building of a vessel for export at a domestic shipyard with funds loaned by the Bank of Export and Import, if the ship was in one of the following categories: first, having a long-term, loading-cargo contract of more than two years with a shipper and engaging in the transport of imports into Japan; second, having a speed of fifteen knots and over and planning to work as a non-conference ship on the liner routes where Japanese shipping firms had sailing rights; and last, having a long-term chartering contract of more than two years with a Japanese operator.[32] Moreover, in the first half of the 1970s, when there occurred an imbalance between demand and supply for tonnage in the near-sea market, the MoT introduced provisos that construction of Japanese vessels for the near-sea market was forbidden in 1972 and 1973, and during these years the export of a vessel was permitted only if the ship could not be utilized in the Japanese short sea trade.[33] In the meantime, therefore, the construction of a ship for export was allowed only by tendering to the MoT a written pledge not to enter into service in the near-sea market. Some 145 written-pledge vessels (1.12 million grt) were built for export.[34] These restrictive policies reflected the government's belief that chartered

---

[32]Yunyukamotsu Yuso Kyogikai [Council for Transport of Imported Cargoes], *20 nen shi* [*Twenty-year History*] (Tokyo, 1984), 229-300.

[33]*Ibid.*, 389.

[34]Nippon Senshu Kyokai, *Kinkai Kaiun no Mondaiten*, 23. This system for restricting the sailing areas of new foreign vessels was not practically effective because most of the written-pledge ships were, with seamen from developing countries on board, deployed in the near-sea market. Doi, "Kinkai Kaiun," 5.

foreign vessels should supplement the Japanese merchant fleet, in which Japanese-flag vessels should cater for the bulk of Japan's seaborne trade.

Competitive decline in parts of the Japanese merchant fleet beginning in the late 1960s, and a series of phenomena accompanying it, such as the sale overseas of tonnage on a large scale and the diffusion of anomalous practices of the charter-back ship and *maru*-ship, narrowed employment opportunities for Japanese seamen. The All Japan Seamen's Union, the sole seafarers' union in Japan, claimed that shipowners should conjointly take responsibility for seamen's employment, and that while the Union could not approve overseas sales of ships which would generate a further surplus of reserve seamen, shipowners should provide a replacement ship for such a sold or returned ship. The shipowners resisted joint responsibility for recruitment on the grounds that employment should be at their own discretion.[35] In October 1972, however, the Employers' Associations for Ocean-Going Shipping reached an agreement with the Union about the formation of a *keiretsu* (group) employment council.[36] Hereafter, shipowners had to ask for the Union's consent before selling their vessels abroad, and thus they took on an obligation to prepare a replacement ship in principle in the ratio of one to one.[37] And if shipowners could not provide the ship in the ratio of one to one, they had to secure employment opportunities for seafarers by making arrangements to send their seamen on loan to ships owned by other shipowners.[38]

[35]Zen Nippon Kai'in Kumiai, *40 nen shi*, 373.

[36] *Ibid.*, 372.

[37]Shinwa Kaiun Kaisha, *Shinwa Kaiun 30 nen shi* (*Thirty-year History of Shinwa Kaiun*] (Tokyo, 1992), 301.

[38]*Ibid.*, 298, 301. During leave periods, seamen received a proportion of their salaries in the form of differentials from the head offices. On the other hand, as the seamen's cost was determined on the base of a dollar-quoted cost of foreign seamen, and the yen's exchange value rose, the difference between receipts from other shipowners and expenditures on their seamen began to widen, leaving shipowners to bear heavy burdens. *Ibid.*, 329.

Flagging Out, Late 1970s-Early 1980s

Since the mid-1970s, the Japanese economy has experienced a relatively low, if steady rate of growth. It became unrealistic to expect a repeat of the previous period's remarkable increase in the demand for shipping services centred upon Japan. In addition, the adoption of the floating exchange rate system in 1973 strengthened the yen, further inhibiting trade. These environmental changes, as well as the continuing rise in the cost of labour, forced shipping companies to impose drastic cutbacks in expenditure. This meant that the wave of globalization, which started in the near-sea trades, surged through the ocean-going market, and it therefore became necessary to reconsider the position of Japanese-flag vessels in the national merchant fleet.

In this second period, the secession of vessels from the Japanese-flag became an irreversible trend which affected Japan's ocean-going shipping as a whole. As shown in column 2 of appendix 1, the number of ocean-going vessels on the Japanese register peaked in 1972. The subsequent decline was remorseless, despite two measures taken by the government in the late 1970s, which might otherwise have increased both the number and tonnage of Japanese-flag vessels. One was a buy-back in 1978 of fifty tie-in ships in order to reduce Japan's foreign currency holdings with the aim of alleviating the pressure on the appreciating yen. The other was a building programme amounting to 3,000,000 gross tons under the Emergency Program for Building Ocean-Going Vessels carried out during the fiscal years 1979-1981, which was intended to relieve the Japanese shipbuilding industry which was severely depressed.[39]

Underlying such a shrinkage was the fact that Japanese-flagged and manned vessels could no longer expect to win contracts for large-scale, specialized work which had sustained the growth of the Japanese merchant fleet. For example, in 1975 when a shipping company entered into negotiations with a steel maker for the renewal of a ten-year, cargo-guaranteed contract for a specialized vessel, seamen's wage disparities among Japanese shipping companies were no longer certified by the shipper, and the firm with the lowest wage level was adopted. Thus, in renewing contracts, the long-term freight rate included the cost of seamen,

[39]Japan Maritime Research Institute, *Zoku Nippon Kaiun Sengo Joseishi* [*The Postwar History of Japanese Shipping Subsidies: A Sequel*] (Tokyo, 1985), 152-154 and 196-197.

and accordingly this was set at the wage level of foreign seamen.[40] Because of the wage differential between Japanese and other Asian seamen, this virtually entailed the "de-Japanization" of specialized vessels. Large shippers such as steel makers harshly requested that shipping firms should reconsider the cost structure of specialized, ocean-going vessels in which a long-term freight rate had previously been determined by adding a certain margin of profit to the costs calculated in yen. As a result, Japanese-flag vessels which could not acquire renewed contracts were sold abroad or scrapped. On the other hand, even if newly built, it became more and more difficult for ships with all-Japanese crews to gain long-term contracts. In addition, after 1975, when the interest subsidy for shipping finance was suspended, there was no saving of capital costs even if a shipowner could build a Japanese-flag vessel with the assistance of the Programmed Shipbuilding Scheme. If he built a tie-in ship, he could avoid fluctuations in foreign exchange rates with dollarization of capital costs, as well as labour costs, and, moreover, he could be exempted from the obligatory assurance of seamen's employment on the sale of a Japanese-flag ship.[41] Although it is difficult to quantify the tie-in ships owned by subsidiaries of Japanese shipping companies, according to the statistical data compiled on open-registry fleets by UNCTAD, the increase of FOC tonnage in Japan between 1978 and 1984 was 4.82 million dwt, ranked fourth in terms of absolute tonnage increase after Norway, the UK, and Korea during the same period.[42]

In line with the circumstances stimulating such de-Japanization, Japanese shipowners began to demand that foreign ships under their control should be considered as part of the Japanese merchant fleet. In June 1975, Shojiro Kikuchi, president of NYK and chairman of the Japanese Shipowners' Association, published an article advocating cognitive legitimacy for the first time by shipowners. He argued that as large-scale vessels, like medium-sized vessels, were losing their competitiveness, vessels under the control of Japanese shipping companies, such as tie-in ships, should be recognized as quasi-Japanese vessels, and thus

---

[40]Yamashita Shinnihon Kisen, *Shasi*, 158.

[41]Nippon Yusen Kaisha, *Yusen 100 nen shi* [*One Hundred-Year History of NYK*] (Tokyo, 1988), 743.

[42]UNCTAD, *Review of Maritime Transport*, 1981-1989.

it should be necessary to maintain and enlarge the fleet of purely Japanese vessels by raising the earning powers of shipping firms with the effective utilization of such quasi-Japanese vessels.[43] The move to recognize chartered foreign vessels under the control of Japanese shipowners as quasi-Japanese vessels went beyond Kikuchi's personal opinion, to become the basic policy of the Japanese Shipowners' Association. A pamphlet, published in 1977 by the Association to summarize their requests to the government, claimed that the government should provide official financing for building a tie-in ship and also treat it equally with a Japanese vessel with regard to tax payment.[44]

Faced with the ceaseless secession of vessels from the Japanese register, and the strong lobbying of the Shipowners' Association, the government was forced to change its shipping policy. Its first decisive step was the publication in 1978 of a report entitled *A Long-Term Policy of Ocean-Going Shipping in the Future*, prepared for the MoT by a sub-committee of the "Council for the Rationalization of the Shipping and Shipbuilding Industries." This inquiry advocated changes in the fundamental policy of enlarging the Japanese fleet to the utmost. That is, it proposed that shipping firms should maintain their international competitiveness by "reducing the total costs with efficient combination of Japanese-flag ships and chartered foreign ships." This signifies that the sub-committee recognized chartered foreign vessels under the effective control of Japanese shipowners as quasi-Japanese vessels, and considered them as complementing the Japanese merchant fleet.[45] At the same time, however, the sub-committee expressed the view that it would not be necessary to give particular consideration to such chartered foreign vessels on the grounds that most were FOC ships, and that the extent of chartering foreign vessels reflected the decisions of shipping firms. Instead, consideration should be given to the shrinkage of Japanese-flag tonnage as a result of the increase in chartered foreign vessels.[46] In order to restore

---

[43]S. Kikuchi, "Atarashii Nippon Kaiun no Kadai [A New Problem of Japanaese Shipping]," *Kai'un* (June 1975), 7.

[44]Nippon Senshu Kyokai, *Henbo suru Nippon Kaiun*, 99-100.

[45]Japan Maritime Research Institute, *Zoku Nippon Kaiun*, 142.

[46]*Ibid.*, 143-144.

the international competitiveness of Japanese-flag vessels, the sub-committee advocated maintaining the Programmed Shipbuilding Scheme, which was expected to remain effective in the curtailment of capital costs, and the adoption of concrete measures, in collaboration with labour and management, to lower labour costs.[47] The Report's recommendations indicated the way forward for labour and management, both sides being concerned by the surplus of reserve seamen. After the Report, the government, the union, and management together attempted to form a new fleet of modernized ships, and to reform working practices on board.

Table 3
The Total Number of Modernized Ships, 1983-1995

Year	Type A	Type B	Type C	Pioneer	Mixed	Total
1983	11					11
1984	65					65
1985	114					114
1986	184					184
1987	93	119				212
1988	65	148				213
1989	43	96	45			184
1990	33	88	48			169
1991	24	74	50			148
1992	15	51	50			116
1993	10	38	14	31		93
1994	4	28	7	32	7	78
1995	2	24	6	27	39	98

Notes: Mid-year figures except in 1983, which was taken at the end of the year. Pioneer: Pioneer ships; Mixed: Mixed-manned ships.

Source: Sen'in Seido Kindaika I'inkai, *Sen'in Seido Kindaika* (Tokyo, 1997), 394.

[47] *Ibid.*, 142.

The concept of the modernized ship was based on the premise that Japanese-flag vessels, with all-Japanese crews, should be placed at the central core of Japan's merchant fleet. It was believed that this would restore the international competitiveness of Japanese-flag ships through the employment of a smaller number of more skilled and more productive seamen. To this end, experiments using merchant ships in the service of shipping firms were planned, and if it proved feasible, an appropriate policy relating to working practices, would be implemented. To supervise the experiments, and devise the new working methods, the Committee for Modernization of Seamen Working System (CMSWS) was established in April 1979.[48] Comprising academics and representatives of the maritime bodies, shipping firms and the union, the Committee was administered by officials of the MoT.

The CMSWS conducted step by step experiments to inquire into the possibility of new work regimes. The first experiment (Stage A) commenced in February, 1981, and aimed at reducing the average complement from twenty-two to eighteen seafarers.[49] Stages B (crews of sixteen) and C (crews of fourteen) commenced in August 1982 and June 1986, respectively.[50] Based on the results of each stage, new standards of equipment in a ship and new systems of working aboard were legally arranged. That is, the modernized ship was to be a machine-zero ship (with the engine room unmanned and operated by a control system), and equipped with automated equipment such as navigation satellite system, auto-pilot, and remote cargo handling system.[51] With regard to labour, new qualifications for seamanship were introduced with watch officers and dual purpose crew members. Each qualification required seamen to acquire skills in both navigation and engineering. By gradually extending these qualifications from a lower ranking of seamen to an upper ranking, it became possible to reduce the complement of seamen on board step by step. Moreover, the curricula of the educational institutes for seamen,

---

[48]Sen'in Seido Kindaika Iinkai [The Committee for Modernization of Seamen Working System (CMSWS)], *Sen'in Seido Kindaika* [*Modernization of Seamen Working System*] (Tokyo, 1997), 12-13.

[49]*Ibid.*, 83 and 86.

[50]*Ibid.*, 174 and 206.

[51]*Ibid.*, 400 and 403-405.

including maritime universities, were re-arranged for teaching the requisite skills in a more systematic manner.[52]

Ships with the new working regimes entered into service one after another as table 3 shows.[53] It was CMSWS policy that the types of ships for experiments should be impartially selected, but numerically large, specialized vessels were in the majority. Of the ships selected for an empirically-proved experiment at each stage, three types of specialized vessel, namely ore carrier, tanker, and PCC (pure car carrier), accounted for eighty-one percent (118 vessels out of the total of 145) at Stage A, eighty-two percent (ninety-three out of 114) at Stage B, and seventy-seven percent (twenty out of twenty-six) at Stage C.[54] Container ships, on liner services, were seldom selected as modernized ships because they were mostly tie-in ships, and were already manned by both Japanese and foreign seamen. It is possible that this pattern of selection was biased towards a type of vessel that had a strong transactional relationship with Japan's larger shippers, but at the same time was under cost-cutting pressure from those shippers.

While the number of modernized ships with all-Japanese seamen was intended to reach 350 (20 million tons), the actual number of modernized ships in service peaked at 219 (12.77 million tons) by the end of March 1988. Even so, modernized ships were at the heart of the Japanese-flag fleet, accounting for some thirty-four percent by number, and fifty-two percent by tonnage, of the ocean-going vessels at that time.[55]

---

[52]*Ibid.*, 153-155 and 333-336.

[53]The two laws relating to the working practices of seamen came into force on 30 April 1983. Legally, the government designated (in the case of "The Mariners Law of Japan"), or authorized (in the case of "The Law for Ship's Officers") the ship as a "modernized ship," which was then approved by the CMSWS as an experimental ship. Zen Nippon Kai'in Kumiai, *40 nen shi*, 498.

[54]CMSWS, *Sen'in Seido Kindaika*, 134, 138, 191 and 237.

[55]*Ibid.*, 198-199; and Association of Japanese Seamanship, *Kokusaika Jidai ni okeru Gaikokaiun to Sen'in* [*Ocean-Going Shipping and Seamen in the Era of Internationalization*] (Tokyo, 1991), 14.

After the Plaza Accord in 1985

The "modernized ship" plan, designed by government, union and shipowners to restore the international competitiveness of Japanese shipping, collapsed due to the appreciation of the yen after the Plaza Accord of 1985. In 1981, when the first experiments into the viability of modernized ship started, the exchange rate of the yen against the US dollar was 240 yen; the plan was designed to keep aggregate labour costs down to about one million dollars per vessel. Yet as can be seen in column 10 of appendix 1, the appreciation of the yen would upset the assumption that a modernized ship could maintain its cost-competitiveness. If the rate of yen to the dollar had been 240, the seamen's cost in a modernized ship would have remained at 1.1 million dollars with a complement of eighteen seamen, or 0.9 million dollars with a complement of sixteen seamen. However, as the rate of yen to the dollar continued to rise to 125 yen or more, the seamen's cost soared to 2.1 or 1.75 million dollars, exceeding the target cost of 1 million dollars (see table 4). Not surprisingly, conventional ships with an all-Japanese crew lost their cost-competitiveness entirely. Even a "pioneer ship," which was the latest modernized ship with a Japanese complement of eleven seamen, had higher labour costs than that of a mixed manned ship with four Japanese seamen on board (see table 4). Now, it became impossible to maintain and operate vessels with all-Japanese crews.

Ships which lost their cost competitiveness were sold abroad on a massive scale, and thus "flagging out" became a realistic option in Japan. Between 1986 and 1989, 700 vessels totalling 18.5 million grt were sold abroad. Even modernized ships, particularly the earlier models, were sold overseas or changed into *maru*-ships. Thus, in the twelve months commencing in September 1990, there was a loss of twenty-one modernized ships — of which ten were Type A, and eleven were Type B — with nine ships sold overseas and twelve converted into *maru*-ships.[56] This reflects the failure of the plan to place Japanese-flag ships with all-Japanese seamen in the central core of Japan's merchant fleet.

Naturally, disposal on such a scale was only made possible because drastic measures relating to seamen's employment were taken. Conditions of service, which had been sacrosanct, were now a major issue

[56] *Ibid.*, 7-8.

between the union and management. Massive dismissals began. In March 1987, the union and employers' associations reached agreement about emergency measures on employment. There were two main points of consent. First, during two years April 1987-31 March 1989, an optional early retirement scheme was to be put into force. If a seaman chose this option, he would receive an extra retirement allowance. Second, redundant seamen were to be given help finding a new job.[57] As a result, the number of seamen, belonging to two employers' associations of ocean-going shipping, decreased from about 22,000 in 1985 to less than 8000 in 1988 (see appendix 1). Modernized ships had also failed to guarantee seamen's employment opportunities and skill enhancement.

Table 4
Comparative Annual Costs of Seamen per Vessel by Each Type of Working System on Board, at the End of the Year 1988

Manning system	$ million
All-Japanese manning	
24 seamen in an ordinary ship	2.65
18 seamen in a modernized ship	2.10
15 seamen in a modernized ship	1.75
11 seamen in a pioneer ship	1.30
Mixed-manning	
9 Japanese seamen plus 15 southeast Asian seamen	1.25
4 Japanese seamen plus 20 Southeast Asian seamen	0.80
All-Southeast Asian seamen	0.35

Notes: Calculated at the exchange rate of 125 yen per dollar.

Source: Working Group of the Council for the Rationalization of Shipping and Shipbuilding Industries, *For the Prevention of Flagging Out* (Tokyo, 1988).

While a large volume of tonnage, including modernized ships, was sold overseas, a Working Group of the Council for the Rationalization of Shipping and Shipbuilding Industries was set up to investigate ways of countering flagging out. Its report, *For the Prevention of Flagging Out*,

[57]Zen Nippon Kai'in Kumiai, *Kaijho Rodo Undo 50 nen no Kiseki* [*Fifty-Year History of Seamen's Labour Movement*] (Tokyo, 1995), 197.

published in December 1988, advocated a review of the plan to place modernized ships at the core of Japan's merchant fleet, and to extend the *maru*-ship device from near-sea shipping to ocean-going vessels as a whole.[58] The new policy laid down that the mixed manning system should be extended from near-sea ships to ocean-going ships to restore the competitiveness of the Japanese fleet.

Accepting the so-called "new *maru*-ship," in October 1988, the union and management arrived at an agreement about mixed manning on these vessels. The main points were as follows: that new maru-ships should in principle be newly-built vessels; that at least six Japanese officers and nine Japanese seamen should be on board; and that foreign officers should have certificates of competency issued by countries which had ratified the treaty of STCW.[59] In fact, much of this agreement was based on an idea that had been proposed by the Shipowners' Association at a meeting of the Council for Rationalization held in 1984, just before the Plaza Accord.[60] With major changes such as the rapidly rising value of the yen after the Plaza Accord, and the emergency measures regarding employment, the idea was revived and mixed manning was put into practice in March 1990. By the end of May 1993, eighty-five new maru-ships were in service.[61]

Modernized ships were not among these new maru-ships. The Council for Transport Policy, however, perceived in its 1991 report, *Ocean-Going Shipping as It Ought to be in the Era of Growing Internationalization*, that so far as competitiveness was concerned, it would be difficult to place modernized ships with all-Japanese crews in the central core of Japan's merchant fleet, and advocated that modernized ships should be reconsidered in terms of a mixed manning system.[62] Following this report, the CMSWS examined the issue, and in June 1992 determined

---

[58]MoT, *Nippon Kaiun no Genkyo 1989*, 106.

[59]MoT, *Nippon Kaiun no Genkyo 1990*, 69.

[60]Zen Nippon Kai'in Kumiai, *Gaiko Kaiun to Nippon Sen'in* [*Ocean-Going Shipping and Japanese Seamen*] (Tokyo, 1985), 18-19.

[61]MoT, *Nippon Kaiun no Genkyo 1993*, 25.

[62]CMSWS, *Sen'in Seido Kinkaika*, 343.

to adopt the mixed-manned modernized ship, whether newly-built or not.[63] Thus, in May 1993, eight vessels were recognized as mixed-manned, modernized experimental ships, which had eight or nine Japanese seamen and thirteen to fifteen foreign seamen aboard;[64] in October 1994, seven experimental vessels were added to extend the modernization with a mixed manning system, each with six or seven Japanese seamen.[65] Nevertheless, the annual cost of seamen in a mixed-manned ship, with nine Japanese seamen on board, on a dollar-quoted basis, is more than three times the cost of a ship manned entirely by southeast Asian seamen.[66] Thus, up to the present day, it has proved difficult to ensure that truly Japanese vessels remain competitive within the Japanese merchant fleet.[67] In fact, the CMSWS has been disbanded since the last experiment of extending the modernization scheme to mixed-manned ships.

The problems facing Japanese shipping are not restricted to the modernized ship. As the focus of trade shifted more and more to east Asia during this period, the situation in which Japan's shipowners could survive if they maintained their transactional relationships with large domestic shippers was rapidly disappearing. New entry into growing markets was necessary for shipping companies to maintain and enlarge their seaborne cargo traffic. Thus, they were forced to globalize not only fleet assets and the workforce but also management functions. Two factors explained this change: first, there was the dollarization of administrative expenses at head offices; and, second, there was the decentralization of decision

---

[63] *Ibid.*, 351.

[64] *Ibid.*, 360.

[65] *Ibid.*, 373 and 376.

[66] Calculated at the exchange rate of 105 yen per dollar. MoT, *Nippon Kaiun no Genkyo 1994,* 20.

[67] This does not mean the total abolition of a modernized ship with all Japanese seamen. In November 1994, it was agreed at the Central Conference between the union and management that the shipping firms should put twenty-eight ships into service as pioneer ships with all Japanese seamen, including eight NYK vessels, eight belonging to MOL, and eight from the K Line, in order to enhance seamanship. The losses incurred in operating these vessels are to be borne by each firm. K. Nakayama, "Industrial Relations of Seamen" (Unpublished discussion paper read at a group for study of shipping economics, 25 November 1994).

making. The former is a move to separate company headquarters and ship management functions — vessel maintenance and repair, and the recruiting and training of seamen — and to delegate those functions to ship management companies established abroad. Accordingly, in 1995, out of about 500 ocean-going vessels owned or controlled by Japan's five largest shipping companies, only five percent was managed directly by company headquarters, sixty percent was left with ship management firms established as subsidiaries in Japan, while the remainder were run by overseas ship management companies (fifteen percent with subsidiaries and twenty percent with independent companies).[68]

The second change, the localization of decision making, reflects the shift in seaborne trade from Japan to east Asia. This shift is prominent in liner services, where the share of cross-trade between foreign countries in container cargo traffic carried by the Japanese merchant fleet rose from twenty-five percent in 1985 to fifty-one percent in 1991, while the share of the same trade in tramp cargo traffic only increased from nineteen to twenty-one percent during the same period.[69]

Thus, the increasing prominence of the cross-trade necessitated the transfer of decision-making on pricing, container positioning, and ship management to regional headquarters or subsidiaries aboard. The globalization of management functions is just beginning.

Globalization and International Competition

Since the Second World War, the proportion of Japan's overseas trade carried in Japanese-flag vessels has fallen. In terms of the volume of goods, as appendix 1 indicates, the loading ratios for exports and imports have contracted steadily to reach three percent and twenty percent respectively in 1995. Does this long-run trend confirm that there has been a decline in the international competitiveness of Japanese ocean-going shipping? One should not draw such a simple conclusion, for the globalization of an industry means that aggregate and ethnocentric statistical data is not necessarily an accurate reflection of the actual situation in the industry concerned.

---

[68]MoT, *Nippon Kaiun no Genkyo 1996*, 54.

[69]*Ibid.*, 45 and 48.

When these loading ratios are classified by cargoes, or considered with chartered foreign vessels, a different picture emerges. With regard to imports, which amounting to almost ten times the volume of exports, iron ore, coal and crude oil are the three major cargoes, together accounting for sixty-five percent of Japan's total volume of imports in 1965 and sixty-three percent in 1995 (see appendix 2).[70] The Japanese-flag vessels' loading ratios for these cargoes had been well maintained until the Plaza Accord. On the whole, these are long haul cargoes, with iron ore coming from Australia, coal brought in from Australia and the US, and crude oil from the Middle East. A large, specialized vessel is therefore required to carry these cargoes. Thus, all of the crude oil conveyed by Japanese-flag vessels, almost all of the iron ore, and nearly eighty percent of the coal, is transported by specialized vessels. In other words, the area in which the Japanese-flag fleet could maintain a relatively high loading ratio was the segment served by large, specialized vessels, well suited for the carriage of major, long-haul cargoes. It is possible that the rationalization efforts of the second period, such as the introduction of the modernized ship and improved working practices contributed to these high loading ratios. Furthermore, if chartered foreign vessels are included, it is evident that the loading ratios of lumber and wood, a major bulk cargo in the near-sea market, have remained, like iron ore, coal and crude oil, at a high level since the Plaza Accord. That is, judging from the loading ratio of imports, the international competitiveness of the Japanese merchant fleet, including chartered foreign vessels, has been relatively well sustained. Among these chartered foreign vessels, needless to say,

[70]There are a few cases in which loading ratios, calculated in terms of deadweight tonnage, exceed 100 percent. This is because the Ministry of Finance, being responsible for preparing statistics of Japanese imports and exports, publishes custom clearance figures relating to all imported or exported commodities every year. The published quantities, however, are not unified in terms of units; for example, automobiles are measured in cars, coal in tons, etc. Thus, it is necessary to convert the trade volume expressed in terms of different units into deadweight tons, a task being carried out by the Ministry of Transport, using its own conversion ratio table. The result is used as a denominator to calculate each loading ratio. The numerator is calculated on the basis of figures reported to the MoT by Japanese shipping companies relating to cargoes loaded in their own and chartered foreign vessels. Here again, the companies' figures are not all expressed in dwt, some items of cargo being measured in freight tons, a unit of tonnage for freight rates. It is necessary to convert freight tons into deadweight tons. Thus, the two unit conversions needed for some cargo items, one a denominator and the other a numerator, generate data errors, such as loading ratios above 100 percent.

are many ships that are effectively controlled by Japanese shipowners. Thus, devices such as the tie-in ship and the *maru*-ship, which have been deployed by Japanese shipowners to counter the worst effects of globalization, have largely proved effective.

The large scale flagging-out of Japanese vessels has led the MoT to urge shipowners to adopt measures which will arrest the depletion of Japanese-flag vessels. But the MoT's policy goal of ensuring that strategically important materials are carried only in Japanese vessels, which it has pursued consistently since the war, has only been sustained recently by the multi-nationalization of the management resources of Japanese shipping companies. Continuing globalization will be accompanied by further diminution of Japanese-flag vessels, and a further reduction in loading ratios, thereby leaving the MoT much less scope to execute its shipping policy using Japanese-flag vessels. However, more recent manifestations of the globalization process, notably with regard to management practices, are now essential to the survival and future development of the Japanese merchant fleet as a whole.

Appendix 1
Japan's Ocean-Going Shipping, 1965-1995

	Japanese Merchant Fleet			Chartered Foreign Vessels	Japanese-flag Vessels' Loading Ratio		Vessels Sold overseas	Vessels built by the PSS	Seamen for Ocean-going Vessels	Foreign Exchange Rates Yen
	Total	Japanese-flag			Import	Export				
	nos.	nos.	'000 grt	nos.	%	%	'000 grt	'000 grt	nos.	per dollar
Year	-1	-2	-3	-4	-5	-6	-7	-8	-9	-10
1965	1019	803	8303	216	43.5	37.6		1825	41101	360
1966	1103	876	10316	227	45.9	37		1909	42965	360
1967	1200	963	12447	237	47	37.4		2033	43905	360
1968	1574	1278	16098	296	47.7	36.4	217	2308	46485	360
1969	1660	1424	19259	236	48.1	38.8	626	2474	48495	360
1970	1970	1508	21185	462	44.6	38.6	1005	2624	49334	360
1971	2123	1531	24130	592	45	34.2	1112	3218	49291	308
1972	2235	1580	27933	655	41.9	28.7	2286	3304	45274	308
1973	2296	1476	30623	820	43.7	26.6	1480	1985	42266	308
1974	2400	1427	32620	973	40.6	23.8	1056	1939	42335	308
1975	2469	1317	33485	1152	45.6	23.3	2051	945	42196	308
1976	2416	1274	34649	1142	46.8	20.6	2375	164	40356	308

	Japanese Merchant Fleet				Japanese-flag Vessels' Loading Ratio		Vessels Sold overseas	Vessels built by the PSS	Seamen for Ocean-going Vessels	Foreign Exchange Rates Yen
	Total	Japanese-flag		Chartered Foreign Vessels	Import	Export				
	nos.	nos.	'000 grt	nos.	%	%	'000 grt	'000 grt	nos.	per dollar
1977	2408	1234	33722	1174	44.4	20.8	2701	258	38049	308
1978	2494	1204	33030	1290	41.6	20.8	2642	302	35451	234
1979	2388	1188	33344	1200	38.8	20.8	2154	1927	32067	206
1980	2505	1176	34240	1329	37.4	20.5	2322	1839	30776	242
1981	2405	1173	34465	1232	36.6	21.5	2652	1802	29860	210
1982	2340	1175	35058	1165	40.4	22.5	3556	679	29140	233
1983	2175	1140	34100	1035	43.8	20.7	2962	998	26087	237
1984	2135	1055	33249	1080	41.4	19.6	2635	1565	24168	231
1985	2435	1028	33470	1407	41	18.3	2743	1215	22323	254
1986	2249	957	30809	1292	42.4	15.7	5341	1280	17517	185
1987	2082	816	28200	1266	38.5	13.8	5611	51	12753	151
1988	2127	640	24582	1487	35.4	10.5	4122	166	7935	127
1989	2002	532	21691	1470	32.7	8.4	3408	574	6138	130
1990	1992	449	20406	1543	28.6	6.9	1695	623	5508	150
1991	2060	419	19815	1641	27.5	6.5	2023	846	5070	135

	Japanese Merchant Fleet				Japanese-flag Vessels' Loading Ratio		Vessels Sold overseas	Vessels built by the PSS	Seamen for Ocean-going Vessels	Foreign Exchange Rates Yen
				Chartered Foreign Vessels	Import	Export				
	Total nos.	Japanese-flag nos.	'000 grt	nos.	%	%	'000 grt	'000 grt	nos.	per dollar
1992	2013	376	18669	1637	26.9	6.2	1432	598	3128	130
1993	2048	340	18420	1708	26	4.7	2903	977	2904	118
1994	1990	280	16669	1710	23.2	3.8	2616		2797	107
1995	1999	218	13849	1781	20.2	3	2675		2443	93

Notes: (1) - (4): Ocean-going vessels of 3000 grt and over until 1967, since then of 2000 grt and over. Figures taken mid-year, except for Japanese-flag vessels at the end of March 1965-1967. (5) - (6): in a calendar year. (7): vessels of 1000 grt and over 1968 to 1971, since then of 2000 grt and over. (9): on the 1st of October, each year. (10): basic rate.

Sources: Japanese Shipowners' Association, *A Statistical Survey of Shipping*, Management and Coordination Agency, *Japan Statistical Yearbook*.

Appendix 2: Imports Classified by cargo (000 M/T) and Loading Ratios, 1965-1994

	1965 (calendar year)			1975 (fiscal year)			1985 (fiscal year)			1994 (fiscal year)		
	imports	loading ratio(%)		imports	loading ratio(%)		imports	loading ratio(%)		imports	loading ratio(%)	
cargo		(a)	(b)		(a)	(b)		(a)	(b)		(a)	(b)
rice	967	54.3	63.8	28	42.9	82.1				1,739	2.6	71.2
wheat	3,645	12.5	27.4	5,726	20.4	90.7	5,503	21.1	78.1	6,429	0.7	86.8
soybean	1,847	20.5	23.8	3,208	8.4	45.6	4,855	9.2	20.4	4,619	0.3	23.6
sugar	1,723	14.3	14.3	2,253	6.3	23.5	1,831	5.4	23.6	1,736	0.0	2.9
lumber	12,508	78.6	82.0	26,891	41.2	75.3	23,042	24.8	61.9	39,676	5.7	82.9
wool	248	51.6	53.2	253	39.1	65.2	198	16.7	33.3	134	11.9	30.6
raw cotton	702	50.4	59.4	682	34.2	52.2	702	13.2	24.2	445	5.4	21.1
phosphate rock	2,418	38.3	46.4	2,565	25.0	71.0	2,426	22.6	91.6	1,235	1.1	160.2
potash	1,083	59.2	71.0	1,248	22.4	60.7	1,354	21.6	63.0	1,235	0.2	30.3
salt	3,543	53.7	65.3	6,378	6.6	50.1	6,471	10.2	57.7	7,572	1.7	74.6
iron ore	39,018	36.3	60.5	130,864	46.1	75.1	123,397	52.4	70.0	119,396	37.0	80.4
coal	17,080	30.4	37.0	62,446	33.8	73.7	93,936	53.8	81.1	121,073	27.5	92.8
others	25,481	29.3	33.8	58,833	34.9	67.3	94,471	19.4	51.6	119,874	3.5	36.2
sub-total	110,263	38.3	50.6	301,375	38.6	72.2	358,186	39.8	66.5	425,163	19.8	70.7
crude oil	73,095	57.7	73.4	226,450	59.3	82.8	169,023	50.9	82.3	234,337	28.8	80.6
petroleum products	15,276	12.9	18.9	26,226	21.0	37.5	67,423	22.7	33.7	87,384	17.6	34.0
treacle	749	67.3	67.3	845	36.8	52.8	707	50.8	73.4	378	3.7	106.9
sub-total	89,120	50.1	64.0	253,524	55.3	78.1	237,153	42.9	68.5	322,099	25.7	68.0
grand total	199,383	43.6	56.6	554,897	46.2	74.9	595,338	41.0	67.3	747,262	22.4	69.5

Notes: (a) Japanese-flag vessels; (b) total fleet, including chartered foreign vessels. Ratios over 100 % reflect errors in original data.

Source: Japanese Shipowners' Association, *A Statistical Survey of Shipping*, each year.

Containerization and the Globalization of Liner Shipping

Frank Broeze

"Getting that 'third ocean' is a goal every liner operator is pursuing right now, representing the great leap towards a global service."[1]

"[The future of our company resides in] ever larger ships and further company mergers or take-overs .... in order to service the increasing number of global customers."[2]

"Container shipping is a mature global service industry."[3]

The purpose of this chapter is to analyze the development of container shipping from the mid-1960s to the present day. As it would be patently impossible to cover the subject in a fully comprehensive fashion, the discussion will focus on the following pivotal questions: what have been the reasons for the introduction and the rapid diffusion of containerization in the world's liner shipping industry? what has been the impact of containerization on the structure of individual companies and the industry as a whole? and, how has containerization changed the relationship of shipowners with other modes of transport, the ports and port systems of the world, and the agencies that acquire their cargoes? Positioning these questions within the overall theme of "global markets," I shall specifically argue that containerization has globalized both the liner shipping industry

---

[1]*Fairplay*, 29 August 1996. See also *Lloyd's List*, April 1993, Containerisation Supplement: "One of the 'buzz' words in the container shipping sector at present is 'globalisation.'"

[2]Thomas Anderson, managing director of Maersk UK, quoted in *Fairplay*, 24 April 1997.

[3]Mary R. Brooks, "International Competitiveness — Assessing and Exploring Competitive Advantage by Ocean Container Carriers," *Logistics and Transportation Review*, XXIX, No. 3 (1993), 275.

and the self-image and outlook of the major companies. This is meant not just in terms of the general internationalization of the post-1945 shipping industry in its ownership, investment capital, flags, seafarers, shipyards, cargoes, destinations, etc., but especially also in specific aspects of the liner industry, particularly global services and agency networks, intimate international cooperation and mergers, and functional diversification into port facilities and the related maritime and non-maritime modes of transport. Liner shipping always contained significant elements of both internationalization and functional integration, but containerization carried these tendencies onto an entirely higher level.

Revolution and Chain Reaction

Containerization resulted directly from the crisis that faced many of the world's major liner companies in the early 1960s.[4] Liner shipping was increasingly suffering from the severe financial burdens placed on it by the current technological state of cargo-handling in port. The loading and discharging of large numbers of individual packages, boxes, bags, crates etc. of often bewildering varieties of shapes and sizes caused long turnround times in port and huge wastage in capital invested. In the USA and also Australia, whose shipping industries suffered from high-cost levels and maritime union militancy, containers were introduced as a radical measure to turn the tide. Ships loaded a much smaller number of the rectangular, standard-sized boxes which could be stacked on top of each other. As time in port was limited to that required to move the containers between wharf and ship, time at sea — i.e. the production of transport — was dramatically increased. Significantly, one of the pioneering companies (appropriately named Sea-Land) was in origin a trucking company while the other, Matson, had a long-standing monopoly in the California-Hawaii trade.[5]

---

[4]The best review of the causes, nature and impact of containerization remains H. J. Witthöft, *Container. Transportrevolution unseres Jahrhunderts* (2nd ed., Herford, 1978). An excellent case study that also discusses the principles involved is G. Devos and G. Elewaut, *CMB 100. Een eeuw maritiem ondernemerschap* (Tielt, 1995), chs. 9-10.

[5]Witthöft, *Container*, 13-14; Sam Ignarski (ed.), *The Box. An Anthology Celebrating 25 Years of Containerisation and the TT Club* (London, 1996), chs. 1-2; and William L. Worden, *Cargoes: Matson's First Century in the Pacific* (Honolulu, 1981).

Sea-Land, under its dynamic leader, Malcolm McLean, rapidly expanded its New York-based network (including the "West Side Story" shuttle to San Juan, Puerto Rico) and built up an extensive agency network. Two standard-size boxes were adopted with dimensions of twenty by eight feet by eight feet and forty by eight by eight feet; the size of the smaller box, expressed as the Twenty-foot Equivalent Unit (TEU), became the unit to measure the capacity of containerships, turnover of ports and terminals, etc. In April 1966 Sea-Land started the revolution when its *Fairland* was despatched to open a service between New York and North Europe with calls at Rotterdam, Bremen and Grangemouth. McLean had prepared his ground carefully by building a dense network of agents in Europe, contracting with 325 European truckers and reducing his risks by a long-term contract to supply the US Army in Germany – hence the call at Bremen. Emphasizing the significance of its challenge to the status quo, in its first port-of-call, Rotterdam, Sea-Land did not use an existing liner agency but bulk-cargo specialist Frans Swarttouw.[6]

The historical importance of McLean's initiative was, in the first instance, that the capital-intensiveness of container shipping enabled the high-cost USA to re-enter the business, take a leading role and maintain a high profile until the present day. Several other companies, including US Lines and Seatrain, launched container services across the Atlantic, while Matson sent its vessels to Japan. In 1971 the USA owned seventy-five containerships (of a world total of 231), aggregating 1,067,468 grt (world: 2,780,681 grt); Britain was in second place (fifty-one ships, 627,448 grt) with Germany and Japan about equal third with about 350,000 grt. Although America's advantage could not be maintained over the long term, in 1981 it was still the largest individual participant (111,000 TEU, 14.2% of a world capacity of 783,000 TEU) and as late as October 1995 Sea-Land (160,000 TEU) was still the largest individual operator, with American President Lines (APL) a creditable tenth.[7] More

[6]At the reception given to celebrate the opening of the service, the representatives of Rotterdam's liner agencies gave Swarttouw such a hard time that he burst into tears (Ignarski, *The Box*, 20). Swarttouw, nevertheless, had the last laugh, as he became Chief Executive Officer of Rotterdam's Europe Container Terminus and made the company into Europe's leading terminal operator.

[7]Fairplay, *Containerisation Yearbook 1996*, 2.

importantly, Sea-Land's initiative caused a chain reaction around the world as no operator could afford to watch passively.

The degree to which liner cargoes could be containerized surpassed all expectations. As one of the great European veterans of containerization, Karl-Heinz Sager, put it:

> I still remember how piles of cargo manifests for certain trades were analysed at our [i.e. North German Lloyd] offices, in order to establish which goods could reasonably be packed in containers. At the time we arrived at a proportion of only about 25-30 per cent for the North Atlantic, though today [1981] 80-90 per cent of all cargo there is carried in containers. For the US-Far East trade our calculations were only slightly more encouraging.[8]

Containerization, however, advanced much faster than Sager had foreseen and was boosted by the unprecedented economic growth of Asian countries such as Japan, Korea, Taiwan, Singapore and Hong Kong.[9] From the late 1970s container shipping broke out of the confines of trade between fully-developed economies with modern transport and information technology infrastructures, and cascaded rapidly to the lesser-developed sections of the world economy. By 1995 the degree of containerization of liner cargoes had risen to an astounding ninety-five percent and the end of expansion was not yet in sight. Some of the major companies, for example, through a rapid increase in the number of refrigerated containers invaded the hitherto specialized reefer market.[10] As intercontinental trunk routes swelled in volume, regional feeder services grew in intensity and intricacy, and *vice versa*. The relative importance of the main trading regions in 1993 is shown in table 1.

---

[8]Quoted in Ignarski, *The Box*, 68. See also Hermann Schreiber, *Verkehr. Schienenbahnen, Schiffahrt, Luftverkehr* (Darmstadt, 1972), 114.

[9]An idiosyncratic but enlightening overview is offered by Paul Kennedy, *Preparing for the Twenty-First Century* (London, 1993); see also Mark Borthwick (ed.), *Pacific Century* (Sydney, 1992). It was actually NYK that put the first "post-Sea-Land" containership into service.

[10]*Fairplay*, 4 July 1996 and 2 January 1997. See also *Fairplay, Newbuildings*, 17 July 1997; and *Asian Shipping*, August 1997.

Table 1
World Container Traffic, 1993

Trade Route	Million TEU	Share in %
Transatlantic	3.2	11.1
Eastbound	1.3	4.5
Westbound	1.9	6.6
Transpacific	8.2	28
Eastbound	4.6	15.9
Westbound	3.6	12.1
Europe-Far East	4	13.9
Eastbound	1.9	6.6
Westbound	2.1	7.3
Short-sea	12.9	44.3
Europe	5.2	18
East Asia	3.5	12.1
USA/Caribbean	1.1	3.8
India/Middle East	3	10.4
Other Routes	0.8	2.8
Total	**28.9**	**100**

Source: Niko Wijnolst and Tor Wergeland, *Shipping* (Delft, 1996), 37-38.

Structural Change at All Levels

The most striking characteristic of the European response to Sea-Land's challenge was the adoption of collaborative strategies by most traditional companies as they faced the introduction of containers on all main routes. Above all, the huge investments required and the massive freight volumes to be acquired in order to offer services of equal frequency with the much more productive containerships forced companies to join forces in more intimate arrangements than the existing shipping conferences offered (conferences, after all, are only a mechanism to regulate competition).[11] Joint ventures became indispensable, becoming known as syndicates or consortia, in which the fleets and acquisition networks of the participating companies were integrated. The first of these consortia were the purely British Overseas Containers Limited (OCL) and Associated Container Transport (ACT),[12] but soon national boundaries counted for little. The first transatlantic consortium, the Atlantic Container Line (ACL), included Cunard, Holland-America Line, Compagnie Générale Transatlantique, and three Swedish members, Swedish-America Line, Transatlantic and Wallenius. In the Europe-Australia trade the Seabridge consortium brought together Nedlloyd, Hapag-Lloyd, Messageries Maritimes and Lloyd Triestino. The Compagnie Maritime Belge was refused membership by ACL, negotiated with the Hamburg-America Line, North German Lloyd and US Lines but had to be satisfied with forming the Dart Container Line with Bristol City Line and Clarke Traffic Services.[13] As participants and trade conditions differed from route to route, these consortia were — with one major exception — restricted to specific trade routes. Companies with many services became members of different consortia. Nedlloyd, for example, in 1981 operated thirty-six different services, nineteen through consortia.[14] It was associated with no less than thirty-two other companies and one autonomous consortium, a remarkable form of tactical flexibility and global behaviour. Nedlloyd's partners included Hapag-Lloyd and the Compagnie Maritime Belge, Japan's NYK and MOL, Neptune Orient Lines (NOL, Singapore), Transportacion

---

[11]The standard estimate was that one containership replaced five conventional vessels. To illustrate the frequency problem, a company operating a weekly service with ten vessels would only be able to maintain a frequency of one sailing every five weeks with the two containerships replacing the ten conventional ones.

[12]An interesting insider's account is James Taylor, *Ellermans. A Wealth of Shipping* (London, 1976), ch. 21. Taylor recounts how Ellerman was rebuffed by the partners in OCL and forced into a rather unwanted coalition.

[13]Devos and Elewaut, *CMB 100*, 208-209. Clarke was a freight-forwarding firm in Montréal. Dart concentrated on the Europe-Canada trade, failing to gain a significant place in the US business.

[14]Nedlloyd, *Annual Report 1982*.

Maritima Mexicana (TMM), Compania Sud Americana de Vapores (CSAV, Chile), and the Australian National Line.

As the range of Nedlloyd's partners shows, containerization globalized the liner shipping industry as it was embraced by many newcomers, especially in what Europeans then still rather dismissively called "non-traditional" maritime countries. Many factors contributed to this phenomenon, including the UNCTAD push for a 40-40-20 division of international liner traffic,[15] the fundamental "Third World economic nationalism" on which this strategy rested, the desire of many governments to obtain a "window" into conferences, and the belief that valuable foreign exchange and other beneficial spin-offs could be obtained through investments in national shipping. No region was more active in that respect than the Asia-Pacific Rim. Singapore, Malaysia, Taiwan, China, Hong Kong, Korea, and Australia on its western littoral, and later also Mexico and Chile on the east coast, joined leaders USA and Japan. Amongst the most prominent of these newcomers were Taiwan's Evergreen and Yang Ming, NOL, Malaysian International Shipping Corporation (MISC), Overseas Orient Container Line (OOCL, Hong Kong), China Ocean Shipping Company (COSCO), Hanjin, Cho Yang and Hyundai (all Korean),[16] CSAV and TMM. There were also aggressive and efficient new European players, above all Maersk.

The one autonomous consortium was Overseas Containers Ltd., originally formed by five British companies, including traditional rivals P&O and Ocean Steamship Co., for the Australian trade. OCL's five participating companies decided to continue their collaboration on the Europe-Far East run and OCL itself became a member of consortia, including the largest yet combination of forces, the TRIO-group (Europe-Far East) with Ben Line (Edinburgh), Hapag-Lloyd and also, significantly, the Japanese traditionals NYK and MOL. The productivity explosion caused by containerization and the heavy cost of ships and containers

[15]This meant that forty percent of the trade to be carried by shipping flying the flag of each of the exporting and importing states, with twenty percent remaining for cross-traders.

[16]On the spectacular rise of Korean shipping see Helen A. Thanopoulou, Dong-Keun Ryoo and Tae-Woo Lee, "Korean Liner Shipping in the Era of Global Alliances" (unpublished paper, 1997). I am most grateful to Dr. Lee for making a copy available to me.

made it imperative to pool freight acquisition at both ends of the line, as was also demonstrated by the accession of MISC to the ScanDutch consortium, a joint venture of Nedlloyd and three Scandinavian companies. This unprecedented collaboration caused a highly paradoxical and ultimately unstable situation in which, on the one hand, forces were bundled in consortia, yet, on the other, there was an immense fragmentation of power through the existence of scores of different consortia. A second paradox existed in the fact that the huge capital investments required for containerization did not prevent newcomers from entering the industry. On the contrary, containerization was used by many, both high- and low-cost, countries to enter the business and by the late 1970s there were signs of acute over-tonnaging which, a few years later, during a deep recession in world trade, turned many trade routes into financial blood baths. Yet the expotentional growth of the business created great opportunities for ambitious and successful solo players like Maersk and Evergreen. The resulting instability, which created considerable doubt about the survival of the conference system, in turn gave additional impetus to the already existing process of concentration and new cooperative arrangements, notably slot-leasing. The evolution of that process was extremely complex, continuously propelled by the entry of newcomers and the elimination of weak players.

During the earliest stages of containerization it became obvious that concentration was the strategy for the future. In 1970 containerships managed what passenger liners had never been able to achieve: the merger between the Hamburg-America Line (or Hapag) and the North German Lloyd into Hapag-Lloyd; it was this bundling of forces that allowed the Germans to remain independent. Another striking example was Nedlloyd, which between 1970 and 1980 absorbed virtually all Dutch overseas liner companies and, in the process, moved all Amsterdam-based services to Rotterdam.[17] Even more than Hapag-Lloyd it became its nation's uncontested national carrier. Likewise, during the 1970s, the Australian National Line took over all Australia's privately-owned container interests, and many other mergers and takeovers took place. ACL became a purely Swedish company as first Broström acquired the

---

[17]H. van Driel, *Een verenigde nederlandse scheepvaart. De fusie tussen Nedlloyd en KNSM, 1980-81* (Rotterdam, 1988).

non-Swedish participation and then, in 1983, sold out to Transatlantic.[18] Elsewhere the multinational United Arab Shipping Company (UASC) represented the bundling of Arab purpose within the specific Gulf context.[19] In France Messageries Maritimes and Compagnie Générale Transatlantique merged into the Compagnie Générale Maritime (CGM), which in the mid 1990s was taken over by the privately owned Compagnie Maritime d'Affrètement (CMA). A special example was P&O, which went through various crises during the late 1970s and early 1980s, but after becoming part of Lord Sterling's financial group in the mid-1980s bought out one partner of OCL after another and gradually turned the consortium into a division under the P&O name. In other words, P&O used OCL to achieve a national dominance in Britain similar to what Nedlloyd and Hapag-Lloyd had achieved in their countries.

Table 2, which shows the ranking of the world's fifteen largest container companies at the end of 1981, provides a fascinating snapshot of the varying dynamics that determined the pattern of growth of container shipping at that stage, with pioneering Americans, traditional Europeans, fast-rising Asians, and a number of independent buccaneers. By 1981 container shipping was under enormous pressures. The influx of newcomers, many of which employed cheap crews, coincided with rapid expansion of the Soviet fleet. Global excess tonnage was estimated at twenty percent, and on the North Atlantic at double that rate.[20] Freight rates collapsed, as did many conferences. Flexible Rate Agreements were introduced on many routes, but prominent outsiders like Evergreen and Maersk largely maintained their independence, believing their quality of service, market share and competitive pricing gave them the edge.[21] A number of prominent companies, like Hapag-Lloyd, P&O, Nedlloyd,

---

[18]Martin Fritz and Kent Olsson, "Twentieth-Century Shipping Strategies: Broström and Transatlantic, Gothenburg's Leading Shipping Companies," in Simon P. Ville and David M. Williams (eds.), *Management, Finance and Industrial Relations: Essays in International Maritime and Business History* (St. John's, 1994), 107-108.

[19]Its founding owners were the state governments of Kuwait, Bahrain, Qatar, United Arab Emirates and Iraq; Jordan joined later.

[20]Devos and Elewaut, *CMB 100*, 244.

[21]Only after "more than a decade of increasingly aggressive independent operation" did Evergreen, in 1982, join its first conference (*Fairplay*, 2 September 1982).

NYK and Japan Line, had additional financial problems caused by ill-timed investments in bulk carriers and/or oil tankers. Weak participants were ruthlessly weeded out; others had to resort to desperate measures to survive. As early as 1980, Farrell Lines abandoned the North Atlantic, leaving Amsterdam without a service to the USA,[22] before going bankrupt in 1983. C.Y. Tung's OOCL was bailed out by Beijing money. Several large firms, including Cunard, P&O and CMB, became subsidiaries of large conglomerates but retained their own corporate identities.

Table 2
The Largest 15 Container Companies, 1981

Rank	Company	Country	Ships	Capacity in TEU	%
1	Sea-Land	USA	30	41713	5.3
2	Hapag-Lloyd	Germany	27	40491	5.2
3	Maersk	Denmark	25	36552	4.7
4	OCL	Great Britain	18	35180	4.5
5	NYK	Japan	26	29047	3.7
6	OOCL	Hong Kong	21	27742	3.5
7	CGM	France	18	22713	2.9
8	Evergreen	Taiwan	15	20768	2.7
9	APL	USA	14	19689	2.5
10	US Lines	USA	19	19346	2.5
11	Mitsui-OSK	Japan	13	18614	2.4
12	NOL	Singapore	9	16539	2.1
13	Nedlloyd	Netherlands	11	15927	2
14	ZIM	Israel	12	14982	1.9
15	Kawasaki K-Line	Japan	13	14641	1.9

Source: Australian, 29 July 1982.

[22] *Dagblad voor de Scheepvaart*, 17 October 1980.

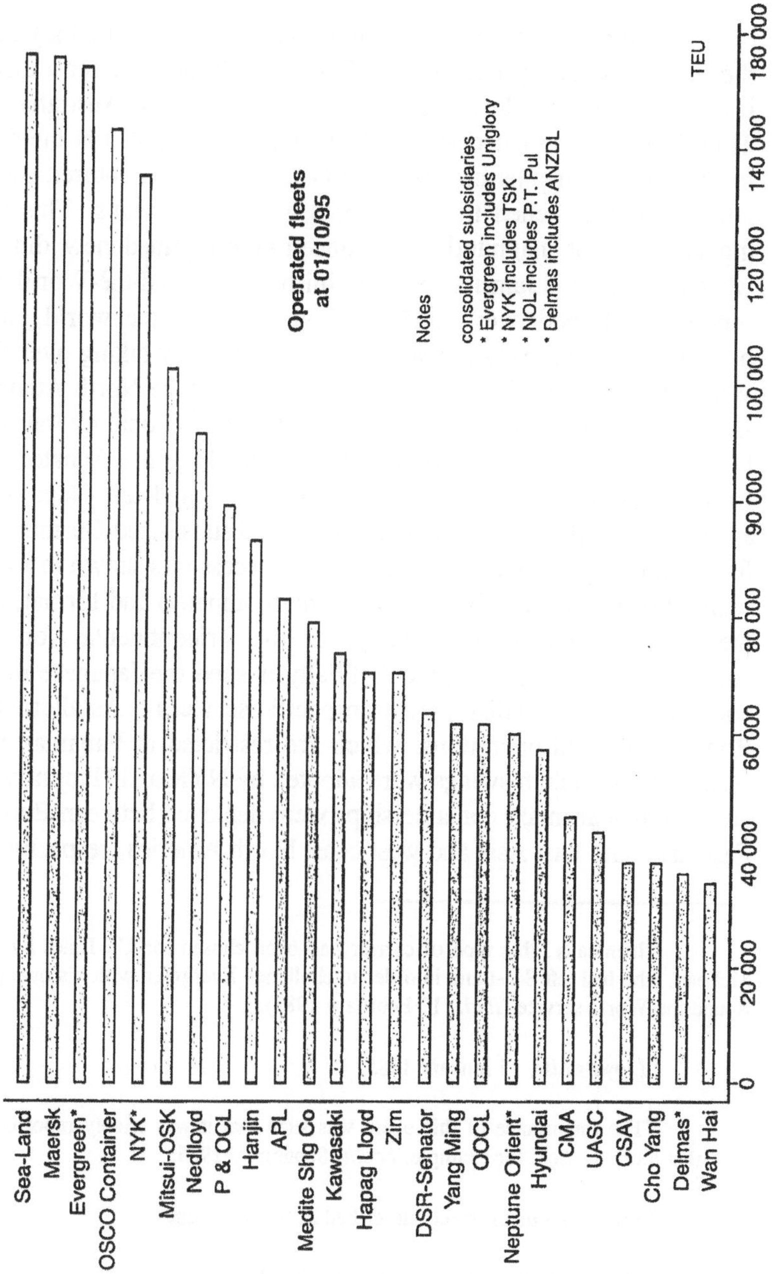

Figure 1: Top twenty-five container ship operators.

Source: *Fairplay Container Operators Directory 1996* (London, 1996), 2.

After the crisis, a rejuvenated P&O and Nedlloyd jointly acquired the fleets and agency networks of US Lines (bankrupt after a disastrous investment in twelve slow-steaming mega-carriers)[23] and Australian-owned Trans Freight Lines (successor to the bankrupt Seatrain). For the first time in their 100 year-plus histories, P&O and Nedlloyd entered the North Atlantic and stretched their networks across all oceans. This push to higher levels of magnitude and concentration gained new dimensions when Evergreen in January 1985 established its Round-the-World service, sending fleets both west- and east-bound around the world, and thus becoming the first truly global carrier.[24] OOCL, by taking over Furness Withy, had been the first Asian company to enter the North Atlantic, but Evergreen's move was an historical landmark.[25] Global operations now became the aim of all major players, especially since Senator Line of Bremen (brainchild of Karl-Heinz Sager who had left Hapag-Lloyd), sweeping up a fleet of largely speculative and subsidized German ships,[26] followed Evergreen's example. Senator's success was shown in its merger with DSR (the former East German liner company) and formation, with the Korean company Cho Yang, of the Tricontinental (or Tricon) consortium. These developments finally pushed the Japanese majors to cooperate and rationalize their transpacific services.[27] As alternatives to Round-the-World operations, which are restricted to Panamax vessels, systems of pendulum swings were adopted by NYK and Hanjin, whereby larger, post-Panamax, containerships were deployed between Europe and East Asia, and East Asia and west coast North America, respectively.[28] In

[23]Ironically, this type of carrier had been chosen for US Lines by Malcolm McLean, who had left Sea-Land in order to challenge Evergreen with his own projected Round-the-World service (*Ibid.*, 17 February 1983).

[24]*Lloyd's List*, 15 January 1985.

[25]The importance of this event was such that it was widely reported in non-specialist journals. See, for example, *South*, September 1985.

[26]Sometimes dismissively described as "dentists' ducks."

[27]*Lloyd's Maritime Asia*, June 1991, 29-31.

[28]*Containerisation International*, December 1991, 27-33; *Lloyd's Shipping Economist*, November 1992, 18-19; and *Containerisation International*, September 1994, 47-51.

the process container shipping became truly globalized as Asian companies added the Atlantic to their services, Europeans returned to the Pacific from which they had withdrawn after the Second World War, and American companies that focused on East Asia turned toward Europe and *vice versa*. As *Fairplay* put it in August 1996: "Getting that 'third ocean' is a goal every liner operator is pursuing right now, representing the great leap towards a global service."[29]

The desire for continued enlargement of scale characterized the policies of all major players from the late 1980s. It broke up many of the existing consortia as members jockeyed for position, new mergers shifted balances of power, and slot-leasing became a major integratory strategy.[30] P&O re-established itself as an "imperial" power as it took over the Shipping Corporation of New Zealand and almost walked away with the Australian National Line (when twenty-five percent of Australia's state-owned airline company Qantas was bought by British Airways). Across the North Sea Maersk combined the rapid expansion of its fleet with the takeover of "oldtimer" East Asiatic, which itself had just swallowed Ben Line. The motives driving the companies are as yet difficult to assess, but appear to originate both from ambitions of the companies' leaders and the competitive conditions of the period in which freight rates were chronically under pressure and enlargement of scale and market share were seen methods for survival and growth. A throwback to late nineteenth-century Social-Darwinist tendencies inherent in current theories of economic rationalism also became visible in the aggressive market behaviour of many companies.[31]

A comparison of the world's twenty-five largest liner companies in 1995 (see figure 1) with the rankings of 1981 demonstrates the remarkable and continued growth of the industry by a factor of about four. Sea-Land and Maersk maintained their leading positions, but the most prominent change was the rise of East Asian companies, above all Evergreen. The Europeans, by contrast, experienced mixed fortunes with traditionals Nedlloyd rising as much as P&O (OCL) had fallen, and the

---

[29] *Fairplay*, 29 August 1996.

[30] For a professional snapshot that well caught the fluidity in the system, see *Containerisation International*, March 1990, 29-33.

[31] *Lloyd's Shipping Economist*, August 1994, 6-9.

presence of newcomers Mediterranean and Senator-DSR. Together with Asian newcomers COSCO, Hanjin and Hyundai, they demonstrated the fluidity of the market, albeit in entirely different modes: while the Asian owners grew on the back of their rapidly growing national economies, the Europeans had no such, often state-supported, market assistance.

Stability seemed to be achieved in 1994 with the formation of two super-coalitions: the "Grand Alliance" of P&O, Hapag-Lloyd, NOL and NYK, and the "Global Alliance" of Nedlloyd, MOL, MISC, APL and OOCL, especially as Sea-Land and Maersk also found each other in a "Worldwide Alliance." These alliances represented more than just an enlargement of scale in consortium formation as cooperation between the partners was extended to all routes worldwide where they operated.[32] Designed to achieve economies of scale and assurances of efficiency and quality of service (such as "just-in-time" commitments and immediate transshipment), the alliances set out to rationalize maritime and shore resources to an unprecedented extent. But, as it turned out, the final configuration and the optimal level of magnitude had not yet been achieved.

The size of the largest, post-Panamax, containerships had been gradually creeping up to 5000 TEU when, suddenly in early 1996, Maersk revealed the first of its new series of twelve vessels, the *Regina Maersk*, to have a 6000-TEU capacity; half a year later it became known that P&O had ordered a new series of ships exceeding 6600 TEU. The imminent arrival of such gigantic ships caused big waves and it was with a sigh of relief that the market in October 1996 received the astounding news of a merger between P&O and Nedlloyd which would give the new British-Dutch company (à la Royal Dutch Shell and Unilever) the largest individual container fleet. This move was justified as guaranteeing the survival of both companies, and it was revealed that Nedlloyd's financial position had been perilous. P&O-Nedlloyd soon afterwards negotiated a

---

[32]It was from this time, too, that similar alliance formation took place in civil aviation; by late 1997, for example, the "Star Alliance" comprised United Airlines (USA), Air Canada, SAS (Denmark, Sweden, Norway), Lufthansa (Germany), Thai and Varig (Brazil). Those flying to Australia (UA, Thai and Lufthansa) teamed up with Ansett Australia, Air New Zealand, Malaysian Airlines and South African Airlines as the "official carriers" for the 2000 Sydney Olympics.

credit facility to the tune of $1 billion.[33] At the same time, Cho Yang emerged as a buyer of its ailing Tricon partner Senator-DSR and moved to closer cooperation with both Korea's largest company Hanjin and the resurgent United Arab Shipping Corporation. During the mid 1990s, Canadian Pacific [CP Ships] bought out its partners in Canada Maritime (the Montréal-Europe consortium), took over Cast, the US-based Lykes Lines and Contship, a lively newcomer with a global network,[34] and became the largest individual operator on the North Atlantic.[35] Elsewhere in the Americas, TMM, benefiting from booming exports in cool Mexican wheat beers and NAFTA-promoted industrialization, took over Ecuador's container company and strengthened itself for a power play with its large Asian and American rivals, several of whom began entering the north-south American business. The P&O-Nedlloyd merger, however, only moved instability onto a higher level as the two partners were members of different Alliances. Further uncertainty — but also concentration of power — was created by the far-reaching slot agreement between Hyandai and the Global Alliance for the transpacific and Asia-Europe routes.[36]

A second bombshell exploded when Singapore-based (and Global Alliance member) NOL announced it was taking over Grand Alliance member American President Lines. Paying some $825 million, a forty-seven percent premium over the current market price, NOL swallowed a company that owned about double its tonnage of container vessels but, more importantly, also possessed a highly regarded American brand name, an extensive logistics network in the States and, in cooperation with TMM, on the west coast of Latin America.[37] NOL's strategy was

---

[33]*Fairplay*, 5 December 1996.

[34]*Ibid.*, 21 August 1997 and 6 November 1997, 7; Contship operated the following services: Europe-Australasia, Europe-Middle East-India; Round-the-World, Mediterranean-Gulf of Mexico, and North Europe-east coast Latin America. Contship was (and still is) the only company managed by a woman, Cecilia Battistello.

[35]*Ibid.*, 1 February 1996.

[36]*Asian Shipping*, August 1997.

[37]*Fairplay*, 24 April and 1 May 1997. TMM reportedly was also interested in buying parts of the soon to be privatized Mexican railways, thus enabling it to become the intermodal leader "south of the border;" *Ibid.*, 4 July 1996.

splendid, but the premium paid (which forced it to increase its gearing ratio from 2:1 to 3.9:1) raised many questions. NOL chairman Herman Hochstadt maintained he had acted to protect the relatively small NOL but also acknowledged that he had been inspired in his decision by the P&O Nedlloyd merger.[38] It must also be borne in mind that Singapore was too small a base for a mega-carrier and that only a larger identity could bring security. Interestingly, it became known that APL had been on the market for some time and, *inter alia*, had been offered to Hapag-Lloyd.[39] That company, however, although keen to swallow Germany's third major container operator Hamburg-Süd, was in no position to act (it was soon taken over by its major shareholder, Preussag, which intended to strip it by selling the container sector). Also ACL — since the 1980s in Swedish hands — was put on the market for sale, evidently to non-Swedish buyers.[40]

Developments since 1994 have left no doubt that the turbulence has by no means reached its end. The awesome hunger of the ever larger containerships, culminating in Maersk's and P&O Nedlloyd's 6000+ TEU carriers, and the unlimited ambitions of their owners have shaken every company and every port to its foundations. Evergreen and its feeder branch, Uniglory, in early 1997 had no less than twenty-six newbuildings on order.[41] Thomas Anderson, managing director of Maersk UK, expressed his company's vision to be "ever larger ships and further company mergers or take-overs...in order to service the increasing number of global customers."[42] Maersk also brought four ships under the American flag to enhance its USA-Mediterranean service.[43] The result was the break-up of many traditional loyalties and recently formed alliances.

---

[38]*Ibid.*, 24 April 1997.

[39]*Ibid.*, 5 December 1996.

[40]*Ibid.*, 24 April 1997.

[41]*Ibid.*, 9 January 1997.

[42]*Ibid.*, 24 April 1997. It is only fair to relate a rival's comment: "[but] even Maersk has to face up to its costs." (Angiolino Vignodelli, chief executive officer of Lloyd Triestino, quoted in *ibid.*, 26 June 1997).

[43]*Ibid.*, 27 February 1997.

Despite continued growth in the volume of container traffic, moreover, huge newbuilding programmes have maintained a structural overcapacity and depressed freight rates and company revenues.[44] The North Atlantic was reported to have caught "Asian flu" when its seventeen lines were joined by COSCO, Yang Ming and K-Line, who did not hesitate to offer discounts.[45] In this Social-Darwinist jungle — which in so many ways resembles the world of the 1890s — the players appear to be largely driven, as P&O Nedlloyd's Chief Executive, Tim Harris, expressed it, by "commercial considerations" and what "will enable us to make the most economic use of our capital assets."[46] Under these conditions, the insider judgement, "Chaos threatens liner trades,"[47] succinctly summed up the state of affairs.

Ports and Port Systems

The impact of containerization on the ports and port systems of the world was as revolutionary as that which transformed the shipping industry.[48] First and foremost, the loading and discharging of containerships required specialized and dedicated port facilities. To be part of the new container world, ports needed to undergo a complete metamorphosis. Container terminals must have huge slabs of open, but well-founded, space to park and arrange containers for shipment; appropriate equipment to move containers across the terminal; specialized container cranes; and, ideally, on-the-spot connections with rail, road and/or water transport facilities (the latter both inland and/or short-sea). *Mutatis mutandis*, from the late 1960s a similar struggle was fought between the ports of the world to be part of the top-quality network of intercontinental liner services as had

---

[44]See the interview with MOL's president, Masaharu Ikuta, in *ibid.*, 3 July 1997.

[45]*Ibid.*, 29 May 1997.

[46]Quoted in *ibid.*, 26 June 1997.

[47]*Ibid.*, 2 January 1997.

[48]I cannot deal in this paper with the social and industrial relations consequences of containerization, but in these spheres a new order has also come into being. The main change has been the marked contraction of port labour forces — another factor that has helped to weaken the traditional nexus between liner companies and their home ports.

been the case in the mid-nineteenth century after the introduction of subsidized mail services. With the exponential growth of container shipping the ports of the world had to undergo dramatic physical transformations, in which the traffic that previously had been handled by large numbers of individual wharves, finger piers and docks were now centralized in a handful of huge terminals. More often than not such space could not be made available in existing conventional port areas. Following the example set from the early 1950s by bulk-handling facilities, the new container terminals were built further out towards the sea, leaving in their wake obsolete inner-city facilities that once had been the heart of the liner trades of the world. Antwerp and Bremerhaven followed this pattern as much as Singapore and Shanghai. In Kobe the container terminals were built on an artificial island, while Rotterdam pushed its Maasvlakte ever further out into the North Sea. Sydney's Port Jackson, which had served it since 1788, could not cope with containerization, by 1980 had moved all operations to Sydney's second port, Botany Bay.[49] Some ports had to build satellites. Marseilles located its container operations at the site of its bulk-shipping harbour, Fos. Bangkok's congestion problems were manifold with both its river and the city almost choking with traffic, so Laem Prabang, a little over 100 kms. to the southeast was built on a virgin site. In 1996, its turnover had sky-rocketed to some 700,000 TEU.[50]

As the example of Laem Prabang suggests, containerization dramatically changed the network of the world's liner ports and the nature of port rivalry. Civil engineers could (and did) construct ports and container terminals at virtually any site. Naturally, all existing ports wished to join the container revolution but the possibility for newcomers to enter the field thoroughly destabilized existing port systems. The aim of every major port was to be included in as many high-quality services to as many overseas destinations as possible, and also that it should enjoy the highest frequency of sailings, the lowest transit times, the largest choice of lines, and the best forward connections from overseas ports to the ultimate destination of the exports. In addition to these competitive dynamics, three further, ever stronger factors boosted the creation of new ports. First, the rapid improvement in all economically developed

---

[49]P.R. Proudfoot, "Sydney and its Two Seaports," *International Journal of Maritime History*, I (1989), 141-184.

[50]*Fairplay*, 20 February 1997.

countries in their inland transport infrastructure through the construction, from the 1950s, of elaborate networks of highways, freeways, autoroutes, Autobahnen, etc., and, from the early 1980s, greatly revitalized railroad systems, so that ports could be located more favourably than the established ports with regard to both their maritime situation and access to their hinterlands. Second, the increasing importance given to port industrialization for the promotion of economic growth, foreign trade and regional revitalization. Prime examples of countries whose economic growth was planned around seaports are Japan and China,[51] but there is hardly a container port in the world that does not have a "special economic zone" or an "industrial area" of one kind or another with it. Container ports stand at the very heart of development policy.

The third factor relates directly to container shipping itself. To reduce costs and maximize sailing-time, operators looked for possibilities to shorten routes and cut overall time spent in port. Increasingly they reviewed the geographical lay-out of their networks. Theoretically, revenue can be maximized by ships shuttling between two terminus ports. In reality, there were very few trade routes where this was commercially possible. Owners found it impossible to avoid serving a number of ports at either or both ends of long-distance services in order to achieve maximum load factors. Moreover, they found that any number of ports vied for their business. In consequence, two contradictory tendencies have dominated the development of the world's container network: on the one hand, there has been a concentration of traffic in a small number of regional and/or national leaders, but, on the other, there has also been a fragmenting effect as both existing and new ports attempted to maintain or gain direct access to the ocean super-highway and as many direct sailings to intercontinental destinations as possible. Container ports evidently were instruments of national economic policy.

The containership operator's task thus became one of choosing the optimal geographical configuration of his liner network. For analytical purposes any liner service can be seen as the combination of two or more

---

[51]See, for example, Yue-man Yeung and Xu-wei Hu (eds.), *China's Coastal Cities. Catalysts for Modernization* (Honolulu, 1992); and P.R. Rimmer with Taniuchi Toru, "Japan's Seaports and Regional Development during the Era of High-Speed Growth," in Frank Broeze (ed.), *Gateways of Asia. Port Cities of Asia from the 13th to the 20th Centuries* (London, 1997), 339-366.

of the following alternatives: termini[52] and hubs which represent concentration, and strings and loops which signify fragmentation. Four kinds of port calls can be distinguished:

- terminus: the first and last port of a service;
- hub: a port, of which a large proportion of its trade is transshipped by feeders to other ports in its region; it may be the first or last call in a service but more often is located en route;
- string: a series of successive ports of call, roughly located in a straight geographical direction;
- loop: a series of successive ports of call of a circular pattern; shipping enters and exits the area through the same strait.

The interplay of the forces of concentration and fragmentation may, in the first instance, be illustrated by the development of the British container port system. Broadly speaking, Britain's conventional trade had been carried by London and Liverpool, with minor shares going to Glasgow and Hull. Only a few years after containerization began, however, Felixstowe, a private port that until then had never been served by long-distance liner traffic, had by far the largest turnover of containers in the country, some 700,000 TEU by 1983. Although the fact that it operated outside the system of state-owned British ports was undoubtedly of great importance, Felixstowe's sudden rise to prominence was equally the result of its experimentation with roll-on roll-off traffic and its favourable location in relation to both its British hinterland and the countries on the opposite side of the North Sea that were served by short-sea feeders and ferries.[53] The trade which Felixstowe attracted, inevitably, was taken from established ports. The British freight market was simply too small for the great consortia to call at more than one or, at the most, two ports. As containers could be easily moved by rail or road meant that the choice of port for imports and/or exports was not any more determined by that

---

[52]I specifically use the term "terminus" and not terminal to avoid confusion with the term "terminal" as used in container terminal, which merely refers to a specialized port facility.

[53]J.H.W. Northfield, "Port Management and Operations at Felixstowe," in Institution of Civil Engineers (ed.), *Port Engineering and Operation* (London, 1985), 111-121.

port's situation in relation to a particular hinterland but, rather, by its situation in relation to the foreland. Thus, when OCL entered the Europe-Far East trade, as part of the giant TRIO-group, neither London nor Liverpool were deemed adequate; instead, it selected Southampton from where a network of motorways covered the whole length and breadth of the country.[54]

The big losers were the ports with traditional industrial relations and/or unfavourable location once Britain became a one-port destination. Glasgow was annihilated, while Hull lost to newcomers like Immingham and Felixstowe. The most dramatic developments occurred in London and Liverpool. The latter, formerly "Gateway of Empire,"[55] whose extensive global network of shipping lines as late as 1960 had been celebrated in George Chandler's review of the city's shipping industry,[56] was deserted as its companies were liquidated or submerged in consortia that directed their ships elsewhere. In the 1980s Liverpool was a third-rate backwater with a turnover of about 50,000 TEU per annum before its fortune turned. The privately-owned Royal Seaforth Dock concentrated on trades in which Liverpool had a locational advantage: Canada, northern Russia and, reviving a traditional trade, the Mediterranean. Liverpool re-emerged as a modest participant and in 1993 achieved a record turnover of 385,000 TEU, its new identity defined by its publicity brochure, *Liverpool — The UK HUB Port*. London followed much the same pattern, although OCL kept the Australian trade at Tilbury. It was only in the late 1980s, when P&O emerged as the strongest British operator, that Tilbury advanced again. In 1994 the Port of London Authority, of which Tilbury is the "quality label," handled more than 900,000 TEU.[57] By this stage Rotterdam and Hamburg had surpassed 4,500,000 TEU and 2,700,000 TEU per year. In northwestern Europe, the rivalry between traditional and new ports is sharper than ever, as the entire region can be served from almost

---

[54]A highly interesting account by an insider of the genesis and first years of Southampton is John Hovey, *A Tale of Two Ports. London and Southampton* (London, 1990).

[55]Tony Lane, *Liverpool, Gateway of Empire* (London, 1987).

[56]George Chandler, *Liverpool Shipping* (London, 1960).

[57]*Port of London Handbook 1997*, a widely publicized and distributed volume, with the ambitious sub-title "the Great British Port."

any location, including Zeebrugge and Flushing. London's rivals lie across the sea as well as in its own land: privately-owned Thamesport in 1995 handled 300,000 TEU and was on the way to attracting more majors.[58]

Table 3

European Ports of Call of Major Europe-Far East Operators, 1996

Global Alliance:
Japan service: Rotterdam, Hamburg, Southampton, Le Havre
China/Korea service: Southampton, Le Havre, Bremerhaven, Rotterdam
China express: Bremerhaven, Rotterdam, Southampton
from the Mediterranean: LaSpezia, Barcelona, Fos, Damietta
Grand Alliance:
service A: Hamburg, Rotterdam, Southampton
service B: Antwerp, Hamburg, Le Havre, Malta
service C: Le Havre, Hamburg, Rotterdam, Southampton
service D: Rotterdam, Bremerhaven, Southampton
K-Line/Yang Ming:
Japan service: Rotterdam, Hamburg, Felixstowe, Le Havre
China service: Le Havre, Felixstowe, Hamburg, Antwerp
Maersk/Sea-Land:
Japan service: Hamburg, Gothenburg, Rotterdam, Southampton, Algeciras
China/Korea service: Hamburg, Felixstowe, Rotterdam, Le Havre, Algeciras
Mediterranean service (orig. from USA): Algeciras, Gioia Tauro
Tricon (DSR-Senator/Cho Yang):
Le Havre, Rotterdam, Bremerhaven, Hamburg, Felixstowe, Antwerp
Tricon/Hanjin:
Mediterranean: Cadiz, Valencia, La Spezia, Gioia Tauro
Hanjin:
Rotterdam, Hamburg, Felixstowe, Le Havre
Hyandai/MSC/Norasia:
Rotterdam, Felixstowe, Le Havre, Barcelona, Genoa, Malta
COSCO:
Hamburg, Rotterdam, Felixstowe, Antwerp, Le Havre
Mediterranean: Limassol, Valencia, Barcelona, Fos, Genoa, Naples
Evergreen:
Rotterdam, Hamburg, Thamesport, Zeebrugge, Le Havre
Mediterranean: Larnaca, Piraeus, La Spezia, Fos, Barcelona, Valencia, Trieste
combined: Felixstowe, Bremerhaven, Antwerp, Gioia Tauro

Source: Based on Michel Neumeister, "Extrême orient: l'axe majeur," *Journal de la marine marchande*, 11 October 1996. The designation of the various services has been simplified. Note that on all services a call is made at Singapore for Southeast Asian destinations.

---

[58] *Fairplay*, 22 August 1996.

Significantly, no operator has dared as yet to centralize all container cargo in one port.[59] Despite the theoretical trend towards concentration, the ever larger capacity of the individual ships and services can only be met by multiple calls on a variety of loops as is shown in table 3.

The rough "league table" of northern ports, based on the number of visits, shows the dynamic mix of old and new. The ranking is Rotterdam fourteen, Hamburg and Le Havre twelve, Felixstowe eight, Southampton seven, Bremerhaven and Antwerp five, and three with only one: London and Liverpool shine by their absence. A similar situation exists in East Asian waters where a number of Japanese, Chinese and Taiwanese ports is included in every major service. The rivalry between Tokyo and Yokohama, and between the Tokyo Bay ports and those of Osaka Bay,[60] is in every way as fierce as that between Antwerp and Zeebrugge,[61] or the ports of the Havre-Hamburg range. Evergreen's recent pendular service, on its westwards passage from the USA to Europe, called in succession at Sendai, Tokyo, Osaka, Hakata, Keelung, Kaohsiung, Hong Kong and Singapore.[62] The unprecedented growth of Shanghai is accompanied by the inclusion of several other Chinese ports, especially by COSCO and OOCL. When American President Lines

---

[59]According to OOCL (Europe)'s CEO, Jim Poon, 5000-TEU carriers certainly warranted major operators looking at reducing the number of calls to two or even one, but the efficiency of European railways, in comparison with those in North America, was too low to be able to cope with the cargo flows generated by such maritime rationalization (*Ibid.*, 16 January 1997). The construction of the "Betuwelijn" from Rotterdam to the Ruhrgebiet may well be the decisive catalyst towards full-scale intermodalism in northern Europe.

[60]The rivalry between Japanese ports is engagingly discussed by Francis E. Phillips in *Containerisation International*, October 1986, 59-65, and November 1986, 62-67.

[61]See F. Suykens, *et al.*, *Antwerp. A Port for All Seasons* (Antwerp, 1986), 514-530; and the interesting article in *Dagblad voor de Scheepvaart*, 7 April 1978.

[62]Neumeister, "Extrême orient."

returned after forty-six years to China, in 1995, it called at the new ports of Yantian and Chiwan as well as Hong Kong.[63]

The unprecedented economic growth of East Asia has made this region the world's most dynamic centre for container shipping. During the 1980s Hong Kong and Singapore grew into by far the largest container ports in the world. Hong Kong, as a major producer itself and the gateway of southern China, in 1995 handled more than 12,600,000 TEU;[64] Singapore passed the 10,000,000 TEU mark in 1994. Singapore's continued programme of port expansion, as well as its repair and maintenance facilities, its leadership as the world's largest refuelling port,[65] its established pattern of liner services, and a wealth of ancillary maritime services, enabled it to maintain its role as virtually unchallengeable regional, and even hemispheric, hub, with a strong hold over the region's secondary ports such as Bangkok, Jakarta, Kuching, Ho Chi Minh City, Port Kelang, and Fremantle.[66] In 1994 Singapore handled no less than thirty-five percent of all ASEAN's seaborne trade, with a shipping network of 530 lines operating to over 700 ports worldwide. Every week nineteen container ships left for Rotterdam and eighteen for Hamburg.[67] As table 1 shows, from the 1980s the intra-Asian trade has increased greatly in importance so that the networks of short- and medium-distance services transcended their original feeder purposes.

While both East Asia and northern Europe are characterized by loop services supplemented by regional feeders, the huge volume of the total trade of Singapore and Hong Kong, and their supremacy as hubs,

---

[63] *Fairplay*, 19 January 1995. An interesting sketch of APL is in *Containerisation Annual*, July 1992, 29-37. A brief overview of the major US container partnerships and the types and number of their services in *American Shipper*, August 1993. Yantian itself is becoming a "micro" container hub with feeders to be set up to Nanhai, Jiuzhou, Gaolan and Gaosha (*Fairplay*, 13 July 1995).

[64] *Fairplay*, 13 June 1996.

[65] *Lloyd's Maritime Asia*, April 1994.

[66] For a general overview of Southeast Asia see Keith Trace, "ASEAN ports since 1945: Maritime Change and Port Rivalry," in Broeze (ed.), *Gateways of Asia*, 318-338. On Port Kelang, see *Fairplay*, 13 April 1995; and *Asian Shipping*, August 1997, 38-39.

[67] *Fairplay*, 6 October 1994.

created significant contrasts between the two port systems.[68] On the east coast of North America an altogether different configuration of ports and port rivalry came into existence. In the first instance, containerization led to a much greater concentration on the leading port, New York. But soon, as in Europe, others saw a chance to capture a share of the trade and by the 1980s Jacksonville, Savannah, Charleston, Norfolk and others became alternative gateways.[69] The dense network of interstate highways throughout the USA gave virtually every port direct access to a vast hinterland, and most also benefited from the rejuvenation of railroad networks.[70] Port rivalry gained an entirely new dimension from the moment, in 1984, that Evergreen opened its first Round-the-World service. These included loops in northern Europe and East Asia, and an innovatory string on the American east coast. This pattern was followed by virtually all majors operating Round-the-World or post-Panamax pendular services. Especially in the former case, southern ports like Charleston or Jacksonville benefitted, while traditionals to the northward came under pressure. Montréal was too remote for inclusion in global services but as terminus took full advantage of its inland location and railroad connections with midwest USA; by the mid 1990s its CP Ships was the largest individual container carrier on the North Atlantic.

The west coast of North America offers a totally different picture again. San Francisco was the undisputed regional leader but containerization almost entirely killed off its port as its waterfront and transport

---

[68]In 1984 Hong Kong and Singapore had still ranked third and sixth, with TEU turnovers of 2.1 million and 1.6 million respectively; the largest ports then had been Rotterdam (2.5 million) and New York (2.3 million) (*Fairplay Pacific*, 27 February 1986).

[69]The major ports of the North American east and Gulf coasts in 1994 were New York/New Jersey 2.0m TEU; Charleston 1.0m; Hampden Roads 0.9m; Montréal 0.7m; Houston 0.6m; Savannah 0.6m; Baltimore 0.5m; and Jacksonville 0.5m TEU (*Containerisation International*, 30 February 1997); Philadelphia and Boston were well behind.

[70]Last of all, paradoxically (although, remembering the origins of Sea-Land, perhaps not) New York/New Jersey, after the takeover of Conrail by CSX Corporation and Norfolk Southern in 1997 (*Fairplay*, 19 June 1997). In 1996 Union Pacific and Southern Pacific had merged (*Ibid.*, 22 August 1996).

infrastructure were woefully inadequate.[71] Matson moved its operations to Oakland,[72] and soon ports within the entire range from Vancouver to San Diego benefited from the exponential growth of transpacific trade. Seattle, Tacoma, Portland, Oakland, and especially Los Angeles and Long Beach emerged strongly.[73] Crucial factors were competitive pricing and the quality of intermodal sea-rail traffic to the population centres of the USA.[74] All west coast ports functioned predominantly as single terminus gateways, as no major company operated any loops or strings. With four railroad systems across North America their flexibility and rivalry are considerable.

The Mediterranean possessed quite different characteristics again, with calls in the Europe-East Asia trade, as table 3 shows. Due to its political fragmentation and geographical shape the Mediterranean has always had a large number of ports and containerization initially brought little change. Traffic was fragmented over many ports as Barcelona (four), Algeciras, Valencia, Fos, La Spezia,[75] and Gioia Tauro (three each) led a large pack of ports in the number of calls made by the great international combines and companies; very few countries had only one

---

[71]In 1996 San Francisco hit rock bottom with a turnover of no more than 5500 TEU; *Ibid.*, 10 April 1997.

[72]Worden, *Cargoes*, 155.

[73]The "league table" in 1994 was Long Beach 2.6m TEU; Los Angeles 2.5m; Oakland 1.5m; Seattle 1.4m; Tacoma 1.0m; Vancouver 0.5m; and Portland 0.3m (*Containerisation International*, 30 February 1997). As can be imagined, this pattern of transpacific maritime highways left no space for Honolulu to develop into a central oceanic hub. See Edward D. Beechert, *Honolulu. Crossroads of the Pacific* (Columbia, SC, 1991), 168.

[74]See *Fairplay*, 3 October 1996 and 10 April 1997.

[75]La Spezia's presence was entirely due to Genoa's long-standing failure to embrace containerization as strong restrictive work practices paralyzed the port for many years; these problems, however, were resolved in the early 1990s and the short artificial summer of La Spezia, like that of Zeebrugge, is rapidly coming to an end as Genoa's superior situation can be fully exploited again; *Ibid.*, 22 May 1997, 3 July 1997, and "Genoa: The Mediterranean Gateway," supplement to *Ibid.*, 30 April 1998.

representative.[76] Like Southeast Asia, the Mediterranean is both a terminal region and a thoroughfare; some of the largest global operators did not even stop in the Mediterranean and/or had separate services beginning and terminating there. As a result several different patterns became superimposed on each other. Some services used loops and strings, with calls at both traditional gateways (such as Barcelona and La Spezia/Genoa) and regional hubs, as the sequences of the Global Alliance (four calls) and Evergreen (six calls) show. Hyundai's schedule included only three ports and used both Barcelona and Malta as hubs. For others three calls is still too much. Maersk/Sea-Land's USA-Mediterranean-East Asia line, for example, only called at Algeciras and Gioia Tauro, Grand Alliance's "service B" only at Malta, and Evergreen's combined service only at Gioia Tauro. These three ports represented the pure hub, which has also appeared in the Indian Ocean and Gulf.

Traditionally, the major ports in the Indian Ocean were the linchpins of European colonialism, especially Bombay, Madras, Calcutta and Karachi, and the coaling stations and entrepôts, Aden, Colombo and Singapore.[77] When containerization came to South Asia, however, India's ports were unable to respond to this challenge, and Sri Lanka's Colombo grew to be the regional hub where both its own country's and a large part of India's container traffic became centralized.[78] In 1993 Colombo was 16th in the rank order of Asian ports, with Karachi the only other South Asian port amongst the top twenty, with just over 700,000 TEU; in 1996 it surpassed the 1,000,000 TEU mark.[79] By that time, finally, India had

---

[76]In 1994 the rank order in TEU turnover of Mediterranean ports was Algeciras 1.0m TEU; La Spezia 0.8m; Barcelona 0.6m; Genoa 0.5m; and Fos 0.4m (*Containerisation International*, 30 February 1997). By 1998 Genoa was poised to overtake Algeciras: "Genoa: The Mediterranean Gateway," 3.

[77]See the overview in Frank Broeze, "The Ports and Port Systems of the Asian Seas: An Overview with Historical Perspective from c. 1750," in Agustin Guimerá and Dolores Romero (eds.), *Puertos y Sistemas Portuarios (Siglos XVI-XX)* (Madrid, 1996), 99-121.

[78]*Fairplay*, 11 March 1993. For an historical perspective see K. Dharmasena, "Bombay and Colombo 1948-1984: A Study in Port Development with Special Reference to Containerization," *The Great Circle*, IX (1987), 119-133. See also K.V. Hariharan, *Containerisation Era in India. Prospects and Problems* (Bombay, 1995).

[79]*Fairplay*, 24 July 1997.

begun to grasp the nettle and the intermodalist policy adopted in 1988 began bearing fruit.[80] Between 1990-1991 and 1993-1994, Bombay (with Jawaharlal Nehru Port) increased turnover from 324,000 to 560,000 TEU, and Madras from 109,000 to 162,000 TEU. But, although the number of direct overseas services increased,[81] India was still mainly served by feeders from Colombo, Singapore, and the Middle East.

The Middle East developed a port system similar to that of the Mediterranean with which it shared the characteristic of being both terminus and port of call for ships sailing between the Atlantic and East Asia. During the 1970s boom a rush of established companies and newcomers flooded into Jiddah and a series of ports in the Gulf.[82] Operators, including local multinational UASC, at first continued traditional varieties of loops and strings along the multitude of ports that reflected the political fragmentation of the Gulf. The two Gulf Wars (1980-1988 and 1990-1991) and the trade crisis of the mid-1980s accelerated the trend towards concentration, as most of the Gulf became a high-risk zone. Dubai rapidly gained dominance as regional hub with an intensive network of short-sea feeders and rose to be among the top ten Asian container ports.[83] But at the same time two entirely new ports were created outside the Straits of Hormuz, Fujairah and Khor Fakkan, from both of which Dubai could be reached by land.[84] By 1993 Fujairah was the eighteenth largest Asian container port with a throughput of 650,000 TEU.[85] With Khor Fakkan, in 1993 ranked twentieth and boasting a bonded "mini-bridge" to its capital Sharjah, Fujairah is the epitome of the

---

[80]Hariharan, *Containerisation Era in India*, ch. 2; port statistics, 38.

[81]See, *Fairplay*, 22 June 1995.

[82]On the "supreme example of port disunity," the UAE, see *ibid.*, 29 August 1991, and also earlier publications, such as *Lloyd's Port Bulletin*, November 1986, 8-11.

[83]*Fairplay*, 21 November 1991 and 13 February 1992; *Lloyd's Maritime Asia*, November 1993 and May 1994.

[84]*Fairplay*, 13 February 1992.

[85]*Ibid.*, 6 July 1995.

new generation of regional hubs.[86] The success of Fujairah and Khor Fakkan inspired others in the region, including Aden, which after the demise of the People's Democratic Republic of Yemen emerged from its Cold War isolation.[87]

The result of the complex interplay between global and regional patterns of production and consumption, port and company politics, and network lay-outs can be seen in table 4, the "league table" of the world's container ports in 1994:

Table 4
The Top Twenty Container Ports in the World, 1994
turnover in TEU [world total: c. 125,000,000 TEU]

rank	port	country	traffic	%
1.	Hong Kong	Hong Kong	11,050,000	8.8
2.	Singapore	Singapore	10,399,000	8.3
3.	Kaohsiung	Taiwan	4,900,000	3.9
4.	Rotterdam	Netherlands	4,539,000	3.6
5.	Busan	Korea	3,213,000	2.6
6.	Kobe	Japan	2,916,000	2.3
7.	Hamburg	Germany	2,726,000	2.2
8.	Long Beach	USA (west)	2,574,000	2.1
9.	Los Angeles	USA (west)	2,519,000	2.0
10.	Yokohama	Japan	2,317,000	1.9
11.	Antwerp	Belgium	2,208,000	1.8
12.	Keelung	Taiwan	2,035,000	1.6
13.	New York/New Jersey	USA (east)	2,034,000	1.6
14.	Dubai	UAE (Gulf)	1,882,000	1.5
15.	Tokyo	Japan	1,865,000	1.5
16.	Felixstowe	UK	1,734,000	1.4
17.	San Juan	USA (Caribbean)	1,522,000	1.2
18.	Bremen/Bremerhaven	Germany	1,503,000	1.2
19.	Manila	Philippines	1,502,000	1.2
20.	Oakland	USA (west)	1,491,000	1.2

Source: *Containerisation International*, August 1995.

[86]*Ibid.*, 29 August 1991, 30 January 1992 and 27 July 1995. Fujairah regards itself also as a sea-air transshipment point, claiming that cargo discharged there is already on a plane at Dubai before the ship could have reached that port. Its "sexy" advertisements highlighted the "Ferrari red" of its cranes (see figure 3); Khor Fakkan in June 1997 introduced the first Liebherr "super post-Panamax" gantry cranes capable of servicing ships with eighteen tiers of boxes.

[87]See *ibid.*, 15 February and 5 September 1996.

Figure 2: Carrying the logo and name inland: a Scandutch container with the Matterhorn.

Source: *Eric Jennings, Cargoes. A Centenary Story of the Far Eastern Freight Conference* (Singapore, 1980), 71.

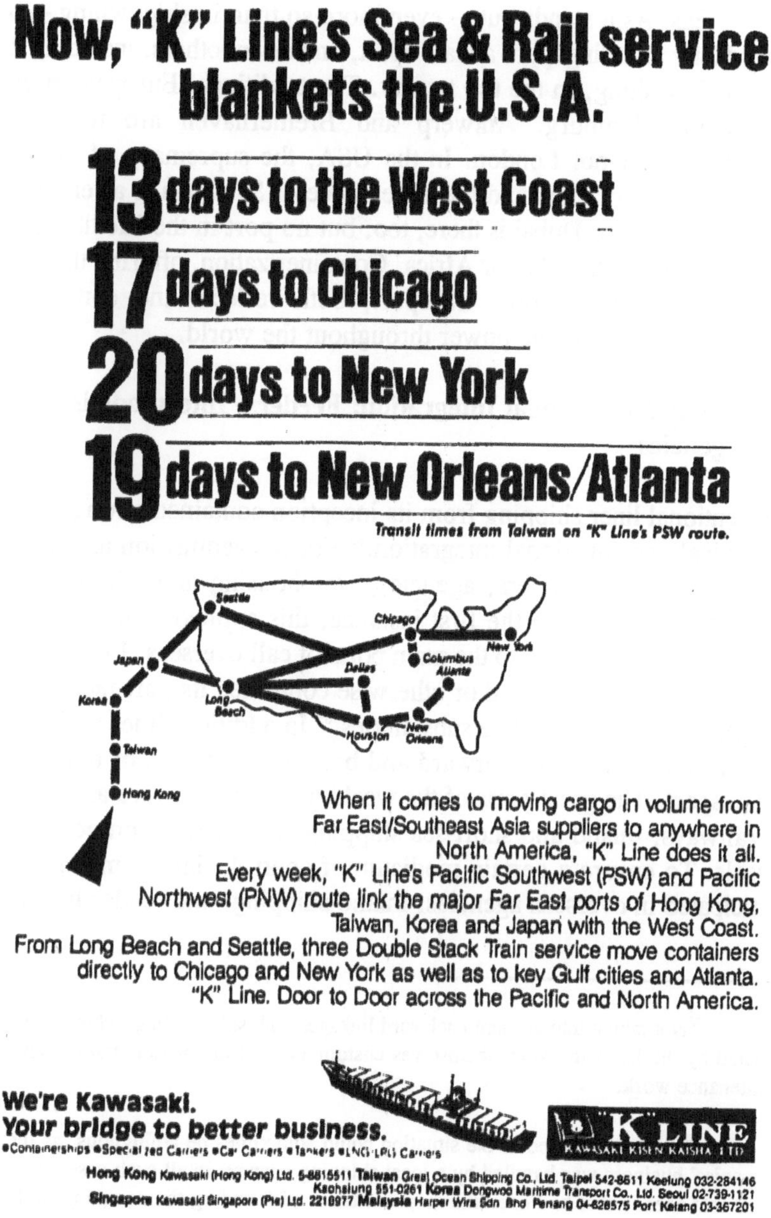

Figure 3: Intermodalism

Source: K-Line publicity brochure, c. 1988.

East Asia stands out — even more so than in shipowning — with Hong Kong and Singapore a class apart, and seven others, including third ranked Kaohsiung, in the top twenty. The traditional European ports of Rotterdam, Hamburg, Antwerp and Bremerhaven are there, with Felixstowe, but not London. In the USA, the supremacy of the trans-pacific trade is marked and the appearance of San Juan is a reminder of where it all began. Dubai is there, too, but no port in the Mediterranean, Latin America, Australia, or Africa. Containerization, offering the highest quality form of maritime transport, both reflects and confirms the distribution of economic power throughout the world.

Vertical and Functional Integration: Feeders, Intermodalism, Ports and Agencies

Conventional liner shipping from its inception contained strong elements of vertical and functional integration.[88] For the acquisition and handling of freight and passengers, agencies, warehousing and wharfage space were indispensable. In the first instance, this applied to the company's home port but often also to the main ports of call overseas. In many cases, the company owned, leased or otherwise controlled its port facilities, and its agencies abroad could be subsidiaries.[89] In addition, liner traffic could not function without the forward and backward services of other modes of transport. The great ports of the world traditionally were as dependent on railways, inland and short-sea shipping as they were on ocean-going vessels. To ensure a certain modicum of control, liner companies often participated in overseas agencies, inland shipping, and feeder lines,[90] but

---

[88]Not taking into account backward linkages with shipbuilding, which were often initiated by the latter to assure themselves customers for construction and/or repair and maintenance work.

[89]In their home ports the situation could sometimes be ambiguous, as the liner companies' business was handled by a local shipping agency; in all such cases, however, it was that agency that had been the major initiator of founding the company in the first place.

[90]See Devos and Elewaut, *CMB 100*; Frank Broeze, "Rederij," *Maritieme Geschiedenis der Nederlanden*, IV (Bussum, 1978), 210, table 7; and H. W. Dick and S. A. Kentwell, *Beancaker to Boxboat. Steamship Companies in Chinese Waters* (Canberra, 1988), 1.

generally speaking, the various modes of transport were largely independent.

It was precisely this entrepreneurial autonomy that clashed fundamentally with the purpose of containerization to smooth the passage of boxes from the original producer to the ultimate consumer. The maritime leg of the transport chain must be integrated as closely as possible with backward and forward transport links. Ports, but also all other modes of transport, must be physically adapted and the relations between them and shipping optimalized. Fortuitously (but not quite, when one considers McLean's background!), containerization trailed, by about a decade or so, the road transport revolution with its door-to-door pick-up and delivery to the most land-locked destinations. A significant cultural phenomenon, trucks carrying the logos and names of companies and consortia, made them household names across all continents (see figure 2). But short-sea and inland shipping, and railroads, were also swept up in the container revolution. Speed and reliability of wharfside handling and transfer to other modes of transport, and the quality of onward transport became issues of vital concern for shipowners in their quest for greater market share and economies of scale. With rising competitive pressures, only marginal differences in the physical quality of service, demand for shorter passage times and "just-in-time" schedules, shipowners came to regard functional diversification and integration as the best method to ensure quality control. Integration became all the more important with the scheduling of high-volume long-distance, pendulum or Round-the-World services and stimulated the alliance formation and mergers of the 1990s. Shipowners, in particular, targeted three main areas of corporate expansion: port facilities, feeders and other modes of transport, and ship's agency.

From the beginning the need for dedicated terminals made container operators work closely together with port authorities. Sea-Land had its facilities in Port Elizabeth, NJ. OCL designed and controlled its own terminals at Tilbury and Southampton.[91] Most major companies across the world, ranging from the ANL in Melbourne to CP Ships in Montréal, came to own or control dedicated facilities in their home ports. The next step forward was made when OOCL, in 1978, went overseas

[91]Hovey, *Tale of Two Ports*. Nedlloyd and CMB invested in large terminals (ECT and Gylsen) that also served other customers. The continuation of the trend was shown by CP Ships, which in the early 1990s acquired Montréal Terminals.

and bought Felixstowe.[92] Soon similar arrangements were made in many ports all over the world, with the specific details depending on local conditions. Two alternative, yet often mutually supportive, strategies emerged. First, there is the increasingly frequent occurrence of major operators leasing terminal facilities, a policy followed, for example, by companies such as OOCL, Maersk, NYK, P&O and COSCO.[93] After a sharp confrontation with the USA, Japan in October 1997 tentatively agreed to allow foreign companies to handle their own cargo, outside the reach of the *yakuza*-dominated Japan Harbour Transport Association.[94] Second, following the fashion set by governments in the mid 1980s in other sectors, came the privatization of entire ports or of their management. A number of specialist firms emerged from the port sector itself, above all the Hutchinson Group which in Hong Kong controls c.7.5% of the world's turnover.[95] The Port of Singapore Authority, while leasing dedicated terminals to individual companies, also became active in developing and managing ports in other Asian countries, as did Manila's ICTSI whose ambition is to be "global."[96] But several majors became remarkably active. P&O has shown itself probably the most aggressive and expansionist participant with a significant investment in Britain, Australia, India, Pakistan, Argentina, China and several other countries.[97] In July 1995, a project, estimated to cost US$615 million, was initiated to

---

[92]Northfield, "Port Management and Operations at Felixstowe," 113-115.

[93]Melbourne was the location for a bitter contest between P&O and OOCL, which the latter seemed to have won, when the Victorian state government suddenly changed the rules. OOCL is now said to be interested in developing a terminal together with COSCO at Botany Bay, Sydney. See *Fairplay*, 20 February 1997; and *Australian Financial Review*, 1 September 1997.

[94]*Fairplay*, 30 October 1997.

[95]*Ibid.*, 13 February 1997.

[96]*Ibid.*, 13 June 1996. ICSTI stands for International Container Terminal Services Inc.; it operates terminals at Manila, Subic Bay, Buenos Aires, Veracruz and soon also Karachi, Aden, and Dammam.

[97]*Ibid.*, 13 June 1996 and 27 February 1997.

develop Colombo's container facility Queen Elizabeth Quay.[98] P&O and three other majors (NYK, NOL and Evergreen) backed the expansion which aims at boosting annual throughput from 230,000 to 1 million TEU. In the creation of new ports, shipping companies played an especially active role: APL, for example, was the driving force behind both Cochin and Fujairah, and Evergreen at Manzanillo, its projected hub at the northern exit of the Panama Canal.[99] In Aden, hoping to become the main hub of the western Indian Ocean, P&O (in addition to ICTSI and the Port of Singapore Authority) became involved.[100] The growing financial and entrepreneurial involvement of container companies in port development cannot but further sharpen their competition.

Control over intermodal transfers could be decisively extended if the shipowner also controlled the onward mode of transport. The first two areas for such expansion were trucking and feeder shipping. Many owners in the late 1960s bought trucking companies (Sea-Land's reverse example, again, providing the model) but in the course of time they moved out of the business, satisfied to rely on long-term contracts with independents. Short-sea shipping was a more natural extension of their core business, and beyond concluding slot leasing arrangements on dedicated carriers, some began operating their own feeder lines, either as joint ventures or on their own account. As early as 1970 CMB started the Ibesca Line as a European feeder for Dart,[101] and from then the practice spread gradually through the industry. Evergreen (with its regional subsidiary, Uniglory), Maersk and Sea-Land became leaders in this field and from the 1980s major-owned regional networks expanded at a pace with general traffic. As main lines grew, global services multiplied and post-Panamax vessels were introduced, the "feeder" concept was gradually stretched to also include long-distance north-south trades like the route from California down the west coast of Latin America. This certainly does not mean that

---

[98]*Ibid.*, 20 July 1995.

[99]APL believed "Fujairah is ideally placed to take advantage of the potential new development in Pakistan, as well as markets in the Gulf, the Red Sea and East Africa." *Ibid.*, 28 September 1989. For Manzanillo, see *Asian Shipping*, August 1997.

[100]*Fairplay*, 4 April 1996 and 30 October 1997.

[101]Devos and Elewaut, *CMB 100*, 210.

the independent feeder company has disappeared, as the examples of Bell Line, probably the oldest in northern Europe, and Med Feeder, one of the most recent newcomers in the Mediterranean, demonstrate.

But the most significant innovation was the development of true "intermodalism" through the integration of shipping, port and railway services. The earliest and largest opportunity rested in the insatiable demand in the USA for East Asian electronic goods. From the early 1980s this was met by dedicating large parts of the east-west US railroad system to container traffic. APL was the first to realise the need to "control its own destiny" on the rails, and in 1982, partly also in response to the Round-the-World plans of Evergreen and US Lines, it developed the double-stack train.[102] Other leading American, Japanese and Taiwanese companies, notably Sea-Land, NYK, K-Line and Evergreen followed APL's lead and concluded agreements with railroad companies which enabled them to off-load containers in west coast ports on dedicated double-stack trains scheduled to depart without delay to cities in the central and eastern states (see figure 3).[103] This functional and organizational intermodalism represented a far greater degree of sea-land transport integration than the classical "land bridge" of the Transsiberian Railway and, although nowhere imitated on the scale of the USA, created widespread interest in developing similar port-hinterland integration. In China, OOCL is cooperating with the state railways to develop intermodalism,[104] while Thailand's new container port, Laem Chabang, quickly adopted dedicated freight trains to help overcome the chronic congestion of Bangkok. India, in 1988, adopted a systematic policy of transforming its railway network into an intermodal feeder and distribution system.[105] Containerization has also made its mark in air freight where considerable growth has resulted from standardization and

---

[102]*Lloyd's Maritime Asia*, May 1989, 10.

[103]See *Fairplay*, 11 April and 11 July 1985; and *Containerisation International* (April 1987), 32.

[104]Interestingly, also in this field the Port of Singapore Authority has become active by assisting with the opening of a container service from Dalian Container Terminal, in which it owns a share, to Harbin. See *Fairplay*, 22 May 1997.

[105]Hariharan, *Containerisation Era in India*, ch. 2.

economies of scale. Ambitious and strategically located sea- and airports, like Dubai, became leaders in shipping-aviation intermodalism.

The last area of functional integration was that of shipping agencies. Traditionally, most liner shipping companies used well-established independent commercial and/or agency firms to handle their overseas business, the major exceptions being "imperial" companies like P&O and CMB. Initially, container operators followed the same practice, but from the late 1980s the larger companies and consortia increasingly desired undivided loyalties and turned over enough business to warrant keeping the agency business in-house.[106] Again, the real innovators were Maersk and Evergreen, "whose concepts of global organisation and aggressive image-making have been years ahead of other lines."[107] Long-standing connections were jettisoned as quality control and, above all, exclusive market information were regarded as vital ingredients to successful management.[108] As advertising gurus strongly believed in the success of projecting company colours and logos, container operators during the 1990s "mopped up" independent agencies in the main ports of call, often taking their employees into their own service. Yet, as globalizing operators continued to penetrate new markets, they still needed to collaborate with local entrepreneurs as well.

Conclusion

Containerization rescued liner shipping from stagnation and decline, but in the process transformed the industry dramatically and with profound repercussions for all modes in the transport chain between producer and consumer. As containerization spread geographically, it also increased in intensity, so that by the mid 1990s approximately ninety-five percent of all liner cargo had been containerized. In contrast with the USA, in Europe and East Asia many individual companies combined forces in national or international consortia in order to make the transition to container shipping. Cooperation was deemed to be indispensable for many reasons, amongst which the high investment costs and the need to

---

[106]*Lloyd's Maritime Asia*, June 1989.

[107]*Fairplay*, 15 August 1996.

[108]*Fairplay Container Operators 1996* (London, 1996), 154 and 259-260.

maintain an adequate frequency of service were most important. In addition to revolutionizing the structure, outlook and operations of both individual companies and the industry as a whole, containerization also enabled many newcomers, both in "traditional" and other maritime nations, to enter the liner business. Widespread internationalization, enlargement of scale and new methods of investment funding enabled independent companies, like Maersk and Evergreen, to emerge. Although consortia did not disappear, many were dissolved, changed in membership or saw their more powerful members reassert their independence. The continued growth of main lines and feeders further stimulated the process of concentration as shrewd shipowners realized that, because of the fundamental flexibility of the containership, their operations were not limited to their traditional trade routes.

True globalization was achieved from the mid 1980s with the introduction of Round-the-World and pendulum services, closer forms of integration through slot-leasing arrangements, takeovers and mergers, new forms of collaboration, and increasing the capacity of the largest carriers to 6000 TEU and beyond. Global networks, which at least theoretically offered significant economies of scale, became the dynamic core of the industry spearheading further changes throughout the system. As a result of this globalization the close nexus which had traditionally existed between many liner shipping companies and their home ports was gradually loosened; international mergers confirmed that several majors were becoming multinational corporations.

Containerization also affected land-based transport infrastructure, both at home and abroad, much more profoundly than conventional liner shipping had ever done. To achieve economies of scale, maximize the returns on their specialized and highly capital-intensive vessels and ensure quality of service, many companies functionally diversified and invested heavily in overseas facilities. They became involved in controlling, planning, managing and owning container terminals to ensure quality of service; with the rise of global and post-Panamax pendulum services, this also affected regional port systems. Ownership and/or control over feeders, agencies, and (mostly in North America) railroad operations greatly increased the power of container companies in their overseas hinterlands.

But, as the largest companies globalized in terms of their networks, strategic coalitions, corporate strategies and self-image, the beginnings of a process of "de-nationalisation" have become evident, i.e., a lessening of the economic, political, social and ideological ties that traditionally bound high-quality liner shipping companies to the interests of their home ports and countries.[109] In its never-ending search for rationalization and economies of scale, container shipping has assumed many of the characteristics of those sectors of the world economy that have moved beyond the stage of internationalization, such as the electronic media and information technology, civil aviation, car manufacturing, and, the first and still most prominent exponent of all, the oil industry.

[109]This applies equally to the executives as to the companies, but a prosopographical analysis is beyond the scope of this essay.

Printed and bound by CPI Group (UK) Ltd, Croydon, CR0 4YY

16/09/2026

14963469-0005